INTERNATIONAL INTELLECTUAL PROPERTY AND THE ASEAN WAY

The Association of Southeast Asian Nations (ASEAN) is actively seeking ways for member countries to enhance their individual economic development within the context of overall regional advancement. Central to this is the creation of a regional intellectual property framework. This book examines the efforts to move beyond sovereign protections of intellectual property rights and establish meaningful interstate cooperation on intellectual property issues. Rather than aim for intellectual property harmonization, ASEAN recognizes its internal diversity and pursues an agenda of "IP Interoperability." The chapters in this collection examine the unique dynamics of "interoperability," analyzing the administration of intellectual property in a part of the world that is of increasing importance. The book enables the reader to compare and contrast the ASEAN model to other approaches in regional cooperation, such as Europe and Latin America, and also explores private international law as a potential vehicle for interoperability.

Elizabeth Siew-Kuan Ng is Deputy Chairwoman and Director of the Intellectual Property Unit at the E.W. Barker Centre for Law and Business, and Associate Professor of Law at the National University of Singapore's Law School. She was appointed *amicus curiae* by the Singapore Court of Appeal on IP matters and is an IP Adjudicator of the Intellectual Property Office of Singapore. She is a Barrister-at-law of Middle Temple (England) and Advocate and Solicitor (Supreme Court, Singapore). A Fellow of Cambridge Commonwealth Society, she was a consultant of the World Intellectual Property Organization (Switzerland). She obtained an LLM (First Class) (University of Cambridge, England) on a Cambridge Commonwealth Trust scholarship.

Graeme Austin is Professor of Law at Melbourne University with a joint appointment as Chair of Private Law at Victoria University of Wellington. He is the coauthor of the pathbreaking text *Human Rights and Intellectual Property: Mapping the Global Interface* (Cambridge University Press, 2011). Before returning to Australasia in 2011, he was the J. Byron McCormick Professor of Law at the University of Arizona, where he convened the intellectual property program. He is a former member of the New Zealand Copyright Tribunal.

International Intellectual Property and the ASEAN Way

PATHWAYS TO INTEROPERABILITY

Edited by
ELIZABETH SIEW-KUAN NG
National University of Singapore
GRAEME W. AUSTIN
Victoria University of Wellington
Melbourne University

CAMBRIDGE
UNIVERSITY PRESS

CAMBRIDGE
UNIVERSITY PRESS

University Printing House, Cambridge CB2 8BS, United Kingdom

One Liberty Plaza, 20th Floor, New York, NY 10006, USA

477 Williamstown Road, Port Melbourne, VIC 3207, Australia

4843/24, 2nd Floor, Ansari Road, Daryaganj, Delhi – 110002, India

79 Anson Road, #06–04/06, Singapore 079906

Cambridge University Press is part of the University of Cambridge.

It furthers the University's mission by disseminating knowledge in the pursuit of education, learning, and research at the highest international levels of excellence.

www.cambridge.org
Information on this title: www.cambridge.org/9781107167209
DOI: 10.1017/9781316711606

First published 2017

Printed in the United States of America by Sheridan Books, Inc.

A catalogue record for this publication is available from the British Library

ISBN 978-1-107-16720-9 Hardback

For my dad and mum: From Elizabeth

For my mother: From Graeme

Contents

Figures

Contributors

Graeme W. Austin is Chair in Private Law at Victoria University of Wellington and a professor in law at Melbourne University. Prior positions include the J. Byron McCormick Professor of Law at the University of Arizona, where he co-convened the intellectual property program. He has been a visiting professor at Wuhan University Law School and the National University of Singapore. An elected member of the American Law Institute, he was appointed as an advisor to its panel on Principles Governing Jurisdiction, Choice of Law, and Judgments in Transnational Disputes. He has been a Herchel Smith Lecturer at Cambridge University and is a 2017 fellow of the Oxford University Intellectual Property Research Centre. He holds a JSD and LLM from Columbia University, where he was the Burton Fellow in Intellectual Property.

Diyanah Binte Baharudin is a senior legal counsel in the Intellectual Property Office of Singapore (IPOS), where she specializes in copyright law, IP dispute resolution and international IP law related matters. Her work includes attending international negotiations, drafting policy papers and conducting legislative reviews. Prior to her current appointment at IPOS, Diyanah was a general litigation lawyer in one of Singapore's oldest law firms, practicing in commercial, criminal, insurance, and intellectual property law. She was also an assistant registrar of trade marks.

Ricardo R. Blancaflor has held a range of leading positions including the director general of the Intellectual Property Office of the Philippines. In 2012, he was named by *IP Magazine* as one of the top fifty most influential people in the world, in recognition of his role in spearheading significant amendments to the Philippines Intellectual Property Code and his holistic approach to intellectual property rights enforcement. His extensive governmental experience includes law reform, defense, security, and crisis management. He has led judicial education initiatives, and has played a significant role in the training of Philippines legal practitioners.

Ignacio de Medrano Caballero is an IP lawyer and a senior official at the European Union Intellectual Property Office (EUIPO). He is currently based in Thailand, managing EU-ASEAN technical cooperation programs on intellectual property. He holds a law degree from the Universidad Autónoma de Madrid, along with specialist degrees in comparative law from Université Libre de Bruxelles, and in European and international law from the Université Catholique de Louvain. He also holds a master's degree in public administration from the Instituto de Empresa. After working as a lawyer specializing in intellectual property in Spain, he joined the European Union Intellectual Property Office (EUIPO). He was then appointed as a legal clerk of the Task Force on Intellectual Property within the cabinet of the president of the European Union General Court in Luxembourg. He then returned to EUIPO to hold several managerial positions such as deputy director for legal and institutional affairs and for human resources.

Chew Phye Keat is a senior partner of the Malaysian law firm Raja, Darryl & Loh. He has been active in the practice of intellectual property law since his call to the Malaysian Bar in 1987. He is a Malaysian registered patent agent, trade mark agent, and industrial design agent. Phye Keat is the immediate past president and was a founding member of of the ASEAN Intellectual Property Association. He is the current president of the Malaysian Intellectual Property Association.

Denis Croze is the director of the Singapore regional office of the World Intellectual Property Organization (WIPO). This appointment follows service in other leading positions at WIPO, including director of the Assemblies and Documentation Affairs Division in the Office of the Director General and as head of the International Law Development Section and Secretary of the Standing Committee on the Law of Trademarks, Industrial Designs and Geographical Indications. Prior to his WIPO service, he was appointed to the International Chamber of Commerce in Paris as head of the Legal Division and as an attorney with the Office of Legal Affairs of the United Nations in New York. Other appointments include heading the Multilateral Affairs Department of the French Patent and Trademark Office (INPI) in Paris. He holds a DEA (master's) in International Economic Law from the University of Paris I (Panthéon-Sorbonne) and a DEA in Political Science from the University of Paris II (Panthéon-Assas).

Carlos Adrián Garaventa is a professor of legal aspects of regional integration processes and an investigator in fields related to constitutional authorization of supranationality at the University of Buenos Aires. He has a postgraduate degree in Development, Public Policies and Regional Integration from the the Facultad Latinoamericana de Ciencias Sociales. He has written several book chapters and academic essays published in specialized magazines and has taught courses and presented conference papers on the effects of regional integration of constitutional and administrative law. He has worked at the Kors Noviks Law Firm in Buenos Aires, and has recently been selected to serve as a coordinator at the National Transport Ministry Legal Affairs Office. He is also the editor-in-chief of the law review *En Letra*.

Richard Garnett is a professor of private international law at the University of Melbourne and a consultant to Herbert Smith Freehills. He regularly advises on cross-border litigation and arbitration matters and has appeared as an advocate before a number of tribunals including the High Court of Australia. He has written extensively in the fields of private international law and arbitration, with his work cited by leading tribunals around the world, including the International Court of Justice, the European Court of Human Rights, the English Court of Appeal, US federal district courts, the Singapore Court of Appeal, and Australian superior courts. His publications include *Substance and Procedure in Private International Law* in the Oxford Private International Law Series. Since 2004, he has served as an expert member of the Australian government delegation to the Hague Conference on Private International Law, to negotiate the 2005 Hague Convention on Choice of Court Agreements and most recently the Draft Convention on Recognition and Enforcement of Foreign Judgments. He has also been an adviser to the American Law Institute on its Principles Governing Jurisdiction, Choice of Law, and Judgments in Transnational Intellectual Property Disputes, and was co-rapporteur on the International Law Association project on transnational group actions and a Director of the Australian Centre for International Commercial Arbitration. He has an LLM from Harvard University, where he was a Lionel Murphy and Fulbright scholar.

Reto Hilty is Director of Intellectual Property and Competition Law at the Max Planck Institute for Innovation and Competition, and holds an appointment as a full professor ad personam at the University of Zurich. He has studied at the Swiss Federal Institute of Technology Zurich (ETH Zurich; first intermediate exam), and has a doctorate from the University of Zurich, School of Law. Prior appointments include head of department and member of the Board of Directors at the Swiss Federal Institute of Intellectual Property, and as a full professor at the Swiss Federal Institute of Technology Zurich. He holds honorary professorships at a number of universities, including at the Ludwig Maximilians University in Munich.

Khin Mar Yee is a professor and head of the Department of Law at the University of Yangon, Myanmar. In 2007–2008, she was a member of the Drafting Commission of the Constitution of the Republic of the Union of Myanmar. She has also acted as a member of the Myanmar delegation in the negotiation regarding the Delimitation of Maritime Boundary between Bangladesh and Myanmar. In 2012, she was a visiting professor at Toulouse University of France, teaching intellectual property law. She has been a delegate at a number of leading international conferences and events, including the 7th Worldwide Conference of the Global Alliance for Justice Education in India. She has also served as a member of the Myanmar Education Policy Committee. She holds a doctorate in intellectual property from the University of Yangon.

Jakkrit Kuanpoth is Research Director for Economic Laws in the Thailand Development Research Institute. He is also a visiting professorial fellow, Faculty of Law, Humanities and the Arts of University of Wollongong, where, for more than ten years he was an associate professor, teaching intellectual property law and laws on property and trusts. His extensive publications on intellectual property law include *Patent Rights in Pharmaceuticals in Developing Countries* (2010). He has been involved in drafting legislation for Thailand on intellectual property–related issues such as patents and pharmaceuticals, plant variety protection, geographical indications, biodiversity, trademarks, and traditional medicines, and has acted as a consultant to various agencies on intellectual property–related issues, including the Ford Foundation, International Centre for Trade and Sustainable Development, Oxfam, and the World Health Organization. He is counsel at the law firm Tillike and Gibbins in Bangkok, Thailand. He holds a doctorate from the University of Aberdeen.

Annette Kur recently stepped down from her position as a senior member of the research staff and head of unit at the Max Planck Institute for Intellectual Property, Competition and Tax Law. She is an affiliated professor at the University of Stockholm and an honorary professor at the University of Munich. She also teaches at the Munich Intellectual Property Law Centre. A former president of the International Association for the Advancement of Teaching and Research in Intellectual Property (ATRIP), she has held visiting professorships at New York University Law School (Hauser Global Law School Program), the National University of Singapore, as well as at several European universities. She has published extensively in the field of national, European, and international trademarks; unfair competition and industrial design law; and on international jurisdiction and choice of law. She has a doctorate from the University of Munich, and has been awarded honorary doctorates from the University of Stockholm and the Swedish School of Economics (Hanken).

Lê Thi Thu Hà is an associate professor in intellectual property at the Foreign Trade University in Vietnam. She has a master's degree in international business law from Tours University and a PhD in intellectual property law from the Foreign Trade University. She has held appointments as a visiting lecturer at the University of Rennes, University of Tours, and University of Bern. A specialist on Geographical Indications, she consults regularly for a variety of stakeholders, from government, provincial authorities, Vietnamese enterprises, and foreign partners.

Mark Lim is a chief legal counsel at the Intellectual Property Office of Singapore (IPOS), where he heads the Hearings & Mediation Department. He advises the Singapore government and public agencies in Singapore on intellectual property matters and is regularly invited to speak at both national and international IP conferences. Before joining IPOS in 2010, Mark was a lawyer in private practice for fifteen years, and served as vice chairman for the Singapore Law Society's IP Committee. He has published many articles in both local and international journals, and provided insights and/or new perspectives on a broad spectrum of IP issues. A senior faculty at the IP Academy, he oversees the development of IP training programs for the legal and public sector in Singapore.

Delphine Marie-Vivien is a graduate in chemistry and intellectual property law and holds a PhD in law. After two years as a patent engineer, she joined CIRAD, a French public research institute dedicated to agricultural research for developing countries, to work on intellectual property and genetic resources issues. Her PhD thesis, *The law of Geographical Indications in India compared to French, European and International Laws*, has been published. Since 2012 she has been based in Vietnam, working on research and development projects regarding the protection of Geographical Indications (GIs). She has published widely on the topic of GIs and is a consultant for the French development agency (Agence Française de Développement – AFD) project on reinforcing GIs in Vietnam and the AFD/FAO project on GIs and rural development in Thailand, Cambodia, Lao PDR, and Vietnam.

Elizabeth Siew-Kuan Ng is the deputy chairwoman and director (Intellectual Property Unit) at the E. W. Barker Centre for Law & Business; director of the Graduate Certificate in Intellectual Property program; and an associate professor of law, National University of Singapore's Law School. She has been appointed amicus curiae by the Singapore Court of Appeal on intellectual property matters and is an intellectual property adjudicator of the Intellectual Property Office of Singapore. She graduated with an LL.B. (Honors) (Queen Mary College, University of London), where she was awarded the Sweet & Maxwell Law prize and Faculty of Law prize. She is a barrister-at-law of Middle Temple (England) and an advocate and solicitor (Supreme Court, Singapore). A Fellow of the Cambridge Commonwealth Society, she was a consultant of the World Intellectual Property Organization. She has held visiting positions at the Max Planck Institute (Germany), at the City University of Hong Kong (China), and at the US Court of Appeals for the Federal Circuit (US). She has delivered more than ninety invited papers including in Australia, China, Fiji, Hong Kong, Malaysia, Mongolia, Myanmar, South Korea, Singapore, Sri Lanka, Switzerland, and Thailand and convened many major public IP conferences. She publishes extensively in Europe, United Kingdom, India, South Korea, Switzerland, Thailand, the United States, Australia, and Singapore, and is an author of studies commissioned by the World Intellectual Property Organization. She obtained an LLM (First Class) (University of Cambridge, England) on a Cambridge Commonwealth Trust scholarship and was conferred the Clough prize.

Sovath Phin leads the practice group in intellectual property and co-leads the corporate and dispute resolution practice group at Bun & Associates, where he specializes in advising on the protection, commercialization, and enforcement of intellectual property rights. He holds a doctorate from Nagoya University Graduate School of Law, Japan, and is an adjunct professor at Pannasastra University of Cambodia. He has also acted as a national legal adviser for international organizations by assisting the Ministry of Commerce of Cambodia in drafting competition law and the law on food safety and the Ministry of Health of Cambodia in drafting the law concerning public health and intellectual property and food safety regulations. He has been admitted to the Bar Association of the Kingdom of Cambodia. One of Cambodia's first selected commercial arbitrators, he is a member of the National Commercial Arbitration Centre (NCAC) and a Fellow of the Singapore Institute of Arbitration. He is currently the vice chairman of the Executive Board of the NCAC. He is also a qualified trademark agent in Cambodia, registered with the Ministry of Commerce. His publications focus on Cambodian intellectual property law.

Roberto Romandini is a senior research fellow, Intellectual Property and Competition Law, at the Max Planck Institute for Innovation and Competition and is a faculty member of the Munich Intellectual Property Law Center. He obtained his first degree in law from the University of Pisa and his LLM degree from the University of Munich with specialization in patent law. Following the completion of his Ph.D. thesis on the patentability of human stem cells, he practiced at a leading intellectual property law firm in Milan. His special area of interest is European and international patent law, legal protection of biotechnological inventions, plant variety rights, and trade secrets.

Agus Sardjono is a lecturer and researcher at the Faculty of Law, University of Indonesia. With a doctorate in law, his primary areas of research include Indonesian business law and intellectual property law. He is an alumnus of the World Intellectual Property Organization Worldwide Academy Turin University program. Together with fellow researchers from American University; New York University; Cambridge University; North Carolina University; Brown University; Social Science Research Council, New York; and Indonesian nongovernmental organizations, he has conducted research on intellectual property rights and traditional cultural expression throughout Indonesia. He has published widely on intellectual property and traditional knowledge, designs, and commercial law.

See Tho Sok Yee joined the Intellectual Property Office of Singapore (IPOS) after several years in private practice. Her work has included assisting the Singapore government in the field of copyright as a member of the IP Inter-Ministerial Committee and as Singapore's representative at the World Intellectual Property Standing Committee on Copyright and Related Rights. She was also involved in the implementation of the US–Singapore Free Trade Agreement. She is now part of the team that makes up the Hearings and Mediation Department. As principal assistant registrar, she manages and adjudicates intellectual property disputes involving trademarks and patents, and has a special interest in alternative dispute resolution for intellectual property disputes. As principal legal counsel, Sok Yee is also involved in legislative, policy, and process review and has a particular interest in access to justice issues. She drew up competency standards as part of the Working Committee (Intellectual Property Protection) under the nationwide IP Competency Framework (IPCF) initiative and served on validation committees that review and validate training and assessment plans against IPCF standards.

Sim Sokheng was appointed as the Cambodian Director-General for International Trade in 2016. Other appointments include director of the Cambodian

Department of Intellectual Property Rights and president of the Secretariat of the National Committee for Intellectual Property Rights of Cambodia. He is a national coordinator for the World Intellectual Property Organization (WIPO)/ASEAN/EU project on Intellectual Property and the ASEAN Working Group on Intellectual Property Cooperation, and is a national consultant for the WIPO on Drafting Cambodian National Intellectual Property Strategy. He also teaches intellectual property law at Pannasastra University of Cambodia and at the Royal University of Law and Economics, Phnom Penh. A graduate in law and business from Royal University of Law and Economics and National University of Management in Phnom Penh, he also holds a master's degree in law from Kyushu University (Japan) and a master's in business administration from the University of the Thai Chamber of Commerce in Bangkok.

Soh Kar Liang is an advocate and solicitor and a registered patent attorney in Singapore, and is the managing director of Ella Cheong LLC, a boutique intellectual property firm, based in Singapore. A graduate of the National University of Singapore, he has been practicing intellectual property law for more than twenty years. He regularly adjudicates on domain name disputes under the World Intellectual Property Organization (WIPO) Uniform Dispute Resolution Policy. He is an active participant in various local and foreign professional and business organizations and currently serves as president of the Singapore Group of the Asian Patent Attorneys Association, and as the Singapore head of the ASEAN Intellectual Property Association. Regularly invited to present at seminars and conferences, he holds leadership positions in other organizations including the International Trademark Association and the Law Society of Singapore.

Pisawat Sukonthapan is an associate professor of law at the Assumption University Law School, Thailand, where she has served in many senior leadership roles. She is also the executive director of Mekong Region Law Center. She has received numerous fellowships and grants, including from The Asia Foundation, McGill University, Harvard-Yenching, the Max Planck Institute (Munich), the Association for Overseas Technical Scholarship, and the Institute of Developing Economies Japan. Her many appointments include membership of Special Committees Considering the Copyright Bill (that was passed into the Copyright Act, B.E. 2537), as an arbitrator, and as an associate judge and mediator of the Central Intellectual Property and International Court of Thailand. She has published widely on intellectual property issues, and has participated in numerous research projects in this field. She holds degrees from Thammasat University (LLB), McGill University (LLM), the

Institute of Social Studies, The Hague (Graduate Diploma in International Law and Development), and Stanford Law School (JSD).

Pablo Wegbrait is a partner at the law firm Kors Noviks (Buenos Aires, Argentina). He also holds positions as a professor of law and as a member of the UNESCO Copyright Chair at the University of Buenos Aires. He is a member of the *Centro de Estudios Interdisciplinarios de Derecho Industrial y Económico* and the Argentine group of the *Association Littéraire et Artistique Internationale* (ALAI). He has written several articles and commentaries on intellectual property, and has lectured about the subject in Argentina and abroad.

Giulio C. Zanetti is an independent international consultant, supporting developing countries to use intellectual property as a development tool. He holds appointments as an adjunct professor at Loyola University Chicago (in Rome), and serves as a visiting professor in the Turin University Master of Laws in Intellectual Property program, an initiative jointly organized with the World Intellectual Property Organization (WIPO). He has also held an appointment as director of the Training and Networks Department and as an intellectual property specialist at the International Development Law Organization, where he was responsible for the design and implementation of national, regional, and international capacity building programs for the benefit of developing country stakeholders in Asia, Africa, Latin America, and Eastern Europe. He created and managed the IP & Development Program, which has been implemented in forty-one developing countries. Prior to working in senior positions in WIPO, he worked as an intellectual property consultant with Società Italiana Brevetti SpA, managing clients' trademark portfolios. He has published several papers on adult learning methodologies and on various aspects of intellectual property and development.

Foreword

This collection of essays on intellectual property "interoperability" in ASEAN could not be more timely. With unprecedented levels of connectivity and increasing international trade, coordination between the intellectual property systems of the different nations is required as never before. At the same time, there are parallel developments that suggest we can no longer assume that intellectual property will evolve toward a harmonized form of multilateralism. The impending exit of the United Kingdom from the European Union, and setbacks for plurilateral initiatives such as the Trans-Pacific Partnership, come to mind in this connection. Indeed, relatively little progress has been made toward harmonization since the Agreement on Trade-Related Aspects of Intellectual Property (TRIPS) came into effect in 1995.

In this context, the "ASEAN Way" could offer some useful lessons. The ASEAN Way envisages greater cooperation and collaboration among member states, and this is likely to be boosted by the establishment of the ASEAN Economic Community and the adoption of the ASEAN Economic Community Blueprint of 2025. At the same time, initiatives such as these are undergirded by an acknowledgment of, and deep respect for, national sovereignty and diversity. ASEAN is a vibrant group of ten nations that together constitute the world's sixth largest economy (as of 2015) and is projected to become the world's fourth-largest regional economy by 2050. The ASEAN member states reflect different legal traditions – common law, civil law, and amalgams of the two. They have different political systems and are at different stages of development. The ASEAN Way reflects a desire to live well together in a spirit of cooperation and harmony, while recognizing the reality that "one size" seldom fits all and might sometimes fit none. In this context, intellectual property has emerged as one of the key policy platforms for ASEAN, but its intellectual property agenda is one of working together (or "interoperability"), not harmonization. If it transpires that the age of multilateralism is indeed over, "ASEAN interoperability" might well offer a useful lens through which to view the new realities of the international intellectual property order.

The editors of this book, Professors Elizabeth Siew Kuan Ng and Graeme Austin, have brought together an impressive group of scholars, officials and administrators, and practitioners to explore different aspects of intellectual property interoperability. The chapters discuss important substantive law questions; cooperative initiatives between the different intellectual property offices of the various ASEAN nations; and other initiatives, such as customs regulation. There is also a comparative aspect: chapters explore models of intellectual property coordination in Latin America and in Europe. The book also explores the potential for developments in private international law to facilitate greater interoperability among diverse intellectual property systems.

The editors and contributors are to be congratulated for a collection that will be of enduring significance for intellectual property in ASEAN and beyond.

Sundaresh Menon
Chief Justice
Supreme Court of Singapore

Preface

Perspectives on Intellectual Property Interoperability

The current policy platforms for the Association of Southeast Asian Nations (ASEAN) include enhancing cooperation in the administration of intellectual property. The ASEAN members are Indonesia, Malaysia, the Philippines, Singapore, Thailand, Brunei, Vietnam, Laos, Myanmar, and Cambodia. It will be apparent that between and among these nations considerable diversity exists across many dimensions: languages, culture, history, political systems, legal systems, and stages of economic development. With intellectual property, as with all areas of economic and social regulation, this diversity presents unique challenges for the ASEAN cooperation agenda. ASEAN has responded by adopting an "interoperability" approach. This approach pursues an agenda of increased cross-border trade, cooperation, and investment, while respecting the sovereignty of individual ASEAN nation-states and each nation's unique perspective. Interoperability thus aligns with what has become known as the "ASEAN Way." For intellectual property, the ASEAN Way involves working together while respecting and accommodating differences.

This collection of essays presents different perspectives on the theme of intellectual property interoperability. In many respects, the diversity of the perspectives presented here itself reflects the ASEAN Way. Each chapter presents unique insights on ASEAN interoperability in the intellectual property context. Some champion the benefits that are seen to accompany enhanced cooperation between member states' intellectual property systems. Others take a more critical stance, questioning the viability of greater interoperability in countries where intellectual property laws are only of marginal relevance to ordinary people, or where significant impediments are in the way of efficient administration of intellectual property. The authors are all experts in their fields, and their analyses draw on their different experiences as academics, administrators, and practitioners. Most of the chapters focus specifically on ASEAN jurisdictions and cooperation between them, and discuss important substantive law questions and issues relating to intellectual property administration. By way of comparison, we have also included perspectives from Europe and Latin America in chapters that discuss different approaches to regional cooperation. Two chapters focus on private international law matters, reflecting our belief that private international law is itself a potential vehicle for interoperability, to the extent that it is premised on mutual recognition of, and respect for, different nations' legal systems.

We hope that the volume will provide insights as to the administration of intellectual property in a part of the world that is of increasing economic significance. To that end, the final section of the book presents a matrix on ASEAN intellectual property systems. The segment summarizes the intellectual property laws and frameworks of the ten ASEAN countries. Comprising six parts, it presents general information on their intellectual property systems, as well as specific data with respect to trademarks, patents, designs, copyright, and other related rights, such as trade secrets, privacy, and personal data protection.

At the same time, the project is animated by a broader agenda. The management of relationships between different nations' intellectual property systems distils a set of profound challenges for intellectual property law. Intellectual property is, or has the potential to be, relevant to almost every area of life. If intellectual property law is understood as one of many social policy levers available to the nation-state, it is inevitable that intellectual property laws will be deployed by different nations in ways that reflect different visions of the good life. Given this, it is inevitable that nations will, to the extent permitted by international law, approach some intellectual property issues in different ways. This might involve deliberative intellectual property policy choices: whether, for example, to adopt a "fair use" defense, or decisions about the breadth of an "experimental use" exception. But they could also reflect choices about where to direct "law reform resources," to the extent that the state of domestic intellectual property laws reflects choices as to how to manage legislative and policy priorities.

We have already noted the diversity that exists between different ASEAN member states. But, in a number of contexts, we are also witnessing a rising skepticism about the kind of economic multilateralism that has driven much of the harmonization agenda in intellectual property. In international forums, within individual nations, and in civil society groups, and among indigenous peoples there is now a diversity of views as to how best to approach the regulation of intellectual property. In some contexts, this has led to demands for greater political accountability. This new politics of intellectual property has foregrounded the need for nations' intellectual property systems to work together without necessarily relying on harmonization or top-down fiat. It is here that the ASEAN interoperability agenda may provide useful insights for other groups of countries that see the benefits of greater cooperation in the intellectual property space, while seeking to maintain domestic differences – or, at least, reserving the *potential* to pursue different policy agendas through the fashioning of their domestic intellectual property regimes.

We are grateful to all the contributors to this volume for their willingness to share their expertise on the cluster of important issues that inform the ASEAN interoperability agenda. We both have benefitted from the enlightening discussions and exchanges of ideas that their papers have provoked. The book has benefited from the diversity of perspectives, including those derived from some authors' work in official capacities in various ASEAN member states. (Of course all chapters represent the authors' personal perspectives, and should not be taken as indications of institutional positions.) The support of the Intellectual Property Unit at the Centre for Law & Business at the National University of Singapore's Law School, which provided much of the funding for this project, is gratefully acknowledged. We have also been honored by the contribution of a Foreword by the Chief Justice of Singapore, Hon. Sundaresh Menon. Excellent research and administrative assistance was provided by Scott Fletcher, Yihang Ng, Claudia Lee, and Finna Wong. We also thank John Berger of Cambridge University Press (New York) for his continued support and encouragement of this endeavor.

Finally, we note that the perspectives presented here only scratch the surface of the complex range of issues that will engage the intellectual property community as the ASEAN interoperability agenda evolves. We have greatly enjoyed working on this current project – but our hope is that intellectual property "interoperability" will be a topic that continues to inspire the attention it deserves.

Elizabeth Siew-Kuan Ng
Singapore
and
Graeme W. Austin
Wellington, New Zealand

2017

PART I

INTELLECTUAL PROPERTY INTEROPERABILITY AND THE ASEAN WAY

In Chapter 1, Elizabeth Siew Kuan Ng presents the interoperability agenda as one solution for international intellectual property cooperation. The next four chapters highlight the unique challenges to intellectual property interoperability in ASEAN and beyond.

First, in Chapter 2 Denis Croze shares his views on integrating intellectual property multilateralism in light of bilateral, regional, and plurilateral developments. The author examines the challenges and competition faced by international organizations from a multiplicity of new actors and stakeholders in a rapidly changing technological and geopolitical landscape. Analyzing the factors that have put intellectual property at a crossroad, Croze concludes optimistically that multilateralism can continue to function effectively alongside regionalism and plurilateralism.

In Chapter 3, Agus Sardjono discusses the challenges to interoperability in the context of cultural heritage. Sharing lessons learned from his extensive research on the traditional values imbued in batik, which has come to be regarded as part of Indonesia's national identity, Professor Sardjono stresses that the interoperability agenda must pay more attention to how intellectual property laws actually align with the realities of the lives of the people. Without such an understanding, the author forewarns that the development of formal intellectual property norms will be inconsistent with the views of the people concerned, and will inevitably lead to system dysfunction.

The next two chapters focus on the trademark systems of Myanmar and Cambodia, two of the newer ASEAN member states. In Chapter 4, Khin Mar Yee provides insights into Myanmar's current trademark system based, inter alia, on the Penal Code of 1861 and the common law. To complement its recent transformation from a socialist regime to a more developed market economy, Myanmar has embarked on modernizing its laws including those in respect of trademarks. Providing useful glimpses on the new draft Trademark

Law, Professor Khin Mar Yee emphasizes that the promulgation of the new TRIPS-compliant intellectual property laws will enhance opportunities for greater interoperability with the intellectual property laws and systems of other ASEAN member states. In Chapter 5, Sokheng Sim, Sovath Phin, and Giulio Zanetti share Cambodia's experience in creating an interoperable trademark system, the branch of intellectual property law which has seen the greatest development in the country. Briefly tracing the historical and policy developments of Cambodia's trademark system, the chapter then centers discussion on the recently adopted national intellectual property development policies and strategies directed mainly at the use of intellectual property to support Cambodia's economic development. The authors highlight the essential features of Cambodia's trademark system and examine several initiatives aimed at enhancing greater trademark interoperability among ASEAN members. They determine that Cambodia's greatest challenges currently lie in its institutional fragmentation, application, and enforcement of intellectual property laws and regulations. Notwithstanding these obstacles, Sim, Phin, and Zanetti conclude that because of the diverse levels of development among ASEAN member states, interoperability may proceed faster and more smoothly in some areas while being delayed or challenged in others.

1

Intellectual Property Interoperability in ASEAN and Beyond

An Integration Model

Elizabeth Siew-Kuan Ng

1.1 INTRODUCTION

In August 2017, the Association of Southeast Asian Nations (ASEAN) will commemorate its fiftieth anniversary. Established by the five founding member countries of Indonesia, Malaysia, the Philippines, Singapore, and Thailand, it later expanded to encompass Brunei Darussalam, Vietnam, Lao People's Democratic Republic (Lao PDR/Laos), Myanmar, and Cambodia. Bonded together by history, geography, and culture, this diverse ten-member grouping has developed in a peaceful and conciliatory manner, with mutual cooperation and friendship. Safeguarding the independence and sovereignty of its member states, the "ASEAN Way" of regional cooperation entrenches the core principles of consensus and noninterference in the internal affairs of other nations. Holding firmly to these key tenets, ASEAN has elevated regional integration to transform Southeast Asia into a key economic bloc. Significant milestones toward accomplishing its goal of establishing an ASEAN Economic Community (AEC) by 2025 include the launch of the ASEAN Economic Community in 2015[1] and the adoption of the ASEAN Economic Community Blueprint of 2025,[2] acclaimed by the secretary-general of ASEAN, His Excellency Le Luong

[1] As of 2015, the ASEAN Economic Community comprises the ASEAN Political-Security Community, the ASEAN Economic Community, and the ASEAN Socio-Cultural Community. It was launched on November 22, 2015 at the 27th ASEAN Summit in Kuala Lumpur, Malaysia. *See The Kuala Lumpur Declaration on ASEAN 2025: Forging Ahead Together* (2015), *available at* www.asean.org/storage/2015/12/ASEAN-2025-Forging-Ahead-Together-final.pdf.

[2] ASEAN Economic Community (AEC) Blueprint 2025 was adopted as part of the "Kuala Lumpur Declaration 2025: Forging Ahead Together," which also includes the ASEAN Community Vision 2025, ASEAN Political-Security Community Blueprint 2025, and ASEAN Socio-Cultural Community Blueprint 2025. *See The AEC Blueprint, available at* www.asean.org/wp-content/uploads/images/2015/November/aec-page/AEC-Blueprint-2025-FINAL.pdf and *The Kuala Lumpur Declaration 2025, available at* www

Minh, as the "biggest milestone in the history of evolution and development of ASEAN since its founding in 1967."[3]

To complement the advancement of economic competitiveness in its region, one of ASEAN's central policy focuses is to enhance regional intellectual property cooperation. Cognizant of the vastly different levels of development among its member states, and desiring to give due recognition to these divergences, ASEAN realized that intellectual property integration should not be centered on substantive harmonization, the approach taken by the European Union (at least not for the near term). As Annette Kur highlights, any convergence efforts in the ASEAN context will not be aimed at perfecting harmonization but rather on facilitating and encouraging cross-border trade and investment.[4] Toward this end, ASEAN has embraced an inclusive supranational intellectual property cooperation framework premised on an interoperability agenda. As Yih San Tan emphasizes, interoperability does not necessarily mean harmonization, but aims at building an intellectual property regime that creators will be able to utilize for overseas market access.[5] Such an integration model enables nations to move forward collectively at varying paces; it is premised on consensus and noninterference and on respect for the national sovereignty of each nation and support for a member's use of existing flexibilities in customizing its domestic policy subject to regional and international commitments. For despite the absence of an intellectual property harmonization agenda, all of the ASEAN member states have acceded to the World Trade Organization (WTO)[6] and are bound by the standards imposed under the Agreement on Trade-Related Aspects of Intellectual Property Rights (TRIPS), among other international treaties. Still, as Rochelle

.asean.org/wp-content/uploads/images/2015/November/KL-Declaration/ASEAN%202025%20Forging%20Ahead%20Together%20final.pdf.

3 *See H. E. Le Luong Minh, Welcome Remarks by H. E. Le Luong Minh, Secretary-General of ASEAN 2016 ASEAN Day Celebration, available at* www.asean.org/storage/2012/05/SG-Remarks-for-49th-ASEAN-Day-Jakarta-2016-final.pdf.

4 *See* Annette Kur, *The EUIPO Convergence Program Model for ASEAN?, in* Elizabeth Siew-Kuan Ng & Graeme Austin (eds.), International Intellectual Property and the ASEAN Way: Pathways to Interoperability, Chapter 15.

5 *See* Tan Yih San, Speech by Mr. Tan Yih San, Chief Executive of IPOS at the NUS Centre for Business and Law (August 15, 2014), *available at* www.ipos.gov.sg/MediaEvents/Readnews/tabid/873/articleid/290/category/Speeches/parentId/80/year/2014/Default.aspx

6 Except for Cambodia, Laos, and Vietnam, all of the other ASEAN member states were also signatories to the General Agreement on Tariffs and Trade (GATT), the multilateral trading system that was replaced by the World Trade Organization (WTO) on January 1, 1995. *See* the WTO, *available at* www.wto.org/. For a discussion on TRIPS, *see, e.g.*, Daniel J. Gervais, The Trips Agreement – Drafting History and Analysis (4th ed., 2012).

Dreyfuss and Graeme Dinwoodie compellingly argue, TRIPS reflects a "neo-federalist regime" in which member states agree to "operate within an international framework"[7] but retain considerable discretion to do so.

Building on my earlier study,[8] this chapter proffers an integration model based on "intellectual property interoperability," drawing on the experience of ASEAN. First, I begin by briefly reviewing the background of ASEAN diversity and diplomacy based on the ASEAN Way, including insights into the Treaty of Amity and Cooperation in Southeast Asia[9] (Treaty of Amity). Second, a short analysis of the patent and trademark filing data will be presented to illustrate the diverging levels of intellectual property creation and utilization in the ASEAN region. The chapter then reflects on ASEAN's inclusive regional cooperation model. Specifically, it highlights the provisions and key aspects of the ASEAN Intellectual Property Action Plan of 2016–2025 to illustrate the pathways of intellectual property interoperability that are being implemented over that timeframe. Third, I ultimately suggest that in a highly integrated but uncertain global economy, a supranational intellectual property interoperability model based on the ASEAN Way may be a plausible way forward. For as Graeme Austin illuminates, intellectual property rights are not ends in themselves but social policy levers that countries can deploy to reflect their visions of the good life.[10]

7 Graeme B. Dinwoodie & Rochelle C. Dreyfuss, A Neofederalist Vision of TRIPS – The Resilience of the International Intellectual Property Regime 5 (2012). *See also* Graeme B. Dinwoodie & Rochelle C. Dreyfuss, *Diversifying without Discriminating: Complying with the Mandates of the TRIPS Agreement*, 13 Mich. Telecomm. & Tech. L. Rev. 445 (2007). These issues are also discussed in detail in a study commissioned by and presented to the WIPO: Elizabeth Siew-Kuan Ng, Effective Use of Patent Related Flexibilities and Their Implementation at the National or Regional Level in Selected Asian Countries (2011, revised 2013), where the author proffered that some "developing countries in Asia have not fully utilized the policy space afforded by international treaties such as the TRIPS-permitted patent flexibilities . . . [and] urged that due care should be taken to avoid any haste in compelling countries at different levels of development to adopt a 'one-size fits all' model if adverse outcomes are to be avoided. On the contrary, a differentiated response may be imperative given the divergence in the social, economic and technological indicators among nations."

8 Elizabeth Siew-Kuan Ng, *ASEAN IP Harmonization: Striking the Delicate Balance*, 25 Pace Int'l. L. Rev. 129 (2013). Some of the material in this chapter is based on this earlier work.

9 *Treaty of Amity and Cooperation in Southeast Asia Indonesia of February 24, 1976, available at* www.asean.org/treaty-amity-cooperation-southeast-asia-indonesia-24-february-1976/.

10 *See* Graeme Austin, *Cooperation through Conflict of Laws: The Justiciability of Cross-Border Copyright Infringement, in* Elizabeth Siew-Kuan Ng & Graeme Austin (eds.), International Intellectual Property and the ASEAN Way: Pathways to Interoperability, Chapter 8.

1.2 ASEAN AND DIPLOMACY: THE ASEAN WAY

1.2.1 *ASEAN: A Brief Overview*

ASEAN was founded to represent "the collective will of the nations of Southeast Asia to bind themselves together in friendship and cooperation and, through joint efforts and sacrifices, secure for their peoples and for posterity the blessings of peace, freedom and prosperity."[11] Set amidst the tumultuous conflict in the Indochina region at that time, the five founding members of Indonesia, Malaysia, the Philippines, Singapore, and Thailand signed the ASEAN Declaration (known also as the Bangkok Declaration) on August 8, 1967, which aimed at building an inclusive community comprising and belonging to all Southeast Asian nations. As such, membership to the Association was kept open to all states in the region. By 1999, the ASEAN community had expanded into a ten-member grouping including Brunei Darussalam, Vietnam, Lao People's Democratic Republic (Lao PDR/Laos), Myanmar, and Cambodia. ASEAN functioned on a "totally informal basis"[12] for around forty years until the conclusion of the ASEAN Charter in 2007. Aimed at creating an ASEAN legal and institutional framework by codifying all of its rules, values, and norms,[13] with a particular focus on conflict resolution mechanisms, the Charter came into force on December 15, 2008. On the international front, all of the ASEAN member states are now members of the WTO, following Laos's accession in 2013.

Situated on a total land area of around 4.49 million square kilometers in a dynamic part of Southeast Asia, ASEAN is the third most populous region in the world, with approximately 629 million residents. Ranked third in terms of the region's global market size after China and India, it also has the third largest (and one of the youngest) labor forces in the world, with around 65 percent of its workers under the age of thirty-five years old. More than 90 percent of the companies in ASEAN are small and medium-sized enterprises.[14] In 2015, ASEAN was ranked as the sixth largest economy worldwide and the third largest in Asia. With a robust and vibrant economy generating a gross domestic product (GDP) of US$2.4 trillion and a GDP per capita (at current prices) of US$3,867 in 2015, some analysts have predicted that ASEAN could become the

[11] ASEAN, *History: The Founding of ASEAN*, *available at* www.asean.org/asean/about-asean/history/. *See generally*, LEE YOONG YOONG (ed.), ASEAN MATTERS! REFLECTING ON THE ASSOCIATION OF SOUTHEAST ASIAN NATIONS (2011).

[12] WALTER WOON, THE ASEAN CHARTER: A COMMENTARY 18 (2016).

[13] *Id.*

[14] Based on the data of the US Mission to ASEAN on the YSEALI – ASEAN Infographics (March 25, 2016), *available at* https://asean.usmission.gov/yseali-asean-infographic-3/.

fourth largest economy in the world by 2050.[15] In terms of global exports, the ASEAN region accounts for around 7 percent of total exports worldwide and is ranked as the fourth largest exporting region in the world, after the European Union, North America, and China/Hong Kong.[16] Intra-ASEAN foreign direct investment (FDI) in 2015 was ASEAN's highest source of FDI, followed by the European Union, Japan, the United States, and China.[17] Similarly, intra-ASEAN trade in 2015 comprised the largest share of ASEAN's total trade by partner, followed by China, Japan, the European Union, and the United States.[18] With the continued deepening of economic regional integration, intra-ASEAN trade is expected to increase substantially.

Notwithstanding ASEAN's impressive data when viewed as a region, it should not be assumed that ASEAN is a monolithic bloc. In fact, it is composed mainly of developing countries with immense variation in their levels of economic, technological, social, and political development. A few examples may serve to further illuminate this diversity:

- Economic divergence: If we look at the data from 2015, a comparison of the GDP between Indonesia and Laos, for example, reveals a wide gap of around US$845 billion. Similarly, the GDP per capita (at current prices) for Singapore was more than fifty times higher than for Myanmar and Cambodia, or a differential of more than US$50,000. Again, if we look at international trade figures,[19] such as those of Thailand and Brunei, there is a disparity of more than US$400 billion. A similar trend emerges in relation to FDI inflow, with Singapore receiving around US$60 billion and the Philippines standing at US$5 billion.[20]
- Digital divide: Singapore is the only ASEAN nation ranked in the category of "Stand-out Country"[21] in the Digital Evolution Index 2013. It is

[15] *See* Vinayak HV, Fraser Thompson, & Oliver Tonby, *Understanding ASEAN: Seven Things You Need to Know* (May 2014), *available at* www.mckinsey.com/industries/public-sector/our-insights/understanding-asean-seven-things-you-need-to-know. *See also* Vivian Balakrishnan, Edited Transcript of Keynote Address by Minister for Foreign Affairs Dr. Vivian Balakrishnan at the 3rd South Asia Diaspora Convention, July 18, 2016, *available at* www.mfa.gov.sg/content/mfa/media_centre/press_room/pr/2016/201607/transcript-of-keynote-address-by-minister-minister-for-foreign-a.printable.html?status=1.

[16] Vinayak et al., *id.* [17] Based on data from the ASEAN Secretariat. [18] *Id.*

[19] The ASEAN IMTS Database 2015 figures as of August 30, 2016; *See* ASEAN website, http://asean.org/.

[20] The figures include equity, reinvested earnings, and intercompany. They are preliminary as of June 30, 2016. *Id.*

[21] The Index ranks countries into four trajectory zones: 1. Stand Out: Nations having high digital evolution and strong momentum; 2. Stall Out: Nations with high digital evolution but weak momentum; 3. Break Out: Nations having low digital evolution but strong momentum;

predicted that it will take many years for the other top ASEAN countries to catch up with Singapore's digital evolution. Based on existing benchmarks (assuming no change in policy or innovation) it is projected that the time taken for the top five ASEAN countries to reach Singapore's current level of digital development will be around 13 years for Indonesia; 12 years for the Philippines; 10 years for Vietnam; and 9 years and 8 years for Thailand and Malaysia respectively.[22]

- Population variance: Indonesia is the most populous country in ASEAN, with a population of more than 255 million. This is more than 600 times higher than that of Brunei, with a population of slightly more than 417,000; more than 50 times higher than Singapore, with around 5 million; and more than 35 times higher than Laos, with approximately 7 million.[23]
- Political distinctiveness: Some ASEAN countries, such as, Singapore, Malaysia, Indonesia, and the Philippines, are democracies. Myanmar, on the other hand, was ruled by a military junta for around fifty years until a civilian government was installed in 2011, followed recently by the country's landmark general election in 2016.[24]
- Religious diversity: More than 85 percent of Indonesia's population identifies as Muslim; around 80 percent of the Philippines identifies as Catholic; in Thailand and Cambodia more than 95 percent of the population identify as Buddhists[25]; and in Myanmar there is a mix of Buddhists, Christians, and Muslims.[26]
- Social/cultural dissimilarities: The ASEAN community comprises diverse cultural groups emphasizing to varying extents differing social values, such as attitudes on communal and inclusive rights. This divergence poses great challenges to ASEAN's intellectual property integration. For example, some social cultures emphasize "commonality" or the belief

4. Watch Out: These nations have low digital evolution and weak momentum. *See* Tufts University, The Fletcher School of Law and Diplomacy, *The Digital Evolution Index of Fletcher School*, *available at* www19.iadb.org/intal/intalcdi/PE/2016/16259.pdf.

[22] *See* Bhaskar Chakravorti, *Where the Digital Economy Is Moving Fastest* (Summary of a Harvard Business Review Webinar of March 9, 2016), *available at* www19.iadb.org/intal/intalcdi/PE/2016/16259.pdf.

[23] Based on country projection data as of August 2016 from the ASEAN website, *supra* note 19.

[24] BBC News, *Myanmar's 2015 Landmark Elections Explained* (December 3, 2015), *available at* www.bbc.com/news/world-asia-33547036 and BBC News, *Myanmar Opens New Parliament Session after Military Rule* (February 1, 2016), *available at* www.bbc.com/news/world-asia-35456982.

[25] Vinayak et al., *supra* note 15. *See also the Nation Master: Religion – Countries Compared*, *available at* www.nationmaster.com/country-info/stats/Religion/Religions.

[26] Burma Center Prague, *Myanmar Fact Sheet*, *available at* www.burma-center.org/burma-myanmar-fact-sheet/.

> that the creative and innovative outputs should be freely shared as "community property."[27] One example highlighted by Agus Sardjono relates to Indonesia's batik cultural heritage, which has been viewed as belonging to the Indonesian people as a community for hundreds of years.[28] In addition, ASEAN is also confronted by a broad diversity of languages. The ASEAN community converses in more than 12 languages including Malay, English, Khmer, Indonesian, Laos, Mandarin Chinese, Tamil, Myanmar, Filipino, Spanish, Thai, and Vietnamese.[29]

Despite the immense diversity among its member states, ASEAN has persevered in its goal of enhancing regional integration. The launch of the ASEAN Community 2015 centered on three key pillars[30] – Political Security, Economic Community, and Sociocultural Community – marked a significant milestone in demonstrating the Association's perseverance and resilience in advancing the goals of coming together as one community, to share one vision and forge one identity. Recognizing the importance of sustaining peace in the Southeast Asian region, ASEAN member states remain guided by the ASEAN Way in dealing with intra- and interstate relations. Take, for example, the Declaration on the Conduct of Parties in the South China Sea of 2002 (DOC) signed by the ASEAN member states and the People's Republic of China and the Code of Conduct in the South China Sea (COC), which inter alia sought to promote self-restraint, maritime cooperation, and the peaceful settlement of disputes in the South China Sea.[31] Others aimed at setting up a reliable dispute settlement mechanism in ASEAN include the ASEAN Protocol on Enhanced Dispute Settlement Mechanism of 2004[32] and the ASEAN Charter on Dispute Settlement Mechanisms of 2010.[33]

27 *See, e.g.*, Dongwook Chun, *Patent Law Harmonization in the Age of Globalization: The Necessity and Strategy for a Pragmatic Outcome*, 93 J. PAT. & TRADEMARK OFF. SOC'Y. 127, 131–132 (2011).

28 Agus Sardjono, *Challenges for ASEAN Interoperability: Lessons from Research on Cultural Heritage Protection in Indonesia*, *in* ELIZABETH SIEW-KUAN NG & GRAEME AUSTIN (eds.), INTERNATIONAL INTELLECTUAL PROPERTY AND THE ASEAN WAY: PATHWAYS TO INTEROPERABILITY, Chapter 3.

29 *See* information on ASEAN member states, *available at* http://asean.org/asean/asean-member-states/.

30 *See* the *ASEAN Community Fact Sheet*, *available at* http://asean.org/storage/2012/05/11a.-April-2016-Fact-Sheet-of-ASEAN-Community.pdf.

31 *Id.*

32 *See* the *ASEAN Protocol on Enhanced Dispute Settlement Mechanism*, *available at* http://agreement.asean.org/media/download/20141217102933.pdf.

33 *See* the *ASEAN Charter on Dispute Settlement Mechanisms*, *available at* https://cil.nus.edu.sg/2010/2010-protocol-to-the-asean-charter-on-dispute-settlement-mechanisms/; *ASEAN Secretariat, Protocol on Dispute Settlement Mechanisms Signed Ha Noi*, April 8, 2010, *available*

1.2.2 *Diplomacy*

The ASEAN Way has acted as the bedrock guiding principle for the Southeast Asian region over the past fifty years. Entrenched in the Treaty of Amity, which was concluded in February 1976 to govern intra- and interstate relations in the Southeast Asian region, it emphasizes perpetual regional peace, stability, friendship, and mutual cooperation in the region. Inspired by the principles of the Charter of the United Nations, it favors a nonadversarial and informal method of dispute resolution in the settlement of interstate differences in Southeast Asia. In the spirit of ASEAN solidarity, the Association's members undertake to create conditions conducive to promote peaceful cooperation based on mutual respect and benefit among the nations of Southeast Asia.[34] Originally created to govern intra-ASEAN relationships, the Treaty was later extended to states outside Southeast Asia that desire to adhere to the ASEAN Way.[35] Further extensions were made in 2010 to include regional organizations whose members are sovereign states.[36] In 2016, ASEAN celebrated the fortieth anniversary of the Treaty of Amity with twenty-two non-ASEAN parties to the Treaty,[37] including Australia, Bangladesh, Brazil, Canada, the Democratic People's Republic of Korea, the European Union, France, India,

at http://asean.org/?static_post=protocol-on-dispute-settlement-mechanisms-signed-ha-noi-8-april-2010.

34 *See The Declaration of ASEAN Concord 1976 (Bali Concord I) Preamble Para 7, available at* http://asean.org/?static_post=declaration-of-asean-concord-indonesia-24-february-1976; *also available at* www.icnl.org/research/library/files/Transnational/1976Declaration.pdf. The Declaration was adopted by the Heads of State/Government at the First ASEAN Summit in Bali, Indonesia on February 24, 1976. *See also* Koh Kheng-Lian & Nicholas A. Robinson, *Strengthening Sustainable Development in Regional Inter-Governmental Governance: Lessons from the 'ASEAN Way'*, 6 SING. J. INT.'L & COMP. L. 640 (2002); and Gillian Goh, *The 'ASEAN Way' Non-Intervention and ASEAN's Role in Conflict Management*, 3 STAN. J.E. ASIAN AFF. 113 (2003).

35 Such an extension was made subject to the consent of all ASEAN member states. *See* the First and the Second Protocols Amending the Treaty of Amity and Cooperation in Southeast Asia, which were signed on December 15, 1987 and on July 25, 1998 respectively. *See, e.g.*, Article 1 of the First Protocol of 1987 amending Article 18 of the Treaty of Amity: "... States outside Southeast Asia may also accede to this Treaty by the consent of all the States in Southeast Asia which are signatories to this Treaty and Brunei Darussalam." *See* also Article 1 of the Second Protocol of 1998, which amends Article 18 of the Treaty of Amity: "States outside Southeast Asia may also accede to this Treaty with the consent of all the States in Southeast Asia ... "

36 *See* the THIRD PROTOCOL AMENDING THE TREATY OF AMITY AND COOPERATION IN SOUTHEAST ASIA 2010, Article 1, stating that the Treaty: "shall be open for accession by States outside Southeast Asia and regional organizations whose members are only sovereign States subject to the consent of all the States in Southeast Asia ... "

37 *See ASEAN Foreign Ministers' Statement on the Occasion of the 40th Anniversary of the Treaty of Amity and Cooperation in Southeast Asia (TAC)* (adopted by the 49th ASEAN Foreign Ministers' Meeting, Vientiane, July 24, 2016), *available at* http://asean.org/storage/2016/07/Statement-of-the-40th-Anniversary-of-the-TAC-ADOPTED.pdf. *See also* the 1976 *Treaty of Amity and*

Japan, Mongolia, New Zealand, Norway, the People's Republic of China, Pakistan, the Republic of Korea, Russia, Sri Lanka, Timor-Leste, Turkey, the United Kingdom, and the United States.

Even at global dialogues, ASEAN continues to hold steadfastly to this key code of conduct deeply rooted in the "principles of independence, sovereignty, equality, territorial integrity, non-interference and national identity of all nations."[38] Despite immense scrutiny and criticism, particularly from some countries in the West, the ASEAN cooperation model was recently vindicated by the recent dramatic transformation in Myanmar, proving what one commentator has aptly termed the "futility of the West's preference for sanctions and isolation."[39]

1.3 INTELLECTUAL PROPERTY INTEROPERABILITY IN ASEAN

1.3.1 *Developing a Competitive ASEAN Economy through Intellectual Property Integration*

One of the key aims of ASEAN's dynamic pursuit of a competitive economy in the global marketplace is enhancing its intellectual property cooperation. To meet the challenges of an interdependent global economy propelled by rapid advancements in science and technology, ASEAN aims to transform the Southeast Asian region into a creative and innovative community. Toward this end, it sought to develop an intra-ASEAN intellectual property framework, while strengthening inter-ASEAN intellectual property cooperation with key external partners and international organizations.[40]

Cooperation in Southeast Asia, which was signed on February 24, 1976 in Bali, Indonesia, *available at* https://cil.nus.edu.sg/1976/1976-treaty-of-amity-and-cooperation-in-southeast-asia-signed-on-24-february-1976-in-bali-indonesia-by-the-heads-of-stategovernment/.

38 *See Bali Declaration on ASEAN Community in a Global Community of Nations (Bali Concord III) Para A.1.a., available at* www.asean.org/storage/archive/documents/19th%20summit/Bali%20Concord%20III.pdf.

39 Tommy Koh, *The World in 2011*, The Straits Times (December 31, 2011).

40 *See, e.g.*, the EC-ASEAN Patent and Trade Marks Program (ECAP I) implemented from 1993–1997 to assist ASEAN countries to promote industrial property protection; EC-ASEAN Intellectual Property Rights Cooperation Program (ECAP II) sought to enhance harmonization and capacity building in ASEAN countries by expanding the scope of activities to cover all fields of intellectual property. Funding was extended to cover a third phase of the ECAP program, namely, the EU-ASEAN Project on the Protection of Intellectual Property Rights (ECAP III) focused on regional harmonization and aimed at aligning the activities to the ASEAN Intellectual Property Action Plan. *See ECAP Project Overview (1993–2016), available at* www.ecap-project.org/about/ecap-project-overview-1993–2016; ECAP III, *available at* www.ecap3.org/.

Initial efforts to forge a common regional intellectual property profile included the creation of an ASEAN Framework Agreement on Intellectual Property Cooperation in 1995 and the formation of the ASEAN Working Group on Intellectual Property Cooperation a year later. The Working Group comprising the intellectual property offices of the ASEAN member states is tasked with developing, implementing, and coordinating the intellectual property and related activities in Southeast Asia.[41] Early roadmaps included the Hanoi Plan of Action and the ASEAN Intellectual Property Action Plans of 2004–2010 and the Work Plan on Copyright. Aimed at conceiving a substantively harmonized regional intellectual property system imbued with one set of regional intellectual property laws, these earlier attempts faced numerous setbacks and had to be abandoned (or at least deferred).[42] As ASEAN accelerated its economic integration and brought forward the launch of the ASEAN Economic Community from 2020 to 2015, a new ASEAN Intellectual Property Action Plan of 2011–2015 was formulated aimed at supporting this objective. This Action Plan built on the earlier ones by advancing regional intellectual property integration through a more fluid cooperation model. These initiatives have been discussed elsewhere[43] and will not be repeated here.

Instead, I will examine the post-2015 ASEAN environment. Particular emphasis will be placed on discussing the "new" strategic goals set forth in the recently adopted ASEAN Intellectual Property Rights Action Plan of 2016–2025 to illustrate the pathways of intellectual property cooperation based on the interoperability agenda. Before proceeding, a short analysis of ASEAN's differing levels of participation in the intellectual property system may provide a useful background.

1.3.2 *Divergence in ASEAN Member States' Participation in the Intellectual Property System*

An analysis of the trademark and patent filing data for 2014 in the ASEAN region discloses a high divergence in intellectual property creation and utilization at both inter- and intra-ASEAN levels.

41 Elizabeth Ng, ASEAN IP, *supra* note 8, at 137.

42 For a discussion on the constraints that ASEAN faced in substantive harmonization, *see* Elizabeth Ng, ASEAN IP, *supra* note 8, at 137–138. *See also* Emma Barraclough, *ASEAN Scales Back IP Plans*, Manag. Intell. Prop., 14 (December 2004–January 2005) and *see generally* Christopher Antons et al. (eds.), Intellectual Property Harmonisation within ASEAN and APEC (2004), and in particular Weerawit Weeraworawit, *The Harmonisation of Intellectual Property Rights in ASEAN*, *in* Christopher Antons et al. (eds.), Intellectual Property Harmonisation within ASEAN and APEC 205, 208 (2004).

43 *Id.*

At the intra-ASEAN level, the data disclosed that the total number of trademark applications (about 219,000) filed in all of the ASEAN intellectual property offices is more than five times higher than that for patents (around 42,000). This huge disparity is nearly two times higher than the global average, where the total number of trademark applications filed worldwide stands at only around 2.7 times higher than those for patents.[44] This seems to indicate a low level of utilization of the patent system in ASEAN member states. A divergence in the proportion of applications filed by residents and nonresidents was also observed with respect to both trademark and patent applications. On the trademark front, although ASEAN residents filed around 1.3 times more trademark applications (approximately 125,000) in the ASEAN region than nonresidents (about 93,000), this ratio is significantly lower than the global average, where the share of resident filings is about three times higher than that of nonresidents (based on the combined data from intellectual property offices worldwide).[45] A converse position emerged with respect to patent applications filed in the ASEAN region. The nonresident share of patent applications filed was substantially higher (around seven times higher) than that filed by ASEAN residents. This trend is an inverse variation from the global scene, where two-thirds of all patent applications worldwide were filed by residents with their domestic patent offices.[46] A high disparity was also observed in the total number of patent and trademark applications filed in the various ASEAN intellectual property offices, with numbers fluctuating considerably from one office to another. For example, the number of patents filed with the Singapore intellectual property office was more than 150 times higher than the number filed in Cambodia, 88 times higher than in Brunei, and about 3 times higher than in the Philippines. A similar trend emerges with respect to trademark filings, where the number of applications filed with the Indonesian intellectual property office was about thirty-nine times higher than that of Brunei, roughly ten times higher than in Cambodia, and around two times higher than Singapore.

Turning to the inter-ASEAN landscape, the share of patent applications filed in the ASEAN region pales significantly when compared with those of the top three countries globally. It was about twenty-two times lower than that in China, fourteen times lower than in the United States, and more than

44 *See WIPO IP Facts and Figures (2015), available at* www.wipo.int/edocs/pubdocs/en/wipo_pub_943_2015.pdf. Globally the patent applications in 2014 were approximately 2.7 million, compared with trademark applications of 7.4 million.

45 Based on the WIPO data in 2014, the resident share was about three-quarters of trademark applications filed worldwide (based on class counts). *Id.*

46 In 2014, the WIPO data revealed that an estimated two-thirds of all patent applications globally were filed by residents with their domestic offices. *Id.*

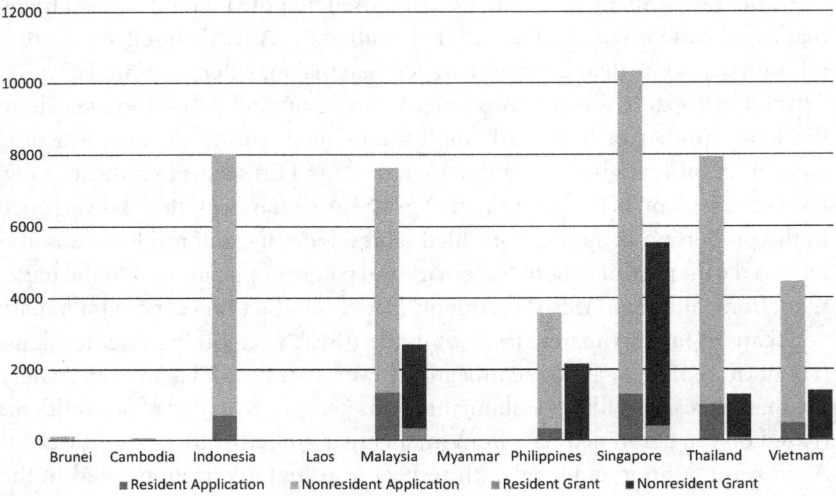

FIGURE 1.1 Patent applications and grants in ASEAN countries (2014).

seven times lower than in Japan. Variance was also perceived (albeit to a lesser extent) when contrasting the trademark applications filed in the ASEAN region with the top three countries worldwide. ASEAN filings stood at around ten times lower than those in China, 1.5 times lower than in the United States, and roughly the same number as in India (the country with the third largest trademarks filings globally).

See Figures 1.1 to 1.4[47] for further details.

Based on the foregoing, a few postulations may be proffered on ASEAN's technological development (assuming that patent data can be considered indicators or measures of innovation). First, viewed holistically as a region, ASEAN's level of technological development seems to lag considerably behind those of the global leaders of China, United States, and Japan. In addition, the ownership (and control) of patented technologies in the ASEAN region appears to be concentrated predominantly in the hands of foreigners (non-ASEAN residents).[48] Being mindful of this gap, ASEAN has stepped up efforts

47 My thanks to Claudia Lee for assisting with the charts that are based on data obtained from the WIPO IP statistics data center for 2014 (as at December 2015).

48 *See* Figure 1.1 on patent grant in the ASEAN countries. For a discussion on the impact of patent rights on developing countries, *see generally*, a study commissioned by the WIPO and published in six languages (English, French, Spanish, Arabic, Chinese, Russian) at the Assemblies of the Member States of WIPO, Thirty-Ninth Series of Meetings, Geneva, September 22 to October 1, 2003: Elizabeth Siew-Kuan Ng, The Impact of the International Patent System on Developing Countries (2003), *available at* www.wipo.int/meetings/en/doc_details.jsp?doc_id=17557.

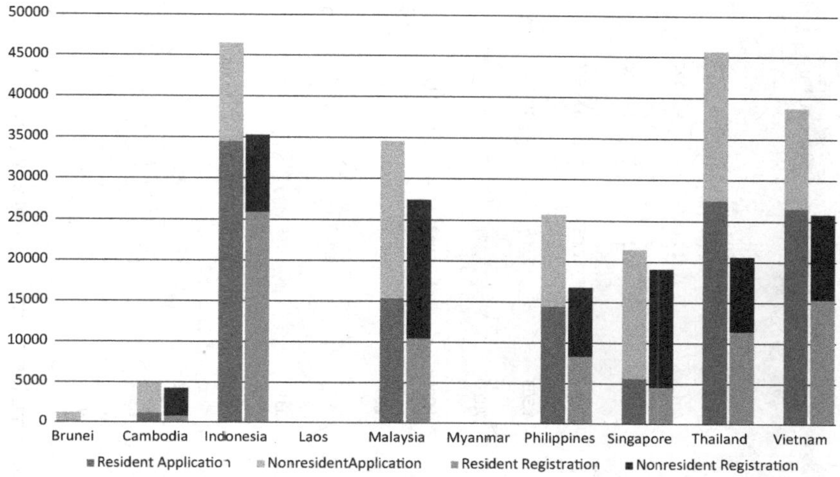

FIGURE 1.2 Trademark applications and registrations in ASEAN countries (2014).

to bolster the utilization of intellectual property through enhancing regional intellectual property integration. The recently adopted ASEAN Intellectual Property Action Plan of 2016–2025 is one case in point.

1.3.3 *ASEAN Intellectual Property Rights Action Plan 2016–2025*

The ASEAN Intellectual Property Rights Action Plan 2016–2025 was formulated to forge a more robust regional intellectual property regime, increase technology transfer, and expand technological capabilities in the region. Under this new ten-year plan, regional intellectual property offices will act as one of the key drivers of innovation in the region by bolstering engagement with the scientific and technological sector, reinforcing the intellectual property ecosystem, and expanding technology diffusion.[49] Four strategic goals aimed at enhancing the interoperability of intellectual property regimes among the ASEAN member states have been formulated[50]:

[49] *See* ASEAN Chairman's Statement of the 28th and 29th ASEAN Summits "Turning vision into reality for a dynamic ASEAN community," Vientiane, September 6–7, 2016.

[50] Note: At the time of writing, the precise details of the ASEAN Intellectual Property Rights Action Plan 2016–2025 have not yet been made available to the public, save for an abstract among others. *See, e.g.*, the information made available at the ASEAN–IPA Annual Meeting and Conference (March 4–6, 2016), *available at* www.aseanipa.org/attachments/article/653/01.%20AWGIPC-ASEAN%20IP%20Plan.pdf.

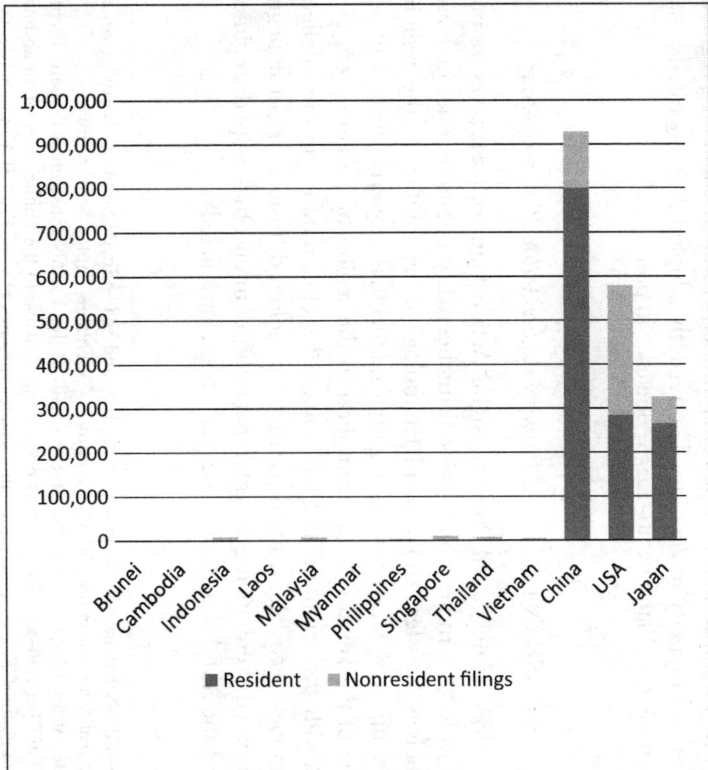

COUNTRY	RESIDENT	NON-RESIDENT	TOTAL
CHINA	801,135	127,042	928,177
US	285,096	293,706	578,802
JAPAN	265,959	60,030	325,989
SINGAPORE	1,303	9,009	10,312
INDONESIA	702	7,321	8,023
THAILAND	1,006	6,924	7,930
MALAYSIA	1,353	6,267	7,620
VIETNAM	487	3,960	4,447
PHILIPPINES	334	3,255	3,589
BRUNEI	26	91	117
CAMBODIA	2	65	67
LAOS	0	0	0
MYANMAR	0	0	0

FIGURE 1.3 Patent applications in ASEAN: Comparison with applications in top three countries globally (2014).

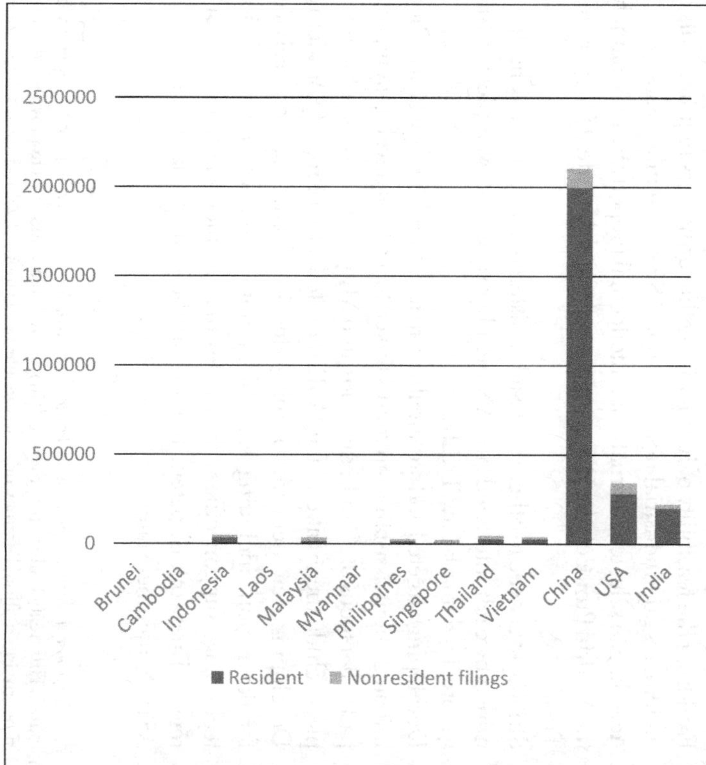

COUNTRY	RESIDENT	NONRESIDENT	TOTAL
CHINA	1,997,014	107,520	2,104,534
US	283,230	58,672	341,902
INDIA	200,137	22,098	222,235
INDONESIA	34,521	11,931	46,452
THAILAND	27,517	18,144	45,661
VIETNAM	26,563	12,181	38,744
MALAYSIA	15,400	19,171	34,571
PHILIPPINES	14,490	11,240	25,730
SINGAPORE	5,635	15,870	21,505
CAMBODIA	1,182	3,706	4,888
BRUNEI	101	1,074	1,175
LAOS	0	0	0
MYANMAR	0	0	0

FIGURE 1.4 Trademark applications in ASEAN: Comparison with applications in top three countries globally (2014).

1. Create a more robust ASEAN intellectual property system through strengthening intellectual property offices and building intellectual property infrastructure in the region.
2. Develop regional intellectual property platforms and infrastructures, thereby contributing toward enhancing the AEC.
3. Promote an expanded and inclusive ASEAN intellectual property ecosystem.
4. Enhance regional mechanisms to foster asset creation and commercialization, especially in the areas of geographical indications and traditional knowledge.

To meet these targets, nineteen initiatives were set forth, aimed at

1. Improving patent, trademark, and industrial design services.
2. Promoting the improvement of intellectual property services through timely and quality output.
3. Fostering excellence in collective management organizations, particularly transparency, accountability, and governance.
4. Exploring the feasibility of harmonizing the formalities requirements of trademarks and industrial design among ASEAN member states.
5. Acceding to selected international intellectual property treaties, namely, the Madrid Protocol, the Hague Agreement, and the Patent Cooperation Treaty.
6. Striving to accede to other WIPO-administered treaties (as may be determined by each interested ASEAN member state), for example, the Singapore Trademark Law Treaty.[51]
7. Developing targeted and sustainable capacity building, as well as office-initiated client-assistance programs linked to levels of development, with particular focus on Cambodia, Laos, and Myanmar. This may, for example, include the creation of an ASEAN Intellectual Property Academy.
8. Developing new networks of integrated intellectual property services for the region, including technology transfer offices and innovation technology support offices. Examples may include the setting up of a regional network of patent libraries in the educational institutions of ASEAN member states.

[51] *See* the *Singapore Treaty on the Law of Trademarks*, *available at* www.wipo.int/treaties/en/ip/singapore/. This treaty builds upon the Trademark Law Treaty and aims to provide a dynamic and modern international framework for the harmonization of administrative registration procedures on trademark.

9. Improving online services of ASEAN member states, including patent, trademark, copyright, and industrial design search systems, as well as implementing online filing systems for patents, trademarks, and industrial designs.
10. Modernizing information technology systems to improve regional service quality including developing an automated system (including translation) for electronic correspondence and dossier systems for trademarks, online filing, sharing of patent and copyright information through regional databases, and improving the regional databases for industrial designs and trademarks.
11. Improving and centralizing the management of the ASEAN Intellectual Property Portal by ensuring regular and timely updates of statistical data, such as the number of filings, registrations, grants, and pendency periods.
12. Implementing a regional Action Plan on intellectual property rights enforcement, which may include designing an online centralized regional platform or mechanism to coordinate information and enhance regional intellectual property enforcement.
13. Establishing an ASEAN Intellectual Property network for members of the judiciary, customs, and enforcement agencies.
14. Enhancing intra- and extra-ASEAN engagements with its stakeholders and external partners, such as through the establishment of online helpdesks.
15. Creating a regional accreditation system for intellectual property practitioners (if appropriate).
16. Enhancing awareness and respect of intellectual property for promoting its protection and utilization to support the branding of a "Creative ASEAN."
17. Developing intellectual property valuation services and raising awareness of intellectual property as valuable financial assets.
18. Promoting the commercialization of geographical indications in ASEAN through protection and branding strategies.
19. Promoting mechanisms for protecting genetic resources, traditional knowledge, and traditional cultural expression.[52]

As with the earlier Action Plan of 2011–2015, this latest Plan also emphasizes teamwork and collective responsibility by appointing specific ASEAN country

[52] *See, e.g.*, Ajeng Widianty (Directorate of Economic and Socio-Cultural Treaties of the Ministry of Foreign Affairs of the Republic of Indonesia), *National Database on GRTKTCE: The Need to Protect Genetic Resources and Traditional Knowledge in Kuala Lumpur, Malaysia* (July 11, 2012), *available at* www.unescap.org/sites/default/files/trips2012-ajeng.pdf.

champions to lead the specific initiatives with defined deliverables and detailed performance indicators. For example, the Philippines is the country champion on intellectual property enforcement, while Indonesia, Laos, and Vietnam will be the main leaders for the genetic resource, traditional knowledge, and traditional cultural expression agenda. Thailand and Indonesia will jointly lead the establishment of an ASEAN Copyright Notification/Recordation Network. Some of these initiatives have been expounded upon in this book by indigenous authors from the respective country champions[53] and will not be elaborated here.

It seems clear that the initiatives aimed at enhancing the pathways to interoperability in the ASEAN region seek broadly to align national intellectual property laws and policies within the AEC framework to promote cross-border trade and technical and procedural convergence, such as through establishing regional intellectual property platforms and infrastructure for the exchange of data among member states. Other proposals aimed at easing the workload and reducing costs and turnaround time for patent applications and prosecutions in the region include the ASEAN Patent Search and Examination Cooperation (ASPEC).[54] ASPEC is the first regional patent cooperation program to facilitate the sharing of patent search and examination results among the nine participating ASEAN intellectual property offices.[55] It is a nonbinding work-sharing process that seeks inter alia to minimize duplication and

[53] *See, e.g.*, the chapters by Pisawat Sukonthapan (Thailand), *Copyright Interoperability in ASEAN: Current and Future Issues* (Chapter 10); Agus Sardjono (Indonesia), *Challenges for ASEAN Interoperability: Lessons from Research on Cultural Heritage Protection in Indonesia* (Chapter 3); Ricardo Blancaflor (Philippines), *Enforcement of Intellectual Property Rights and the Challenges of ASEAN Integration* (Chapter 7). Other chapters written by ASEAN authors include Sokheng Sim, Sovath Phin, & Giulio Zanetti (Cambodia), *Trademark System in Cambodia* (Chapter 5); Lê Thi Thu Hà & Delphine Marie-Vivien (Vietnam), *Notification and Registration System of Geographical Indications: ASEAN's Perspective* (Chapter 11); Khin Mar Yee (Myanmar), *Trademark Protection in Myanmar: Current Issues and Future Directions* (Chapter 4); Jakkrit Kuanpoth (Thailand), *Challenges for Protection and Administration of Intellectual Property: Thailand's Perspective* (Chapter 14); Mark Lim, See Tho Sok Yee, & Diyanah Binte Baharudin (Singapore), *Singapore's Intellectual Property Dispute Resolution Experience and ASEAN Interoperability* (Chapter 6), Soh Kar Liang (Singapore) & Chew Phye Keat (Malaysia), *Proposal for a PAN-ASEAN Trademark Registration: A Case for the Practical Application of the Interoperability Principle* (Chapter 13). For other proposals on interoperability, *see, e.g.*, Ignacio de Medrano Caballero, *Connectivity, Interoperability, and Regional Integration of the ASEAN Trademark and Design Systems* (Chapter 12), *in* ELIZABETH SIEW-KUAN NG & GRAEME AUSTIN (eds.), INTERNATIONAL INTELLECTUAL PROPERTY AND THE ASEAN WAY: PATHWAYS TO INTEROPERABILITY.

[54] *See* the *ASEAN Patent Examination Co-operation (ASPEC), available at* www.ipos.gov.sg/AboutIP/TypesofIPWhatisIntellectualProperty/Whatisapatent/Applyingforapatent/ASEANPatentExaminationCo-operationASPEC.aspx.

[55] Except for Myanmar, all of the ASEAN intellectual property offices are participants in ASPEC.

multiplicity of work. As at August 2016, a total of 154 ASPEC requests have been submitted. Another example is the establishment of the ASEAN Intellectual Property Direct,[56] an online "one-stop" intellectual property resource directory.[57] Moving further afield, ASEAN has also laid out plans to enhance integration beyond intellectual property.

1.3.4 *Beyond Intellectual Property: Other Pathways to Interoperability*

ASEAN has also pursued other pathways to facilitate interagency dialogue and cooperation. Take, for example, the establishment of the Council of ASEAN Chief Justices to promote closer collaboration among the judiciaries in the region to share best practices and other judicial matters; and work plans on e-commerce and good regulatory practices to support regional trade liberalization and to advance freer movements of goods in ASEAN.[58] Others, such as the establishment of a National Trade Repository by all ASEAN member states, aim at linking them subsequently to form an ASEAN Trade Repository, a one-stop online database of information on ASEAN trade and customs.

Mindful that some ASEAN members may lack the capacity to participate in all of its initiatives, ASEAN has piloted several programs aimed at selected groups of countries (at least during the initial stages). Examples include the exchange of live data in the ASEAN Single Window environment to expedite customs clearance. Participating countries include Indonesia, Singapore, and Thailand; and the ASEAN Customs Transit System to facilitate movement of transit goods across borders – where Malaysia, Singapore, and Thailand are participants. Anticipating that other ASEAN member states will eventually join these and other platforms when they are ready, these programs aim to create a seamless, standardized, and harmonized system within the region, with ASEAN reiterating its commitment to narrow the developmental gap among ASEAN member states (especially the newer members of Cambodia, Laos, and Myanmar).

In the longer term, it is envisaged that the effective utilization and exploitation of intellectual property in the ASEAN region will contribute toward higher exports and greater in-flows of both domestic and foreign investment to Southeast Asia. Toward this end, ASEAN has intensified negotiation on the

[56] *See ASEAN IP Direct Portal, available at* www.ipos.gov.sg/AboutIP/IPResources/UsefulLinks/RegionalOrganisations/ASEANIPDirect.aspx.

[57] These initiatives have been examined in the author's earlier work and will not be reiterated here; *see* Elizabeth Ng, ASEAN IP, *supra* note 8, at 149–153.

[58] *See* ASEAN Chairman's Statement, *supra* note 49.

Regional Comprehensive Economic Partnership with its six free trade partners of Australia, China, India, Japan, Korea, and New Zealand,[59] and strengthened the relationship with its Dialogue Partners and other external parties. The recent adoption of a five-year Plan of Action 2016–2020 with Russia testifies to ASEAN's resolve to deepen inter-ASEAN relations.

1.4 CONCLUSION

ASEAN has evolved peacefully for the last fifty years, building an inclusive, dynamic, sustainable, and resilient community within a global community of nations.[60] ASEAN's goal of developing a politically cohesive, economically integrated, socially responsible, and truly people-centered and rules-based community[61] may provide useful lessons for the broader global community. For as Graeme Austin explains, the challenges faced by ASEAN's diversity are not unique to the region; rather they are shared by many nations worldwide.

As a microcosm of the world, ASEAN's fluid integration framework, anchored on consensus and noninterference, upholding the sovereignty of nations, and enabling nations to move forward together cooperatively at varying paces may be a much needed panacea in this new age of uncertainty.

Despite the promises held out by deep harmonization of law and practices (such as cost reduction in acquisition and enforcement of rights), the current realities of a highly integrated but nonhomogeneous world portend toward a collaborative interoperable model as the better way forward in the turbulent times ahead. Indeed, the interoperability agenda can extend beyond ASEAN to other settings, such as the judicial processes of private international law and cross-border enforcement.[62] As this model continues to evolve and adapt to changing times, lessons can also be drawn from other regional and

[59] Information on the Regional Comprehensive Economic Partnership is available on various websites including those of the Ministry of Trade and Industry Singapore, *available at* www.mti.gov.sg/MTIInsights/SiteAssets/Pages/FACTSHEET-WHAT-YOU-NEED-TO-KNOW-ABOUT/Factsheet%20on%20RCEP%20(June%202014).pdf; Asia Regional Integration Centre, *available at* https://aric.adb.org/fta/regional-comprehensive-economic-partnership; China FTA Network, *available at* http://fta.mofcom.gov.cn/list/rcepen/enrcepnews/1/encateinfo.html; New Zealand Foreign Affairs and Trade, *available at* https://www.mfat.govt.nz/en/trade/free-trade-agreements/agreements-under-negotiation/rcep/.

[60] *See* Bali Concord III, *supra* note 38.

[61] *See* the Nay Pyi Taw Declaration on the ASEAN Community's Post-2015 Vision (November 12, 2014), *available at* www.asean.org/storage/images/pdf/2014_upload/Nay%20Pyi%20Taw%20Declaration%20on%20the%20ASEAN%20Communitys%20Post%202015%20Vision%20w.annex.pdf.

[62] *See, e.g.*, Graeme Austin, *Cooperation Through Conflict of Laws*, *supra* note 10; Richard Garnett, *Intellectual Property Remedies Across Borders*, *in* Elizabeth Siew-Kuan Ng & Graeme

international systems.[63] As Jerome Reichman and Rochelle Dreyfuss counsel: "[I]nstead of moving forward with harmonization for its own sake, the international intellectual property community must first identify and test trustworthy, empirically supportable solutions likely to benefit humanity at large."[64]

The interoperability agenda based on cooperation the ASEAN Way is presented as one such solution in this work.

AUSTIN (eds.), INTERNATIONAL INTELLECTUAL PROPERTY AND THE ASEAN WAY: PATHWAYS TO INTEROPERABILITY, CHAPTER 9.

[63] *See, e.g.*, Annette Kur, *Convergence Program*, *supra* note 4; Reto Hilty & Roberto Romandini, *Developing a Common Patent System: Lessons to Be Learned from the European Experience* (Chapter 16), *in* ELIZABETH SIEW-KUAN NG & GRAEME AUSTIN (eds.), INTERNATIONAL INTELLECTUAL PROPERTY AND THE ASEAN WAY: PATHWAYS TO INTEROPERABILITY; Carlos Adrián Garaventa & Pablo Wegbrait, *Integration in Intellectual Property in Latin America*, *in* ELIZABETH SIEW-KUAN NG & GRAEME AUSTIN (eds.), INTERNATIONAL INTELLECTUAL PROPERTY AND THE ASEAN WAY: PATHWAYS TO INTEROPERABILITY, CHAPTER 17; and Denis Croze, *Integrating Intellectual Property Systems in Light of Plurilateral and Regional Agreements*, *in* ELIZABETH SIEW-KUAN NG & GRAEME AUSTIN (eds.), INTERNATIONAL INTELLECTUAL PROPERTY AND THE ASEAN WAY: PATHWAYS TO INTEROPERABILITY, Chapter 2.

[64] Jerome H. Reichman & Rochelle Cooper Dreyfuss, *Harmonization without Consensus: Critical Reflections on Drafting a Substantive Patent Law Treaty*, 57 DUKE L.J. 85, 130 (2007).

2

Integrating Intellectual Property Systems in Light of Plurilateral and Regional Agreements

Denis Croze

2.1 INTRODUCTION

It is not uncommon to hear that multilateralism is experiencing a crisis.[1] The development of bilateral, regional, and plurilateral agreements is said to be, if not a cause, at least a demonstration of the difficulties in getting worldwide consensus when seeking adoption of new international norms. Debates in multilateral forums are getting more and more politicized, creating tensions between countries on most issues. These tensions affect not only substantive law but also technical questions, such as those relating to the harmonization of formalities and practices.[2] Moreover, international organizations are facing competition from a multiplicity of new actors, including coalitions of like-minded countries, private foundations, civil society groups, and consumers.*

In this context, there was no reason for intellectual property to be exempt from these phenomena. As Doris Long opined:

> The strong integrating movements of intellectual property multilateralism in the latter decades of the 20th century and the first decade of the 21st century have given way to a period of increasing dis-integration. The period that saw the rise of the Agreement on Trade-Related Aspects of Intellectual Property Rights (TRIPS) and diverse regional and multilateral treaties defining the boundaries of intellectual property rights in the digital universe has been replaced by an era of "dis-integration" marked by a rise in multi-forum

* The views expressed in this chapter are personal and do not represent the views of WIPO or the member states of the World Intellectual Property Organization (WIPO).

[1] *See* World Trade Organization, *Is Multilateralism in Crisis?* WTO Public Forum 2012, Workshop 3, *available at* www.wto.org/english/res_e/booksp_e/public_forum12_e.pdf.

[2] *See* Sundaresh Menon, *Transnational Commercial Law: Realities, Challenges and a Call for Meaningful Convergence*, 2 SING. J.L.S. 231 (2013).

> standard-making enterprises, many directed by non-governmental organizations (NGOs) and other previously un-empowered actors who have found a voice through the greater communicative abilities of the Internet and other digital mobilizing media.[3]

Francis Gurry, director general of the World Intellectual Property Organization (WIPO), identified[4] four main factors that have contributed, in the past two decades, to the challenges faced by traditional international organizations. First, there is the tension between the pace of technological change and the pace of universal multilateral response: "The speed of technological change poses a severe challenge for organizations whose procedures and processes are built upon the slow accumulation of historical experience."[5] The slow multilateral processes therefore provide an incentive to choose other forums for those countries that want to make rapid progress and quickly conclude an agreement.

Second, there is the increasing speed of geopolitical change. The growing disjunction between economic reality and political architecture presents a challenge of adaptation for international organizations:

> The political architecture of the multilateral system, whether in terms of the institutionalized distribution of power, definitions of political groupings, or location on the scale of development, is based on the economic reality of the world at the end of Second World War and the decades that followed it until the 1990s. . . . A lack of correspondence between economic reality and political architecture is a fertile breeding ground for lack of trust, that fragile commodity upon which the possibility of a shared view of a problem and its solution and, thus, agreement rests.[6]

This geopolitical shift is particularly obvious when looking at Patent Cooperation Treaty (PCT) filings (Asia 38%, Europe 31%, and USA 27%) or creative industries (North America 33%, Asia 33%, and Europe 33%).

Third, the past two decades have seen a blurring of the "distinction between public and private" in many parts of the world, with the massive involvement of the private sector in public policy challenges. As Dr. Gurry said:

[3] *See* Doris Estelle Long, *Deviant Globalization and the Rise of Diverse Interests in the Multilateral Protection of Intellectual Property*, *in* IRENE CALBOLI & SRIVIDHYA RAGAVAN (eds.), DIVERSITY IN INTELLECTUAL PROPERTY: IDENTITIES, INTERESTS AND INTERSECTIONS, 58–75 (2015).

[4] *See* Francis Gurry, Director General, WIPO, *Lakshman Kadirgamar Memorial Oration 2013: Challenges for International Organizations and Multilateralism* (November 13, 2013), *available at* www.wipo.int/about-wipo/en/dgo/speeches/dg_colombo_2013.html.

[5] *Id.* [6] *Id.*

The entry of private individuals, organizations and foundations into fields traditionally managed by public organizations has increased the competition for voluntary funding on which so many of the international organizations have come to rely in addition to their regular budgets in order to prosecute their programs – competition, it might be added, from actors who are necessarily more agile and adaptable than the international organizations.[7]

Finally, the new digital environment – the internet and social media notably – has also introduced a multiplicity of implications and consequences for international organizations. Dr. Gurry again:

"The Internet has facilitated the creation of networks of all conceivable varieties – social, political, economic, cultural, scientific and technological" and "empowered more actors, notably non-governmental organizations (NGOs) to participate in policy discussions by putting them on an equal information footing with States and by linking them throughout the world."[8]

Considering the different methods of accessing and reporting on information and the different ways to communicate, Dr. Gurry wonders whether "international organizations [can] capture the imagination of the public without engaging in a radical change of communication methods" and he asks whether member states will allow secretariats to do so.[9] As Gurry further opines:

What results from this brief review of some of the salient agents of change affecting international organizations is a picture of great complexity. International cooperation now takes place in a world of multiple speeds and layers (national, bilateral, plurilateral and multilateral), multiple dimensions (public, private, and a range of mixtures of both) and multiple power balances (economic, financial, political, people, information, idea, diplomatic and military). The one-dimensional world of a single balance of political power seems to be becoming a thing of the past.[10]

Using these insights as a springboard, this chapter focuses on how WIPO is experiencing the integration of intellectual property systems in light of plurilateral and regional agreements. In other words, is interoperability – that is, building coherent services for users when the individual components are technically different and managed by different social, organizational, political, and legal entities – meaningfully possible in the field of intellectual property?

[7] *Id.* [8] *Id.* [9] *Id.* [10] *Id.*

2.2 INTELLECTUAL PROPERTY IS CHALLENGED

At a time when intellectual property rights have been moving from an "arcane area of legal analysis and a policy backwater to the forefront of global economic policymaking,"[11] it is commonly agreed that, for several decades, the very concept of intellectual property has been challenged. As Daniel Gervais states, "IP is viewed as reflecting fundamentally binary and opposing positions of 'right holders' and 'users'."[12] Although WIPO's mandate and aim are to promote the economic, social, and cultural development of all countries through a balanced and effective international intellectual property system, the debate over how the balance between private interests and public policy should be struck (particularly in the area of limitations and exceptions to intellectual property rights) has been going on for some time.[13] It is easily conceivable that this debate – and the tension that it creates – will continue into the future, as many questions have not been addressed. The debate is not the focus of this chapter, and much literature has been written on it already. However, the persistent dichotomy of approaches and the lack of consensus among actors in the intellectual property arena are conducive to the development of plurilateral and regional agreements. Peter Yu has described this phenomenon as an "international intellectual property regime complex, a non-hierarchical, decentralized conglomerate regime that includes not only the traditional area of IP laws and policies but also the overlapping areas in related international regimes or fora."[14]

How far will the extension of the scope, duration, and object of intellectual property rights go? Will limitations and exceptions to intellectual property rights be considered according to developing countries' views? Where will the intellectual property pendulum be stabilized? These open questions, among many, have also been stirred by the "change of the nature" of intellectual property rights, which have moved away from being justified as an incentive for innovation and creativity to being a focus of international trade policy. Intellectual property rights are increasingly considered by businesses as assets, as tools of competition or as effective aids to the marketing and export of

[11] *See* KEITH E. MASKUS, INTELLECTUAL PROPERTY RIGHTS IN THE GLOBAL ECONOMY (2000).

[12] *See* Daniel Gervais, *Is There a "Middle Way" in International Intellectual Property?* 47 (2) INT'L. REV. INTELL. PROP. & COMPET. L. 135, 135–137 (2016), *available at* http://link.springer.com/article/10.1007/s40319-016-0458-9.

[13] *See* Denis Croze, *Sphère privée et patrimoine public: Comment concilier les deux en matière de propriété intellectuelle?*, 65(4) REV. ÉCON. SOC. BULL. SOC. ETUD. ECON. SOC. 153 (2007).

[14] *See* Peter K. Yu, *The Global Intellectual Property Order and Its Undetermined Future*, 1 W.I.P.O.J. 1–15 (2009).

products. Moreover, intellectual property is moving from an object of trade policy to an object of investment policy: intellectual property regimes, notably in plurilateral agreements, expand beyond trade to cover investments, leading to a growing "incentive–investment" divide.[15]

2.3 INTELLECTUAL PROPERTY IS AT A CROSSROADS

Many different factors have also contributed to put intellectual property at a crossroads.[16] One can easily say that intellectual property in the twenty-first century is experiencing a "new frontier." Part of this new frontier is explained by the globalization of international trade and the fact that all economic sectors (industry, trade, culture, health, education, research and development, agriculture, food, environment, etc.) increasingly rely on intellectual property. This interest has brought the topic to new audiences and deepened the discussions and debates around it, while the modern digital environment has opened a new borderless territory that challenges traditional intellectual property territorial structures.

In addition, a huge variety of new actors and stakeholders (IGOs, NGOs, business circles, civil society, etc.) are now participating in the debate and strongly influencing global discussions and individual nations' decisions. New domains of protection (nontraditional marks, business methods, gene patents, etc.) and nonprotection (open access) are being explored while new instruments of protection (traditional knowledge, traditional cultural expressions) are being claimed. The sophistication of technology and its commercialization are introducing new combinations of rights and new combinations of intellectual property owners are further complicating the protection and exploitation of intellectual property rights on a global scale. New techniques of competition ("patent ambush," "patent submarines," "ever-greening," "patent trolls," etc.) are being developed by the business sector, which, as a consequence, is facing additional costs and enforcement challenges.

The accumulation of these new elements and the heterogeneous responses to them are reflected in the lack of common policy approaches at the international level. And therefore the development of bilateral, regional, or plurilateral agreements is often described as symptomatic of a crisis in the multilateral intellectual property system.

[15] *See* Peter K. Yu, *The International Enclosure Movement*, 82 IND. LAW J. 827, 827–907 (2007), *available at* http://ssrn.com/abstract=896134; Peter K. Yu, *The Non-Multilateral Approach to International Intellectual Property Norm-setting, in* DANIEL J. GERVAIS (ed.), INTERNATIONAL INTELLECTUAL PROPERTY: A HANDBOOK OF CONTEMPORARY RESEARCH 83 (2014), *available at* http://ssrn.com/abstract=2325766.

[16] *Id.*

It is obvious that the development of Free Trade Agreements (FTAs) and Economic Partnership Agreements (EPAs), whether regional or plurilateral, raise concerns about the future of multilateralism and question the future integration of intellectual property systems on a global scale. These developments have significant implications for developing and least developed countries. As Peter Yu notes, "the development of new bilateral, plurilateral and regional trade agreements outside the multilateral process has threatened to take away the limited 'policy space' less-developed countries have retained notwithstanding their membership in a number of international treaties."[17] He lists a number of concerns relating to the development of EPAs and FTAs: (1) the risk of undermining the multilateral system, notably by monopolizing the time, resources, and energies of negotiating countries on bilateral or regional negotiations; (2) the fragmentation of the international regulatory system – a "spaghetti bowl"[18] or "noodle bowl"[19] – which may lead to "a mish-mash of overlapping, supporting, and possibly conflicting obligations"[20]; (3) the strengthening of the power asymmetry existing in the international trading system, which increases the risk that developing, and least developed countries will accept standards that may not necessarily reflect their needs; and (4) the temptation of "backdoor lawmaking" from politicians who, under the pressure of domestic trade groups "outsource" the legislative process to an international forum in an effort to create laws that the domestic legislature would not have otherwise enacted.[21]

Moreover, these agreements – sometimes described as "Country Club agreements"[22] where membership rules are agreed to by a limited number of founders and that the newcomers have to accept – often fail to include in the negotiations the countries that will be significantly impacted by the

[17] Yu, *The Global Intellectual Property Order and Its Undetermined Future*, *supra* note 14, at 1.

[18] *See also* JAGDISH N. BHAGWATI & ANNE O. KRUEGER, THE DANGEROUS DRIFT TO PREFERENTIAL TRADE AGREEMENTS 2–3 (1995).

[19] *See also* Richard Baldwin, *Managing the Noodle Bowl: The Fragility of East Asian Regionalism*, 53 SING. ECON. REV. 449 (2008); Jong Woo Kang, *The Noodle Bowl Effect: Stumbling or Building Block?* (Asian Development Bank Economics Working Paper Series No. 446, 2015), *available at* www.adb.org/sites/default/iles/publicaion/172902/ewp-446.pdf.

[20] *See* SIMON LESTER, BRYAN MERCURIO & LORAND BARTELS (eds.), BILATERAL AND REGIONAL TRADE AGREEMENTS: COMMENTARY AND ANALYSIS 4 (2008).

[21] *See* Peter K. Yu, *Anticircumvention and Anti-Anticircumvention*, 84 DENV. U. L. REV. 13, 54–55 (2006).

[22] *See* Daniel Gervais, *Country Clubs, Empiricism, Blogs and Innovation: The Future of International Intellectual Property Norm Making in the Wake of ACTA*, *in* MIRA BURRI & THOMAS COTTIER (eds.), TRADE GOVERNANCE IN THE DIGITAL AGE 324 (2012); Peter. K. Yu, *The ACTA/TPP Country Clubs*, *in* DANA BELDIMAN (ed.), ACCESS TO INFORMATION AND KNOWLEDGE: 21ST CENTURY CHALLENGES IN INTELLECTUAL PROPERTY AND KNOWLEDGE GOVERNANCE 258–283 (2014).

issues at stake. If not all the important players are members, the impact of the agreement is reduced. These agreements are also criticized for not being fully transparent, and those who are not involved in their negotiations raise important issues relating to due process and access to information. In addition, some of these agreements include provisions which introduce investor–state dispute resolution mechanisms or more generally offer the choice of dispute resolution forums, therefore undermining the World Trade Organization (WTO) dispute settlement process. Finally, the development of multiple plurilateral agreements among like-minded countries may contribute to an inflation of plurilateral agreements that further fragment the international regulatory system.

2.4 ARE REGIONAL OR PLURILATERAL AGREEMENTS NECESSARILY A BAD THING FOR MULTILATERALISM?

Should we consider that multilateralism is an outdated approach and that regional and plurilateral agreements are appropriate for setting international intellectual property norms? The historical evolution of the international intellectual property regime has shown that polarized policy debates are not a new thing in intellectual property.[23] Since the Paris and Berne Conventions, actors have changed roles and modified their positions according to their level of development. This path might be followed in a similar way by emerging economies.

Moreover, FTAs and EPAs are no longer the exclusive purview of industrialized countries. Emerging economies such as China and India are increasingly active in negotiating bilateral or, in the case of the Association of Southeast Asian Nations (ASEAN), regional agreements.[24] Another noteworthy regional example is the Regional Comprehensive Economic Partnership (RCEP), which is currently being negotiated between Australia, China, India, Japan, New Zealand, South Korea, and the ASEAN member states.[25] However, as Peter Yu points out,[26] FTAs initiated by emerging economies aim principally

[23] *Id.*

[24] *See* Jayashree Watal, Intellectual Property Rights in the WTO and Developing Countries (2001).

[25] *See* Peter K. Yu, *The RCEP and Intellectual Property Norm-setting in the Asia-Pacific, Intellectual Property Rights and Mega-Regional Trade Agreements* (Global Perspectives and Challenges for the Intellectual Property System, CEIPI-ICTSD Publication Series No. 4) (2016), *available at* http://ssrn.com/abstract=2810579.

[26] *See* Peter K. Yu, *The Non-Multilateral Approach to International Intellectual Property Norm-setting, supra* note 15.

at liberalizing regional trade and do not necessarily focus on intellectual property. Moreover, when they do contain provisions on intellectual property, those provisions do not generally go beyond the requirements of the TRIPS Agreement. Although these agreements do not currently have a significant impact on international intellectual property norm setting, one can legitimately wonder how long emerging economies will stick to minimum intellectual property standards in such agreements. If the discussions in multilateral forums on, for example, traditional knowledge, genetic resources, and traditional cultural expressions continue to drag on for an indefinite time, there is a significant chance that emerging economies will abandon those in favor of bilateral or plurilateral agreements that better reflect their changing circumstances.

Beyond regional economic integrated systems such as those of the European Union there are several examples of successful regional harmonizations of intellectual property standards. The Organisation Africaine de la Propriete Intellectuelle, the African Regional Intellectual Property Organization, and the Eurasian Patent Office are all examples of regional organizations that have demonstrated positive results. Similarly, the Organisation pour l'Harmonisation en Afrique du Droit des Affaires[27] in sixteen African countries and the ASEAN Intellectual Property Rights Action Plans in Southeast Asia provide good examples of regional convergence of laws.

Depending on political perspective, EPAs and FTAs can be seen as providing positive changes to international intellectual property norms. They certainly constitute a more expeditious process than negotiations in multilateral forums. By targeting problematic practices within each country, they may help overcome domestic political resistance within some countries and therefore provide more efficient solutions for them. Moreover, by reducing the number of negotiating parties, countries can also provide "side-payments" that they otherwise would be unable to offer in multilateral fora. Finally, they provide entry points into regional and plurilateral networks and allow countries to explore interstate relationships with a smaller number of countries.

From a multilateral perspective, the most important strength of the EPAs and FTAs is that some of their provisions require the contracting parties to ratify or accede to WIPO treaties. This is often the case for WIPO Treaties such as the PCT, the Protocol Relating to the Madrid Agreement Concerning the International Registration of Marks, or the Hague Agreement Concerning the International Registration of Industrial Designs, all of which are regularly referred to in the provisions of such agreements. EPAs and FTAs can also introduce "multilateral extra" provisions (different from TRIPS-plus provisions

[27] Organization for the Harmonization of Business Law in Africa.

although they may encompass them) that cover issues that fall outside of existing multilateral agreements, increasing the scope and extent of commitments made under existing multilateral agreements. Once a web of agreements has been built, the constituent agreements can help establish norms that will eventually be consolidated through the multilateral process. As Ruth Okediji has pointed out, countries may seek to "consolidate and (perhaps improve) the gains from bilateralism" once they have developed a network of bilateral agreements that is sufficiently dense for that purpose.[28] Cho Sungjoon has suggested that regionalism may contribute to multilateralism under certain circumstances through a "laboratory effect." After experiencing trial and error and learning-by-doing at the regional level, countries may feel confident in ratcheting these regional initiatives to the multilateral forum.[29]

It is commonly agreed that universal multilateral processes are "inherently slow," and that they require "lengthy process in order to enable all nations, with varying degrees of development and major information and knowledge asymmetries, to be comfortable with the perception and analysis of problems and the democratic development of responses."[30] At WIPO, discussions start at the Working Group/Standing Committee level before a decision is submitted to the WIPO General Assemblies, which then decides to convene a diplomatic Conference.[31] Then, at the national level, accession and ratification processes must occur and be fitted onto the agendas of national parliaments and assemblies.

Moreover, it can be difficult to reach agreement as to the form of multilateral agreements or on any changes that should be made to them. Member states may have difficulty reaching consensus on any proposals because of unwillingness to compromise, the number of states involved (WIPO has 189 member states as of 2016), and the risk of states abandoning the process because of the slow pace of negotiations. In this context, some commentators have questioned whether a treaty is necessarily the best approach. If a treaty does not harmonize intellectual property law but rather includes specificities that each country wants to bring to the treaty, a "lowest common denominator" approach runs the risk of appearing as a compilation of each state's laws. If member states are tempted to compromise by agreeing on provisions that

[28] *See* Ruth L. Okediji, *Back to Bilateralism? Pendulum Swings in International Intellectual Property Protection*, 1 U. OTTAWA L. & TECH. J. 124, 143 (2004).

[29] *See* Cho Sungjoon, *A Bridge Too Far: The Fall of the Fifth WTO Ministerial Conference in Cancún and the Future of Trade Constitution*, 7 J. INT'L. ECON. L. 219, 238 (2004).

[30] *See* Francis Gurry, *supra* note 4.

[31] *See* CAROLYN DEERE BIRKBECK, THE WORLD INTELLECTUAL PROPERTY ORGANIZATION (WIPO): A REFERENCE GUIDE 81 (2016).

contain ambiguities, or vague and non-results–oriented terms in order to reach a consensus, it is difficult to be certain of the legal consequences of any resulting treaty. And if the treaty does not sufficiently update existing international norms and leaves aside, because of a lack of consensus, the technical progress that justified it being changed, it also runs the risk of being outdated before even being implemented.

2.5 CONCLUSION: THE FUTURE OF MULTILATERALISM AND WIPO'S ROLE IN THE INTERNATIONAL INTELLECTUAL PROPERTY ARENA

Despite this difficult context, WIPO has been remarkably able in recent years to conclude a number of multilateral agreements. Take, for example, the Beijing Treaty on Audiovisual Performance in 2012; the Marrakesh Treaty to Facilitate Access to Published Works for Persons Who Are Blind, Visually Impaired or Otherwise Print Disabled in 2013; and the Geneva Act of the Lisbon Agreement on Appellations of Origin and on Geographical Indications in 2015. Furthermore, several other projects covering design law, the protection of broadcasting organizations, and genetic resources, traditional knowledge, and traditional cultural expressions are currently being discussed by member states.

This raises the question of how WIPO has been so successful in helping to conclude multilateral agreements. A number of nonexhaustive explanations can be provided: these treaties addressed topics and issues that have not been specifically addressed before in a multilateral agreement or that are wholly new to the international arena; they do not increase the level of intellectual property protection in existing areas but instead relate to new domains; they have a limited scope, and are rather focused and technical in nature; and the process has been transparent and all interested circles (civil society notably) have been involved in the negotiation process.

In addition to its successful adoption of treaties, and notwithstanding the adoption of soft law instruments such as recommendations jointly adopted by the Paris Assembly and the WIPO Assembly,[32] WIPO and its member states have developed platforms for international collaboration outside the traditional treaty-making process. The first example is the Unified Dispute Resolution Policy, which sets out the legal framework for the resolution of disputes between

[32] Joint Recommendation on the Protection of Well-known Marks (1999), Joint Recommendation on Trademark Licenses (2000), and Joint Recommendation on the Protection of Marks on the Internet (2001).

a domain name registrant and a third party, largely based on the recommendations contained in the Report of the WIPO Internet Domain Name Process. Since this policy, a number of new platforms have been created at WIPO's initiative, such as WIPO Green,[33] which provides an interactive marketplace that promotes innovation and diffusion of green technologies; WIPO Re:Search,[34] which catalyzes the development of medical products for neglected tropical diseases, malaria, and tuberculosis through innovative research partnerships and knowledge sharing; and the Accessible Book Consortium,[35] a multistakeholder partnership that aims at increasing the number of books worldwide in accessible formats (such as braille, audio, and large print) and to make them available to people who are blind, have low vision, or are otherwise print disabled.

In conclusion, it appears that it is still possible to have an optimistic view of the multilateral processes surrounding intellectual property. No doubt challenges exist in the multilateral process for intergovernmental organizations. However, regional and plurilateral agreements can contribute in a positive manner to advancing issues to meet evolving member states' needs. WIPO's examples show that multilateralism can still function effectively if certain elements are in place.

33 WIPO Green, *About WIPO Green* (2013), *available at* www3.wipo.int/wipogreen/en/aboutus/.
34 WIPO, *WIPO Re:Search* (2016), *available at* www.wipo.int/research/en/.
35 Accessible Books Consortium, *About Accessible Books Consortium (ABC)*, *available at* www.accessiblebooksconsortium.org/portal/en/index.html.

3

Challenges for ASEAN Interoperability

Lessons from Research on Cultural Heritage Protection in Indonesia

Agus Sardjono

3.1 INTRODUCTION

The commitments of custodian heritage communities contrast markedly with the philosophical bases of intellectual property. The latter are exclusive in nature, whereas the former are communal and inclusive. Accordingly, debates about intellectual property protection for the use of cultural heritage typically focus on whether it is appropriate to apply intellectual property law concepts to cultural heritage at all. This distinction also distills important challenges for the interoperability of intellectual property in the Association of Southeast Asian Nations (ASEAN) context. Within the interoperability agenda, it should not be assumed that the intellectual property system is suitable, or even relevant, for many of the *people* in the nations that comprise the ASEAN group. If it transpires that intellectual property rights have little or no salience to peoples' worldviews, the promises of interoperability will never be fully realized.

This chapter draws from my own research projects on cultural heritage in the Indonesian context[1] with the aim of distilling some of the lessons learned about developing an appropriate protection system for Indonesian cultural heritage. My research on traditional knowledge and cultural heritage in Indonesia

[1] This chapter draws on the following studies: AGUS SARDJONO, PENGETAHUAN TRADISIONAL: STUDI MENGENAI PERLINDUNGAN HAK KEKAYAAN INTELEKTUAL ATAS OBAT-OBATAN [Traditional Knowledge: A Study on the Protection of Intellectual Property Rights on Medicine] (Jakarta: Progam Pasca Sarjana, Fakultas Hukum Universitas Indonesia, 2004); PETER JASZI ET AL., TRADITIONAL ARTS – A MOVE TOWARD PROTECTION IN INDONESIA (2007); AGUS SARDJONO ET AL., PEMANFAATAN HAK KEKAYAAN INTELEKTUAL OLEH PENGUSAHA KERAJINAN MUTIARA DI LOMBOK DAN KERAJINAN ROTAN DI AMUNTA (2012) [The Use of Intellectual Property System by Pearl & Rattan Entrepreneurs in Lombok and Amuntai] (Jakarta: Progam Pasca Sarjana, Fakultas Hukum Universitas Indonesia, 2012); Agus Sardjono et al., *The Implementation of Legal Protection of Mark for Small- and Medium-Scale Batik Entrepreneurs in Pekalongan, Solo, and Yogyakarta* (2013) (paper on file with author).

suggests that intellectual property may be quite irrelevant to the day-to-day lives of many people, and inconsistent with the belief systems that inform the worldviews of those responsible for significant amounts of creative work.

Intellectual property regulations have existed in Indonesia ever since the era of the Dutch Indies. However, during that period intellectual property rules were not applicable to all strata of society, only to Europeans.[2] As Afifah Kusumadara has noted, intellectual property laws are not laws originally developed by the Indonesian nation itself, and were not part of Indonesian customary law.[3] As in many other jurisdictions, the Indonesian government has been under pressure to enact intellectual property laws that are consistent with international norms as a consequence of membership of the World Trade Organization (WTO). Failure to enact or adapt its intellectual property–related laws to the provisions of Trade-Related Aspects of Intellectual Property Rights (TRIPS) would have brought the consequence of trade sanctions being imposed on it.[4] As a consequence of such practice of the transplantation of the law, the implementation of intellectual property laws in Indonesia faces numerous challenges. A key purpose of the research described in this chapter was to assess the way in which intellectual property actually impacted on the lives of artisans in local communities. The research underscores a significant degree of inconsistency between intellectual property and the pattern of Indonesian entrepreneurs' way of thinking and practices. The overarching finding is that intellectual property is frequently irrelevant to these communities.

3.2 INTELLECTUAL PROPERTY RIGHTS AND TRADITIONAL KNOWLEDGE

With its highly diverse population consisting of many different communities, each having its own respective unique culture, Indonesia is a country with a

[2] *See* Article 131 of the *Indische Staatsregeling* (IS) (Ned. S.1854–2, September 2, 1854) or State Administration Rules in Indonesia during the Dutch Government era.

[3] Afifah Kusumadara, *Konflik Hukum HAKI dengan Adat di Indonesia* [The Conflict of IP Law and Custom in Indonesia], 12 J. ARENA HUKUM 2 (2000).

[4] *See* Simon Butt, *Intellectual Property in Indonesia: A Problematic Legal Transplant*, 24(9) E.I.P.R. 429, 436 (2002): "The vast majority of Indonesia's post-independence intellectual property laws have been enacted or amended at the 'insistence' of the United States, either by threats to withdraw preferential tariff treatment under its 'Generalized System of Preferences' ('GSP') scheme or under 'Special 301' of the Trade Act of 1974. Indonesia's most recent revisions and enactments were prompted by the TRIPS Agreement, again instigated by the United States and a number of other industrialized countries. This, of course, was a trade-off for favorable General Agreement on Trade and Tariffs ('GATT') concessions." *See also* AGUS SARDJONO, HAK KEKAYAAN INTELEKTUAL DAN PENGETAHUAN TRADISIONAL [Intellectual Property Rights and Traditional Knowledge] (2010).

rich cultural heritage.[5] One of the prominent characteristics of the respective communities is the value of togetherness (communal and inclusive rights), which is diametrically different from the values underlying intellectual property claims (exclusive rights).

In an early project,[6] my research collaborators and I concluded that the individualistic Western regime is not suitable for the protection of traditional medicine–related knowledge as a form of cultural heritage. We based this conclusion on a number of reasons. First, the intellectual property regime tends to be oriented toward protecting the owners of capital in order to secure their technology and investment. Whereas intellectual property rights facilitate the commercialization of creative endeavor, local communities do not regard traditional medicinal knowledge as an object of commercial activity. Second, the intellectual property rights regime is a foreign regime, the implementation of which has been imposed on developing countries under a system that often stands in stark contrast to the character of their respective communities. Third, the intellectual property rights regime is principally concerned with the economic interests of individual inventors or creators. But local custodian communities regard traditional medicinal knowledge as part of the cultural heritage, rather than as individualized property or an apparatus of commercial life. Fourth, intellectual property rights, and patents in particular, are an extremely complex system. As a legal regime that provides protection to the inventor, patents require the party concerned (the inventor or the inventor's employer) actively to take steps to protect their endeavors. At the same time, local communities tend to have a more "concrete" way of thinking. Local communities are also not used to the written culture which, for example, undergirds the patent regime. In sum, including traditional knowledge in the category of "intellectual property" is not appropriate. Traditional knowledge is not "property" in the economic and material sense of the word; rather, it is more of a cultural property of a nonmaterial nature.

In light of this research, we concluded that Indonesia should not use the intellectual property rights system for the protection of the rights of custodian communities in their cultural heritage. In the author's view, the intellectual property rights system can be applied only to protect *individual* creativity. If such individual creativity is derived from the use of a community's cultural heritage, the individual using it must be prepared to acknowledge the origins

5 *See* M. Junus Melalatoa, Ensiklopedi Suku Bangsa di Indonesia [Encyclopedia of Ethic Groups in Indonesia] (Departemen Pendidikan dan Kebudyaan RI, 1995). In this chapter, references to traditional knowledge and traditional arts will be hereinafter referred to under the term *cultural heritage*, as both are essentially cultural heritages that belong to and live in the custodian community concerned.

6 *See* Agus Sardjono, *supra* note 4, at 391–563.

of his or her creativity. These ideas have been acknowledged by the World Intellectual Property Organization's Intergovernmental Committee on Intellectual Property Rights and Genetic Resources, Traditional Knowledge and Folklore. That Committee emphasized sharing the benefits arising from the use of genetic resources, traditional knowledge, and folklore (benefit sharing).[7]

At a more general level, traditional knowledge exposes a number of issues that concern Indonesia's global relations in the intellectual property context, in addition to the concerns of the interoperability agenda within ASEAN. As a result of international relations and economic globalization, there has been increasing social interaction among nations from industrialized countries and members of local communities living in Indonesia. In such interactions, nations from industrialized countries bring in values of "modernity," while a majority of the Indonesian people still live in their traditional world.

In the author's view, forcing the application of intellectual property onto cultural heritage could actually lead to a process that has the potential to harm the Indonesian people. One risk concerns misappropriation of local cultural knowledge by foreign entities. Many foreign nations look at the economic potential of using traditional medicinal knowledge by creative individuals; within a cultural heritage framework the concern is with how knowledge can be deployed for the common interest and benefit of all. Moreover, the ASEAN interoperability agenda is surely challenged by the responsibility of the Indonesian government to protect *all* of its citizens against the acts of foreigners that may potentially harm their interests, including acts of misappropriation of traditional medicinal knowledge and biodiversity owned by the Indonesian nation. In other words, before it is assumed that greater intellectual property interoperability in ASEAN is desirable, it must first be asked whether that agenda is sufficiently protective of all people within the nations that comprise the ASEAN group of nations.

In the author's view, the Indonesian government needs to take the initiative and undertake measures that genuinely protect its citizens, particularly members of local communities who live in areas spread all over Indonesia's territory. Such measures must adhere to the system of values developing within

7 The idea of acknowledgment has been discussed at various meetings and sessions of the WIPO Committee dealing with IPR issues related to genetic resources, traditional knowledge, and folklore. The 1998–1999 Fact-Finding Missions undertaken by the WIPO revealed the potential of using intellectual property principles to provide effective protection for traditional knowledge. *See, e.g.*, Begoña Venero, *WIPO's Intergovernmental Committee on Intellectual Property, Genetic Resources, Traditional Knowledge and Folklore* (paper presented in Montreal, July 12, 2010), *available at* www.cbd.int/abs/side-events/resumed-abs-9/id2126-wipo.pdf.

the environment of local communities concerned, while also accommodating the demands of international relations. The various alternative measures include legal instruments that add to or complement the existing legal protections. In addition, the implementation of law itself needs to be regarded as an important and necessary alternative measure of choice.

There is therefore a need to acknowledge the tension between legal norms that are animated by individualistic modern values and Indonesian communal traditional values. The tension is not necessarily irreconcilable. For example, the harmonization of the individualistic values underlies intellectual property norms with traditional values could be achieved by amending the legal provisions that recognize the collective right of local communities on their traditional knowledge.[8] Harmonization of the local communities' values of togetherness with Western values of modernity might also be advanced by adopting a *sui generis* law[9] enabling the recognition of collective rights of local communities in the context of global relations, both in the social as well as the economic area.

At both central and regional levels, government should act as custodian of local communities' collective rights and take the initiative in fostering an active role for community members in protecting and defending their rights. Such an active role would include, among other things, ensuring that documentation of cultural heritage is accurate, as well as the creation of an appropriate benefit-sharing mechanism to provide economic benefits to the community concerned in exchange for the use of its traditional knowledge. In addition, various nongovernmental organizations, focusing their attention on the protection and preservation of Indonesia's biodiversity, should more actively protect local communities' rights against the risk of misappropriation. The government should also promote benefit sharing in cases involving the use of traditional knowledge in Indonesia, and where Indonesia's biodiversity is exploited.

That is not to say, however, that the intellectual property rights system cannot be used at all. For example, the intellectual property system can still be used for derivative work that takes its source from cultural heritage material,

8 *See, e.g.*, Article 26, *Indonesian Patent Law* (Law No. 13 of 2016).

9 This initiative undertaken by the Regional House of Representatives of the Republic of Indonesia (*Dewan Perwakilan Daerah Republik Indonesia*) has formulated a Draft Law on the Management of Traditional Knowledge and Traditional Cultural Expression (*RUU Pengelolaan Pengetahuan Tradisional dan Ekspresi Budaya Tradisional*). At the time of writing, although the draft law has been delivered to the Indonesian Parliament (DPR-RI), it has not yet been discussed owing to the legislation schedule.

provided that the legal responses include acknowledgment of the source of the material as well as benefit sharing with its communal owners.

3.3 INTELLECTUAL PROPERTY RIGHTS AND TRADITIONAL ARTS

Similar conclusions were also drawn in subsequent research that was conducted in collaboration with researchers both within and outside Indonesia.[10] This research distilled the following conclusions. First, the issue of acknowledgment is the most prominent concern of traditional artists, ranging from Dalang in shadow-play performances to weavers in villages. From the statements made by these artists, it is clear that the most important issues to them are the misappropriation of their cultural heritage itself and the fact that recourse through the formal legal system is beyond their reach.

Second, it became clear that traditional artists have their own concept of misappropriation, which may be different from the concept of misappropriation that informs the intellectual property system. In international forums, the concept of misappropriation generally refers to a series of practices of using information deemed to be unfair – such as the patenting of new pharmaceuticals based on information obtained from traditional knowledge. However, our research disclosed that traditional artisans are concerned about unfairness in a more concrete commercial reproduction process, done extensively involving materials that originate directly from traditional sources, particularly in arts such as painting, carving, and textiles. The different conceptions of "misappropriation" seem to result from different worldviews. In general, local community members tend to use "concrete" viewpoints. In contrast, a more "abstract" viewpoint informs intellectual property rights. Accordingly, in the author's view, the term of misappropriation needs to be fundamentally redefined if it is to be meaningful to the life and work of traditional artists.

The research also disclosed that problems for traditional artists also arise from the territorial character of the intellectual property laws. The existing intellectual property regime in Indonesia cannot provide protection for traditional arts if intellectual property protection of a portion of such traditional arts has already been sought by the misappropriating party in another country. One of the most salient examples of this involved a case involving a local artist whose traditional art design for jewelry was registered as a design patent in the

[10] The research team consisted of Peter Jaszi (American University), Lorraine V. Aragon (North Carolina University), Jane Anderson (New York University), Agus Sardjono (University of Indonesia), Rizaldi Siagian (Yayasan Karya Cipta Indonesia), Ignatius Haryanto (Lembaga Studi Pers dan Pembangunan), Abdon Nababan (Aliansi Masyarakat Adat Nusantara), Hinca Panjaitan (Indonesia Media Law and Policy Center).

United States. As a result, the artist was unable to continue exporting her own products to the United States, as the design had been registered in the United States.[11]

Finally, the research concluded that conventional intellectual property rights very often do not offer appropriate protections for traditional artists. This research has revealed the myth that intellectual property rights have the ability to enhance economic activities. Considering that the current intellectual property rights regime has been formulated to control knowledge and the market, and that it is derived from the individualistic Western paradigm, its philosophical foundation is inconsistent with the worldviews of traditional artist communities. In sum, the research concluded that conventional intellectual property rights are not adequate to protect the rights of community members with respect to their traditional heritage in the form of traditional arts.

3.4 A STUDY OF LEGAL CULTURE

Subsequent research in Lombok and Amuntai distilled findings that are consistent with the issues discussed in the preceding sections.[12] The purpose of the Lombok and Amuntai research was to achieve a fuller understanding of the manner in which intellectual property laws are implemented in practice, particularly among traditional craftsmen. This research focuses on legal culture, specifically related to intellectual property rights, conducted by applying a quantitative/qualitative method. The quantitative method is aimed at obtaining an objective view of the perceptions that prevail in rural communities concerning the existence of intellectual property rights. The aim of the qualitative method is to obtain a more in-depth view of such perceptions within these communities. The research focused on the concern with barriers in the way of the implementation of the intellectual property system in Indonesia. It drew attention to the lack of evidence suggesting that intellectual property rights are in any way aligned with traditional values in local handicraft business practices. In addition, it is yet to be established how handicraft entrepreneurs

[11] For more details, *see* the author's presentation: Agus Sardjono, *Warisan Budaya Sebagai Sumber Ekonomi Baru: Telaah Aspek Hukum* [Cultural Heritage as New Sources of Indonesian Economy: A Legal Aspect Perspective] (paper presented in Jakarta on July 11, 2007) as reported in Forum Inovatif Pekerja Media [the Innovative Forum Media Workers], *Melindungi Kekayaan Warisan Budaya Bangsa* [Protecting Cultural Heritage Wealth of Nation] (July 16, 2007), *available at* https://johnherf.wordpress.com/2007/07/16/melindungi-kekayaan-warisan-budaya-bangsa/.

[12] The research team consisted of Agus Sardjono, Brian A. Prastyo, Heny Marlina, and Desrezka G. Larasati and the study was conducted between 2013 and 2015.

in the regions actually utilize intellectual property rights in their business activities. Finally, there is no evidence available establishing that intellectual property rights actually contribute to enhancing profits gained by local handicraft businesses.

Importantly, the research shed light on the view conveyed by those who promote intellectual property, including WIPO, and the idea that intellectual property inculcates universal values.[13] More specifically, it exposed the tension in the view that intellectual property is at once "native to all nations and relevant in all cultures, and that it has contributed to the progress of societies," and is "becoming a major element in corporate business management."[14] This view perpetuates the view – a highly-contestable idea in the author's view – that intellectual property is consistent with traditional values and has resonance for all people and all cultures. In addition, World Intellectual Property Organization (WIPO) espouses the view that intellectual property is, or will become, a key business element for every firm.[15] These ideas need to be rigorously scrutinized, especially in the Indonesian context.

The research therefore concerned law in action. That is, it focused on intellectual property law in handicraft industry practices in the regions, as it applies "on the ground." In part, the research was descriptive, to the extent that it is aimed at obtaining a view of the use of intellectual property in a concrete manner by handicraft entrepreneurs in the regions, as well as at obtaining a sense of the way in which handicraft entrepreneurs in the regions view the existence of intellectual property, be it positive or negative. The research methodology also combined the normative legal research method and empirical research method. The normative legal research method was adapted to the task of demonstrating how intellectual property norms should be applied whereas an empirical research method was applied in order to understand the manner in which such norms are actually implemented by community members.

A key reason for focusing on Lombok and Amuntai was that their handicraft products, namely pearls and rattan, are exported overseas. In addition, focusing on these areas provides a useful comparison to research that has already been conducted in Java. The team of researchers used data from the Service Offices of Industry, Trade and Cooperatives of the Municipal Government of Mataram, and the Regency Government of Hulu Sungai Utara. The research

13 WIPO, World Intellectual Property Declaration (WO/GA/26/4 Annex IV), June 2000, *available at* www.wipo.int/edocs/mdocs/govbody/en/wo_ga_26/wo_ga_26_4-annex4.doc.

14 Kamil Idris, Intellectual Property: A Power Tool for Economic Growth 2, 8 (2003).

15 *Id.*

also involved the local regional government apparatus to cooperate in this research by distributing questionnaires and conducting interviews with leading local craftsmen. The researchers posed several questions about factual information to handicraft entrepreneurs. For instance, the research analyzed the number of registered intellectual property rights, the number of intellectual property license agreements entered into, the amount of revenue obtained from intellectual property royalties, the number of summons to parties alleged of misappropriating intellectual property, the number of parties allegedly having misappropriated intellectual property and reported to the police, and so on.

The principal concern was with "legal culture" in the broader sense, which, in the author's view, is more reflective of the legal attitude of the community concerned than formally enacted laws. To that end, the research was informed by Friedman's idea that analysis of the elements of law should not be limited to substantive norms; rather, it also includes legal institutions and legal culture in a broader sense.[16] All of these elements affect the effective implementation of law in a society's everyday life. Law is effectively implemented if members of the society concerned appreciate legal norms as guidance for conduct. When there are gaps between the substance of norms and the outlook on life or values living in the society concerned, such norms become obsolete and ineffective. Especially when the law enforcement apparatus lacks an understanding of the norms concerned, such norms become increasingly abandoned, and end up as a collection of words in laws and regulations. As Tom Tyler has explained, an understanding of levels of compliance with legal norms must start with prior understanding of such a society's perception of values concerning justice and legal obligations.[17] If the values embodied in a legal norm do not align with the values adopted and living in the society concerned, it will not achieve, or, as relevant, may lose, its legitimacy as a norm recognized by the society concerned.

Indonesian society is a communal and religious one. Religious values are formalized in the First Pillar of the *Pancasila*,[18] namely Belief in The One

[16] Lawrence M. Friedman, The Legal System: A Social Science Perspective 11–16 (1975).

[17] Tom Tyler writes: "[a] normative perspective leads to a focus on people's internalized norms of justice and obligation. It suggests the need to explore what citizens think and understand their values. By contrast, an instrumental perspective regards compliance as a form of behavior occurring in response to external factors. It leads to a focus on the extent and nature of the resources that authorities have for shaping public behavior." *See* Tom R. Tyler, Why People Obey the Law 4 (1990).

[18] *Pancasila* is the Foundation of the State of the Republic of Indonesia set out in the Constitution of the Republic of Indonesia. *See The Preamble to the Indonesian Constitution 1945*.

Almighty God (Ketuhanan Yang Maha Esa). The value of belief in The One Almighty God is materialized in the form of a life based on religious ideas. It is not surprising, therefore, that religious norms are in fact obeyed to a greater extent than norms of state law, including, of course, intellectual property laws. Such religious norms are not limited to formal religious norms known in Indonesia, such as Islam, Christian, Catholic, Hindu, and Buddhist norms. They also include spiritual values that constitute the Spirit of life itself. In its turn, this spirituality brings a nuance and spirit into the Indonesian people's outlook on the phenomenon of everyday life. It is not surprising, therefore, that the exclusive nature of individual rights offered by the intellectual property system is regarded as inferior to the deeper values of goodness and virtue. A society informed by these values will inevitably attribute inferior value to the exclusive rights of the intellectual property system offering economic benefits to holders of the relevant rights.

The philosophy of togetherness (*gotong royong*) and spirituality has created values according to which the intellectual excellence of individual members of society (in the form of creative products) should not be monopolized by the individual possessing any distinguishing quality – especially if the monopoly is motivated solely by individual economic profit, as has been the case with corporations who own intellectual property. Whatever the rights of individuals, these rights are tempered by the idea that the individual is an inseparable part of his or her community.[19] Such a way of thinking contrasts with worldviews that put the individual at the center, and valorizes the economic interest of the individual above the interest of other people. In the writer's view, individualism represents the "spirit" of intellectual property rights. It is in stark contrast to the legal culture that governs the lives of many communities in Indonesia. Take, for example, the cultural heritage of batik, which has formed part of the Indonesian community for hundreds of years. The traditional values imbued in batik and its use in major events have come to be regarded as part of Indonesia's national identity and culture, belonging to the people of Indonesia. Its addition by UNESCO to the Intangible Cultural Heritage list in 2009 marked an important recognition and extension of Indonesia's cultural heritage in batik to the rest of the world.

Once the law is taken out of its social context, it fails to achieve its purpose. The main purpose of implementing the intellectual property system is to protect the interests of intellectual property holders against misappropriation by other parties. Other things being equal, this is a very good purpose. However, once it is placed in the context of a society which attributes a higher degree

[19] Sardjono, *supra* note 6, at 16.

of importance to the values of togetherness and spirituality, a contradiction between values becomes inevitable. In a communal and religious community, people who advance only their own economic interests are bound to be regarded as egoistic, asocial, and greedy. Communal societies strive for balance between individual and common interest. The prevailing purpose of the intellectual system loses its legitimacy once its norms are complemented with extreme exclusivism, while the norms are to be applied in the environment of a society based on spirituality and the idea of *gotong royong*. A norm such as this is bound to experience "dysfunction" in its implementation.[20] Once intellectual property is applied in a society that does not adopt the view of individualism and materialism, there is a risk that the laws will experience dysfunction or will fail to achieve their mission.

Based on the research conducted in Lombok and Amuntai, it was concluded that neither of the two views espoused by WIPO that are set forth in the preceding text is correct, at least if applied in the context of Indonesia. In reality, local entrepreneurs in Indonesia are not yet familiar with intellectual property, let alone apply intellectual property in their business activities. It is evident that as a transplanted system, the intellectual property system has remained foreign and difficult to be accepted or understood by its people, particularly in view of the fact that the intellectual property system has a different philosophical background from the way of thinking followed by many of the people who constitute Indonesian society. Of course, the results may very well have been different had the research been conducted on entrepreneurs in Jakarta, an Indonesian center of business. Even so, the results of research conducted in Jakarta could not represent conditions in Indonesia in general.

3.5 CONCLUSION

Drawing from the different research projects described in the preceding sections, it is suggested that the ASEAN interoperability agenda must pay more attention to how intellectual property laws actually align with the realities of the lives of the people who constitute the varied societies of the nations that comprise the ASEAN group of nations. Looking forward, one project that in this author's view could enhance the interoperability agenda would be the development of an ASEAN Model Law on the Management and Protection of Cultural Heritage that is adoptable and applicable among ASEAN

[20] *See* STEVEN VAGO, LAW AND SOCIETY 15 (3rd ed., 1991).

countries.[21] This initiative could significantly enhance cultural heritage management within ASEAN. At the same time, such a project should not be pursued without further work on attempting to understand the rich fabric of legal cultures in the nations concerned. Without such an understanding, focusing on formal intellectual property norms will be inconsistent with the worldviews of the people concerned, and inevitably result in "dysfunction."

[21] This could be modeled, *e.g.*, on Indonesia's Draft Law on the Management of Traditional Knowledge and Traditional Cultural Expression. *See* Draft Law, *supra* note 9.

4

Trademark Protection in Myanmar

Current Issues and Future Directions

Khin Mar Yee

4.1 INTRODUCTION

After more than sixty years of isolation, Myanmar (formerly known as Burma) recently began its transformation from a socialist regime to a more developed market economy. This has opened up tremendous investment opportunities in the country, particularly since 2011 when a civilian government was installed under the Constitution of the Republic of the Union of Myanmar of 2008.[1] The recent landslide victory of the National League for Democracy led by Daw Aung San Suu Kyi in the general election saw the installation of a new government in March 2016.

Realizing the importance of implementing transparent and effective laws to encourage and promote investment – as well as the significance of intellectual property in propelling economic growth – Myanmar has embarked on modernizing its laws including those with respect to intellectual property. To complement these legislative initiatives, a National Intellectual Property Strategy is also being developed by the Ministry of Science and Technology in consultation with relevant stakeholders and assistance from the World Intellectual Property Organization.

To enhance intellectual property awareness in the country, various initiatives have been advanced. Examples include the hosting of training and workshops for members of the judiciary, and the conducting of intellectual property courses (at undergraduate and postgraduate levels) in the law schools of various universities in Myanmar. In July 2016, the Law Department of the University of Yangon launched a Diploma in Intellectual Property Law (DIPL) program.

[1] *See* Constitution of the Republic of the Union of Myanmar, May 29, 2008.

As a member of the Association of Southeast Asian Nations (ASEAN), Myanmar is bound by the ASEAN Framework Agreement on Intellectual Property Cooperation to advance the legal framework to support the ASEAN Economic Community. Additionally, as a member of the World Trade Organization (WTO), it is also bound by the standards set forth in the Agreement on Trade-Related Aspects of Intellectual Property Rights (TRIPS), subject to the flexibilities made available to least-developed members. It is therefore exempted from implementing all substantive TRIPS standards until 2021, and until at least 2033 with respect to the patenting of pharmaceutical products.[2] Nevertheless, Myanmar's draft trademark law (which is expected to be promulgated in 2017) is already TRIPS-compliant and includes provisions such as those relating to the grant of a right of priority as required under the Paris Convention. Myanmar has also given due consideration to the Singapore Treaty on the Law of Trademarks, even though it is not currently a contracting state. To implement these and other initiatives, Myanmar will be establishing an intellectual property office (an entirely new organ in the country). This chapter will be centered on Myanmar's trademark law, and will consider what constitutes a trademark as well as civil and criminal enforcement mechanisms.

4.2 LAWS RELATING TO TRADEMARK RIGHTS

Myanmar's Constitution provides: "The Union shall permit citizens' rights of private property, right of inheritance, right of private initiative and patent in accord with the law."[3] Additionally, it also guarantees as one of the fundamental rights "the right to ownership, the use of property and the right to private invention and patent."[4] Intellectual property laws are enlisted in Schedule 1 of the Union Legislative List of the Constitution, which means that they fall within the purview of the supreme Union Legislative Body (Pyidaungsu Hluttaw) and not regional or state legislative bodies (namely Regional Hluttaw or State Hluttaw). Consequently, intellectual property laws once promulgated will extend to the whole of Myanmar.

Since intellectual property is an intangible asset, laws are essential to its protection. Although copyright is protected under the Myanmar Copyright Act of 1914, there is currently no specific law for trademark registration. A trademark can, however, currently be protected at common law on the basis of its use or registration under related laws. Additional protection is also

[2] *See* WTO, *WTO Members Agree to Extend Drug Patent Exemption for Poorest Members* (November 6, 2015), *available at* www.wto.org/english/news_e/news15_e/trip_06nov15_e.htm.

[3] MYANMAR CONSTITUTION, *supra* note 1, at § 37(c).

[4] *Id.* at § 372.

conferred on well-known trademarks. To give effective protection to the strategic role that trademarks play in commerce and marketing for private enterprises, several civil and criminal laws offer protection for trademark rights, such as the provision of remedies for infringement. These include

- The Penal Code 1861
- Specific Relief Act 1877
- Sea Customs Act 1878
- Land Customs Act 1878
- Myanmar Merchandise Marks Act 1889
- Registration Act 1908

Trademark infringement cases are dealt with in the courts and by out-of-court measures. Customs officials also have experience in handling trademark infringement matters and are empowered to confiscate fake goods and goods bearing infringing trademarks, utilizing provisions in the Sea Customs Act and Land Customs Act. There are also plans to create an intellectual property section within the police force. However, in order to enforce these trademark rights, there must be a protectable trademark under the law. Before proceeding to discuss the various ways in which trademark may be protected in Myanmar, it is helpful to clarify what constitutes a trademark.

4.3 DEFINITION OF TRADEMARK

In order to register a mark as a trademark in Myanmar, the Penal Code of Myanmar[5] provides that the mark be "used for denoting that goods are the manufacture or merchandise of a particular person." Additionally, the Penal Code also provides that a "property mark" is "a mark used for denoting that moveable property belongs to a particular person."[6] To be protected as a trademark, it must be distinctive[7]; this was defined in *Gaw Kan Lye v. Saw Kyone Saing*[8] as meaning that the mark must be capable of distinguishing a particular person's goods from somebody else's by indicating that it was manufactured by that particular person, and not simply any manufacturer of the type of goods.

This was elaborated upon in the case of *U Tin Latt (a) U Sai Lail & I v. U Kyaw Nyein* (Special Appellate Civil Case No. 23, 2000)[9] where the Court held that a trademark is "any sign or symbol applied or attached to goods offered for sale in the market as to distinguish them from similar goods and to identify

5 Myanmar Penal Code § 478 (1861). 6 *Id.* at § 479. 7 *Id.* at § 478.
8 (1939) Y.L.R. 503. 9 (2001) M.L.R. 216.

them with a particular owner. A trade mark includes a device, brand, heading etc. and any combination thereof." The case related to a dispute between the producer of "Taung Gyi Mauk Mai" (a medicated Thanet Kha that is used as cosmetics) and another producer of the same kind of product under a different name, "Shan Maung Mai." Although the names were different there were similarities in the mark, including the size of the plastic container and the instructions on product usage. The court found that there was a likelihood of confusion and granted a temporary injunction in favor of the owner of the "Taung Gyi Mauk Mai" trademark. In another case, *Malaysia Dairy Industries Pte. Ltd. v. Kabushiki Kaisha Yakult Honsha,*[10] a permanent injunction was issued to prevent the use of a trademark in respect of the packaging of a product. In that case, although the name "VITAGEN" used on the bottle of milk yogurt by the plaintiff, Malaysia Dairy Industries Pte. Ltd., is different from the word "Yakult" used by the defendant, the package (bottle) designs were the same. This bottle design should actually be protected under industrial design law. However, as the Industrial Design Law of Myanmar is currently still in draft form, trademark protection was relied upon.

Adopting the TRIPS definition of a trademark, Myanmar's draft new Trademark Law provides that: "Trademark means any sign or any combination of signs, capable of distinguishing the goods or services of one undertaking from those of other undertakings, shall be capable of constituting a trademark. Such signs in particular words including personal names, letters, numerals, figurative elements and combinations of colours as well as any combination of such signs and that signs be visually perceptible. This term includes Trademark, Service mark, Collective mark and Certification mark."

4.4 TRADEMARK REGISTRATION AND PROTECTION AT COMMON LAW

A trademark can be protected on the basis of its usage or registration. Trademark protection on the basis of use is established under the common law. An example is *U Tin Latt (a) U Sai Lail & I v. U Kyaw Nyein*[11] where the court granted the appellant exclusive rights over the "Taung Gyi Mauk Mai" trademark, which had been used since 1994, thereby affirming that trademark rights could be acquired through use of the mark in Myanmar.

Even though there is currently no specific trademark law regulating the registration of trademarks in Myanmar, trademarks may be registered under the Registration Act 1908. Importantly, trademark protection continues to be based on the traditional concept of use of the mark. Registration merely serves

[10] Decree in Original Suit, Civil Regular Suit No. 262 of 2002, Yangon Division Court.
[11] (2001) M.L.R. 216.

to confirm that the rights have been acquired through use. Consequently, in the event of a dispute over trademark ownership, the first user of the trademark will have priority, and not the person who was the first to register the trademark. Under Myanmar's new draft Trademark Law, the first to file principle will apply.

Registration of a trademark is not compulsory for the acquisition of trademark rights, and mere registration does not constitute conclusive proof of ownership of the trademark or user of the mark. Nonetheless, registration may constitute *prima facie* evidence of ownership of the trademark in criminal or civil proceedings. In the author's experience, many trademark owners still believe that the mark must be registered in order to obtain effective protection under the law. Registration may be refused if the mark is likely to be objectionable on moral or legal grounds, or where it is likely to hurt the religious susceptibilities of any class of citizens in Myanmar. Examples include fraud, colorable imitation of a currency note and marks bearing the image of General Aung San. To effect a registration of a trademark, a Declaration of Ownership of Trademark[12] is filed with the Registration Office of the Register of Deeds and Assurances.[13] On registration, an advertisement, announcement, or "Trademark Caution" will be published in the daily newspapers, stating that any fraudulent imitation, unauthorized use of, or infringement of the said trademark will be dealt with according to the law. One of the current loopholes in the registration system is the lack of a proper procedure for conducting an official search of the Register for marks that have already been registered, as the Register is not open for public inspection. Instead, an applicant has to rely on the local practice of requesting private collectors or law firms that have kept records of trademark cautionary notices to conduct such searches.

Unlike the trademark laws of many countries, the Registration Act of Myanmar does not provide for the expiry or renewal of registered trademarks. Hence, registered trademarks will remain perpetually on the Register and no renewal is required. To serve as a notification to the public that a particular trademark

[12] A declaration of ownership is a solemn statement of facts made by the declarant and usually attested by a notary public or a magistrate or some judicial officer. It usually states the rights of the declarant to the trademark, and a specimen of the trademark or label is usually attached to the declaration.

[13] Direction No. 13 of the Inspector General of Registration, as last amended in 1962 and s 18 (F) of the Registration Act, 1908. This office is a branch of the Settlements and Land Records Department under the Ministry of Agriculture and Irrigation. It may sound strange that trademark registration is carried out under the Ministry of Agriculture and Irrigation. The history can be traced from the Settlements and Land Records Department under this Ministry. After the Second World War, the Department carried out the registration of deeds. As a matter of fact, Direction 13 of the Registration Act clearly contemplates trademark as an item that may be registered under s 18 (F) of the Registration Act.

has not been abandoned, it is customary for the cautionary notices to be republished from time to time, around every three years. If a trademark owner wishes to change the proprietor's name, device, address, or covered goods or services and so forth with respect to the registration, the trademark has to be registered again, but the proprietor of the registered trademark can maintain the earliest registration date of the mark over subsequent registration dates. Myanmar's new draft trademark law will provide that the registration of a trademark will be for an initial period of ten years, lasting for periods of ten years for each subsequent renewal.

4.5 TRADEMARK PROTECTION UNDER CRIMINAL LAW

Historically, trademark infringement was provided under the law of passing-off.[14] Today, both civil and criminal remedies are available for infringement of trademarks (though in practice civil remedies are preferred by the trademark proprietor).

The Myanmar Penal Code 1860 governs criminal proceedings relating to infringement of trademarks, property marks, and other marks.[15] An owner of a trademark may take criminal action for an infringement of his trademark for the following offenses:

- Using a false trademark (s 482)[16]
- Counterfeiting a trademark (s 483)[17]
- Making or possessing any instrument for counterfeiting a trademark (s 485)[18]
- Selling goods marked with a counterfeit trademark (s 486)[19]

14 *See John Walker & Sons Ltd. v. U Than Shwe* (1968) M.L.R. 73.

15 *See* Myan. Penal Code §§ 478–489 (1861).

16 § 482 of the Myan. Penal Code (1861) states that, whoever uses any false mark or any false property mark shall, unless he proves that he acted without intent to defraud, be punished with imprisonment of either description for a term that may extend to one year, or with a fine, or with both.

17 § 483 of the Myan. Penal Code provides that, whoever counterfeits any trademark or property mark used by any other person shall be punished with imprisonment of either description for a term that may extend to two years, or with a fine, or with both.

18 § 485 of the Myan. Penal Code states that whoever makes or has in his possession any dye, plate or other instrument for the purpose of counterfeiting a trade mark, or property mark, or has in his possession a trademark or property mark for the merchandise of a person whose manufacture or merchandise they are not, or that they belong to a person to whom they do not belong, shall be punished with imprisonment of either description for a term that may extend to three years, or with a fine or with both.

19 § 486 of the Myan. Penal Code provides that whoever sells or exposes, or has in possession for sale or any purpose of trade or manufacture, any goods or things with a counterfeit trademark

Moreover, it is also an offence to counterfeit any property mark used by a public servant, or a mark used by a public servant to denote qualities of a particular mark (e.g., place of manufacture, the name of the manufacturer, etc.) knowing the same to be counterfeit. Such an offence is punishable by a term of imprisonment of up to three years and/or a fine.[20]

A few cases illustrate these points. In *U Han Kyi (The Creation Myanmar Co. Ltd.) v. Ko Mya Soe*,[21] forged Giordano properties were sold using the "GIORDANO" trademark. The court convicted the accused Ko Mya Soe of Sein Gay Har Store under s 486 of the Penal Code and imposed a fine of K. 20,000 and a four-month prison term. Another case involved the well-known mark "MITSUBISHI" where the court ruled in favor of Mitsubishi Electric Corporation. The defendant was imposed a fine of K. 100,000 and a three-month prison term under s 486 of Penal Code.[22]

Apart from the Penal Code, Myanmar's Merchandise Marks Act[23] also governs offences relating to trademarks and property marks, particularly its provisions relating to forfeiture of goods. Moreover, the Sea Customs Act, the Land Customs Act, and the Myanmar Merchandise Marks Act also empower customs to stop and search vessels to seize goods and conduct arrests where a reasonable suspicion exists of there being prohibited goods (or goods subject to duty) on board, or if there is a reasonable cause to suspect that an offense has been committed. All confiscated goods are kept by the Customs Department and held until a decision is made as to their disposal in accordance with s 181 of the Sea Customs Act. Section 18(d) of the Sea Customs Act 1878[24] and its subsequent amendment also deal with prohibitions with respect to goods with a counterfeit trademark within the meaning of the Penal Code, or a false trade description within the meaning of the Merchandise Marks Act.[25] Under s 167 conviction under the section renders goods liable for confiscation, and persons concerned in the offense to a penalty not exceeding three times the value of the goods, or not exceeding K. 1,000.[26]

Under the new draft Trademark Law, criminal penalties of imprisonment for a term up to three years and/or fines not exceeding 50 lakhs may be imposed for offenses relating to the use of counterfeit marks on products or services;

or property mark shall be punished with imprisonment for a term that may extend to one year or with a fine, or with both.

[20] Myan. Penal Code § 484 (1861).

[21] *U Han Kyi (The Creation Myanmar Co. Ltd.) v. Ko Mya Soe (Sein Gay Har Store), Criminal Regular Case* No. 446/2001.

[22] *U Zayar Lwin, Mitsubishi Electric Corporation & PME Co. Ltd. v. U Hla Myint*, Criminal Regular Case No. 380/2014.

[23] This Act was promulgated on April 1, 1889.

[24] The Myanmar Code, Vol. III, 258–259.

[25] *Id.* at 2.

[26] *Id.*

possession of instruments for the purpose of counterfeiting a trademark; and the sale, distributing, importing, or exporting of goods with counterfeit marks. In cases in which the same crime is repeated within five years, heavier penalties may be imposed, such as three to ten years of imprisonment or fines not exceeding 100 lakhs. Additionally, anyone who abets the offense is liable for the same punishment as the primary offender.

Finally, it should be noted that unlike in normal criminal prosecutions, there is a statutory time limit for commencing such actions. The period of limitation prescribed by s 15 of the Merchandise Marks Act for prosecuting an offender under the Myanmar Penal Code for the use of a false trademark is three years from the date of the commission of the offense charged or one year from the date of discovery by the prosecutor of the offense charged, whichever is less.[27] Under the new draft Trademark Law, limitation periods are prescribed with respect to appeals to the administrative authorities and to the court.

In addition to the common law remedies and criminal sanctions discussed in the foregoing, some civil laws relating to trademark protection are also available. These are discussed below.

4.6 TRADEMARK PROTECTION UNDER CIVIL LAW

Apart from the common law, trademark protection is also available under civil law in Myanmar. In the 1968 case of *John Walker & Sons Ltd. v. U Than Shwe*,[28] the Chief Court, in taking notice of s 54 of the Specific Relief Act,[29] held that a suit for infringement of a trademark was maintainable. On the facts of the case, John Walker failed in its action owing to the lack of a likelihood of confusion as the mark was used on different goods, namely, whisky and blood tonic.

It is worth noting that whether the trademark infringement is brought under the common law of passing-off or under civil law, the relief available is the same: injunction, damages, and other consequential relief.

[27] S 15 of the Myanmar Merchandise Marks Act reads as follows: "No such prosecution ... mentioned in the last foregoing section shall be commenced after the expiration of three years next after the commission of the offence, or one year after the first discovery therefore by the prosecutor, whichever expiration first happens." *See also* the case of *TM. Mohamed Cassini v. G.S.T Shaik Thumby Sahib* (1940) R.L.R. 244.

[28] (1968) M.L.R. 73.

[29] S 54 of the Specific Relief Act (1877), the Burma Code, Vol. No. XI, 415, states that a perpetual injunction may be granted to prevent the breach of an obligation existing in favor of the applicant, whether expressly or by implication.

The case of *Garments Ltd. v. La Chemise Lacoste Co.* illustrates the application of civil liability principles to trademark rights.[30] In that case, the court found that Crocodile Garment Ltd. sold properties similar to the property distributed by La Chemise Lacoste and granted an injunction to prevent the use of the Lacoste trademark.

4.7 PROTECTION OF WELL-KNOWN MARKS, TRADENAMES, AND GEOGRAPHICAL INDICATIONS

A leading case on the protection of well-known marks in Myanmar is the decision of *John Walker & Sons Ltd. v. U Than Shwe*[31] in 1968. Although the Chief Court recognized that a suit for trademark infringement could be brought by John Walker, it failed on the facts of the case as it could not establish a likelihood of confusion in the use of the mark by Than Shwe on goods that were different from John Walker, namely, blood tonic instead of whisky. This case is likely to be decided differently today, since, in this author's view, Myanmar (like many other countries) has increasingly recognized the value of well-known marks, and is likely to confer additional protection on such marks. In any event, it seems clear that the John Walker case will be decided differently under the new draft Trademark Law, where protection will be conferred on well-known marks without any registration requirement, and even without use or trade in the jurisdiction concerned. Moreover, owners of well-known marks can obtain additional protection against certain uses of their marks on dissimilar goods.

[30] *See* Appeal against the Judgment and 2003 in Civil Regular Suit 2002 of Yangon Division Court *Garments Ltd. (Applicant) v. La Chemise Lacoste Company (by its authorized agent) (Respondent)* in 2003. In that case, La Chemise Lacoste Company through its authorized agent sued Crocodile Garments Company for a perpetual injunction against using the trademark of La Chemise Lacoste. A decree was passed in favor of the plaintiff and the Crocodile Garments Company, being dissatisfied with the judgment and decree of Divisional Court, presented this appeal. In the written statement, it argued that the Crocodile trademark and the Crocodile design are neither alike nor similar and that the defendant has the legal right to use the Crocodile trademark and Crocodile device trademark, that accordingly, the plaintiff was not entitled to an injunction. The plaintiff had continually registered the trademark with the picture of a crocodile and advertised many times in the local newspaper. Although the two trademarks may be a little different when compared, it is a counterfeit trademark if the imitation is made similar. If two trademarks are alike and the alleged wrongdoer intends to cheat the buyer of the goods in question, it is sufficient to be a forgery. Therefore, the finding of the divisional Court that Crocodile Garment Ltd., sold the properties similar to the property distributed by La Chemise Lacoste Company is correct. Thus, the appeal was dismissed with costs confirming the judgment and decree of the Division Court.

[31] (1968) M.L.R. 73.

A recent case where the owner of a well-known mark succeeded in protecting its mark (albeit under criminal law) is *U Zayar Lwin, Mitsubishi Electric Corporation & PME Co. Ltd. v. U Hla Myin*. On August 11, 2015, the Pabedan Township Court ruled in favor of Mitsubishi Electric Corporation in a trademark infringement case against an importer and distributor of infringing breakers bearing the well-known mark of MITSUBISHI,[32] and imposed a fine and imprisonment under s 486 of the Penal Code. The court held that the plaintiff's products had been officially distributed by PME Co. Ltd. and sold worldwide under the famous trademark MITSUBISHI registered in more than 140 countries. The defendant had been running a shop selling electrical products for more than 40 years and based on evidence provided by the plaintiff, the famous character of Mitsubishi could not have been unknown to the defendant. Notably, the factors considered by the Court in determining what constitutes a well-known mark include the degree of recognition by the relevant sector of the public in Myanmar; the duration, extent, and geographical area of the use or promotion of the mark; any registrations or applications for registration; and an assessment of value associated with the mark in Myanmar and abroad.

Under the new draft Trademark Law, trade names can obtain protection without registration. Similarly, there will be a chapter in the draft law on protection of Geographical Indications (GI). Any organization or any authority on behalf of the producers of natural resources or natural products, producers of agricultural products, or producers of manufactured goods or handicrafts are entitled to apply for GI registration in line with the prescribed rules. Moreover, it will also provide for alternative dispute resolution in the settlement of trademark disputes.

4.8 CONCLUSION

Currently, Myanmar's trademark law, and intellectual property laws generally, differ significantly from those of other countries, including the ASEAN member states. These differences may be an impediment to intellectual property interoperability among ASEAN countries.

Myanmar has made good progress in modernizing its laws, however, such as the recently enacted Consumer Protection Law of 2014, the Competition Law of 2015, and the Plant Variety Protection Law of 2016. On the promulgation of the new draft Copyright Law, Trademark Law, Patent Law, and Industrial

[32] *U Zayar Lwin*, *supra* note 22.

Design Law, Myanmar's intellectual property laws will be TRIPS-compliant and become more interoperable with those of ASEAN and WTO countries. Moving forward, these initiatives will greatly enhance opportunities for greater interoperability with the intellectual property laws and systems of other ASEAN member states.

5

Trademark System in Cambodia

Sim Sokheng,* Sovath Phin,** and Giulio C. Zanetti

5.1 INTRODUCTION

Cambodia has recently put in place laws and regulations that protect the intellectual property rights of local and international investors. Such efforts have resulted in a wider recognition of various types of intellectual property, namely trademarks, copyrights, patents, industrial designs, utility models, plant breeders' rights, geographical indications, the layout designs of integrated circuits, and acts of unfair competition. In addition to such remarkable efforts, the current legal system has been greatly influenced by and upgraded thanks to various regional and international legal frameworks.

At the international level, Cambodia has been a member of the World Trade Organization (WTO) since September 2004, following a long process of negotiation and accession with other contracting parties. Under the WTO legal framework, Cambodia is bound to comply with the General Agreement on Tariff and Trade and other agreements, including the Agreement on Trade-Related Aspects of Intellectual Property Rights (TRIPS). Under TRIPS, a member is obliged to ensure that its intellectual property laws comply with minimum substantive standards of protection. Overall, Cambodia has complied with these obligations, even though as a Least Developed Country it is not obliged to comply fully with TRIPS until 2021, and until at least 2033 with respect to the patenting of pharmaceutical products.[1]

* This work does not necessarily reflect the views of the institutions that the author worked or is working for. Sokheng Sim would like to thank two research assistants: Sothyvon Eng and Seychanly Tith for collecting and updating the relevant laws and regulations, and data presented in this chapter.

** Sovath Phin would like to thank Rothna Ngorn for research assistance.

[1] *See* WTO, *WTO Members Agree to Extend Drug Patent Exemption for Poorest Members* (November 6, 2015), *available at* www.wto.org/english/news_e/news15_e/trip_06nov15_e.htm. In its draft working party report, Cambodia requested the 2009 transition period. Finally,

At the regional level Cambodia has been a member of the Association of Southeast Asian Nations (ASEAN) since 1999. It is committed to complying with the ASEAN Framework Agreement on Intellectual Property Cooperation of 1995, and subsequent action plans including the ASEAN Intellectual Property Rights Action Plan 2004–2010, the Work Plan for Cooperation on Copyrights, the ASEAN Intellectual Property Rights Action Plan 2011–2015, and the newly updated ASEAN Intellectual Property Rights Action Plan 2016–2025.[2] In addition, Cambodia has also entered into several bilateral and regional investment agreements[3] and remains strongly committed to protecting intellectual property rights.

Cambodia has expended great efforts to ensure interoperability of its intellectual property system with those of ASEAN and beyond. In this chapter, the authors share Cambodia's experience in creating an interoperable trademark system, the branch of intellectual property law that has seen the greatest development in the country. First, it provides an overview of the trademark system in Cambodia including its history and policy developments. Second, it briefly explains the essential features of the trademark system. Third, it discusses the interoperability aspect of the Cambodian trademark system. Finally, it highlights challenges and future directions of the Cambodian intellectual property system, focusing on the trademark regime.

5.2 OVERVIEW OF THE TRADEMARK SYSTEM IN CAMBODIA: HISTORY AND DEVELOPMENT

5.2.1 *Introduction*

In recent years, Cambodia has placed strong emphasis on developing its intellectual property laws and infrastructure, aimed inter alia at enhancing economic development, attracting foreign direct investment, creating jobs, and raising the standard of living for the Cambodian people. Toward this end, it

WTO members pressed Cambodia to accept the 2007 transition period. However, because of the status of Cambodia as a Least Developed Country, it is entitled to the general transitional period agreed on by all WTO members.

2 *See* Elizabeth Siew-Kuan Ng, *Intellectual Property Interoperability in ASEAN and Beyond: An Integration Model, in* ELIZABETH SIEW-KUAN NG & GRAEME AUSTIN (eds.), INTERNATIONAL INTELLECTUAL PROPERTY AND THE ASEAN WAY: PATHWAYS TO INTEROPERABILITY, Chapter 1.

3 Examples of intellectual property—relevant bilateral treaties entered into by Cambodia include the Agreement on Comprehensive Economic Partnership among Japan and member states of the Association of Southeast Asian Nations (December 1, 2009), Agreement between Japan and the Kingdom of Cambodia for the Liberalization, Promotion and Protection of Investment (July 31, 2008), Agreement between the United States of America and the Kingdom of Cambodia on Trade Relations and Intellectual Property Rights Protection (October 4, 1996).

has also signed bilateral trade agreements with many countries, such as the United States,[4] Thailand,[5] China,[6] Japan,[7] Korea[8] and Singapore.[9] One study suggests that, as a result of the Cambodia–US trade relationship, more than 600,000 jobs have been created (generating wages for workers amounting to US$75 million per month), and exports to the United States have risen to approximately US$2 billion to date.[10]

In addition, Cambodia has also signed Memorandums of Understanding aimed at promoting cooperation in the field of intellectual property protection and enforcement. Take, for example, the Memorandum of Understanding on intellectual property cooperation between the Kingdom of Cambodia and the Kingdom of Thailand of March 5, 1997.[11] At the international level, Cambodia is a member of several multilateral intellectual property agreements. These include the World Intellectual Property Organization (WIPO) Convention,[12] the Paris Convention for the Protection of Industrial Property (Paris Convention),[13] TRIPS,[14] the Protocol Relating to the Madrid Agreement Concerning the International Registration of Marks (Madrid Protocol),[15] the

4 *See* Agreement between the United States of America and the Kingdom of Cambodia on Trade relations and Intellectual Property Rights protection, October 4, 1996, *available at* www.wipo.int/wipolex/en/treaties/text.jsp?file_id=241514.

5 *See* Bilateral Investment Treaty between Thailand and Cambodia, March 30, 1995, *available at* www.aseanbriefing.com/search.html?s=bilateral+investment+treaty+between+Thailand+and+Cambodia.

6 *See* Bilateral Investment Treaty between China and Cambodia, July 19, 1996, *available at* www.aseanbriefing.com/userfiles/resources-pdfs/Cambodia/BIT/Cambodia_China_BIT.pdf.

7 *See* Agreement between Japan and the Kingdom of Cambodia for the Liberalization, Promotion and Protection of Investment, June 14, 2007, *available at* www.wipo.int/wipolex/en/other_treaties/text.jsp?file_id=309528.

8 *See* Agreement between the Government of the Kingdom of Cambodia and the Government of the Democratic People's Republic of Korea for the Promotion and Protection of Investments, November 1, 2007, *available at* www.moc.gov.kh/Portals/0/Docs/TradeInfo/TA/2007%2011%2001st,%20Agreement%20between%20Cambodia-%20Nord%20Korea%20English.pdf.

9 *See* Agreement between the Government of the Kingdom of Cambodia and the Government of the Republic of Singapore on the Promotion and Protection of Investments, Nov. 4, 1996, *available at* http://investmentpolicyhub.unctad.org/Download/TreatyFile/583.

10 *See* Sim Sokheng, Intellectual Property (IP) Laws in ASEAN: *IP & FTA in AEC and RCEP: Cambodia's Approach, Opportunities & Challenges*, 7th Annual CSCL Conference at Pannasastra University of Cambodia, Phnom Penh, Cambodia (February 28, 2015). It should be noted that these treaties on trade and investment contain some clauses related to the cooperation in the field of intellectual property.

11 *Available at* www.cambodiaip.gov.kh/DocResources/fa4014d2-c12f-4197-bbfd-5502850346d3_c786a043-b88d-4f64–9429–60a330efdc5f-en.pdf.

12 Cambodia became a member of the WIPO on July 25, 1995.

13 Cambodia became a member of the Paris Union on September 22, 1998.

14 Cambodia became contracting party to TRIPs Agreement on October 13, 2004 when it became a member state of WTO.

15 The Protocol was concluded in 1989 and Cambodia's ratification is dated June 5, 2015.

Patent Cooperation Treaty (PCT),[16] and the Hague Agreement Concerning the International Registration of Industrial Designs (Hague Agreement).[17] As an ASEAN member state Cambodia is also a party to the ASEAN Framework Agreement on Intellectual Property Cooperation,[18] the ASEAN–China Free Trade Agreement,[19] the ASEAN–Australia–New Zealand Free Trade Agreement,[20] and the Agreement on Comprehensive Economic Partnership between Japan and Members States of the ASEAN.[21] A brief review of the history of Cambodia's trademark system may provide a useful backdrop to its current development.

5.2.2 *History and Development of Cambodia's Trademark System*

According to Letter No. 452 of the Minister of Commerce addressed to the President of the Council of Ministers of the State of Cambodia, dated October 10, 1991, trademark registration in Cambodia had begun even before the arrival of the Khmer Rouges and the resulting destruction of the Cambodian legal system.[22] The Letter interestingly revealed that foreign trademarks had been registered and kept at the commercial court and at the tribunal of first instance under the previous regime. Moreover, the Letter requested the Council of Ministers to authorize the Ministry of Commerce to register and maintain the registration of foreign and national trademarks. On that basis, the Bureau of External Relations at the Department of Foreign Trade

[16] Cambodia submitted its instrument of accession to the Patent Cooperation Treaty (PCT) on August 24, 2016 and the PCT became effective as of December 8, 2016.

[17] On November 25, 2016, Cambodia deposited its instrument of accession to the Geneva (1999) Act of the Hague Agreement Concerning the International Registration of Industrial Designs. As of February 25, 2017, Hague System users will be able to designate Cambodia in an international design application.

[18] The Agreement was adopted on December 15, 1995 at Bangkok. Cambodia became contracting party to the Agreement on April 30, 1999 when it became the tenth member of ASEAN.

[19] The Agreement came into force on January 1, 2010.

[20] The Agreement was adopted on February 27, 2009. Cambodia adhered to the Agreement on November 5, 2010.

[21] The Agreement was adopted on March 26, 2008. Cambodia's ratification is dated December 1, 2009.

[22] Before the destruction of the Cambodian legal system by the Khmer Rouge, Cambodia might also have had some legal texts on copyright and related rights. This statement is based on the fact that Cambodia ratified in 1955 the Universal Copyright Convention of September 6, 1952. In 1961, it also became a signatory to the Rome Convention for the protection of performers, producers of phonograms and broadcasting organizations of October 26, 1961. For a detailed discussion regarding the legal, economic, historical and political aspects of the intellectual property regime of Cambodia in general, *see* Peter Ganea, *Cambodia, in* Intellectual Property in Asia: Law, Economics, History and Politics (Paul Goldstein & Joseph Straus, eds., 2009).

of the Ministry of Commerce started to accept applications for trademark registration.

Subsequently, in 1992 during the transitional period Cambodia adopted provisions relating to the Judiciary and Criminal Law and Procedure, including provisions concerning counterfeiting of trademarks and misappropriation of intellectual property rights in general.[23] In 1997, the Bureau was upgraded and renamed the Department of Intellectual Property under the Ministry of Commerce, and a Ministerial Regulation of 1997 ("Prakas No. 368") formed the basic legal framework for the registration and development of trademark law in Cambodia. Under Prakas No. 368, the Department of Intellectual Property was authorized to register and grant trademark and service mark certificates to local and foreign applicants and handle all registration-related problems. It also stipulated the protection period, conditions, and requirements for registration of a mark. Prakas No. 368 was repealed in 2002 by the Law on Marks, Trade Names and Acts of Unfair Competition (Trademark Law), and a Sub-Decree of 2006 implemented the Trademark Law. Since then, the Ministry of Commerce has issued many regulations to implement the 2002 Trademark Law and the 2006 Sub-Decree.[24]

5.2.3 *National Intellectual Property Development Policies and Strategies*

The National Intellectual Property Strategy and Its Implementation

In 2013, Cambodia adopted a comprehensive National Intellectual Property Strategy (NIPS).[25] On behalf of the Royal Government of Cambodia, the National Committee for Intellectual Property Rights (NCIPR)[26] embarked on this project with the support of WIPO, and aimed to establish an intellectual property strategy that harmonized all existing practices to embrace common objectives. The formulation of the NIPS was conducted by WIPO's

[23] *See* arts. 47 & 48 of the Provisions Relating to the Judiciary and Criminal Law and Procedure Applicable in Cambodia during the Transitional Period. Those provisions however were repealed by the new Criminal Code dated November 30, 2009 and the new Criminal Procedure Code dated August 10, 2007.

[24] For a list of those laws and regulations, *see* www.cambodiaip.gov.kh/.

[25] The National Intellectual Property Strategy [hereinafter *NIPS*] was adopted by the National Committee for Intellectual Property Rights of Cambodia.

[26] The National Committee for Intellectual Property Rights [hereinafter *NCIPR*] was created by Sub-Decree No. 142 dated September 18, 2008, the National Committee for the Management of IP Rights is mandated to assure the unique national policy in the field of IP and to reinforce the smooth cooperation between relevant ministries and entities in organizing, promoting, and enforcing the laws and provisions related to intellectual property rights.

international experts and by a team of national experts, taking into account the views of all relevant stakeholders.

NIPS lays down four key objectives to be undertaken by relevant ministries within a certain timeframe:

- Improve the capability and capacity within the Cambodian economy and state institutions to strategically use the intellectual property system to support Cambodia's economic development
- Improve the capability and capacity within the Cambodian government to deliver intellectual property policy, services, and enforcement to support Cambodia's agricultural, commercial, industrial, and cultural sectors as well as the tourism industry
- Improve awareness and understanding within the broader population of the economic role of intellectual property and to increase the strategic use of the intellectual property system by Cambodian businesses
- Align Cambodia's intellectual property legislation with international standards to meet Cambodia's development, economic, and social needs

The four key objectives are broken down into thirty-seven initiatives[27] to be carried out within specific timeframes (short, medium, and long term) under the responsibility of different government institutions.

NIPS forms a crucial and comprehensive guideline to maximizing the utilization of the intellectual property system in numerous sectors of the economy, all of which are seen as having significant economic potential for Cambodia. Trade activities, the emergence of Small and Medium-Sized Enterprises (SMEs), and the flow of investments are all regarded as benefitting from a sound and reliable intellectual property system. The following six sectors of Cambodia's economy are in particular considered to benefit significantly from increased use of the intellectual property system: (1) Agriculture, (2) Culture, (3) Education & Training, (4) Health, (5) Industry & Commerce, and (6) Tourism.

In addition to NIPS, the government of Cambodia has also adopted other policies and strategies that are directly or indirectly related to intellectual property, such as the Rectangular Strategy, the National Strategic Development Plan, the Industrial Development Policy, and Cambodia Trade Integration Strategy. These are briefly reviewed in the sections that follow.

[27] For a detailed explanation, *see NIPS*, *supra* note 24.

The Rectangular Strategy and the National Strategic Development Plan

Cambodia was the first Least Developed Country to join the WTO (in 2004) through the full accession process. As a result of the WTO accession negotiation process, Cambodia adopted a legislative reform agenda to bring its business, investment, and trade regimes in line with international norms. Pursuing this legislative agenda, Cambodia adopted a strategy, among others, to strengthen mechanisms for the protection of intellectual property rights and to prevent illegal copying, reproduction, and use of new techniques and technology. This strategy was spelled out in the so-called 2004 Rectangular Strategy: Economic Policy Agenda of the Royal Government of Cambodia (Rectangular Strategy).

The Rectangular Strategy has been implemented and updated in three consecutive phases. In the third and latest phase of its update and implementation (Rectangular Strategy Phase III), the government assigned the Ministry of Commerce to focus its efforts, inter alia, on the promotion and protection of intellectual property rights.[28] Recognizing the significant progress made in promoting SMEs through the implementation of industrial property policies,[29] including the adoption of the NIPS in 2013, the National Strategic Development Plan 2014–2018 (NSDP 2014–2018) was formulated to implement the Rectangular Strategy Phase III.

Adopted on May 30, 2014, the NSDP 2014–2018 sets out six key policy priorities: (1) Good Governance, (2) Overarching Environment for Implementing the Strategy, (3) Promotion of the Agricultural Sector, (4) The Development of Physical Infrastructure, (5) Private Sector Development and Employment, and (6) Capacity Building and Human Resource Development. Intellectual property is encompassed within policy (5) (Private Sector Development and Employment), and aims to strengthen the private sector and business environment to promote investment. In time, it will also improve the skills and expertise of the Cambodian workforce through technology transfer. For this to be successful, the Ministry of Commerce is mandated to promote the respect of intellectual property rights within the timeframe of 2014–2018.

Industrial Development Policy 2015–2025

Cambodia's recently adopted Industrial Development Policy (IDP) 2015–2025 is designed to promote the country's industrial development to ensure

[28] National Strategic Development Plan 2014–2018, 165, *available at* www.mop.gov.kh/home/nsdp/nsdp20142018/tabid/216/default.aspx.

[29] *Id.* at 58–59.

sustainable and inclusive economic growth, focusing on economic diversification, strengthening competitiveness, and promoting productivity.[30] Toward this end, it instituted a set of comprehensive and interconnected policy measures and action plans with clearly defined responsible institutions leading the implementation process.[31] These policy measures and action plans are directed at improving the regulatory environment, focusing on trade facilitation measures and export promotion, strengthening industrial standards and industrial property rights, facilitation of the payment of tax obligations, and the establishment of a labor market and industrial relations. In relation to industrial property rights, the government has set out the following projects:

- Improving the effectiveness of the process of registering industrial property rights by way of implementing collaborative procedures to recognize registration agents of partner countries and to facilitate the registration of intellectual property rights through automation
- Raising awareness of the importance of standards, metrology, and industrial property rights in order to broaden and attract the interest of entrepreneurs
- Taking practical actions to strengthen the implementation of standards, metrology, and industrial property rights as a tool for promoting competitiveness[32]
- Strengthening the management of the Cambodian Innovation and Invention Center to promote invention and training on industrial property rights[33]

The Cambodia Trade Integration Strategy

The Cambodia Trade Integration Strategy (CTIS) 2014–2018 provides for a number of initiatives to be carried out in order to create "a modern, trade-supportive intellectual property rights framework."[34] Several targets were set with respect to trademarks and designs, such as the registration of more than 1,200 new trademarks by Cambodian businesses and 60 local design registrations by 2018.[35] To achieve this outcome the government is committed to adopting several key recommendations:

30 *See* Cambodia Industrial Development Policy 2015–2025, I, *available at* www.cambodiainvestment.gov.kh/content/uploads/2015/09/IDP-English-Version-FINAL1.pdf.

31 *Id.* at III. 32 *Id.* at 24. 33 *Id.* at 27.

34 *See* Cambodia Trade Integration Strategy 2014–2018, 182, *available at* www.kh.undp.org/content/dam/cambodia/docs/PovRed/Cambodia%20Trade%20Integration%20Strategy%202014–2018.pdf.

35 *Id.*

- The government should develop a clear capacity development plan.
- The development of Cambodia's intellectual property right framework and infrastructure should be "development centered."
- Cambodian policymakers and officials should continue to assess very carefully the costs and benefits of any possible accession to an international agreement, taking into account national interests, institutional and financial capacity limitations, and trade integration considerations.
- Cambodian policymakers and officials should also make use of the new transitional period granted to Least Developed Countries by the WTO TRIPS Council and carefully sequence actions and priorities so that the government's scarce resources are put to the most effective use.[36]

Unlike the IDP (which is mainly focused on industrial property) and like the NIPS, the CTIS covers almost all aspects of intellectual property, with the aim of promoting the protection, registration, and enforcement of intellectual property rights, as well as the balancing of the interests of right holders and the public. For example, the NIPS incorporates the promotion of access to essential medicines so as to ensure that intellectual property development may support public health objectives.

Similarly, the CTIS emphasizes a "Development Centered" approach and indicates that there is a need to increase awareness of intellectual property rights in the public at large and, most importantly, to increase the use of intellectual property rights protection by Cambodian firms and creators. The CTIS also recognizes an urgent need to more aggressively promote the use of intellectual property protection by Cambodian businesses, including SMEs. In addition, the CTIS also incorporated the NSIP and the ASEAN IPR Action Plan 2011–2015 as part of the process of integrating the Cambodian economy into the ASEAN single market.

Whilst the IDP does not refer to any of the above regional instruments, it seems clear that it should nevertheless also take into account the NSIP and the ASEAN IPR Action Plan, as doing so will ensure consistency and interoperability on intellectual property rights in Cambodia and the region. It can thus be argued that all of the above national policies and strategies are designed to foster the integration of Cambodia into the regional and international intellectual property regimes, and to promote the interoperability of the various national systems with those regimes.

[36] For detailed recommendations, *see id.* at 182.

5.2.4 *Impact of International Intellectual Property Treaties on the Cambodian Intellectual Property Systems*

Since 1995 when Cambodia became a member of WIPO, the country has acceded to five international intellectual property treaties: the Paris Convention, TRIPS, the Madrid Protocol, the PCT, and the Hague Agreement.

The Paris Convention

The first major substantive intellectual property treaty that Cambodia signed was the Paris Convention in 1998, an important step in Cambodia's "intellectual property journey" since joining WIPO in 1995. The Paris Convention greatly influenced the development of Cambodian practice on registration of marks, and its principles formed the basis for the Trademark Law of 2002, namely (1) National Treatment, (2) Filing and Registration Conditions, (3) Priority, (4) Use and Cancellation, (5) Grace Period for Renewal, (6) Agent or Representative, (7) Well-Known Marks, (8) State Emblems and Official Signs, and (9) Unfair Competition.[37] Nonetheless, certain loopholes remained in the Trademark Law since the Paris Convention did not provide a comprehensive or detailed framework on trademark protection. For instance, while art. 6 of the Paris Convention stipulates that "conditions for the filing and registration of trademarks shall be determined in each country of the Union by its domestic legislation," it does not provide concrete and specific guide on how it should be implemented in a legislative provision. Hence, guidance was sought from the TRIPS provisions.

Trade-Related Aspects of Intellectual Property Rights

Adoption of a new set of intellectual property laws was one of the conditions for Cambodia's accession to the WTO. Hence, even before Cambodia's WTO accession in 2004, it had already established its national intellectual property laws based on the TRIPS minimum standards of intellectual property protection. The following fundamental aspects were therefore incorporated into the 2002 Trademark Law: (1) Definition of Protectable Marks, (2) Grounds to Refuse Registration, (3) Publication and Opposition, (4) Requirements to Maintain a Registration, (5) Minimum Term of Protection, (6) Exclusive

[37] In other fields of intellectual property, namely patent, utility model, industrial design, and indication of source (geographical indication), the Paris Convention also provides some basic rules to be applied by member states. Those rules are essentially the national treatment, the right of priority, and some other specific requirement for each subject matter. Owing to the length of this chapter, only trademark-related provisions are discussed herein.

Rights, (7) Well-Known Marks, (8) Licensing and Assignment, (9) Determination of Infringement, and (10) Enforcement Provisions.

The Madrid Protocol

Cambodia was the fourth country in the ASEAN Economic Community (AEC) to join the Madrid Protocol, following the Philippines, Singapore, and Vietnam, and was ahead of some larger economies, including Malaysia, Indonesia, and Thailand.[38] The Instrument of Accession to the Protocol relating to the Madrid Agreement concerning the International Registration of Marks was signed and deposited with WIPO in March 2015, and took effect on June 5, 2015. Following this milestone, the Department of Intellectual Property is now drafting the Ministerial Regulation on Implementation of the Protocol. Further, it is worth noting that, because the Bureau of International Mark Registration has not yet been operationalized (despite its establishment on July 24, 2014), an ad hoc team[39] dealing with international trademark registration was established to ensure the functioning of the international registration system.

The PCT

On September 8, 2016, Cambodia became the 151st member state of the PCT. The PCT entered into force in Cambodia on December 8, 2016. From this effective date, the designation of Cambodia will be automatically included in the international application. An international application, filed by a natural or legal person who is a national or resident of Cambodia, will start from a Receiving Office. The Office will then transmit the international application to the International Searching Authority (ISA) and to the International Bureau of WIPO. After receiving the international search report and written opinion of the ISA, the Bureau will publish the PCT patent application and communicate it to the designated national or regional patent office. Based on the international search report and written opinion of the ISA, the latter examines the patentability of the invention and grants a patent only if the requirements for registration provided under its national legislation are met. Being a less

[38] *See* Sim, *supra* note 10. The Madrid Protocol is an international registration system that enables trademark owners to apply for protection in up to 132 member countries, including the European Union, the United States, China, Japan, India, and some ASEAN countries. The system accounts for approximately 80 percent of world trade.

[39] Also known as the Madrid Team where the officials in charge are those from the Bureau of Mark Registration. The Madrid Protocol presents the following advantages: (1) the possibility of filing an international application with one office only instead of filing separate application in the various offices concerned, (2) one single application form, (3) a single procedure, (4) one single language (including English), and (5) lower filing and maintenance fees.

developed country, the international application filed by a national or resident of Cambodia will enjoy a reduction of 90 percent for certain fees, including the international filing fee, applicable during the international phase of the application. However, the national phase of the PCT application is subject to payment of separate fees prescribed by the Cambodian patent office. Thanks to Cambodia's accession to the PCT, an international filing of a patent is possible in the Cambodian jurisdiction.

The Hague Agreement

On November 25, 2016, Cambodia deposited its instrument of accession to the Geneva (1999) Act of the Hague Agreement (1999 Act).[40] The accession of Cambodia to the 1999 Act brings the number of Contracting Parties to this 1999 Act to fifty-two and the total number of Contracting Parties to the Hague Agreement to sixty-six. As of February 25, 2017, Hague System users are able to designate Cambodia in an international design application. The instrument of accession was also accompanied by the following declarations:

- The maximum period for the deferment of the publication of an industrial design where Cambodia is designated in an international registration is twelve months from the filing date or, where priority is claimed, from the priority date.
- The maximum duration of protection provided for by the legislation of Cambodia with respect to industrial designs is fifteen years.
- The application of level two of the standard designation fee, under Rule 12(1)(c)(i) of the Common Regulations under the 1999 Act and the 1960 Act of the Hague Agreement.[41]

5.3 ESSENTIAL FEATURES OF THE CAMBODIAN TRADEMARK SYSTEM

5.3.1 *Cambodian Trademark Law: Essential Features*

One key example of Cambodia's efforts to improve its trademark system is the reduced turnaround time for the registration of trademarks, now guaranteed to be within six months. This result is the outcome of significant efforts put in place by the Cambodian government to create, develop, and reform its

[40] *See Cambodia Joins the Hague System*, *available at* www.wipo.int/hague/en/news/2016/news_0011.html.

[41] *See* WIPO Information Notice No. 13/2016, *available at* www.wipo.int/edocs/hagdocs/en/2016/hague_2016_13.pdf.

trademark system. A few key features of this system are discussed in the text that follows.[42]

Subject -Matter of Trademark Protection

The Trademark Law defines a "mark" as "any visible sign capable of distinguishing the goods (trademark) or service (service mark) of an enterprise."[43] A mark must be distinctive, serving to distinguish the goods or services of one or more enterprises from those of the other enterprises. An application for trademark registration is to be filed with the Department of Intellectual Property. A mark will be registered and protected if it is distinctive and does not fall into any category set out under art. 4 of the Trademark Law. For example, the proposed mark must not be contrary to public order, morality, or good customs. A mark containing a pornographic picture, for example, could not be registered based on morality grounds. A mark "likely to mislead the public or trade circles" may also be refused registration. For example, if product X was made in Cambodia, but it bears a mark "Japan X" it would not be registered if it is found that it is likely to mislead consumers or users with respect to its place of production.

Apart from trademarks, "collective marks" and "trade names" are also registrable.[44] A "trade name" refers to the name and/or designation identifying and distinguishing an enterprise (as opposed to its goods and/or services), while "collective mark" refers to any visible sign "capable of distinguishing the origin or any other common characteristic, including the quality, of goods or services of different enterprises." An application for registering a collective mark shall be accompanied with a copy of the regulation governing its use,[45] and the use of the collective mark will be subject to the consent and control of the registered owner of that collective mark.

The Rights of a Trademark Holder

After registration of a trademark, the exclusive right to use the mark in relation to goods/services is granted to the owner of the mark. The trademark owner is entitled to prohibit others from using the registered mark on similar and/or identical goods/services without his authorization.[46] The duration of protection is limited to ten years from the filing date of the application. It can be

[42] For a detailed explanation of this section, *see* Phin Sovath, *Economic Law: Intellectual Property Rights, in* INTRODUCTION TO CAMBODIAN LAW (Hor Peng, Kong Phallack & Jörg Menzel, eds., 2011).

[43] *See* Trademark Law, art. 2 (2002). Although the Trademark Law refers to "Enterprise," in practice, an individual may also apply and own the trademark.

[44] *Id.* [45] *Id.* at art. 17. [46] *Id.* at art. 11.

indefinitely renewed for further periods of ten years.[47] During the protection period, the registered owner of the mark may institute court proceedings for infringement.[48] In addition, provisional measures and border measures are also available to trademark owners.

Rights over the trademark do not, however, extend to acts in respect of articles that have been put on the market in Cambodia by the registered owner or with his consent. Cambodia therefore adopts the principle of national exhaustion of trademark rights, where the trademark holder cannot prevent consumers from using or reselling the product when it was first put on the market by the trademark owner or any third party authorized by him. The principle of national exhaustion, however, is not applicable to acts relating to infringing products, which were put on the market without consent or authorization from the trademark owner.

Opposition, Invalidation, and Cancellation of Trademark

After registration, a trademark may be subject to opposition, invalidation, and cancellation actions. Any interested party can oppose the registration of a mark within the period of ninety days from the date of its publication in the official gazette.[49] The opposition complaint may be filed on the grounds that one or more of the requirements of arts. 2a, 4, and 5 of the Trademark Law, and the regulations pertaining thereto, are not fulfilled. Under art. 13 of the Trademark Law, any interested person may request the Ministry of Commerce to invalidate the registration of a mark if it can be proved that requirements under the Trademark Law are not fulfilled.[50] Such invalidation shall be deemed to have been effective as of the date of the registration.[51] In addition, the Ministry of Commerce also has the right to cancel registered marks in a number of circumstances, such as when there is no application for renewal or when the owner of the trademark is not the legitimate owner.[52]

Protection against Unfair Competition

The Cambodian Trademark Law also includes provisions relating to acts of unfair competition. The Trademark Law defines any act that is contrary to honest practices in industrial, commercial, and service matters as an act of unfair competition.[53] Article 23 of the Trademark Law lists the following behaviors as acts of unfair competition: (1) all acts of such a nature as to

47 *Id.* at art. 12. 48 *Id.*

49 In order to expedite the registration process, Cambodia legislation does not allow any opposition action before the registration of the mark. In some other countries such as France, the opposition action must be filed before the registration of the mark.

50 *See* Trademark Law, art. 13 (2002). 51 *Id.* 52 *Id.* at art. 14. 53 *Id.* at art. 22.

create confusion; (2) false allegations to discredit the establishment, the goods, or the industrial, commercial, or service activities of a competitor; and (3) indications or allegations that are used to mislead the public as to the nature, the manufacturing process, the characteristics, the suitability for their purpose, or the quantity of the goods. Therefore, any dishonest practice that creates confusion, misleads the public, or discredits a competing establishment will be prohibited as long as it falls into any of the three aforesaid categories.

Application of International Treaties and Interpretation
Cambodia incorporates the provisions of international industrial property treaties to which it is a party into its national trademark law and declares that where there is any conflict, the provisions of the international treaties shall prevail over the provisions of the Trademark Law.[54] Its Trademark Law also incorporated definitions on certain key terms, such as "International Classification," "Paris Convention," "Priority Date," and "Counterfeiting Trademark Goods," which are commonly and internationally recognized.[55] This enhances the interoperability of the Cambodian trademark system with other national, regional, and international systems.

5.3.2 *Trademark Administration*

The Department of Intellectual Property administers the Cambodian trademark system. Pursuant to the Ministerial Regulation on the Organization and Functioning of the Department of Intellectual Property,[56] there are eight subordinate divisions under the supervision of the Department, namely the Division of Mark Registration, the Division of International Mark Registration, the Division of Post Mark Registration, the Division of Geographical Indications and Trade Secrets, the Division of Litigation, the Division of Cooperation and Legal Affairs, the Division of Education and Public Awareness, and the Division of Administration and Information Technology.

The Division of Mark Registration is responsible for the following:

- Preparing procedures and legal regulations pertaining to the registration of marks
- Preparing proposals and implementing projects pertaining to the registration of marks
- Conducting mark searches prior to registration

[54] *Id.* at art. 60. [55] *Id.* at art. 61.

[56] *See* Prakas No. 206 PN.BL.PRK on Organization and Functioning of the Department of Intellectual Property (July 24, 2014).

- Conducting formality examinations of filed marks
- Conducting substantive examinations of filed marks
- Searching and assessing marks and well-known marks
- Receiving and solving complaints and refusals prior to the registration of mark
- Registering marks and granting certificates of registration
- Recording of changes regarding names and addresses of the mark owners, the merging of marks, and the transfer of ownership prior to registration
- Preparing and implementing the automation of mark registration
- Performing other tasks as provided by the leadership

Given the high degree of alignment between the Cambodian trademark system and the requirements of international trademark law, we are of the view that the Cambodian system would not impede interoperability of the intellectual property systems across ASEAN countries. Furthermore, it should be noted that Cambodia has been working on numerous other initiatives aimed at enhancing the interoperability of intellectual property systems. Some of these activities are elaborated below.

5.4 CAMBODIAN INTELLECTUAL PROPERTY INTEROPERABILITY WITH ASEAN COUNTRIES

5.4.1 *Intellectual Property in General*

Substantial efforts have been made to ensure compliance with the requirements of the AEC Blueprint and the ASEAN IPR Action Plan 2011–2015 so as to create a transparent and competitive business environment. Some of these initiatives are aimed at harmonizing procedures, reducing discrepancies, and enhancing cooperation between ASEAN member states, and include

- The establishment of searching tools for trademarks and industrial designs, namely "ASEAN TMview" and "ASEAN DesignView," to facilitate the search within a single database of trademark and design applications and registrations filed and protected in any ASEAN country, including Cambodia.
- Like many ASEAN countries, Cambodia has adopted the "TMclass" system developed by the EU Intellectual Property Office to facilitate classification of trademarks in accordance with the Nice Classification.
- Accession to the Madrid Protocol in July 2015 allows Cambodian trademark owners to obtain protection in more than ninety countries.

- The adoption of a trademark manual (drafted under the auspices of the European Union) to harmonize trademark examination practices in all ASEAN countries. The manual is in the process of being translated into numerous languages of ASEAN countries. A similar initiative in respect of industrial designs is underway, and might be adopted in the near future by Cambodia.
- Discussions with other ASEAN countries on the possible recognition of trademark agents accredited by other member states, thereby enhancing the provision of intellectual property services within ASEAN.
- The adoption of an information technology platform for a trademark databank based on the WIPO-developed Industrial Property Administration System (IPAS), a software commonly used across ASEAN.
- Adoption of the Locarno Classification for the International Classification of Industrial Designs, in-line with numerous other ASEAN countries.
- The signing of Memorandums of Understanding with the Japanese Patent Office and Singaporean Intellectual Property Office to promote cooperation in the field of industry property, and in particular to facilitate the grant of patents by Cambodia.
- Participation in an ASEAN project aimed at creating a common database of intellectual property cases and intellectual property enforcement initiatives. Recently, Cambodia has established a national "Intellectual Property Enforcement Focal Point" to share information and more effectively cooperate in cross-border enforcement endeavors.

5.4.2 *Interoperability of Trademark Administration*

In the specific field of trademark law, Cambodia has undertaken a number of initiatives to enhance greater trademark interoperability among ASEAN members.

Automation of Trademark Administration

The Department of Intellectual Property is launching e-filing of marks in early 2017. A significant amount of work has been done to achieve this ambition. The project of digitalization has been implemented with the deployment of the Electronic Document Management System with the support and assistance of WIPO. More than two million documents have been scanned and stored in digital format, which allows for the data to be managed more efficiently and effectively. In addition, a data validation project was carried out with the support of the World Bank, focusing on the accuracy of the more than 55,000 trademarks registered and more than 45,000 post-registration activities.

Simplified Trademark Workflow

The Industrial Property Automation System has been overhauled, improving efficiency in the registration process. The WIPO-backed Business Process Review has been adopted to simplify the procedures and eliminate unnecessary steps prolonging the registration process. New mark search engines are incorporated, making trademark information even more accessible to the public. ASEAN TMview and WIPO Global Brand have been introduced, making it possible for businesses to conduct their autonomous mark search themselves, saving time and reducing expenses. This has helped to promote transparency and competitiveness in the business environment in Cambodia, by making the intellectual property system more credible.

Enhanced Capacity of the TM Examiners and Attorney/Agent

As of 2015, Cambodia is a leading ASEAN member state in reducing the average turnaround time for the registration of trademarks without objections/opposition to six months (as measured from the date of filing). A manual of substantive examination of marks is now in the drafting process and is expected to be approved in 2017.

Professional training for trademark agents is organized once a year. The very first batch was held in 2014, and it included sixty participants from local law firms and institutions. The third round of training was held in early January 2016 and completed in March 2016.

5.5 CURRENT AND FUTURE CHALLENGES

Perhaps the most significant challenge that Cambodia currently faces in the field of intellectual property is its institutional fragmentation. There are three intellectual property offices in charge of the various intellectual property rights: the Ministry of Commerce is responsible for trademarks and geographical indications; the Ministry of Industry registers patents and industrial designs; and the Ministry of Culture is in charge of copyrights and related rights. To address this issue, the NCIPR was created to coordinate all relevant public stakeholders. The Minister of Commerce acts as Chairman of the Committee and coordinates the intellectual property agenda with representatives of the other fourteen related ministries. The Department of Intellectual Property was assigned as Secretariat of NCIPR. However, there are still challenges for NCIPR and its Secretariat on effective coordination among Ministries and Institutions.

Despite the very significant and tangible improvements achieved in the last ten years (and more noticeably in the last five years) in the field of intellectual property, Cambodia still faces substantial challenges, particularly in the application and enforcement of the intellectual property laws and regulations. Efforts are still needed to enforce these regulatory texts and to achieve their intended goals. These include

- Dissemination and increased awareness of all intellectual property laws and regulations to all relevant stakeholders
- Development of human capital including experts, practitioners, and professionals in all intellectual property sectors
- Capacity building for existing and potential examiners of the various intellectual property rights to respond to the increasing number of applications filed nationally and internationally (particularly in the area of trademarks)
- Promotion and strengthening of enforcement of existing intellectual property laws and regulations
- Adoption and implementation of new regulations to supplement the full implementation of intellectual property laws
- Joining numerous intellectual property–related international treaties and conventions and subsequently enacting or modifying national laws to ensure full implementation of these international instruments
- Provision for regional integration commitments, including AEC and the Regional Comprehensive Economic Partnership Framework

At the regional level, Cambodia is currently trying to support the ASEAN Secretariat to find solutions to some of the most common problems and challenges created by the significant differences in the levels of development among ASEAN member states. Challenges include the substantial differences in the capacity, priorities, and innovation needs of ASEAN member states and differences in the official and working languages, among the states, both of which can represent a significant obstacle to the effective functioning of a harmonized intellectual property system at the regional level. Furthermore, accession to any new treaty, in the short term, is likely to create new financial, institutional, and human resources demands in an environment of "scarce" resources.

As a Least Developed Country, the level of intellectual property awareness in Cambodia is still limited, and requires more attention and public promotion. Because of this, most people, including some rights holders, are not aware of their rights. In order to tackle this problem, Cambodia has been carrying out a number of campaigns to promote intellectual property awareness, especially for the business community. Given the magnitude of the problem, additional efforts and financial resources are needed.

5.6 CONCLUSION

Cambodia is determined to take advantage of the potential inherent in its location at the center of the ASEAN region, and aims to further integrate with neighboring countries. Interoperability with other ASEAN member states in the field of intellectual property is perceived as a precious opportunity to enhance economic growth and integration. However, the very diverse level of development of the various intellectual property regimes may represent a serious obstacle, and interoperability may proceed faster and more smoothly in some areas while being delayed or challenged in others.

PART II

INTELLECTUAL PROPERTY INTEROPERABILITY AND JUDICIAL PROCESSES

The four chapters in this part identify the opportunities for interoperability in the context of dispute resolution and private international law. The first two chapters discuss the intellectual property dispute resolution experience of Singapore and the Philippines; the next two chapters ensue with an appraisal on private international law as a vehicle for achieving interoperability of judicial processes.

First, in Chapter 6 Mark Lim, See Tho Sok Yee, and Diyanah Binte Baharudin share Singapore's intellectual property dispute resolution experience. Tracing Singapore's journey from the early days of its legal system to its current structure, the authors highlight the significant milestones achieved in establishing Singapore's intellectual property dispute resolution system. Situating this development within the broader regional context, Lim, See Tho, and Baharudin emphasize that the differences between ASEAN and the European Union (such as the lack of supranational institutions) present challenges to developing a single, unified intellectual property dispute resolution system in ASEAN. Given these differences, a soft approach in the form of establishing interoperability of systems was preferred to the more hard-nosed style of harmonization for ASEAN. The authors portend that this softer approach could help foster an environment of mutual understanding and trust that is needed for the creation of interoperable intellectual property mechanisms, and contribute significantly toward the development of an ASEAN common market.

In Chapter 7, Ricardo Blancaflor examines the challenges in the integration of intellectual property enforcement in the ASEAN region. Emphasizing that developing and least-developed countries generally view intellectual property from the standpoint of what is beneficial to their individual nations, regional integration of intellectual property enforcement is not usually given high priority in the face of more pressing national interests. Calling for the adoption of a holistic approach to intellectual property enforcement both nationally and regionally, the author points out that the strengthening of rapport between officials from different agencies plays an important role in fostering better cooperation among government agencies and facilitating inter-agency support. Blancaflor concludes that the establishment of an interoperable regional intellectual property regime including enforcement will be crucial to developing a competitive ASEAN economic region.

Chapters 8 and 9 introduce the idea that principles of private international law – or conflict of laws – could provide a useful vehicle for achieving some of the key aims of interoperability: cooperation and alignment without harmonization. Both interoperability and private international law concern the accommodation of differences between different legal systems. In private litigation involving international elements, accommodating difference occurs mostly by necessity, rather than design: private international law *must* engage with differences in different legal systems, as individual litigants pursue particular advantage in one or other of the domestic laws that might plausibly apply to specific aspects of the underlying claim. At the same time, the overarching ends are justice and convenience, which are also key dynamics of the ASEAN Way.

Chapter 8 by Graeme Austin takes up these themes in the context of justiciability in the area of copyright law. Exploring this topic within the common law context, the chapter discusses how justiciability was, until fairly recently, a highly contested topic. Somewhat ironically, common law courts manifested respect for other nations' sovereignty over domestic intellectual property laws by refusing to apply them. Drawing on the concerns of interoperability in the ASEAN context, this chapter suggests that doctrines that enable application of foreign laws by domestic courts might be useful vehicles for achieving a greater degree of interaction between different domestic legal systems. These emerging doctrines have the potential to enable different domestic copyright laws to have effect without overriding each other. In this way, these doctrines further some of the key aims of interoperability: respect for difference and individual policy choices made within distinct polities.

Chapter 9 by Richard Garnett adds further detail to these broad propositions through an examination of remedies in the cross-border intellectual property field, a hitherto underexplored topic. It is one thing to suggest that different nations can and should apply foreign intellectual property laws. But for individual litigants, the ultimate concern is the relief that might be achieved through adopting this strategy. Different nations' laws will not be truly "interoperable" unless individuals and firms can be confident that their litigation will be effective in vindicating rights that are infringed.

The authors of these chapters recognize that within the ASEAN context, there is much work to be done before the apparatus of private international law will become a fully-evolved tool of interoperability. The important differences between ASEAN members' intellectual property laws will also find expression in different approaches to private international law. Even so, within the overarching agenda of achieving a more integrated and aligned intellectual property regime, the ideas explored in these chapters might offer some further avenues of inquiry within the overarching interoperability agenda.

6

Singapore's Intellectual Property Dispute Resolution Experience and ASEAN Interoperability

Mark Lim, See Tho Sok Yee, and Diyanah Binte Baharudin

6.1 INTELLECTUAL PROPERTY AND INTELLECTUAL PROPERTY DISPUTE RESOLUTION WITHIN THE ASEAN ECONOMIC COMMUNITY

Intellectual property dispute resolution mechanisms are key to ensuring that the intellectual property rights granted by each member state are real and effective. To this end, the ASEAN Intellectual Property Rights (IPR) Action Plan 2011–2015 (Action Plan 2011–2015) recognizes the need for the development and implementation of a regional action plan on the enforcement of intellectual property rights.[1] Similarly, the ASEAN Economic Community Blueprint (2008–2015) (AEC Blueprint 2015) recognizes the need to "sustain consultations and information exchanges among national enforcement agencies in IPR protection."[2] The ASEAN Economic Community Blueprint (2015–2025) (AEC Blueprint 2025) repeats the commitment to strengthen intellectual property rights cooperation through several measures, such as expanding the ASEAN intellectual property ecosystem through establishing an ASEAN network of offices (intellectual property, judiciary, customs, and other enforcement agencies) "to enhance effective cooperation on the regional IPR enforcement and to promote building respect for IP."[3]

A strong framework for intellectual property dispute resolution helps to ensure that there is effective enforcement of granted intellectual property

[1] ASEAN, *ASEAN Intellectual Property Rights Action Plan 2011–2015* (July 31, 2011) [hereinafter ASEAN IPR Action Plan 2011–2015] at 7, *available at* www.aseanip.org/Portals/0/PDF/ASEAN%20IPR%20Action%20Plan%202011–2015.pdf.

[2] ASEAN, *ASEAN Economic Community Blueprint (2008–2015)* (November 20, 2007) [hereinafter AEC Blueprint 2015] at 20, [45(iv)], *available at* www.asean.org/storage/images/archive/5187–10.pdf.

[3] ASEAN, *ASEAN Economic Community Blueprint (2015–2025)* (February 19, 2016) [hereinafter AEC Blueprint 2025] at 15, [31(iii)], *available at* www.asean.org/storage/images/2015/November/aec-page/AEC-Blueprint-2025-FINAL.pdf.

rights in each ASEAN member state and to give investors the confidence to allocate funds in this region to support research and development for future innovation, knowing that the fruit of their labor is likely to be protected. This helps to achieve the strategic goal of the AEC Blueprint 2015: "to promote the region as being conducive to the needs of users and generators of IP." It also helps to encourage the development of local innovation and creativity, in line with observations in the AEC Blueprint 2015 that such development would ensure more equitable access and benefits to all stakeholders both in traditional and newer intellectual property rights.[4]

However, it is recognized that developing a harmonized set of dispute resolution procedures, whether for intellectual property or any other subject matter, is challenging because of the innate differences in legal systems within ASEAN and the different socioeconomic climates of each member state. To this end, it is suggested that each country should adopt dispute resolution mechanisms that would be most appropriate to its own unique context.

6.2 SINGAPORE'S INTELLECTUAL PROPERTY DISPUTE RESOLUTION EXPERIENCE: A BRIEF OVERVIEW

Singapore is committed to developing a reputable quality intellectual property dispute resolution system, which will also benefit ASEAN and pave the way for more external trade and investment with ASEAN as a bloc.[5] This section briefly describes Singapore's journey from the early days of its legal system to the significant recommendations for change to Singapore's current system, with a brief discussion of the impact of these changes.[6]

Singapore is a common law jurisdiction that inherited much of its legal tradition from the United Kingdom. The court system is two-tiered, consisting of state courts and the Supreme Court. The state courts are divided into district courts and magistrates' courts[7]. There is also a Small Claims Tribunal dealing

4 *See* AEC Blueprint 2015, *supra* note 2, at 19, [44].

5 *See generally*, IP Steering Committee, *Singapore's Intellectual Property (IP) Hub Master Plan: Developing Singapore as a Global IP Hub in Asia* (March 1, 2013), *available at* www.ipos.gov.sg/Portals/0/Press%20Release/IP%20HUB%20MASTER%20PLAN%20REPORT%202%20APR%202013.pdf.

6 *Infra* note 24.

7 District Courts hear cases exceeding S$60,000 but not exceeding S$250,000 in value (with the exception that, with effect from December 1, 2016, district courts can hear claims not exceeding S$500,000 that arise from road traffic accidents or are based on personal injuries resulting from industrial accidents), while magistrates' Court hear cases not exceeding S$60,000 in value.

with certain matters.[8] The Supreme Court comprises the High Court[9] and the Court of Appeal. The Court of Appeal is the final court of appeal in Singapore and is presided over by the Chief Justice and the Judges of Appeal. There are also two specialist divisions of the High Court: the Family Division and the Singapore International Commercial Court.

In the intellectual property space, the forum for dispute resolution depends on the right in question and the relief sought. A dispute pertaining to preregistration rights (e.g., where a party seeks to oppose a new application to register a trademark), will be heard in the specialist tribunal within the Intellectual Property Office of Singapore (IPOS). As early as 1937, Singapore had a government department within the Ministry of Law called the Registry of Trade Marks and Patents (RTMP) dealing with regulatory functions in respect of trademarks[10] and reregistration of UK patents.[11]

Disputes pertaining to post-registration rights are heard either by the High Court in Singapore or by IPOS. IPOS shares concurrent jurisdiction with the High Court in Singapore for revocation and invalidation under the Trade Marks Act,[12] and revocation under the Registered Designs Act.[13] However, certain matters may be heard only in the High Court, such as infringement of patent, trademark, and registered design rights. And some matters, such as patent revocation (not being part of a counterclaim), are heard at first instance exclusively at IPOS.[14]

8 These matters are sale or purchase of goods, provision of services, tortious damage (not including motor vehicle accident related damage) and contractual disputes relating to a lease of residential property, where the claim does not exceed S$10,000 (or S$20,000 by agreement between the parties). *See* sects. 5(1) and 5(4) of the Small Claims Tribunals Act (Cap. 308, 1998 Rev. Ed. Sing).

9 Civil matters above S$250,000 are generally commenced in the High Court. Criminal cases where the offenses are punishable with death or with imprisonment for a term that exceeds ten years are also heard in the High Court. *See generally*, official website of the Supreme Court of Singapore, *Structure of the Courts* (August 5, 2016), *available at* www.supremecourt.gov.sg/about-us/the-supreme-court/structure-of-the-courts.

10 *E.g.*, processing of applications for the registration of trademarks, renewals, and restoration of trademark registrations, and adjudication of opposition and rectification proceedings for such registration.

11 This was stated by way of introduction at the Second Reading of the Intellectual Property Office of Singapore Bill: *Singapore Parliamentary Debates, Official Report* (February 22, 2001), vol. 72 at col. 1457 (Ho Peng Kee, Minister of State for Law).

12 *See* s 22(5) and s 23(5) of the Trade Marks Act (Cap. 332, 2005 Rev. Ed. Sing.).

13 *See* s 27 of the Registered Designs Act (Cap. 266, 2005 Rev. Ed Sing.).

14 This was stated in the Second Reading of the Patents Bill: *Singapore Parliamentary Debates, Official Report* (March 21, 1994), vol. 62 at col. 1447 (Professor S. Jayakumar, Minister for Law) and in Alban Kang et al., A Guide to Patent Law in Singapore 8.2.1–8.2.2 (2d ed. 2009). There is also an academic interpretation of the Patents Act (Cap. 221, 2005 Rev. Ed. Sing.) that the High Court and IPOS share concurrent jurisdiction for patent revocation: *see* Ng-Loy

As for nonregistrable intellectual property matters (e.g., copyright, passing off, breach of confidence), these could begin at either the state courts or at the High Court, depending on the value of the claim in question. If the claim is for certain copyright licensing matters, where the licensee seeks to change the industry benchmarks that he has to pay for a particular license, such actions would have to go to the Copyright Tribunal.[15] In earlier years, intellectual property cases would be placed on the general list of civil cases at both the High Court and the state courts.

External developments in the world of trade changed the intellectual property space and significantly affected intellectual property dispute resolution. As a member of the World Trade Organization, Singapore ratified the Agreement on Trade-Related Aspects of Intellectual Property Rights (TRIPS) on January 1, 1995. In the same year, a new local patent system was introduced to allow Singapore to accede to certain international treaties such as the Patent Cooperation Treaty, the Budapest Treaty, and the Paris Convention.[16] In 1998, the Copyright Act was amended to give effect to Singapore's obligations under the TRIPS agreement, and the Trade Marks Act was repealed and replaced with the Trade Marks Act 1999 in order to keep pace with international trends and to enable Singapore to accede to the Madrid Protocol.[17]

In the shadow of these developments, the RTMP eventually started to evolve to take on a larger role, evolving from being a government department with mainly regulatory functions to becoming more involved with policy development, law reform, and promotional and facilitation activities.[18] In September 1999, the RTMP was restructured as IPOS and given oversight of the entire range of intellectual property laws. In April 2001, IPOS was converted into a statutory board, established by the Intellectual Property Office of Singapore Act.[19] Among its other functions and duties, IPOS would administer the

WEE LOON, LAW OF INTELLECTUAL PROPERTY OF SINGAPORE 30.0.6 (2d ed. 2014). In Singapore the case of *Dien Ghin Electronic (S) Pte. Ltd. v. Khek Tai Ting (trading as Soon Heng Digitax)* [2011] 3 SLR 227, the plaintiff applied directly to the High Court for patent revocation under s 80 of the Patents Act (Cap. 221, 2005 Rev. Ed. Sing.), and it was heard and decided by the High Court. The issue of jurisdiction was not raised in this case.

15 The tribunal is a specialist, ad hoc tribunal convened at the State Courts. *See generally* Part VII (Copyright Tribunals) in the Copyright Act (Cap. 63, 2006 Rev. Ed. Sing.).

16 *See* Second Reading of the Patents Bill: *Singapore Parliamentary Debates, Official Report* (March 21, 1994), vol. 62 col. 1446 (S. Jayakumar, Minister for Law).

17 *See* Second Reading of the Trade Marks Bill: *Singapore Parliamentary Debates, Official Report* (November 26, 1998), vol. 69 col. 1698 (Ho Peng Kee, Minister of State for Law).

18 *See* Second Reading of the Intellectual Property Office of Singapore Bill: *Singapore Parliamentary Debates, Official Report* (February 22, 2001), vol. 72 col. 1457 (Ho Peng Kee, Minister of State for Law).

19 Cap. 140, 2002 Rev. Ed. Sing.

systems in Singapore for the protection of intellectual property, promote public awareness and effective use of intellectual property rights, represent the government internationally on matters related to intellectual property, and promote or assist in the development of the profession of intellectual property agents or intellectual property advisers.[20] In 2002, shortly after IPOS was established, the Intellectual Property Court was established as a specialist commercial court presided by Judges with experience and expertise in intellectual property law.[21]

The next significant milestone was the introduction of a specialized docketing system for case management of intellectual property cases.[22] Under this system, intellectual property cases would be allocated to a specified assistant registrar who would generally hear all interlocutory applications arising in each intellectual property case. In addition, a designated intellectual property judge would be assigned to hear all interlocutory appeals, "milestone" pretrial conferences,[23] and the substantive trial on liability. This would give the assistant registrar and the judge a better understanding of each case as it developed and would result in quicker and more targeted case management.

Despite the gradual improvements made to Singapore's intellectual property dispute resolution landscape, there is always room for further improvement. Toward this end, a review committee was recently set up to recommend further improvements to the system. The two key objectives of this review are to enhance access to justice in the intellectual property dispute resolution system, and position Singapore as the jurisdiction of choice for intellectual property dispute resolution in Asia. As Chief Justice Sundaresh Menon stated, the committee "will endeavour to devise a system that ensures that costs are not a bar to smaller players who must act to safeguard their IP rights,

[20] Section 6(1)(a) of the Intellectual Property Office of Singapore Act (Cap. 140, 2002 Rev. Ed. Sing.) [hereinafter known as IPOS Act].

[21] For a list of the judges on the Specialised Lists of the High Court (Intellectual Property/Information Technology), *see* Official Website of the Supreme Court of Singapore, *supra* note 9.

[22] *See* Supreme Court of Singapore, *Intellectual Property Court Guide* (September 6, 2013), *available at* www.supremecourt.gov.sg/docs/default-source/default-document-library/about-us/ip-court-guide.pdf [hereinafter the Intellectual Property Court Guide]. The Intellectual Property Court Guide also contains specific instructions as to how an intellectual property case should be managed. For example, a party that wishes to have confidentiality undertakings over its documents is expected to work out the manner in which such confidentiality can be preserved, whether in the form of an order of court, a nondisclosure agreement, or a confidentiality club; *see id.* [17].

[23] A milestone pretrial conference is usually scheduled after the completion of discovery, before the exchange of affidavits, intended to deal with the key administrative decisions in the case.

without hindering the continuing development of our jurisprudence."[24] Its recommendations are currently being considered by the Ministry of Law in conjunction with broader reviews of the civil justice system.[25]

6.3 ASEAN INTELLECTUAL PROPERTY DISPUTE RESOLUTION SYSTEM: KEY CHALLENGES

As may be observed from Singapore's experience, the development in the intellectual property dispute resolution context stemmed from the developments in the broader intellectual property space accommodating global developments in world trade. In ASEAN, these developments have not taken shape at the same pace, given the vastly different political, economic, and social environment of each member state. Each member state has developed autochthonous systems for dealing with intellectual property over the years in tandem with these factors. Given the many different operating systems present within ASEAN today, it would be challenging to have a single, unified intellectual property dispute resolution system.[26]

6.4 DIFFERENCES BETWEEN ASEAN AND THE EU AND CORRESPONDING CHALLENGES TO INTEGRATION WITHIN ASEAN

While the EU is often held up as a model of legal integration, there are important differences between ASEAN and the EU system:

- The different stages of economic development within member states
- The diversity within the different legal systems used by member states
- The lack of supranational institutions within the ASEAN framework
- The different timelines for economic integration

[24] *See* Sundaresh Menon S.C., Chief Justice, Opening of the Legal Year 2016 (January 11, 2016), *available at* www.supremecourt.gov.sg/Data/Editor/Documents/Response%20by%20CJ%20-%20Opening%20of%20the%20Legal%20Year%202016%20on%2011%20January%202016%20(Checked%20against%20Delivery%20110116).pdf [hereinafter CJ OLY Speech 2016].

[25] *See* Sundaresh Menon S.C., Chief Justice, Opening of the Legal Year 2017 (January 9, 2017), *available at* www.supremecourt.gov.sg/Data/Editor/Documents/Opening%20of%20the%20Legal%20Year%20Speech%20(Final).pdf.

[26] *See* ASEAN Intellectual Property Association, *Special Section on ASEAN*, in ELIZABETH NG SIEW-KUAN & GRAEME AUSTIN (eds.), INTERNATIONAL INTELLECTUAL PROPERTY AND THE ASEAN WAY: PATHWAYS TO INTEROPERABILITY, Chapter 18; and Elizabeth Siew-Kuan Ng, *Intellectual Property Interoperability in ASEAN and Beyond: An Integration Model*, in ELIZABETH NG SIEW-KUAN & GRAEME AUSTIN, INTERNATIONAL INTELLECTUAL PROPERTY AND THE ASEAN WAY: PATHWAYS TO INTEROPERABILITY, Chapter 1.

6.4.1 *Different Stages of Economic Development*

The disparity between economic developments in the ASEAN member states is much greater than that of the EU member states. As such, while more EU member states might be ready to advance their intellectual property infrastructure, it may not be a priority for ASEAN member states.

To illustrate, Luxembourg has the highest GDP per capita among EU member states. This is about 2.5 times the EU average. This contrasts markedly with Bulgaria's GDP per capita, being the lowest among EU member states, at about 0.3 times the EU average.[27] About fourteen out of the twenty-eight EU member states have GDP per capita above the EU average. In contrast, Singapore's GDP per capita, the highest among ASEAN member states, is about 4.7 times the ASEAN average,[28] whilst Cambodia's, the lowest among ASEAN member states, is about 0.1 times the ASEAN average.[29] There are just two member states (Singapore and Brunei Darussalam) with GDP per capita rates above the ASEAN average, and most member states have GDP per capita values that are below the average.

6.4.2 *Different Legal Systems*

Any form of harmonization in the ASEAN context would be complicated by the fact that the member states have very different legal systems and are at very different stages of development. Member states such as Singapore, Malaysia, Brunei Darussalam, and Myanmar[30] have common law legal systems inherited from the British. On the other hand, Indonesia, Vietnam, Laos, and Cambodia have civil law legal systems, also inherited in the course of their histories.

[27] Information and statistics taken from Eurostat: Statistics Explained, *GDP per Capita, Consumption per Capita and Price Level Indices* (December 11, 2015), *available at* http://ec.europa.eu/eurostat/statistics-explained/index.php/GDP_per_capita,_consumption_per_capita_and_price_level_indices.

[28] The average GDP in ASEAN member states is US$11,167.19 as compared to Singapore's GDP which is US$52,744 (data correct as of August 2016). *See* ASEAN, *Macroeconomic Indicators – Gross Domestic Product per Capita in ASEAN* (August 2016), *available at* http://asean.org/storage/2015/09/table7.pdf.

[29] Cambodia's GDP per capita is US$1,199 as compared to the ASEAN average of US$11,167.19. *See id.*

[30] As regards the general characteristics of Myanmar's legal system, *see* Hogan Lovells, *Change and Opportunity in Myanmar* (November 11, 2015), *available at* www.hoganlovells.com/~/media/hogan-lovells/pdf/publication/changeandopportunityinmyanmarapril2012_pdf.ashx. It should also be noted that Myanmar has just recently undergone elections in early December 2015, and change may be imminent.

Thailand, which was never colonized, has a civil law legal system with strong common law influences.[31] The Philippines' legal system has been described as "a blend of customary usage, and Roman (civil law) and Anglo-American (common law) systems," depending on the area of law in question.[32] It would be difficult for ASEAN member states to come to agreement on any substantive or procedural multilateral treaty, given these basic differences in legal culture. This is unlike the EU member states, most of which subscribe to the civil law tradition (except for the United Kingdom).

6.4.3 *Lack of Supranational Institutions*

Even if there were sufficient political will to overcome these differences, another challenge to ASEAN lies in the fact that there are no supranational institutions within the framework. The EU, however, has an elected European Parliament and the Council of the European Union, which together have the power to adopt and amend legislative proposals and to decide on the EU budget.[33] The European Parliament alone is made up of 751 members drawn from the 28 member states of the EU, who are elected directly by the EU citizens.[34] These institutions have the support of the European Commission whose role is to promote the general interest of the EU by proposing and enforcing legislation as well as implementing policies and the budget. To ensure that there is a uniform application and interpretation of EU law, a Court of Justice of the European Union was established. As of November 2015, they have issued approximately 28,000 judgments.[35]

31 *See* Joe Leeds, *Introduction to the Legal System and Legal Research of the Kingdom of Thailand* (November 2008), *available at* www.nyulawglobal.org/globalex/Thailand.html.

32 The civil law operates in areas such as family relations, property, succession, and contract and criminal law, while the common law operates in areas such as constitutional law, procedure, corporation law, negotiable instruments, taxation, insurance, labor relations, banking, and currency. *See* ASEAN Law Association, *Legal Systems in ASEAN*, *available at* www.aseanlawassociation.org/papers/phil_chp1.pdf. The ASEAN Law Association is a non-governmental organization that brings together under one roof all the different branches of the law profession – judges, law teachers, law practitioners, and government lawyers: *see* ASEAN Law Association, *About Us*, *available at* www.aseanlawassociation.org/about.html.

33 *See generally*, the official website of the European Union, *EU Institutions and Other Bodies – EU Institutions in Brief* (December 14, 2016), *available at* http://europa.eu/about-eu/institutions-bodies/index_en.htm.

34 *Id.*

35 *See generally*, the official website of the European Court of Justice, *General Presentation* (March 17, 2016), *available at* http://curia.europa.eu/jcms/jcms/Jo2_6999/.

ASEAN, on the other hand, does not have a supranational body with the power to adopt and amend legislative proposals, or to ensure enforcement of the same. The supreme policymaking body of ASEAN is the ASEAN Summit,[36] which comprises the heads of state of the member states, rather than a separate, elected body of members like the European Parliament. There is also an ASEAN Coordinating Council, which does not put forward a specific legislative program, but instead prepares meetings and coordinates the implementation of agreements and decisions of the ASEAN Summit.[37] As a basic principle, disputes are not resolved via a supranational court, but are to be resolved "through dialogue, consultation and negotiation,"[38] unless they are disputes that relate to specific ASEAN instruments for which a specific mechanism may be provided in a separate treaty (e.g., the Treaty of Amity and Cooperation in Southeast Asia).[39]

6.4.4 *Timeline for Economic Integration*

Finally, there is a vast difference in terms of the timeline for economic integration between both blocs. Unlike the EU, which began its process of economic unification around 1945, eventually culminating into the first few treaties in 1951 and 1957, the first articulation of the concept of ASEAN economic integration was revealed in the Framework Agreement on Enhancing ASEAN Economic Cooperation in Singapore in 1992.[40] Further to this, several agreements on economic cooperation were signed in 1992 and 1995 respectively.[41] However, it was not until 2003 that the "ASEAN Economic Community" (AEC) was declared as an agreed goal of regional economic integration.[42] The first AEC Blueprint (2008–2015) was signed only in 2007 in Singapore. Following from the AEC Blueprint, the ASEAN Comprehensive Investment

36 *See The ASEAN Charter* (2015), Chapter IV (Organs), art. 7(2)(a) (February 2015), *available at* www.asean.org/wp-content/uploads/2012/05/11.-October-2015-The-ASEAN-Charter-18th-Reprint-Amended-updated-on-05_-April-2016-IJP.pdf [hereinafter ASEAN Charter].

37 *See* ASEAN Charter, art. 8(2)(a) and (b).

38 *See* ASEAN Charter, art. 22(1).

39 *See generally*, ASEAN Charter, art. 24.

40 *See* ASEAN Secretariat, *A Blueprint for Growth: ASEAN Economic Community 2015 – Progress and Key Achievements* at 4 (January 11, 2016), *available at* www.asean.org/storage/images/2015/November/aec-page/AEC-2015-Progress-and-Key-Achievements.pdf [hereinafter known as AEC Progress Report 2015].

41 *Id.* These were the Agreement on the Common Effective Preferential Tariff Scheme for the ASEAN Free Trade Area (1992) and the ASEAN Framework Agreement on Services (1995).

42 AEC Progress Report 2015, *supra* note 40, at 3.

Agreement was signed in February 2009 to "further enhance regional integration to realize the vision of the AEC."[43] The ASEAN Trade in Goods Agreement (May 2010) was signed to move closer to the AEC Blueprint goal of establishing a single market and production base.[44]

ASEAN has made significant progress in liberalizing trade across the region in terms of tariff elimination among the ASEAN-6 (comprising of Brunei Darussalam, Indonesia, Malaysia, the Philippines, Singapore, and Thailand).[45] However, some tariffs remain on industries of strategic importance, and there has been little progress on nontariff barriers between members.[46] The leaders of ASEAN have just adopted a second blueprint, the AEC Blueprint 2025, to complete the measures initiated under the AEC Blueprint 2008 – 2015, and to take further measures to minimize trade protection and compliance costs in dealing with nontariff barriers.[47]

These ASEAN Blueprints were adopted relatively recently and it may be too early to assess their effectiveness in achieving any form of economic integration. It should be remembered that it has been more than fifty years since the EU first embarked on its project of economic integration, while for ASEAN, this project is a little over ten years old since it was formally conceived. ASEAN is likely to require more time to achieve the degree of economic integration and harmonization found in the EU.

6.5 INTEROPERABILITY, NOT HARMONIZATION

Given the differences between the EU and ASEAN, harmonization may not be a practical goal in the near future for ASEAN at large. The goal that should be put forward in the ASEAN context is that of achieving "interoperability," rather than "harmonization." The difference was put across by Mr. Tan Yih San (IPOS' then-chief executive) as follows: "Interoperability does not necessarily mean harmonization, but rather point[s] us towards the aim

43 ASEAN, *Recital to the ASEAN Comprehensive Investment Agreement*, *available at* http://agreement.asean.org/media/download/20140119035519.pdf.

44 ASEAN, *The ASEAN Trade in Goods Agreement*, *available at* http://investasean.asean.org/index.php/page/view/asean-free-trade-area-agreements/view/757/newsid/872/asean-trade-in-goods-agreement.html.

45 AEC Progress Report 2015, *supra* note 40, at 10.

46 Koster Jeroen, *ASEAN 2015 – Opportunities and Challenges* (November 2014), *available at* www.cliffordchance.com/briefings/2014/11/asean_2015_opportunitiesandchallenges.html.

47 AEC Blueprint 2025, *supra* note 3, at 10(iii)(a),(g).

of building an IP regime that creators will be able to use to access overseas markets."[48]

6.5.1 *The "Soft Approach" – Enabling Dispute Resolution in the ASEAN Intellectual Property Context*

What could "interoperability" mean in the ASEAN context? Do the member states in ASEAN have a shared cultural context that may have a bearing on how they choose to resolve disputes? From the challenges we have observed in the foregoing, it would seem impractical for each member state to adopt a uniform type of dispute resolution system, given the varying legal and socioeconomic backgrounds of each country. However, there are certain commonalities in the intellectual property context that each country would have to consider, for example, discovery of documents, search orders, experiments, confidentiality orders, and damages.

In this regard, it is submitted that a "softer approach" within ASEAN could be much more effective than a hard-nosed legalistic approach, for example, having a supranational court and enforcement mechanism. Such an approach is more suited for ASEAN given its commitment to the "ASEAN Way"[49] that adopts the principles of consensus and noninterference in the internal affairs of its member states. Indeed, perhaps this is simply a reflection of what it means to be ASEAN (or, perhaps, Asian). In the mediation context, for example, it has been suggested that there are three core themes that describe "Asian values"[50]: Confucianism, collectivist inclination, and the prevalence of face concerns (with the important caveat that these are only generalizations).[51] If this rings true, then it may be useful to think of achieving "interoperability" by using a "soft approach," for both procedural standards and substantive legal decision making.

In terms of procedural standards, it would be useful to increase accessibility to each other's legal decisions, statutes, and search and examination results. For substantive legal decision making, it would be useful to develop familiarity with each other's judicial and legal systems and with the decision makers in each other's jurisdictions. Given greater accessibility and understanding of

48 *See* IPOS, *Speech by Mr Tan Yih San, [then] Chief Executive of IPOS at the NUS Centre for Business and Law* (2014), *available at* www.ipos.gov.sg/MediaEvents/Readnews/tabid/873/articleid/290/category/Speeches/parentId/80/year/2014/Default.aspx.

49 The "ASEAN Way" refers to the principle of consensus and noninterference in the internal affairs of its member states. *See* ASEAN Charter, Preamble, and art. 2(2)(a),(d),(e).

50 Or alternatively, "Asian characteristics" or "Asian traits": *see infra* note 67.

51 Joel Lee & Teh Hwee Hwee, An Asian Perspective on Mediation 53–67 (2009).

each other's procedural and substantive laws, it would be a natural, organic step forward for each member state to have some "soft influence" on each other's examination reports and/or legal decisions.[52] For example, a company that intends to conduct litigation in Indonesia, Malaysia, the Philippines, and Singapore would benefit from the certainty of enforcement in each country if the rules applied were the same across the board. Ideally, a firm could start a lawsuit in Malaysia, and on its conclusion use this judgment as persuasive weight for settlement negotiations in the other jurisdictions, or alternatively, use it as persuasive authority in the courts of other countries. The value of the company's intellectual property rights increases if they are backed by a uniform system of enforcement. This would give the company much needed comfort and certainty when conducting business in the region.

For the government and judicial authorities of each country, this would also entail savings in personnel time (and therefore resource and cost savings), since the legal merits of an intellectual property infringement case can be more readily determined with the benefit of substantive decisions in parallel proceedings in ASEAN. In a uniform system of enforcement, the outcomes may be broadly similar unless the particular facts specific to a jurisdiction are markedly different from those in the parallel proceedings. Alternatively, the case would not even have to reach the court if the judgment in another court is used as the basis for settlement among the disputants.

6.5.2 *Singapore's Role in Facilitating Interoperability in Substantive Legal Decision Making and Procedural Standard Setting*

The next few paragraphs will consider Singapore's role in facilitating interoperability of dispute resolution systems within ASEAN by supporting capacity-building projects that set out to create an ASEAN with similar baseline procedures and friendly exchanges that aspire to deepen understanding of each other's substantive decision making.

Interoperability in Substantive Legal Decision Making

In the common law world, it is not uncommon for judges to refer to previously decided cases in other jurisdictions to arrive at their decision. Where there are parallel proceedings in different jurisdictions, a decision in Country X

[52] Another approach to developing interoperability in the practice of law in today's globalized world is to create a set of guidelines to shape the nature and extent of communications between courts in diverse jurisdictions, to develop a network connecting the courts of key commercial centers on a multilateral as well as bilateral basis, as observed by Singapore's Chief Justice Sundaresh Menon: *see* CJ OLY Speech 2016, *supra* note 24.

will of course not be binding on Country Y, which is a different sovereign country. The decision in Country X may, however, be of some persuasive relevance, which would hinge upon the similarity of the laws of the particular jurisdiction with those of (say) Singapore and also on the individual facts of the case.[53] In the context of intellectual property, it clearly does not follow from the fact that if a mark is well-known in Country X, that the mark is necessarily also well known in Country Y. On the other hand, if a party makes certain factual assertions in one jurisdiction, that party should not be permitted to take a completely different position in another jurisdiction.[54] For example, in Singapore, the recent litigation[55] involving the "Ku De Ta" trademarks showed that the court would consider the evidence given by the party in another jurisdiction (Australia) in coming to its decision, even though it had no legal obligation to do so.

In general, Singapore has regarded the decisions of the United Kingdom and Australia as persuasive authority (depending on the legislation concerned), since we adopt much of our legislation from these jurisdictions. For example, the Singapore Trade Marks Act is based largely on the UK Trade Marks Act 1998, and it is common for Singapore courts to cite UK decisions as persuasive authority.

In recent years, the UK courts have similarly had occasion to refer to judgments of the Singapore courts. For example, the UK Supreme Court recently followed what they referred to as "an impressively wide-ranging judgment" by the Singapore Court of Appeal in the area of passing off.[56]

If there were greater interoperability between ASEAN intellectual property dispute resolution systems, it may be possible for ASEAN member states to treat the decisions of each other as persuasive as well, depending on the law and the facts at hand.

In China, some courts are also increasingly open to foreign decisions on intellectual property disputes, especially those in the English language. In

53 *Festina Lotus SA v. Romanson Co. Ltd.* [2010] 4 S.L.R. 552 at [118].

54 *Christie Manson & Woods Limited v. Chritrs Auction Pte. Limited* [2016] I.P.O.S. 1 at [27].

55 *Guy Neale and others v. Nine Squares Pty. Ltd.* [2015] 1 S.L.R. 1097 and *Guy Neale and others v. Ku De Ta SG Pte. Ltd.* [2015] 4 S.L.R. 283.

56 *Starbucks (HK) Ltd. v. British Sky Broadcasting Group plc* [2015] U.K.S.C. 31 at [45] and [66]. The Singapore Court of Appeal judgment referred to is the decision in *Staywell Hospitality Group Pty Ltd. v. Starwood Hotels & Resorts Worldwide Inc* [2014] 1 S.L.R. 911. This was also highlighted by Lord Neuberger, president of the UK Supreme Court in the lecture he gave for the Singapore Academy of Law: *see* Lord Neuberger of Abbotsbury, *Singapore Academy of Law Annual Lecture 2015 – Is Nothing Secret? Privacy and Confidentiality, Privacy, Freedom of Information and Whistleblowing in the Internet Age* (2016) 28 S.Ac.L.J. 1.

2016, Senior Judge Zhang Yongjian, Chief Judge of the Fourth Civil Division, Supreme People's Court of the Republic of China, iterated that China's open economy expects law harmonization in Asia and in the world at large, and described the Chinese courts' efforts in law harmonization.[57] Substantive intellectual property decisions by the courts of ASEAN member states could well come under consideration by the courts in China. If there is more interoperability in substantive legal decision making within ASEAN, in tandem with some interoperability with China's legal decision making, judicial decisions on intellectual property issues in dispute could coalesce over time. A degree of confluence would make ASEAN an even more attractive investment destination for China.

The Singapore International Commercial Court

The Singapore International Commercial Court (SICC) was launched on January 5, 2015, as a specialist division within the High Court,[58] having jurisdiction to hear and try cases that are of an "international and commercial nature"[59] and where the plaintiff and defendant in the originating process has submitted to the SICC's jurisdiction under a written jurisdiction agreement.[60] However, the parties cannot seek relief in the form of or connected with a prerogative order (including a mandatory order, a prohibiting order, a quashing order, or an order for review of detention).[61] The SICC also has the jurisdiction to hear and try cases that are transferred from the High Court in regular civil proceedings,[62] and also committal proceedings in respect of judgments made by the SICC.[63]

Foreign lawyers may also represent parties to SICC proceedings in "offshore cases"[64] and in other specified circumstances.[65] Interestingly, the SICC also

57 At the international conference "Doing Business across Asia: Legal Convergence in an Asian Century" on January 21–22, 2016 in Singapore.

58 Singapore International Commercial Court, *About the SICC – Overview of the SICC* (June 1, 2016), *available at* www.sicc.gov.sg/About.aspx?id=22.

59 Rules of Court (Cap. 332, r 5, 2014 Rev. Ed. Sing.), Order 110, Rule 7(1)(a). The terms "international" and "commercial" are defined in Rule 1(2) of the same Order 110.

60 Rules of Court (Cap. 332, r 5, 2014 Rev. Ed. Sing.), Order 110, Rule 7(1)(b).

61 Rules of Court (Cap. 332, r 5, 2014 Rev. Ed. Sing.), Order 110, Rule 7(1)(c).

62 Rules of Court (Cap. 332, r 5, 2014 Rev. Ed. Sing.), Order 110, Rule 7(2)(a) read with Rule 12.

63 Rules of Court (Cap. 332, r 5, 2014 Rev. Ed. Sing.), Order 110, Rule 7(2)(b).

64 An "offshore case" is defined as "an action which has no substantial connection with Singapore, but does not include an action in rem (against a ship or any other property) under the High Court (Admiralty Jurisdiction) Act (Cap. 123, 2001 Rev. Ed. Sing.)": *see* Rules of Court (Cap. 332, r 5, 2014 Rev. Ed. Sing.), Order 110, Rule 1(1) (Interpretation)).

65 Such as, where there is a joint request or application for a pre-action certificate or when the court exercises its discretion to allow foreign representation for the just, economical, and

allows questions of foreign law to be determined on the basis of submissions instead of proof,[66] and a foreign lawyer can make submissions on such questions, subject to registration requirements under the Legal Profession Act.[67] There are also "more flexible court procedures"[68] allowed in the SICC that would otherwise not be a feature of ordinary commercial litigation in the High Court. SICC's judgments are generally enforceable[69] via existing legislative provisions in the Reciprocal Enforcement of Commonwealth Judgments Act[70] and the Reciprocal Enforcement of Foreign Judgments Act,[71] as well as the Hague Convention on the Choice of Court, recently signed by Singapore on March 25, 2015.[72]

In aligning the SICC with international best practices, there will be greater interoperability in substantive legal decision making in Singapore, since the process of decision making could be made on the basis of internationally

expeditious disposal of the proceedings. The other possible circumstances are listed in the Singapore International Commercial Court Practice Directions at Part IV (Representation), 26(a)–(e), *available at* www.supremecourt.gov.sg/docs/default-source/default-document-library/sicc-practice-directions-(with-effect-from-1-jan-2016)f7782f33f22f6eceb9b0ff0000fcc945.pdf.

66 For both offshore and non-offshore cases: *see* Rules of Court (Cap. 332, r 5, 2014 Rev. Ed. Sing.), Order 110, Rule 25(1).

67 *See* Rules of Court (Cap. 332, r 5, 2014 Rev. Ed.), Order 110, Rule 25(4). A foreign lawyer without the right of audience in Singapore would have to undertake to be registered under s 36P of the Legal Profession Act (Cap. 161, 2009 Rev. Ed. Sing.).

68 Examples include more flexibility in granting confidentiality orders (Rules of Court (Cap. 332, r 5, 2014 Rev. Ed. Sing.), Order 110, Rule 30); ability of the SICC to apply internationally recognized standards of evidence (e.g., the International Bar Association Rules on the Taking of Evidence in International Arbitration) (Rules of Court (Cap. 332, r 5, 2014 Rev. Ed. Sing.), Order 110, Rule 23). *See generally*, SICC, *Brochure on the Singapore International Commercial Court* (January 22, 2016), *available at* www.sicc.gov.sg/documents/docs/SICC%20Brochure_Final.pdf.

69 *See generally*, SICC, *Singapore International Commercial Court Note on Enforcement of SICC Judgments* (December 9, 2015), *available at* www.sicc.gov.sg/documents/docs/SICC_Enforcement_Guide.pdf.

70 The Reciprocal Enforcement of Commonwealth Judgments Act (Cap. 264, 1985 Rev. Ed. Sing.) covers enforcement in Australia (New South Wales, Queensland, South Australia, Tasmania, Victoria, Western Australia, Australian Capital Territory, Norfolk Island, and Northern Territory), New Zealand, Sri Lanka, Malaysia, Windward Islands, Pakistan, Brunei Darussalam, Papua New Guinea, and India (except the State of Jammu and Kashmir): *see generally*, Reciprocal Enforcement of Commonwealth Judgments (Extension) (Consolidation) Notification, The Schedule (Cap. 264, Section 5, Note 1, 1999 Rev. Ed. Sing.).

71 The Reciprocal Enforcement of Foreign Judgments Act (Cap. 265, 2001 Rev. Ed. Sing.) covers enforcement in Hong Kong: *see generally*, Reciprocal Enforcement of Foreign Judgments (Hong Kong Special Administrative Region of the People's Republic of China) Order (Cap. 265, Section 3(1), order 1, 2001 Rev. Ed.).

72 Ministry of Law, *Singapore Signs the Hague Convention of 30 June 2005 on Choice of Court Agreements* (March 26, 2015), *available at* www.mlaw.gov.sg/content/minlaw/en/news/announcements/sg-signs-cocagreement.html.

recognized legal norms and the decision itself could take into consideration submissions on foreign law by foreign lawyers. The SICC's judgments are also likely to be enforceable in certain foreign jurisdictions.[73]

Further to the preceding, it is observed that certain steps have been made toward achieving interoperability via the "soft approach," in terms of developing a set of (nonbinding) examination guidelines, signing memoranda of understanding, and putting together a database of case law. These should assist ASEAN member states to better understand and influence each other's decision-making processes. In addition, legal symposia and exchanges between patent examiners would also enable key decision makers in the judiciary and in intellectual property offices to exchange ideas and understand each other's decision-making processes better. These initiatives are briefly outlined below.

Memorandum of Understanding between Cambodia and Singapore

An encouraging signal of the positive impact that can be achieved with mutual understanding was the recognition of a Singapore patent by Cambodia's Ministry of Industry and Handicrafts on March 4, 2015, on the basis of a positive report by IPOS' Search & Examination Unit. This recognition was pursuant to a Memorandum of Understanding signed between both countries.[74] This was also Cambodia's first-ever granted patent. As stated by Mr. Tan Yih San, IPOS' then-chief executive, this collaboration "simplified and reaffirmed two countries' commitment to better support businesses seeking cross-border investment in the combined market of 20 million people."[75] On January 19, 2016, it was also announced[76] that IPOS has started issuing first-office-action search and examination reports for patent applications filed in Cambodia, as a follow up on commitments under this Memorandum of Understanding. H. E. Dr. Cham Prasidh, Senior Minister, Minister for Industry and Handicraft, recognized that "this brings us a step closer towards IP harmonisation in ASEAN, as the region advances towards being a single IP bloc." This is an example of how ASEAN member states may work together in a concrete way to make

73 SICC Note, *supra* note 69 and Reciprocal Enforcement of Commonwealth Judgments Act, *supra* note 70.

74 Intellectual Property Office of Singapore, *First Singapore Patent Recognised in Cambodia* (March 10, 2015), *available at* www.ipos.gov.sg/MediaEvents/Readnews/tabid/873/articleid/304/category/Press%20Releases/parentId/80/year/2015/Default.aspx.

75 *Id.*

76 Intellectual Property Office of Singapore, *Singapore Furthers IP Cooperation with Cambodia to Expedite Quality Patent Grants* (January 19, 2016), *available at* www.ipos.gov.sg/MediaEvents/Readnews/tabid/873/articleid/330/category/Press%20Releases/parentId/80/year/2016/Default.aspx.

the AEC useful to intellectual property applicants and businesses, and sets the ground for more consistent dispute resolution outcomes.

The Asian Business Law Institute

The Singapore Academy of Law launched the Asian Business Law Institute (ABLI) on January 21, 2016, created with an "Asian" focus to fill the gap in legal knowledge of the national laws of Asian countries for companies doing business in Asia. Unlike other research institutes in universities, it will be more practice oriented, providing practical solutions such as practitioners' handbooks, concrete policy recommendations, and legal tools (e.g., model laws, uniform standards).[77] ABLI will initially focus on three key projects: increasing the recognition and enforcement of foreign court judgments in ASEAN, Australia, China, and India; fleshing out guiding principles for Asian data privacy laws; and developing definitions of principles and cross-border rules for contracts, to create a common frame of reference when drafting the same.[78] Another area that it will look into is streamlining Asian cross-border small claims procedures, which is an area particularly relevant to the rapidly growing e-commerce sector.[79]

Singapore also supports various ASEAN initiatives such as the development of an ASEAN Intellectual Property Case Law Database under the auspices of EU-ASEAN Project on the Protection of Intellectual Property Rights, by providing a team of legal experts to select relevant ASEAN case law, prepare summaries in English, and tag relevant key words and data related to those cases following a standardized approach. The database has gone live and currently includes key decisions from Singapore and Thailand.[80]

Interoperability in Procedural Standard Setting

Besides encouraging greater understanding of substantive legal principles between the ASEAN countries, Singapore has also been engaging ASEAN through the "soft approach" of having legal symposia and exchanges, where

77 *See* Sundaresh Menon S.C., Chief Justice, *Conference Keynote Address, Doing Business across Asia: Legal Convergence in an Asian Century* (January 21, 2016), *available at* www.supremecourt.gov.sg/Data/Editor/Documents/'Doing%20Business%20Across%20Asia%20-%20Legal%20Convergence%20in%20an%20Asian%20Century'%20(Final%20version%20after%20delivery-%2020160116).pdf.

78 *Id.*

79 Grace Leong, *Singapore Leads Asia Business Law Initiative* (November 17, 2015), *available at* www.straitstimes.com/business/companies-markets/singapore-leads-asian-business-law-initiative.

80 ASEAN Intellectual Property Portal, *Statistics and Resources – ASEAN Case Law Database*, *available at* www.aseanip.org/Statistics-Resources/ASEAN-Case-Law-Database.

courts from around the region can benefit from Singapore's experience and also interact with each other to develop best practices. These activities will help to complement the initiatives taken by ASEAN on the broader scale, such as under the AEC Blueprint 2025, where member states are to complete accession to a number of procedural intellectual property treaties such as the Patent Co-operation Treaty, the Madrid Protocol, and the Hague Agreement Concerning the International Registration of Industrial Designs.[81] Indeed, Mr. Daren Tang, IPOS' current chief executive, has suggested that multilateral institutions should focus on interoperability of procedural rather than substantive laws.[82]

Work-Sharing via ASPEC

This is a Singapore-led effort which enables intellectual property offices from participating ASEAN member states to utilize the search and examination result(s) from other participating intellectual property offices as reference(s) for its own search and examination work. The program has received some 154 requests as of August 31, 2016,[83] with the first office action issued within 5.7 months. Of these requests, forty-eight requests have had a final report issued.[84]

ASEAN Patent Examiners' Community of Practice

IPOS has organized annual ASEAN Community of Practice events for patent examiners in Singapore from 2013 to 2016, aimed at familiarizing the ASEAN patent examiners with each other's practices. In the last few years, the topics at this event have become more in-depth and advanced.

Study Visit by Supreme Court, Ministry of Law and IPOS to, inter alia, the Shanghai Intellectual Property Court and Shanghai Intellectual Property Administration

A study visit was made by Singapore to Shanghai, China in October 2015 to understand China's approach to intellectual property enforcement, adjudication, and management. The visit saw many interesting exchanges at the judicial and executive levels, with several areas of concern in common. Similar

81 AEC Blueprint 2025, *supra* note 3, at 31(i)(d).

82 Daren Tang, Chief Executive, Intellectual Property Office of Singapore, Keynote Speech, *Completing the Jigsaw: A View of IP Norm-Making in a Decentralized World* at the Singapore Management University (January 29, 2016) (unpublished).

83 Intellectual Property Office of Singapore, *ASEAN Patent Examination Co-operation: ASPEC Statistics* (October 19, 2016), *available at* www.ipos.gov.sg/AboutIP/TypesofIP WhatisIntellectualProperty/Whatisapatent/Applyingforapatent/ASEANPatentExaminationCo-operationASPEC.aspx.

84 *Id.*

study visits could be arranged between ASEAN countries to facilitate greater understanding and learning from one another.

Singapore Judicial College's Outreach Efforts in ASEAN

The Singapore Judicial College was recently established under the auspices of the Supreme Court of Singapore and is dedicated to the training and development of judges and judicial officers.[85] It comprises both a local and international wing. Under the international wing, there have been several programs conducted by the College under the Ministry of Foreign Affairs' Initiative for ASEAN Integration, which was launched by the former Prime Minister Goh Chok Tong in 2000 with the objective of narrowing the development gap in ASEAN by assisting the newer members in the grouping, namely, Cambodia, Laos, Myanmar, and Vietnam.[86] Between April and November 2016, the College has made seven trips to each of these countries, on the themes "International Framework for Court Excellence," "Court Excellence & Court Dispute Resolution: A Tale of Two Workshops," among others.[87] In addition, the College also conducted courses[88] in Singapore under its international wing. Foreign judges and officials from ASEAN and other parts of the world participated in these courses.

The Singapore–Myanmar Integrated Legal Exchange

In October 2014, Senior Minister of State Indranee Rajah signed a Memorandum of Understanding on the Singapore–Myanmar Integrated Legal Exchange between the Ministry of Law and the Supreme Court of the Union (Myanmar), and also witnessed the signing of a similar Memorandum of Understanding between the Ministry of Law and the Union Attorney-General's Office. Both Memorandums of Understanding seek to enhance greater understanding of the laws, legal systems, and legal and judicial institutions of Singapore and Myanmar. These objectives will be achieved through the exchange

85 Supreme Court of Singapore, *Singapore Judicial College* (April 29, 2016), *available at* www.supremecourt.gov.sg/sjc/home.

86 Embassy of the Republic of Singapore, Press Statements and Speeches *Ministry of Foreign Affairs Press Statement: Singapore's Enhanced Contribution to the Initiative for ASEAN Integration* (November 20, 2007), *available at* www.mfa.gov.sg/content/mfa/media_centre/press_room/pr/2007/200711/press_20071120_08.html.

87 Supreme Court of Singapore, Singapore Judicial College, *International Training Programmes 2016* (December 14, 2016), *available at* www.supremecourt.gov.sg/sjc/judicial-education/international/2016.

88 The courses include (i) Strategies of Case Management: Challenges, Solutions and Innovation (April 4–8, 2016); (ii) End-To-End Court Technology (July 11–15, 2016); and (iii) Innovating Justice Workshop (November 18–19, 2015).

of legal materials, study visits, collaborative seminars and symposiums, attachments, and scholarships for Myanmar officials.[89]

In addition to the efforts listed in the foregoing, Singapore participates in efforts by multilateral institutions to engage in information sharing between judicial officers. For example, Singapore participated in the Regional Colloquium on Intellectual Property Enforcement for Judges organized by the World Intellectual Property Organization in cooperation with the Korean Intellectual Property Office and the Department of Intellectual Property of Thailand on October 28–29, 2015.[90] This session allowed judges from the region and beyond (from China, Philippines, Thailand, Indonesia, Malaysia, Republic of Korea, Singapore, Vietnam, Cambodia, Myanmar, Brunei Darussalam) to share their experiences in civil procedure and remedies for intellectual property infringement.

6.6 CONCLUSION

Although it is challenging to harmonize the laws and practices of all ASEAN member states given the legal, economic, and cultural context unique to each ASEAN country, several positive steps have been taken in the direction of achieving greater understanding between the member states. The "soft approach" could help to foster an environment of mutual understanding and trust that could gradually influence the way processes are conducted and decisions are made. The "camel" used in Walter Woon's analogy, given at the launch of his 2015 book "*The ASEAN Charter: A Commentary*" to describe the ASEAN Charter as serviceable but inelegant, may yet evolve. As observed by the current IPOS Chief Executive, in recent years "there has been a change of attitude and tone" in discussions on intellectual property at the ASEAN level in that intellectual property is no longer seen as a luxury that only developed countries can afford, but is at the center of attention of conversations about how to drive development, remake the economy and even engage in conversations about our tradition and culture.[91] Creating interoperable mechanisms

[89] Ministry of Law, Press Releases, *Senior Minister of State for Law, Ms. Indranee Rajah, Concludes Working Visit to Myanmar* (October 10, 2014), *available at* www.mlaw.gov.sg/content/minlaw/en/news/press-releases/SMS-working-visit-to-myanmar.html.

[90] International Bureau of WIPO, Provisional Program, *WIPO-KIPO-DIP Regional Colloquium on Intellectual Property Enforcement for Judges* (Bangkok, October 28–29, 2015), *available at* www.wipo.int/edocs/mdocs/enforcement/en/wipo_kipo_dip_ipr_ju_bkk_15/wipo_kipo_dip_ipr_ju_bkk_15_inf_1_prov.pdf.

[91] Daren Tang, Chief Executive, Intellectual Property Office of Singapore, *10th Anniversary Celebration of the WIPO Singapore Office on "IPresent – Singapore and the ASEAN Now: Strengths and Opportunities"* (November 24, 2015), *available at* www.ipos.gov.sg/MediaEvents/Readnews/TabID/873/articleid/327/Default.aspx.

for intellectual property to function within ASEAN will enhance the value of intellectual property rights, which in turn would stimulate growth in intellectual property filings, transactions, and dispute resolution, thus contributing positively toward the next phase of development of an ASEAN common market.

7

Enforcement of Intellectual Property Rights and the Challenges of ASEAN Integration

Ricardo R. Blancaflor

7.1 ENFORCEMENT OF INTELLECTUAL PROPERTY RIGHTS IN ASEAN

Among the spectrum of important issues related to intellectual property rights, those pertaining to enforcement have not traditionally been regarded as high priority among the national policy agenda of developing countries. Being treated as private rights,[1] intellectual property rights are exercised on the initiative and efforts of the rights holder, leaving little incentive for state intervention. Hence national policy has generally focused on the sufficiency of intellectual property protection and on ensuring the correct "balance" between incentivizing the creation of intellectual property and preserving the public domain's access to them.[2] Even the Philippine Constitution merely encourages the creation, but not enforcement, of intellectual property rights.[3] States usually focus on regulating the conditions, requirements, and limitations on the grant and use of intellectual property rights. In contrast, intellectual property rights enforcement centers on the availability of remedies and rules of procedure to facilitate investigation, prosecution, and adjudication of intellectual property rights violations.[4]

In the last decade, however, numerous studies have disclosed that widespread intellectual property infringement can have an adverse impact on

[1] "Ownership is acquired either by occupation or by intellectual creation." *See* CIVIL CODE OF PHILIPPINES, art. 712 and 721 (1949).

[2] LOUIS HARMS, THE ENFORCEMENT OF INTELLECTUAL PROPERTY RIGHTS: A CASE BOOK (3d ed. 2012), (*citing Theberge v. Galeri D'Art Du Petit Champlain Inc.*, 2002 SCC 34 [Canada], and *Robertson v. Thompson* Corp., 2006 SCC 43 [Canada]).

[3] CONSTITUTION OF THE REPUBLIC OF THE PHILIPPINES, February 11, 1987, at Article XIV §13.

[4] This would also include the availability of provisional remedies to preserve the status between parties and the relevant evidence in anticipation of a final judgment. *See* Administrative Matter No. 02-1-06 S.C., Rule on Search and Seizure in Civil Actions for Infringement of Intellectual Property Rights (effective February 15, 2002).

countries, and is no longer merely affecting private interests. Examples include the impact of counterfeit drugs and medicines on public health, the use of the financial proceeds from intellectual property–related crimes to support the criminal activities of syndicates and criminal organizations, and economic loss resulting from withdrawal of foreign investments and the winding-up of legitimate businesses.[5] Serving to highlight the need for states to play a more active role in the enforcement of intellectual property rights, there has been a shift in mindset, as seen in the sphere of treaty making. The Agreement on the Trade-Related Aspects of Intellectual Property Rights (TRIPS), for example, sets out minimum standards on intellectual property enforcement including remedies and procedures,[6] marking the possibility for new international norms in intellectual property enforcement.

Similar developments can be observed in the Association of Southeast Asian Nations (ASEAN) as it moves to integrate the political, economic, and social spheres of the ten member states. Initially, the initiatives were aimed at harmonizing the legal systems[7] to ensure that the intellectual property laws in each ASEAN member state were in compliance with the minimum standards set forth in TRIPS. With the adoption of the ASEAN IPR Action Plan of 2011–2015, efforts were directed at establishing effective remedies and procedures for the enforcement of intellectual property rights in the region. Under Initiative 6 of the Action Plan of 2011–2015, ASEAN members were committed to developing and implementing a regional action plan on intellectual property rights enforcement designed to strengthen the capacities of government agencies tasked with this mission. At the same time, it sought to engage the private sector in developing effective intellectual property rights enforcement and the provision of sufficient data and information to ASEAN member states on international best practices.[8]

With the completion of the launch of the ASEAN Economic Community in 2015, some of the challenges in implementing Initiative 6 under the Action Plan of 2011–2015 became clearer. These include difficulties posed by ASEAN intellectual property integration generally, as well as, more specifically, by

5 *See, e.g.*, United Nations Office on Drugs and Crime (UNODC), *Focus on the Illicit Trafficking of Counterfeit Goods and Transnational Organized Crime*, *available at* www.unodc.org/documents/counterfeit/FocusSheet/Counterfeit_focussheet_EN_HIRES.pdf.

6 *Agreement on Trade-Related Aspects of Intellectual Property Rights*, Part III, April 15, 1994, *Marrakesh Agreement Establishing the World Trade Organization*, Annex 1C, 33 I.L.M. 87–88 (1994), *available at* www.wto.org/english/tratop_e/trips_e/t_agmo_e.htm [hereinafter TRIPS].

7 ASEAN Secretariat, *ASEAN Intellectual Property Rights Action Plan 2004–2010, available at* http://asean.org/?static_post=asean.intellectual-property-right-action-plan-2004–2010.

8 ASEAN Secretariat, *ASEAN IP Rights Action Plan 2011–2015*, 7, *available at* www.aseanip.org/Portals/0/PDF/ASEAN%20IPR%20Action%20Plan%202011–2015.pdf.

issues relating to state involvement and intervention in intellectual property rights enforcement.

7.2 CHALLENGES OF ASEAN INTEGRATION

The primary challenge of ASEAN integration is how a regional identity can be developed.[9] This endeavor would involve not only the public, but also all ASEAN government officials including policymakers and executive agencies. Intellectual property rights have generally been viewed from a national standpoint of what is beneficial to individual nations. Hence legislative priorities have tended to focus on the economic advantages and preservation of a nation's culture and creative arts. Conversely, regional integration calls for the adoption of a broader perspective where national policymakers must expand beyond domestic considerations. However, owing to the developmental divergence among the ASEAN member states, it may not be justified to require the developing and least developed members to prioritize intellectual property rights enforcement against other more pressing national interests, particularly when these rights are largely owned by big businesses or foreign investors. The importance of intellectual property rights to economic development through facilitation of foreign direct investments and job creation is not always acknowledged. Moreover, there is little public sentiment favoring the raising of intellectual property standards, especially those on enforcement.[10]

Another problem with raising intellectual property enforcement standards relates to the economic resources of developing and least developed countries. Few are able to prioritize resources to update technological tools and training of government personnel relating to the prosecution of intellectual property rights violations. In view of the financial burdens imposed on these countries, intellectual property enforcement is undertaken with assistance from foreign dialogue partners, which are not always readily accepted by ASEAN member states in view of national interests.

Moreover, intellectual property rights enforcement is not solely within the province of the intellectual property offices; it involves numerous state agencies. A holistic government-wide approach is integral to the success of achieving regional integration of intellectual property rights enforcement.

9 ASEAN Secretariat, *History – ASEAN: One Vision One Identity One Community*, *available at* http://asean.org/asean/about-asean/history/.

10 Emmanuel Hassan, Ohid Yaqub, & Stepanie Diepeveen, *Intellectual Property and Developing Countries: A Review of the Literature* (2010), *available at* www.rand.org/content/dam/rand/pubs/technical_reports/2010/RAND_TR804.pdf.

7.3 ROLE OF INTELLECTUAL PROPERTY OFFICES IN INTELLECTUAL PROPERTY RIGHTS ENFORCEMENT

The primary role of intellectual property offices generally revolves around regulatory functions on administration of national intellectual property laws. These include dealing with applications and grants of intellectual property rights. Resources are focused on increasing the efficiency and effectiveness of performing these primary functions, such as improving regulatory workflows to reduce the processing time. Beyond raising awareness for intellectual property rights, most intellectual property offices in the ASEAN region play a very limited role in intellectual property enforcement, leaving this task to the police, border control agencies, investigative bodies, state prosecutors, and the judiciary.

As a result of the important work undertaken by ASEAN Working Group on Intellectual Property Cooperation (AWGIPC), the role of intellectual property offices in ASEAN has begun to evolve. Previously, the intellectual property offices were merely focused on bureaucratic or regulatory functions. Under the influence of AWGIPC, they now take on developmental advocacies, such as promotion of knowledge creation; technological innovation and transfer; business generation for micro, small, and medium enterprises; and protection of traditional knowledge and cultural expressions.[11] Intellectual Property offices have increasingly assumed the role of policymaking instead of mere policy implementation.[12] Given the rapid expansion of international norms and overlapping of rights, intellectual property offices are now faced with the daunting task of ensuring that the delicate balance between the interests of intellectual property owners, users, and the state is preserved.[13] In the context of intellectual property enforcement, intellectual property offices (as coordinating agencies for ASEAN regional initiatives and programs) should consider establishing a system of intragovernmental coordination between the various government bodies and agencies involved in law enforcement.

7.4 ROLE OF CUSTOMS OFFICIALS IN INTELLECTUAL PROPERTY RIGHTS ENFORCEMENT

In cross-border trade, customs officials occupy a vital position in regional intellectual property rights enforcement and are often the first line of defense. As regional economic integration increases, trade within and between ASEAN

[11] *See* ASEAN Intellectual Property Rights Action Plan 2011–2015, *supra* note 8. [12] *Id.*

[13] Examples include issues relating to anti-circumvention provisions in copyright law and patentability of secondary uses of pharmaceutical products.

countries is expected to surge, increasing the importance of border control measures. The role of custom officials must evolve from its traditional domain of dealing with simplified procedures for trade facilitation toward making a preliminary determination on potential rights violations. For example, when handling applications for the suspension of the release of allegedly counterfeit goods, custom officials are required to make a prima facie determination whether there are grounds to suspect that the goods are infringing.[14] Ex officio action is now also within the exercise of powers of customs authorities, where they are no longer required to act only on receipt of complaints from the rights holders. In fact, under a recordation system, rights holders merely register their intellectual property rights with the customs authorities, which will then inform them if there are any incoming suspicious shipments that may potentially violate their intellectual property rights.[15] On receipt of such information, intellectual property owners may then commence proceedings to suspend the release of goods, and prosecute the consignee if infringement is established on inspection.[16]

Apart from border control measures with respect to imported goods, some countries have placed stringent border control measures with respect to goods for exportation.[17] Notwithstanding the additional burden on customs authorities in terms of the volume of shipments that must be examined and cleared, this seems to be an effective measure for curbing the transshipment of infringing goods from notorious markets.

7.5 ROLE OF OTHER GOVERNMENT AGENCIES IN INTELLECTUAL PROPERTY ENFORCEMENT

With the spilling-over of intellectual property policies into other policy areas, intellectual property rights enforcement is no longer confined to the domain of intellectual property offices, customs officials, or the traditional law enforcement agencies, such as the police or specialized investigative bodies. Government prosecutors and the judiciary also have a crucial role to play, as

[14] *See* Customs Administrative Order No. 6–2002, Rules and Regulations Implementing R.A. 8293, also known as the Intellectual Property Code of the Philippines ("IP Code") in relation to Sections 51–60 of the Trade-Related Aspects of Intellectual Property Rights Agreement ("TRIPS"), amending for the purpose Customs Administrative Order (CAO) No. 7–93 on Customs Border Control (September 23, 2002).

[15] *Id.* [16] *Id.*

[17] For example, in Vietnam, the border control measures of both intellectual property–related imports and exports include the suspension of customs procedures for suspected intellectual property right infringing goods and supervision to detect goods containing signs of infringement of intellectual property rights. *See Vietnamese Law on Customs*, Ch. XVIII §2 art. 216 (2001), *available at* www.asean.org/uploads/archive/20534-vietnam.pdf.

enforcement involves effective prosecution and adjudication requiring prosecutors familiar with intellectual property laws. Likewise, judicial decisions must also be consistent and well reasoned. Better predictability will enable rights holders to exercise their rights more effectively. Other government agencies involved in enforcement include officials from the health ministries[18]; authorities overseeing the misappropriation of cultural rights and those relating to the rights of indigenous peoples/communities; officials from agricultural ministries[19]; and even competition, antitrust, and environmental authorities.

7.6 A HOLISTIC APPROACH TO INTELLECTUAL PROPERTY RIGHTS ENFORCEMENT IN ASEAN

The plethora of stakeholders and relevant government agencies involved in intellectual property rights enforcement serves to underscore the need for a holistic approach both nationally and regionally. Nationally, ASEAN member states must adopt a mechanism that fosters coordination among all government agencies involved in intellectual property rights enforcement and promotes information sharing. Establishing rapport between officials from different agencies is also important to facilitate interagency support. Capacity building and training programs tailored to meet the specific functions of each agency, roundtable discussions among members of the judiciary, and the imposition of penalties for infringement are important to achieving a holistic enforcement approach.

Take, for example, the experience of the Philippines. Faced with a proliferation of counterfeit goods in the Philippines market, often sold in plain view at shopping malls, the Intellectual Property Office of the Philippines (IPOPHL) led a concerted effort involving all government agencies dealing with intellectual property rights enforcement. Working with the Bureau of Customs[20] and the Optical Media Board,[21] agencies granted "visitorial

[18] These health officials may be involved in determining policies for access to medicines and counterfeiting of patented drugs.

[19] For example, officials dealing with the protection of agricultural goods enjoying specific reputations linked with the country's geographical territory.

[20] §2536 of the Tariff and Customs Code of the Philippines; Customs Memorandum Order No.010–06. The Bureau of Customs is authorized to conduct visits at facilities and warehouses that are suspected to be storing goods that have been smuggled or have not paid the appropriate duties and taxes. Because counterfeit goods are always sold below the market value of the genuine goods, and can be considered as undervalued and wrongly declared goods, they are within the purview of customs officials.

[21] Republic Act No. 9239, entitled "An Act Regulating Optical Media, Reorganizing for this purpose the Videogram Regulatory Board, Providing Penalties Therefor, and for Other Purposes."

powers" and inspection powers by law, the counterfeit goods could be seized including from warehouse storage facilities before entering the distribution chain. Additionally, the Philippine National Police and the National Bureau of Investigation conduct "test buys" on suspected retailers of counterfeit items, serving as evidence before the regional trial courts to support the issuance of a judicial writ of search and seizure. Philippine's holistic approach to the enforcement of intellectual property rights is also bolstered by actions such as the cancellation of the registration of business names, companies, and visas of infringers, and the lodging of complaints against infringers for violation of consumer protection laws and for tax evasion (where applicable).

Nonetheless, a differentiated approach may need to be adopted in the other ASEAN member states, in line with their national policy and capacity. Once the national mechanism is in place, it could be elevated to establish a regional level of coordination and cooperation. For instance, there could be greater levels of information sharing, so as to identify patterns of production, shipment, and distribution of counterfeit or pirated goods in the ASEAN region. Actions such as these would help develop a more concerted regional effort toward addressing systematic infringing activities.

Adding to the problems is the limited commonality in the laws of ASEAN member states governing intellectual property rights infringements. For example, only some ASEAN member states, such as Malaysia[22] and Thailand,[23] have specialized intellectual property courts. The Philippines,[24]

The Optical Media Board is authorized to conduct visits on suspected illegal replicators of optical media products, and to seize such machines and instruments used to carry out such activities, thereby facilitating the apprehension at source of large-scale producers of optical media containing pirated copyright works.

[22] The Intellectual Property Court was established in Malaysia in July 2007 in response to the increase in the piracy of copyrighted materials and counterfeiting of goods in Malaysia. The Court consists of fifteen Sessions Courts and six High Courts for the purposes of hearing only intellectual property cases. The Sessions Court (IP) hears only criminal intellectual property matters, whereas the High Court (IP) hears civil cases on intellectual property, appeals from the decisions of the respective registrars, and criminal intellectual property appeals from the decisions of the Sessions Court (IP). *See* Intellectual Property Corporation of Malaysia (MyIPO), *IP Law and Administration in Malaysia*, *available at* www.wipo.int/edocs/mdocs/treaties/en/wipo_smes_kul_11/wipo_smes_kul_11_ref_theme_08_01.pptx.

[23] The Intellectual Property and International Trade Court was established in Thailand in December 1997 to create a "user-friendly" forum with specialized expertise to serve commerce and industry and to assist in the recovery of the Thai economy in the 1990s. *See* Vichai Ariyanuntaka, *Intellectual Property and International Trade Court: A New Dimension for IP Rights Enforcement in Thailand*, *available at* www.wipo.int/wipolex/en/text.jsp?file_id=185591.

[24] The Philippines does not have specialized courts for managing intellectual property cases. The Philippines Supreme Court issued a resolution in June 2003 transferring all intellectual property cases to the newly designated Special Commercial Courts. These Special Commercial

Indonesia[25], and Cambodia[26] have designated commercial courts that deal with intellectual property cases. In the author's view, it is imperative that legal and judicial reforms be instituted to forge strong linkages and cooperation among ASEAN member states in line with the interoperability agenda.[27] The creation of an interoperable enforcement framework, such as establishing a centralized database of intellectual property rights enforcement data, statistics, operations, prosecution, and decisions, is of utmost importance. Toward this end, the author proposes that each ASEAN member state begins by laying the institutional foundations for intellectual property rights enforcement in accordance with the ASEAN Intellectual Property Rights Action Plan of 2011–2015.

7.7 CONCLUSION

In conclusion, it must be highlighted that intellectual property rights enforcement cannot operate in a vacuum. In the author's view, it is dependent on high-quality granting of intellectual property rights, a culture of respect for intellectual property rights, and the appropriate incentive for the creation of intellectual property. Effective intellectual property rights enforcement is only one pillar of a good intellectual property system. Despite the differences in the level of development, language, culture, and political systems, the establishment of an interoperable regional intellectual property regime, including enforcement, will be crucial to developing a competitive ASEAN economic region.

Courts handle all intellectual property–related cases filed in the regular Philippines courts and handle cases formerly adjudicated by the Securities and Exchange Commission. *See* OFFICE OF THE UNITED STATES TRADE REPRESENTATIVE, 2005 NATIONAL TRADE ESTIMATE REPORT ON FOREIGN TRADE BARRIERS 498 (2005).

25 In Indonesia, cases involving intellectual property issues are delegated to specialized commercial courts set up in the early 2000s to build up expertise in the legal system and speed up the litigation process. These specialized commercial courts are based in Jakarta and intellectual property cases are heard by a bench of three to four judges who have received special intellectual property training. *See* OECD, NATIONAL INTELLECTUAL PROPERTY SYSTEMS, INNOVATION AND ECONOMIC DEVELOPMENT: WITH PERSPECTIVES ON COLOMBIA AND INDONESIA 156 (2014).

26 *See*, U.S. Department of State, 2015 *Investment Climate Statement – Cambodia* (at 45), *available at* www.state.gov/e/eb/rls/othr/ics/2015/241508.htm, highlighting that the Cambodian government had enacted the Law on Court Structure in July 2014 under which the Commercial Court was created.

27 *See* Elizabeth Siew-Kuan Ng, *Intellectual Property Interoperability in ASEAN and Beyond: An Integration Model* in ELIZABETH SIEW-KUAN NG & GRAEME AUSTIN (eds.), INTERNATIONAL INTELLECTUAL PROPERTY AND THE ASEAN WAY: PATHWAYS TO INTEROPERABILITY, Chapter 1.

8

Cooperation through Conflict of Laws

The Justiciability of Cross-Border Copyright Infringement

Graeme W. Austin

8.1 INTRODUCTION

This chapter discusses ways that conflict of laws (or private international laws) might contribute to the broader aims of intellectual property interoperability – that is, the working together of different nations' intellectual property systems in contexts where harmonization is not a realistic possibility. As Elizabeth Ng has explained, the "ASEAN Way" emphasizes consensus, noninterference, and respectful recognition of each nation's sovereignty interests, with at the same time a desire to move forward together in a cooperative manner, while giving due recognition to different levels of development.[1] These issues are by no means unique to the Association of Southeast Asian Nations (ASEAN). Across the globe, different nations enjoy different levels of technological and economic development, and their laws and governance reflect different cultural and social values and different histories and traditions.

As a tool for shaping markets for innovation and cultural life,[2] intellectual property laws reflect these differences. The challenge is how to develop vehicles for achieving greater integration in the intellectual property field, while respecting those differences. These differences exist in part because intellectual property rights are not ends in themselves. They are social policy levers that, to the extent permitted by public international law obligations, individual nations can deploy in ways that reflect different visions of the good life. As is explained later in this chapter, it is possible to apply the principle of choice

[1] Elizabeth Siew-Kuan Ng, *ASEAN IP Harmonization: Striking the Delicate Balance*, 25 PACE INT'L. L. REV. 129 (2013).

[2] *See* RONALD V. BETTIG, COPYRIGHT CULTURE: THE POLITICAL ECONOMY OF INTELLECTUAL PROPERTY (1996); ROSEMARY COOMBE, THE CULTURAL LIFE OF INTELLECTUAL PROPERTY: AUTHORSHIP, APPROPRIATION, AND THE LAW (1998).

of law in a way that facilitates cross-border integration, while acknowledging national differences.

To that end, this chapter addresses a question of relatively narrow technical compass – the justiciability of foreign copyright disputes – and considers it in the light of some of the dynamics that characterize the ASEAN Way. It details three different approaches to choice of law in cases of cross-border copyright infringement: (1) the rule that infringement of copyright in another territory is not justiciable, a rule that held considerable sway in English law until the recent watershed decision of the Supreme Court in *Lucasfilm v. Ainsworth*[3]; (2) the rule that domestic copyright law can, under some circumstances, reach conduct in foreign territories – a principle that has been developed in some US courts; and (3) the principle recently embraced by the UK Supreme Court in *Lucasfilm* that infringement of copyright under foreign laws is indeed justiciable. In so doing, it considers which of these approaches best accords with the values of consensus, cooperation, noninterference, and respectful recognition of sovereign interests inherent in the ASEAN Way.

8.2 THE PUBLIC INTERNATIONAL LAW SETTING

While public international law has been the principal vehicle for achieving standardization, public international law obligations in the intellectual property context do not obliterate all scope for expression of different domestic policy choices. In Rochelle Dreyfuss and Graeme Dinwoodie's analysis,[4] the Agreement on Trade-Related Aspects of Intellectual Property Rights (TRIPS)[5] does not, or does not entirely, impose a one-size-fits-all approach, smothering all possibility of domestic variation or innovation. Instead, TRIPS offers important possibilities for a kind of international "intellectual property federalism," a sharing of powers and responsibilities within different regimes. Moreover, there are many key areas, such as intellectual property ownership,[6] where

[3] [2011] UKSC 39. As Richard Garnett explains in his chapter, in some jurisdictions, including Australia, the jurisprudence on cross-border enforcement of intellectual property rights remains unclear in a number of jurisdictions. *See* Richard Garnett, *Intellectual Property Remedies across Borders, in* Elizabeth Siew-Kuan Ng & Graeme Austin, International Intellectual Property and the ASEAN Way: Pathways to Interoperability, Chapter 9.

[4] Graeme B. Dinwoodie & Rochelle C. Dreyfuss, A Neofederalist Vision of TRIPS: The Resilience of the International Intellectual Property Regime (2012).

[5] Agreement on Trade Related Aspects of Intellectual Property Rights, April 15, 1994, Marrakesh Agreement Establishing the World Trade Organization, Annex 1C, 33 I.L.M. 87–88 (1994) [hereinafter TRIPS].

[6] *See* Graeme W. Austin, *Intellectual Property Politics and the Private International Law of Copyright Ownership*, 30 Brook. J. Int'l. L. 899 (2005).

nothing remotely resembling intellectual property harmonization has been achieved. And some kinds of intellectual property, such as personality rights, fall entirely outside of the harmonization agenda.

The governing principle that accounts for the continued relevance of the nation-state in intellectual property regulation is "territoriality." From the beginning of modern international intellectual property relations, with the completion of the Berne[7] and the Paris[8] Conventions in the nineteenth century, it has been recognized that a genuinely "international" intellectual property code, giving rise to a uniform domestic laws, would be impossible to achieve.[9] Instead, international intellectual property relations evolved an approach that required "national treatment" and the application of minimal standards, creating a "mosaic" of distinct national laws, which in combination provide the potential for international protection of intellectual property rights. The Paris Convention, for example, expressly references the idea through the principle of independence of rights.[10] National treatment is grounded in territoriality: the principle is needed because domestic intellectual property laws are assumed to operate only within domestic borders.[11] For copyright works protected under the Berne Convention,[12] protection no longer stopped at the

[7] *See, e.g.*, Berne Convention for the Protection of Literary and Artistic Works, September 9, 1896, S. TREATY DOC. NO. 99–27 (1986) (as revised at Paris July 4, 1971 and amended September 28, 1979) [hereinafter Berne Convention].

[8] Paris Convention for the Protection of Industrial Property, March 20, 1883, 21 U.S.T. 1583, 828 U.N.T.S. 305 [hereinafter Paris Convention].

[9] As to the Berne Convention, *see* STEPHEN STEWART, INTERNATIONAL COPYRIGHT AND NEIGHBORING RIGHTS para 3.08 (2d ed. 1989) (discussing the thwarted desideratum of achieving a universally applicable international copyright code); SAM RICKETSON & JANE GINSBURG, INTERNATIONAL COPYRIGHT NEIGHBOURING RIGHTS: THE BERNE CONVENTION AND BEYOND 41–52 (2d ed. 2005) (discussing the drafting history of the Berne Convention).

[10] Paris Convention, art. 4 *bis* (1): "Patents applied for in the various countries of the Union by nationals of countries of the Union shall be independent of patents obtained for the same invention in other countries, whether members of the Union or not"; art. 6(3): "A mark duly registered in a country of the Union shall be regarded as independent of marks registered in the other countries of the Union, including the country of origin."

[11] Curtis A. Bradley, *Territorial Intellectual Property Rights in an Age of Globalism*, 37 VA. J. INT'L. L. 505 (1997).

[12] As described by the US legislature, the five original objectives of the Berne Convention were as follows: (1) the development of copyright laws favorable to authors in all civilized countries; (2) the elimination of basing rights on reciprocity; (3) the end of discrimination between foreign and domestic authors; (4) the abolition of formalities as a condition of protection; and (5) the promotion of uniform international law for the protection of copyrightable works. H.R. REP. No. 609 (1988), at 12 (recounting the history of Berne Convention). *See also* Sam Ricketson, *The Birth of the Berne Union*, 11 COLUM.-VLA J. LAW & ARTS 9 (1986). Reciprocity remains a connecting factor in a few instruments. *See, e.g.*, Directive 96/9/EC of the European Parliament and of the Council of 11 March 1996 on the Legal Protection of Databases, 1996

borders,[13] but protection within those borders depended on the domestic laws in force there.

While globalization and the rise of digital networks have challenged the territoriality premise,[14] the principle endures. Some twelve years ago, I suggested that it would be inappropriate "to assume (or even hope) that we are partway through a grand narrative that has the demise of territoriality and the achievement of standardized, supranational intellectual property laws as its inevitable dénouement."[15] That view was animated by some of the normative claims that can be made for preserving the possibility of domestic variation in intellectual property laws, for the very reason that these laws reflect different socioeconomic choices; and it was informed by a concern for the efficiency gains that can flow from regulatory experimentation in different national contexts. Relatedly, other scholars have greeted with considerable skepticism many of the heady ideas about the demise of the nation-state,[16] and suggested, with no small amount of prescience, that nation-states would realize that there was much at stake in the loosening of control over digital networks and that they would act in ways that reinforced, and jealously protected, domestic sovereignty interests.[17] In the intellectual property context, the so-called reverse domain name hijacking provisions of the US Lanham Act is a notable (and perhaps notorious) example.[18]

At the same time, the forces of globalization and the international reach of digital distribution platforms are requiring intellectual property law to adapt. Global connectivity opens up new channels of commerce, enhanced opportunities for cross-border collaborations, new methods of gathering and processing vast amounts of data, a reduction in the friction formerly associated with global

O.J. (L 77) 20, art. 11 (conditioning protection of databases made outside the EU by non-EU residents on a determination that the relevant foreign nation offers comparable protections).

13 *See generally* Hamish Sandison, *The Berne Union and the Universal Copyright Convention: The American Experience*, 11 COLUM.-VLA J. LAW & ARTS 89 (1986) (describing the pre-Berne unremunerated exploitation of works by foreign authors).

14 In the trademark context, for example, *see* IRENE CALBOLI AND EDWARD LEE (eds.), TRADEMARK PROTECTION AND TERRITORIALITY CHALLENGES IN A GLOBAL ECONOMY (2014).

15 Graeme W. Austin, *Valuing "Domestic Self-Determination" in International Intellectual Property Jurisprudence*, 77 CHI.-KENT L. REV. 1155, 1158 (2002).

16 David R. Johnson & David G. Post, *Law and Borders – The Rise of Law in Cyberspace*, 48 STAN. L. REV. 1367 (1996); John T. Delacourt, *Recent Development: The International Impact of Internet Regulation*, 38 HARV. INT'L. L.J. 207 (1997).

17 *See, e.g.*, Jack L. Goldsmith & Alan O. Sykes, *The Internet and the Dormant Commerce Clause*, 110 YALE L.J. 785 (2001); Jack L. Goldsmith, *Against Cyberanarchy*, 65 U. CHI. L. REV. 1199, 1221–24 (1998).

18 Codified at 15 U.S.C. § 1125(d)(1)(A) (2012). For an illustration of the application of this provision, *see Barcelona.com, Inc. v. Excelentisimo Ayuntamiento de Barcelona*, 330 F.3d 617 (4th Cir. 2003).

supply chains, and increased interest in creative endeavor from remote geographical areas. Increasingly, there is a Canute-like quality to the insistence on geographically segregated markets for intellectual property-rich products, hitherto a corollary of formal legal distinctions between different territorially confined intellectual property rights. Many consumers know what digital content is available elsewhere, and seem to have little tolerance for geoblocking software that enables content proprietors to divide markets along geographical borders. And now, geoblocking is under scrutiny as a matter of competition policy.[19] As Marketa Trimble notes,[20] among many internet users, we are witnessing a "territoriality referendum," as consumers deploy increasingly sophisticated technologies that enable evasion of geoblocking software. For example, in New Zealand, a widely available service known as "global mode" has enabled New Zealanders to access foreign streaming sites such as HBO Now and Amazon TV using a VPN service provided by ISPs.[21] As a result of a legal challenge from broadcasters against ISPs, a settlement has been reached that resulted in the discontinuation of these services.[22] It has been suggested that across the Tasman, in Australia, more than 684,000 Australians use VPN services to access overseas content that is cheaper and more varied than they can otherwise access, such as Hulu, the well-known US streaming platform.[23]

While the forces of globalization generate many new opportunities for intellectual property owners, these opportunities are accompanied by new threats. Just as digital distribution platforms significantly enhance opportunities for global marketing, they also create new vulnerabilities to infringement. Intellectual property piracy is of course nothing new.[24] But global digital networks enable something different in kind: a shift from *seriatim* copying, whether licensed or not, to simultaneous and geographically pervasive[25] availability.

19 *European Commission, Digital Single Market Strategy: European Commission Agrees Areas for Action*, Brussels, March 25, 2015, *available at* http://europa.eu/rapid/press-release_IP-15-4653_en.htm.

20 Marketa Trimble, *The Territoriality Referendum*, 6 WIPO J. 89 (2015).

21 Adam Turner, *How Hard Will It Be for Kiwis to Sneak into HBO Now?* (March 8, 2015), *available at* www.stuff.co.nz/entertainment/tv-radio/67099134/how-hard-will-it-be-for-kiwis-to-sneak-into-hbo-now.

22 John Drinnan, *Global Mode Goes Dark – Broadcasters Win Legal Fight*, N. Z. Herald (online ed, Auckland, June 24, 2015).

23 Monica Tan, *VPNs Could Be Blocked Under Proposed Australian Copyright Legislation, Say Choice*, The Guardian (online ed, London, April 17, 2015).

24 *See, e.g.*, Ricketson, *supra* note 12.

25 Jane C. Ginsburg, *Berne without Borders? Geographic Indiscretion and Digital Communications* (Stephen Stewart Memorial Lecture, Intellectual Property Institute London U.K., October 29, 2001) (November 2001) at 6, *see* Columbia Law School, Pub. Law Research Paper No. 01–30, *available at* http://ssrn.com/abstract–292010.

How should copyright law respond? At the international level, an important early response was the two 1996 World Intellectual Property Organization (WIPO) "Internet Treaties," the WIPO Copyright Treaty (WCT)[26] and the WIPO Performances and Phonograms Treaty (WPPT).[27] These were responses to technological challenges that were not addressed by the TRIPS Agreement. The third recital of the former document captures this theme: "Recognizing the profound impact of the development and convergence of information and communication technologies on the creation and use of literary and artistic works."[28] With minor changes dictated by context, identical language is used in the WPPT. These treaties enhance and adapt protections for copyright and related rights in ways that are better tailored to the digital distribution, and create new disciplines in areas such as digital rights management information and anti-circumvention technologies. These initiatives have continued with the completion in 2012 of the Beijing Treaty on Audiovisual Performances.[29] The two WIPO internet treaties are given "teeth" by their incorporation into bilateral and regional free trade agreements (FTAs), the FTA between the United States and Singapore being a prominent early example.[30]

While these public international law initiatives created new standards of protection, they did not speak to a key puzzle distilled by the exploitation of intellectual property across global networks: the question of applicable law. Indeed, the public international law of intellectual property is for the most part silent on such questions,[31] or, when it does speak, it does not do so clearly.[32] Yet these issues are critical to the international exploitation and enforcement

[26] World Intellectual Property Organization Copyright Treaty, December 20, 1996, 36 I.L.M. 65 (1997) (hereinafter WCT).

[27] WIPO Performances and Phonograms Treaty, December 20, 1996, 36 I.L.M. 76 (1997) (hereinafter WPPT).

[28] WCT, *supra* note 26, at recital 3.

[29] World Intellectual Property Organization, Beijing Treaty on Audiovisual Performances, WIPO Doc. AVP/DC/20 (June 24, 2012).

[30] Singapore/U.S. Free Trade Agreement, art. 16.1.2(a) (requiring compliance with *inter alia* the WCT and the WPPT).

[31] An exception is art. 14 *bis* (1)(a) of the Berne Convention, which states that *(a)* Ownership of copyright in a cinematographic work shall be a matter for legislation in the country where protection is claimed.

[32] An important example is art. 5(2) of the Berne Convention, which provides that "apart from the provisions of this Convention, the extent of protection, as well as the means of redress afforded to the author to protect his rights, shall be governed exclusively by the laws of the country where protection is claimed." This admits of a number of meanings. On its face, the meaning of the phrase "the laws of the country where protection is claimed" could mean the *lex fori*, that is, the laws of the forum where the plaintiff initiates infringement proceedings. Alternatively, it could mean the country "for which" protection is claimed, a territorial reading that is more consistent with the national treatment principle.

of intellectual property through digital networks. This gap in the international intellectual property regime was one of the catalysts for the initiative by different groups of scholars to develop a coherent set of principles to address private international law issues in the intellectual property context.[33] The results include the American Law Institute's *Intellectual Property: Principles Governing Jurisdiction, Choice of Law, and Judgments in Transnational Disputes*, published in 2008, and the Max-Planck Institute's *Principles for Conflict of Laws in Intellectual Property*, published in 2013.[34] In Asia, there have been two broadly similar initiatives.[35] The detailed set of issues distilled by the project of crafting a coherent conflict of laws regime are now being discussed within the International Law Association[36] and at the World Intellectual Property Organization.[37]

8.3 THREE APPROACHES TO CHOICE OF LAW

8.3.1 *Nonjusticiability of Foreign Copyright Infringement*

Until the recent decision of the UK Supreme Court in *Lucasfilm*, the prevailing orthodoxy was that infringement of foreign copyrights was not justiciable in a domestic forum. A rigid jurisdictional prohibition, the rule went further

33 A further set of initiatives was the proposal by the Hague Conference on Private International Law to develop a Convention on Jurisdiction and Foreign Judgments in Civil and Commercial Matters Hague Conference on Private International Law, The Judgments Project – preliminary work, *available at* www.hcch.net/index_en.php?act=text.display&tid=154. The broader initiative ultimately failed, but led to a Convention on Choice of Court Agreements limited to the B2B context: Convention on Choice of Court Agreements, June 30, 2005, *available at* www.hcch.net/index_en.php?act=conventions.text&cid=98.

34 The American Law Institute, Intellectual Property: Principles Governing Jurisdiction, Choice of Law, and Judgments in Transnational Disputes (2008) [hereinafter ALI Principles]; European Max-Planck Group for Conflict of Laws in Intellectual Property, Conflict of Laws in Intellectual Property: The Clip Principles and Commentary (2013).

35 Transparency Proposal on Jurisdiction, Choice of Law, Recognition Enforcement of Foreign Judgments in Intellectual Property, Transparency of Japanese Law Project (2009); Korean Private Int'l. Law Assoc., Principles on Intellectual Property Litigation (2010).

36 *See* International Law Association Committee, Intellectual Property and Private International Law, *available at* www.ila-hq.org/en/committees/index.cfm/cid/1037 (working papers).

37 *See* WIPO, *Seminar on Intellectual Property and Private International Law*, WIPO-ILA/IP/GE/15/INF/1 Pov.1 (November 24, 2014), *available at* www.wipo.int/edocs/mdocs/enforcement/en/wipo_ila_ip_ge_15/wipo_ila_ip_ge_15_inf_1_prov.pdf. A recent contribution to this literature is the discussion paper published by WIPO: Andrew F. Christie, Private International Law Issues in Online Intellectual Property Infringement Disputes with Cross-Border Elements: an Analysis of National Approaches (2015).

than the principle that choice of law questions might influence decisions as to the appropriate forum. As the Singapore Court of Appeal has noted, "The relevance of choice of law considerations in a *jurisdictional* enquiry . . . lies in the general proposition that where a dispute is governed by a foreign *lex causae*, the forum would be less adept in applying this law than the courts of the jurisdiction from which the *lex causae* originates."[38] The Court also noted that "[w]hile it is true that the courts of a country (for example, Singapore courts) can apply the laws of another country (for example, German law) to a dispute, there will clearly be savings in time and resources if a court applies the law of its own jurisdiction to the substantive dispute."[39] Accordingly, choice of law considerations can be a significant factor in determining the appropriate forum to hear a dispute. In intellectual property cases, however, the traditional approach has been to apply a rigid rule precluding jurisdiction, rather than a more subtle factored analysis.

Some cases had suggested otherwise, including the first instance decision in *Lucasfilm*.[40] There have been a small handful of New Zealand decisions along the same lines.[41] However, in *Lucasfilm* the Court of Appeal attempted, as a matter of common law principle,[42] to shut the door firmly against adjudicating such cases. In broad outline, *Lucasfilm* concerned copyright infringement proceedings brought by the owners of the relevant intellectual property rights in helmets worn in the *Starwars* movies by the Stormtrooper characters. These allegations were advanced against a party domiciled in England. The Stormtrooper helmets were held not to be protected under UK copyright law; however, it was accepted that by selling the helmets in the United States the defendant had infringed the claimant's rights under US copyright law. The claimant had secured a default judgement in a US federal district court (including treble damages under the US Lanham Act),[43] but this judgement was held to be unenforceable.[44] Accordingly, the claimant would be afforded relief only if infringement of US copyright law were justiciable in an English forum.

38 *Rickshaw Investments v. Nicolai Baron von Uexkull* [2006] 1 SLR (R) 377 at [42].

39 *Id.*

40 *Lucasfilm Ltd. v. Ainsworth* [2008] EWHC 1878 (Ch).

41 *Kabushiki Kaisha Sony Computer Entertainment v. van Veen* (unreported) High Court, New Zealand, CIV.-2004–485–1520 (October 16, 2006).

42 *Cf. Pearce v. Ove Arup Partnership Ltd. (Jurisdiction)* [2000] Ch. 403 (jurisdiction required under the Convention on Jurisdiction and Enforcement of Judgments in Civil and Commercial Matters); *see* now: Council Regulation (EC) no. 44/2001 on Jurisdiction and the Recognition and Enforcement of Judgments in Civil and Commercial Matters, 2001 O.J. (L 12) 1.

43 *Lucasfilm Ltd. v. Shepperton Design Studios Ltd.*, 2006 WL 6672241 (C.D. Cal., 2006).

44 The decision was held to be unenforceable according to the principles in *Adams v. Cape Industries plc.* [1990] Ch. 433.

The judge at first instance held that the US infringements were justiciable.[45] Mann J reasoned that infringement of foreign copyright could be determined by an English court, so long as questions of validity of the copyright were not put in issue. The decision was overturned by the Court of Appeal. In a detailed judgment, Sir Robin Jacob emphasized the "local" character of intellectual property disputes, reasoning that "infringement of an intellectual property right (especially copyright, which is largely unharmonized) is essentially a local matter involving local policies and local public interest. It is a matter for local judges."[46] Accordingly, the *Moçambique* rule,[47] precluding jurisdiction over foreign immovables, applied with full force to such claims. In this passage, the phrase "especially copyright" is telling: it is often assumed that copyrights are *less* localized than other kinds of intellectual property, especially patents and registered trademarks.[48] Unlike that of a copyright, the existence of a patent or a registered trademark depends on the act of a foreign official, exercising a kind of delegated sovereignty. Indeed, in some copyright statutes within the Anglo tradition, copyrights are expressly characterized as "movable" property.[49]

Moreover, the statement seems to imply, at least by negative inference, that the greater the level of harmonization, the more appropriate will be the adjudication of foreign rights. This view underscores other reasons advanced by the Court of Appeal for declining jurisdiction. The Court noted that enforcement might involve clashes between the intellectual property policies of different countries. His Lordship considered the *Lucasfilm* case itself to exemplify the problem: the defendant's actions in the United Kingdom were lawful; the same acts were apparently unlawful according to US copyright law.[50] Relatedly, the

45 [2008] EWHC 1878 (Ch.).
46 [2010] Ch. 503, 548.
47 *British South Africa Co v. Cia de Moçambique* [1893] A.C. 602. The jurisdictional prohibition in copyright cases can be traced to an Australian case involving infringement of foreign patent rights (technically, a case of infringement of rights arising under a different Australian State): *Potter v. Broken Hill Pty Co Ltd.* (1906) 3 C.L.R. 479. *Potter* was applied by analogy to copyrights. *See* Graeme W. Austin, *The Concept of 'Justiciability' in Foreign Copyright Infringement Cases*, 40(4) INT'L. REV. INTELL. PROP. & COMPET. L. 393, 395–399 (2009) (tracing the rise of the jurisdictional prohibition in copyright cases).
48 *See, e.g.*, Joost Blom, *Star Wars Storm Troopers, the Next Episode: Lucasfilm in the United Kingdom Supreme Court* 24 I.P.J. 15, 27 (2011) (suggesting that the justiciability of infringement of foreign registered rights raises more difficult questions than copyright).
49 *See, e.g.*, Copyright, Designs and Patents Act 1988 s 90(1) (UK).
50 It should be noted that the conclusion that the defendant's actions were unlawful under US law was based on a default judgment in which the point was not ventilated, and, it appears, an agreement between the parties. *See Lucasfilm Ltd. v. Shepperton Design Studios Ltd.*, 2006 WL 6672241 (C.D. Cal., 2006). Whether a costume *is* protected according to US "useful article" doctrine (*see* 17 U.S.C. § 101 (definition of "useful article")), is a fiercely complex question: *see,*

Court reiterated a point raised in a number of patent cases, most prominently by Aldous J., as he then was, in *Plastus Kreativ AB v. Minnesota Mining and Manufacturing Company*[51]: extraterritorial jurisdiction "will involve (and does here) a restraint on actions in another country – an interference which prima facie a foreign judge should avoid." The Court noted that, in the particular case, the defendant has no intention of actually going to the United States, but the Court warned that "if the jurisdiction exists one could easily imagine such a case." This concern is distilled by the monopolistic character of intellectual property rights, which, in the view of Aldous J., should cause judges in one country to be reticent about adjudicating cases that could, for example, have the effect of raising prices in foreign markets.[52]

The reasoning of the Court of Appeal, reasoning that has also been followed in the Republic of South Africa,[53] is grounded in concerns for comity and respect for the law making powers and domestic policies of foreign sovereigns, an attitude underscored by courts' recourse to the *Moçambique* principle. In a famous modern restatement of this principle in *Hesperides Hotels Ltd. v. Aegean Turkish Holidays Ltd.*,[54] Lord Wilberforce emphasized the close relationship between foreign immovable and domestic sovereign power. For a foreign court to adjudicate on infringement of these rights would, according to this theory, interfere with foreign sovereignty interests.

In the intellectual property context at least, the principal difficulty with such an approach is that respect for foreign sovereignty interests becomes a template for lack of enforcement. *Lucasfilm* itself illustrates the point. Assuming that a valid claim under US copyright laws existed, the English court was the *only* forum in which that claim could be given effect, given the location of the defendant's domicile. To be sure, one sovereign cannot generally create substantive rights that have effect in another's territory[55]: but this should not support a corollary principle of judicial reticence dictating a refusal to give effect to rights created by a foreign sovereign. Indeed, the recognition and enforcement of foreign copyrights seems to accord greater respect to foreign sovereignty than a refusal to enforce these rights at all. In the *Lucasfilm* case, the

e.g., *Whimsicality, Inc. v. Rubie's Costume* Co 891 F.2d 452 (2d Cir. 1989) (Halloween costumes deemed useful, and not protected). Differences between national copyright laws are regularly exploited. It is hardly a clash of policies if a Richard Strauss opera remains within copyright in life-plus 70 *pma* countries, but is in the public domain in countries that hew to the Berne Convention minimum of life plus 50 *pma*.

51 [1995] R.P.C. 438. 52 *Id.* at 447.

53 *Gallo Africa v. Sting Music (40/10)* [2010] ZASCA 96 (September 3, 2010) (Supreme Court of Appeal of South Africa).

54 [1979] A.C. 508.

55 *See, e.g., Peer International Corp v. Termidor Music Publishers Ltd. (No.1)* [2004] Ch. 212.

relevant US rules reflected deliberate policy choices as to the scope of domestic copyright laws – in this case, in utilitarian three-dimensional objects. Many countries' copyright laws engage with this problem – and there are subtle distinctions between the different approaches to the issue of ensuring that copyrights do not trespass into rights more appropriately regulated through patent or designs law.[56] Even so, those carefully crafted policy distinctions will count for little unless the rights are enforceable.

8.3.2 *Extraterritorial Application of Domestic Laws*

Another approach to cross-border infringement has been the adoption of what I have described elsewhere as a "single governing law" approach to cross-border copyright infringement.[57] In a number of cases, US courts have held that a domestic court may give relief for foreign infringements where a "predicate" infringing act occurred within the United States.[58] In some cases, this principle renders a plaintiff entitled to recover pecuniary relief *under United States copyright law* for acts of infringement that occurred abroad.[59]

This approach also has parallels in a strand of US trademark doctrine. In the 1952 decision in *Steele v. Bulova Watch Co*,[60] the United States Supreme Court held, over a strenuous dissent, that the federal Lanham Act could reach the defendant's activities in Mexico.[61] The *Bulova* case has spawned

56 For a recent case illustrating the distinction between Australian and New Zealand law, *see Jeanswest Corporation (New Zealand) Limited v. G-Star RAW* [2015] NZCA 14.

57 Graeme W. Austin, *Social Policy Choices and Choice of law for Copyright Infringement in Cyberspace*, 79 OREGON L. R. 575 (2000).

58 *Los Angeles News Serv. v. Reuters Television Int'l, Ltd.*, 149 F.3d 987 (9th Cir. 1998); *De Bardossy v. Puski*, 763 F. Supp. 1239 (S.D.N.Y. 1991); *Ahbez v. Edwin H. Morris & Co.*, 548 F. Supp. 664 (S.D.N.Y. 1982). *Robert Stigwood Group Ltd. v. O'Reilly*, 530 F.2d 1096 (2d Cir.), *cert. denied*, 429 U.S. 848 (1976).

59 At least one US court has assumed that common law courts in other jurisdictions would also adopt this theory. In *Creative Technology Ltd. v. Aztech System Pte Ltd.*, 61 F.3d 696 (9th Cir. 1995), the US Court of Appeals for the Ninth Circuit dismissed on *forum non conveniens* grounds a copyright case involving two Singaporean firms. The court not only considered that Singapore would be a more convenient forum; it also surmised that there would be "no barrier" to the adoption by the Singaporean courts of the single governing law approach that had developed in US copyright jurisprudence. In other words, the US court appeared to assume that a Singaporean court would apply Singaporean law to all infringements, domestic or foreign.

60 344 U.S. 280 (1952). *See generally*, Graeme Austin, *The Story of Steele v Bulova: Trademarks on the Line, in* JANE C. GINSBURG & ROCHELLE C. DREYFUSS (eds.), INTELLECTUAL PROPERTY STORIES 395 (2006).

61 In the Anglo tradition, there are perhaps some parallels with the principle that domestic laws can be applied so as to prevent the use of an instrument of fraud in foreign markets. Some US courts have been more resistant to the opposite scenario: applying the Supreme Court's

a detailed jurisprudence on the application of the *Bulova* principle beyond its core facts.[62] In the Ninth Circuit, for example, to determine if there is a cause of action for trademark infringement a court balances a range of factors, including the degree of conflict with foreign law or policy, the nationalities of the parties, and the location of their principal places of business; how likely it is that the infringing party will comply with either US law or the law of any other foreign nation; the relative significance of the conduct on US commerce compared with the effects on other nations' commerce; the intentions of the defendant; and the relative importance of any violations of US rights compared with violations of rights under foreign trademark laws. As this list indicates, lower courts have recognized that the application of domestic laws to activities in foreign nations can be in tension with the sovereignty interests of those jurisdictions.

In contrast, these sovereignty concerns have not informed the analysis in the US copyright case law in which plaintiffs have secured relief under US law for activities in foreign territories. Indeed, the contrary position has sometimes expressly been adopted. The leading decision in the Second Circuit Court of Appeals concerned exploitation abroad of a movie that was made in breach of the plaintiff's copyright in a dramatic work.[63] The court ruled that as soon as the defendant received profits from the exploitation of the movie – either domestically or in foreign territories – a constructive trust was impressed upon those profits for the benefit of the copyright owner.[64] Most telling, however, was the court's acknowledgement that "The plaintiffs made no proof of foreign law, and we cannot say that the exhibition of the [film] abroad was a tort."[65] In other words, the court was indifferent to the content of the laws of the territories in which it was said that exploitation of the film breached the plaintiff's copyright in the underlying dramatic work.

It will be interesting to see if these extraterritorial applications of US copyright will survive the current "anti-extraterritorial" trend that has surfaced in recent US jurisprudence. In a case involving allegations of infringement of patented software, the Supreme Court refused to apply US patent law to

"zone of interests" test (*see Lexmark Int'l., Inc. v. Static Control Components, Inc.*, – U.S. –, 134 S.Ct. 1377, 188 L.Ed.2d 392 (2014)) a district court has recently held that the ownership of trademark rights under Mexican law does not provide a party with standing under the Lanham Act. *Belmora LLC v. Bayer Consumer Care AG*, – F.Supp.3d –, 2015 WL 518571 (E.D. Va., 2015).

62 *See Vanity Fair Mills v. Eaton Co.*, 234 F.2d 633 (2d Cir. 1956); *Wells Fargo & Co v. Wells Fargo Express Co.*, 556 F.2d 406 (9th Cir. 1977); *Star-Kist Foods, Inc. v. P.J. Rhodes & Co.*, 769 F.2d 1393 (9th Cir. 1985); *McBee v. Delica Co.*, 417 F.3d 107 (1st Cir. 2005).

63 *Sheldon v. Metro-Goldwyn Pictures Corp.*, 106 F.2d 45 (2d Cir. 1939) *aff'd*, 309 U.S. 390 (1940).

64 *Id.* at 52. 65 *Id.*

the copying and loading of software onto computers that occurred outside the United States, in circumstances in which the computers were to be distributed outside of the jurisdiction.[66] The Court emphasized that foreign conduct is usually the domain of foreign law, which "may embody different policy judgments about the relative rights of inventors, competitors, and the public."[67] The appropriate response, the Court opined, was to seek relief under the relevant foreign patent laws, observing that the canon against extraterritorial application of domestic laws reflects the "presumption that United States law governs domestically but does not rule the world."[68]

In *F. Hoffman-La Riche Ltd. v. Empagran*,[69] a decision from 2004, the Court had adopted a similar attitude to the extraterritorial application of US antitrust laws. Justice Breyer reasoned:

> Where foreign anticompetitive conduct plays a significant role and where foreign injury is independent of domestic effects, Congress might have hoped that America's antitrust laws, so fundamental a component of our own economic system, would commend themselves to other nations as well. But, if America's antitrust policies could not win their own way in the international marketplace for such ideas, Congress, we must assume, would not have tried to impose them, in an act of legal imperialism, through legislative fiat.[70]

Interestingly, this view has quite a lot in common with the dissenting opinion by Justice Douglas in the *Bulova* case.[71] There, Justice Douglas objected that the application of US law to acts done in Mexico would bring US law "into conflict with the laws and practices of other nations, fully capable of punishing infractions of their own laws."[72] It remains to be seen whether US courts will apply this concern for respect of other nations' sovereignty interests that are reflected in domestic intellectual property laws. The winding back of extraterritorial application of antitrust laws might, of course, provoke a cynic to observe that while some US courts are prepared to "export" its copyright laws, the same is not possible with antitrust laws – a source of principles that might serve to constrain overly expansive intellectual property rights. On the

66 *Microsoft Corp. v. AT & T Corp.*, 550 U.S. 437 (2007).

67 *See also Pennoyer v. Neff*, 95 U.S. 714, 722 (1877) ("no State can exercise direct jurisdiction and authority over persons or property without its territory.").

68 *Microsoft Corp. v. AT & T Corp.*, 550 U.S. 437, 454 (2007). The Court has recently reiterated this view in a case involving application of the U.S. Alien Foreign Tort Statute. *Kiobel v. Royal Dutch Petroleum Co.*, 133 S. Ct. 1659, 1664 (2013).

69 542 U.S. 155 (2004).

70 *Id.* at 169.

71 *See* Graeme W. Austin, *Intellectual Property Politics and the Private International Law of Copyright Ownership*, 30 BROOK. J INT'L L. 899, 907 (2005).

72 *Steele v. Bulova*, 344 U.S. 280, 292 (1952).

other hand, it is possible that some of the more general lessons from the recent cases constraining extraterritorial application of domestic law might also be applied to the copyright context.

While this kind of "single governing law" approach to international copyright infringement has a number of efficiency advantages, it may be insufficiently sensitive to the domestic sovereignty interests of the nation-states to which it applies. To the extent that copyright law represents a balancing of various interests, the single governing law approach risks overriding the expression of that balancing exercise that domestic copyright laws represent. Moreover, in a regional context, if one nation were to become a magnet for complex cross-border litigation, there is a further risk that *its* laws will dominate in intellectual property litigation, even with respect to conduct outside its borders. In the ASEAN context, this is hardly a blueprint for furthering values such as cooperation and mutual respect for different nations' distinct approaches to intellectual property policy.

8.3.3 *Justiciability of Foreign Copyright Infringement*

The approach to cross-border copyright infringement that best aligns with the principles of cooperation and mutual respect is for a domestic court to be willing to apply domestic laws to infringements within the forum, and the relevant foreign laws to the infringement in foreign territories. In *Lucasfilm*, the UK Supreme Court largely dismissed the relevance of concerns grounded in comity to the question of adjudication of foreign copyright infringement. It recognized *obiter* that such concerns might inform the adjudication of foreign registered rights, but, in the Court's analysis, no such concerns should inform the adjudication of copyright disputes. Indeed, the Court emphasized that the opposite is likely to be true, reasoning that "there are no issues of policy which militate against the enforcement of foreign copyright." There might be specific instances where foreign sovereignty interests are implicated: reference was made to a case from 1972, in which an English court had to engage with the copyright consequences of the international circulation of a book of which it was claimed that it had been first published through "underground" circulation in the former USSR.[73] But this is not the same as the claim that adjudication of infringement under foreign copyright laws *in itself* raises comity questions that should provoke a domestic court to decline jurisdiction.[74]

[73] *Bodley Head Ltd. v. Alec Flegon* [1972] 1 W.L.R. 680.

[74] *See, e.g.*, the very full and enlightening discussion of this point in Benedetta Ubertazzi, Exclusive Jurisdiction in Intellectual Property 128–136 (2012).

If *Lucasfilm* gains widespread acceptance in the common law world, foreign copyright infringement should, at the very least, be justiciable in the forum in which the defendant is domiciled. In theory, at least, this will mean that courts may be required to ascertain and apply the laws of a number of different foreign states. The approach is consistent with another strand of US copyright jurisprudence, in which courts have entertained the idea that foreign infringements of copyright are justiciable in a US forum. The leading case is the Second Circuit's decision in *Boosey & Hawkes Music Publishers, Ltd. v. Walt Disney*,[75] an old license/new media case. The music publisher alleged that the Walt Disney Company had infringed the copyright in Stravinsky's *Rite of Spring*, claiming that Disney's reissuing on videocassette of the movie *Fantasia* was not covered by the original synchronization license for the inclusion of the composition in the 1939 movie. Disney, which had released the movie in some nineteen foreign countries, argued that foreign copyright infringement was not justiciable in a US domestic court. If correct, this would have served to atomize the claim, forcing the music publisher to litigate in each of these countries.

The Second Circuit held that infringement of foreign copyrights was indeed justiciable. Even so, it remitted the case to the lower court for consideration of an interpretive question arising out of the original license; had *Disney* won on that issue, it may have demolished *Boosey & Hawkes'* claim altogether. In the meantime, the parties settled.[76] The Second Circuit's decision probably tilted the negotiation table in favor of the music publisher: the ability to consolidate its claims, domestic and foreign, would have made it easier for Boosey & Hawkes to pursue its claim. At the same time, by withholding from a final determination of the case, the court probably encouraged the parties to settle. Very helpfully, the court's ruling left both sides with much at stake – provoking the kind of settlement that can be expected to follow from the recognition that US courts will not force parties to litigate foreign copyright infringement cases forum by forum.

8.4 COOPERATION THROUGH CONFLICT OF LAWS

Implicit in the preceding discussion is the idea that conflict of laws rules reflect different kinds of values. The "no jurisdiction" approach is one that conceives of intellectual property as essentially localized disputes – and reflects a perception of intellectual property cases as requiring the kind of specialized knowledge that only the local practicing profession possess. However, this

75 145 F.3d 481 (2d Cir. 1998).

76 *See* Austin, *The Concept of Justiciability*, *supra* note 47, at 408.

approach also generates a paradox: the same respect for the kinds of domestic policy choices that might be reflected in the framing of distinct intellectual property regimes can lead to underenforcement of the very intellectual property rights that were created under the sovereign power that courts adopting this view seek to protect. As a matter of brute reality, some parties will not have the resources, in time, money, and the opportunity costs associated with litigation, to pursue claims *seriatim*. Moreover, as *Lucasfilm* illustrates, when the claim is against an individual defendant, intractable problems of enforcement are likely to arise.

In contrast, the "single governing law" approach has a number of advantages in terms of efficiency and simplicity. Court and litigants are not required to ascertain the content of the foreign laws. In addition, the parties are likely to have significant connections to the forum, making the global application of the forum's law more palatable, at least for the individual parties. On the other hand, single governing law approaches may be insufficiently respectful of the territoriality principle, and of the distinctions that may exist between different domestic copyright regimes. To be sure, in many cases there may not be *actual* distinctions between different legal systems – although, as the *Lucasfilm* case illustrates, meaningful distinctions can occasionally be quite important to the parties' rights and obligations. Moreover, as the US Supreme Court has recently emphasized, for one nation to attempt to "rule the world" – at least insofar as choice of law principles are concerned – is likely to prove unhelpful and unsustainable.

The approach in cases such as *Lucasfilm* and *Boosey & Hawkes* offers the possibility of a kind of "co-operation though conflict of laws." It requires the forum's door to be open to infringement claims involving foreign copyrights, which means that parties have an opportunity to get meaningful relief for infringement of their rights. At the same time, by insisting that *foreign laws apply to foreign infringement* the approach is respectful of distinctions between different countries. It is a coordinated approach that is well suited for sovereign nations that want to live together while respecting important distinctions between them. In an era in which there is increasing concern for the value of intellectual property, it also means that copyright owners have a better chance of achieving meaningful enforcement in cross-border commerce.

8.5 CONCLUSION

The emerging reality is likely to be a kind of "half-way house." In private litigation, private parties have significant control of the way issues are conceptualized and presented – a fortiori for alternative dispute resolution. We are likely to see parties selecting representative jurisdictions, and even to agree between themselves that the relevant laws are the same. Alternatively, we might see the development of principles and practices that enable courts to focus sharply on relevant distinctions between different regimes – where, for example, defenses are shaped slightly differently – so as to allow some conduct to be permissible in one country but not in others.

Particularly difficult questions may arise in the context of widespread or "ubiquitous" international piracy. In these circumstances the American Law Institute has proposed that the governing law should be the law with the closest relationship to the parties, focusing on factors such as the place of residence, the center of the parties' relationship, and so on.[77] This kind of simplification represents a compromise, in a document that, for the most part, hews closely to the principle of territoriality. With ubiquitous infringement, however, to start with a principle of territoriality, for all that it would represent respect for national differences, is likely to be too demanding for the litigants. In these kinds of cases, it may be worthwhile foregoing a little of the respectful recognition of different nations' copyright laws in favor of a principle that will facilitate meaningful enforcement.

77 ALI Principles of Intellectual Property, *supra* note 34: "§ 321 Law or Laws to Be Applied in Cases of Ubiquitous Infringement: (1) When the alleged infringing activity is ubiquitous and the laws of multiple States are pleaded, the court may choose to apply to the issues of existence, validity, duration, attributes, and infringement of intellectual property rights and remedies for their infringement, the law or laws of the State or States with close connections to the dispute, as evidenced, for example, by:

(a) where the parties reside;
(b) where the parties' relationship, if any, is centered;
(c) the extent of the activities and the investment of the parties; and
(d) the principal markets toward which the parties directed their activities.

(2) Notwithstanding the State or States designated pursuant to subsection (1), a party may prove that, with respect to particular States covered by the action, the solution provided by any of those States' laws differs from that obtained under the law(s) chosen to apply to the case as a whole. The court shall take into account such differences in determining the scope of liability and remedies."

9

Intellectual Property Remedies across Borders

Richard Garnett

9.1 INTRODUCTION

The theme of the chapters in this book is the "interoperability" of intellectual property law in the Association of Southeast Asian Nations (ASEAN) region in a context in which harmonization of substantive laws is unlikely to be achieved in the near future. One way of understanding interoperability may be through the prism of the private international law doctrine of comity, which encourages national courts to respect and give effect to the laws and judgments of other countries in appropriate circumstances. As Graeme Austin notes in his chapter[1] and as discussed later, courts in common law countries have become more willing in recent years to recognize claims involving foreign intellectual property rights and, to this extent, are fulfilling the aims of comity and hence, interoperability. Such developments may therefore be worthy of adoption in ASEAN countries more generally. Of course, however, these goals can be attained only where intellectual property rights owners have access to meaningful forms of relief in cross-border cases. Consequently, remedies are the focus of this chapter.

Historically the vast majority of intellectual property disputes have been wholly domestic in nature, concerning parties within a single national territory, rights conferred by the law of that territory, and infringements taking place there. Cross-border intellectual property disputes were rare and courts generally did not have to consider the application or adaptation of the existing rules to cases involving foreign elements. In particular, principles of private international law (jurisdiction, applicable law, and the recognition and

[1] Graeme Austin, *Cooperation through Conflict of Laws: The Justiciability of Cross-Border Copyright Infringement, in* ELIZABETH NG SIEW-KUAN & GRAEME AUSTIN (eds.), INTERNATIONAL INTELLECTUAL PROPERTY AND THE ASEAN WAY: PATHWAYS TO INTEROPERABILITY, Chapter 8.

enforcement of foreign judgments) infrequently arose in intellectual property cases compared to transnational contracts and torts.

The emergence of new forms of technology in the past twenty years combined with the greater mobility of goods and services has dramatically altered this position. Most importantly, the digital networked environment has created scope for simultaneous, multiterritorial communication of works and trade symbols with the consequent risk of globally widespread infringements of rights in such material.[2] Rights holders are now more exposed than ever to infringement by persons located in foreign countries. The fundamental problem is that, even if claimants have intellectual property protection under the laws of multiple countries, they may have serious difficulty in enforcing such rights.

The discussion that follows will concentrate on the relief that may be available to a claimant in a cross-border intellectual property dispute and the procedural strategies and techniques that may be employed by a defendant to frustrate the obtaining of redress. For the purposes of this chapter, the concept of "remedy" will focus on measures open to both claimants and defendants in the context of cross-border disputes.

The two most common remedies for claimants in intellectual property disputes for infringement of rights are compensatory damages and the injunction. To challenge ownership or validity of rights, a declaration is commonly sought. Each remedy will be considered separately for the purpose of examining the unique problems that arise in the transnational context and the relevance to interoperability.

9.2 DAMAGES

9.2.1 *Damages Claims: Local Intellectual Property Rights*

In the case of an action for damages for infringement of a statutory intellectual property right such as a trademark, copyright, or patent the forum court must first determine whether it has personal jurisdiction over the defendant. Where the defendant is a local resident or corporation carrying on business in the forum, personal jurisdiction is normally easy to satisfy under common law principles by service of the originating process on the defendant. Occasionally, however, the problem is that the defendant is located outside the territory of

[2] The American Law Institute, Intellectual Property: Principles Governing Jurisdiction, Choice of Law, and Judgments in Transnational Disputes 3 (2008) [hereinafter ALI Principles].

the forum court and in such a case the claimant must satisfy the statutory rules for service out of the jurisdiction. Such rules typically require a link between the forum court and the cause of action. In Commonwealth countries the most commonly relied upon grounds for service in intellectual property infringement cases are that the claim is based on infringement of a forum statute, that the infringement (classified as a tort) occurred in the forum, that damage was suffered there from an infringement wherever occurring, or that the subject matter concerns property in the forum.[3] In the United Kingdom there are also special rules of personal jurisdiction under the Brussels I Regulation (recast)[4] for defendants domiciled in a European Union (EU) member state.

Such grounds sound relatively generous to claimants but in practice they are of limited utility in a case of infringement of a forum intellectual property statute unless the claimant can also show that such infringement occurred *in the forum*. The reason for this conclusion is that in common law countries rights granted under intellectual property statutes are generally territorially limited: that is, an infringement action can be brought only where the claimant can show that the infringement took place in the forum. So, for example, a Singapore court can adjudicate a claim for infringement of a Singapore copyright only where the breach occurred in Singapore. This territorial limitation may be described as a "subject matter" jurisdiction or justiciability limitation on the power of courts to adjudicate actions for breach of local intellectual property laws.[5]

Note that where the intellectual property right is derived not from statute but from the common law, such as claims for passing off or breach of confidence, no such subject matter jurisdiction restriction applies and a claimant is entitled to effect service out of the jurisdiction on a foreign defendant where either the wrong occurred in the forum or damage was suffered there. In a commercial context, the damage ground, at least in Australian law, has been widely interpreted to embrace any loss of business or financial harm to the claimant in the forum.[6] Where a breach of confidence claim is framed in

3 *See, e.g.*, the Australian state of New South Wales, Uniform Civil Procedure Rules 2005, Sch. 6 (d), (e), (j), (r).

4 Regulation (EU) No. 1215/2012 of the European Parliament and of the Council of 12 December 2012 on the Jurisdiction and the Recognition and Enforcement of Judgments in Civil and Commercial Matters (recast), 2012 O.J. (L 351) 1.

5 *See, e.g.*, in Australia, Copyright Act 1968 (Cth) § 36(1). For a criticism of this principle, *see* J. FAWCETT & P. TORREMANS, INTELLECTUAL PROPERTY AND PRIVATE INTERNATIONAL LAW 323–327 (2d ed. 2011).

6 *Flaherty v. Girgis* (1985) 4 NSWLR 248 at 266.

contract, then service out of the jurisdiction is permissible where the contract was made or breached in the forum, was governed by forum law, or included a submission to the forum courts' jurisdiction.[7]

Hence, from the point of view of service out of the jurisdiction, pursuing a common law claim in the context of cross-border intellectual property infringement has some forensic advantages.

There has been much discussion therefore among commentators and national courts as to where infringement of an intellectual property right occurs. It is beyond the scope of this chapter to examine this question, although the outcome seems to depend very much on the particular right infringed with different analyses for trademark, patent, and copyright and also the way in which individual national intellectual property laws define the nature of the right in each case.

The requirement of territoriality, in providing that an actionable infringement must have occurred in the forum, reinforces the objective of interoperability by preventing courts from asserting jurisdiction over claims with insufficient connection to the forum. In that way, the "sovereignty interests of other nations" are respected.

9.2.2 *Damages Claims: Foreign Intellectual Property Rights*

The position is different where a claimant seeks to recover damages for a breach of its intellectual property rights existing under *foreign* laws. Until very recently in common law countries it was not possible to sue for infringement of a foreign intellectual property right, whether derived from statute or the common law. The court was said to lack "subject matter jurisdiction" over the claim or it was "nonjusticiable." There were typically two reasons given for such a limitation. The first was that foreign intellectual property rights were analogous to land under the common law principle in *British South Africa Co v. Companhia de Moçambique*,[8] which prevents a court adjudicating upon questions of title or trespass to foreign land. The second basis, which appears confined to Australian and US law,[9] was that the claim could not be heard because it engaged the "act of state" doctrine, which prevents a court adjudicating upon the acts of a foreign state's officials on its territory.

[7] *See, e.g.*, in the Australian state of New South Wales, Uniform Civil Procedure Rules 2005 Sch. 6 (b), (c), (h).

[8] [1893] AC 602 (HL).

[9] *See* the discussion of the UK Supreme Court in *Lucasfilm Ltd. v. Ainsworth* [2012] 1 AC 208 at [81]–[86].

The subject matter jurisdiction limitation had profound consequences for a claimant, particularly where it held intellectual property rights under the laws of multiple countries and was a victim of simultaneous, multiterritorial infringement, the potential for which has become much greater in the digital era. The claimant in such cases would have to bring separate actions in each country where infringement was alleged – obviously a highly impractical and expensive course of action. Recently, however, the position has changed: courts in England, New Zealand, and Hong Kong have now recognized a limited scope for claimants to sue for breaches of foreign statutory intellectual property rights. Such an approach offers the potential, for the first time, of claimants being able to consolidate all infringements in one action in a single forum, an outcome that has long been advocated by commentators on the grounds of access to justice and efficiency of litigation.[10]

In *Lucasfilm Ltd. v. Ainsworth*[11] the United Kingdom Supreme Court allowed a claimant to sue in England to recover damages for infringement of copyright committed outside the EU in breach of the copyright law of a non-EU state. In support of this conclusion, the court noted "the modern trend in favor of the enforcement of foreign intellectual property rights"[12] and that "there are no issues of policy which militate against the enforcement of foreign copyright" with states having "an interest in the international recognition and enforcement of their copyrights."[13]

A conclusion identical to that in *Lucasfilm* had been reached five years earlier by MacKenzie J of the High Court of New Zealand in *KK Sony Computer Entertainment v. Van Veen*,[14] with the court holding that claims for breaches of UK and Hong Kong copyright were justiciable in New Zealand. The correctness of this decision has been recently confirmed in *Jedis Ltd. v. Vodafone New Zealand Ltd.*,[15] where the court opined that a contrary conclusion "could potentially turn New Zealand into a sanctuary for international copyright pirates."[16]

While the *Lucasfilm* case was limited to infringements of foreign copyright, the logic of the decision suggested that infringements of all foreign statutory intellectual property rights should now be justiciable. Consequently, English and New Zealand courts have now accepted that claims for damages for

[10] *See, e.g.*, ALI PRINCIPLES, *supra* note 2, at Ch. 3 §§ 221–223; Fawcett & Torremans, *supra* note 5, at 311; Graeme Austin, *Copyright Infringement in New Zealand's Private International Law*, 19 *NZULR* 1, 12 (2000).

[11] [2012] 1 AC 208.

[12] *Id.* at [108].

[13] *Id.* at [109]; for a fuller discussion, *see* Austin, *supra* note 1.

[14] (2006) 71 IPR 179.

[15] [2012] NZHC 2448.

[16] *Id.* at [36].

infringements of foreign patents[17] and trademarks[18] may be instituted. Furthermore, in Hong Kong, it seems that a similar approach has been adopted,[19] with the Court of Appeal accepting that a claim for infringement of a foreign patent could be adjudicated in the forum.

The position in Australia regarding suits for damages for foreign statutory intellectual property rights remains unclear. In an early decision of the High Court of Australia, *Potter v. Broken Hill Proprietary Ltd.*,[20] the court refused to determine an action relating to the infringement of a patent granted in another state on the basis that the issue was nonjusticiable. The court reached this decision by two distinct, although related paths. Griffith CJ relied on the principle in the *Moçambique* case to the effect that a foreign patent was a form of immovable property, the title to or possession of which could not be determined by the forum. Griffith CJ and two other judges, Barton and O'Connor JJ, then applied the act of state doctrine as a further ground to deny justiciability, holding that the grant of a patent was an act of a foreign government on its own territory that was unreviewable. Arguably, however, the High Court's decision in *Potter* was influenced by the fact that the defendant had also raised the question of the *validity* of the patent in its defense a matter that, as discussed in the text that follows, remains beyond the subject matter jurisdiction of common law courts. Had the issue in *Potter* been one of infringement alone then possibly the court may have been willing to adjudicate.

While courts in later Australian decisions (in *obiter dicta*) have interpreted *Potter* as precluding all suits for damages for infringement,[21] at least one judge[22] has noted the distinction between infringement and validity questions (with infringement claims being justiciable). Moreover, there have also been other developments that suggest a possible willingness to reconsider the status of foreign statutory intellectual property rights in Australia. First, the state of New

17 *Stewart v. Franmara Inc. (No. 2)* [2012] NZHC 1771.

18 *Converse Inc. v. Conley (UK) Ltd. & Ors* [2012] EWPCC 24.

19 *See Esquel Enterprises Ltd. v. Tal Apparel Ltd.* [2006] HKCFA 34, although the proceeding was subsequently stayed on the ground that Hong Kong was an inappropriate forum.

20 (1906) 3 CLR 479; for a fuller discussion of this case *see* Richard Garnett, *Potter v. Broken Hill: Misuse of Precedent in Cross-Border IP Litigation*, in ANDREW T. KENYON, MEGAN RICHARDSON & SAM RICKETSON (eds.), LANDMARKS IN AUSTRALIAN INTELLECTUAL PROPERTY LAW 1 (2009).

21 *Tritech Technology Pty Ltd. v. Gordon* (2000) 48 *IPR* 52 at [27]; *Norbert Steinhardt & Son Ltd. v. Meth* (1960) 105 *CLR* 440 at 443.

22 *TS Production LLC v. Drew Pictures Pty. Ltd.* (2008) 172 *FCR* 473 at [16] (Finkelstein J). In *Re Interlego AG and Lego Australia Pty. Ltd. v. Croner Trading Pty. Ltd.* (1992) 25 *IPR* 65 at 98, Gummow J (with whom Black CJ and Lockhart J agreed) seemed to appreciate the limited scope of the *Potter* decision, noting that it 'says no more than that the grant of a patent is an act of sovereignty behind which the courts of another state will not go'.

South Wales has abolished the *Moçambique* rule by statute[23] and second, the High Court has indicated that it has "reserved for further consideration" the standing of the *Potter* decision.[24]

In Singapore, there have been no decisions on the issue although the 2003 report of the Singapore Academy of Law on choice of law in torts[25] assumed that actions for damages for infringement of foreign statutory intellectual property rights could not be brought in a Singapore court. The Academy recommended that such actions be justiciable and that the *Moçambique* principle be read down to permit infringement suits.[26] The Academy agreed that the increased scope for consolidation of claims for multiterritorial infringements in a single action in one forum was a valuable objective supporting such an approach.[27]

The wider scope for enforcement of foreign intellectual property rights is also relevant to the themes of interoperability and comity, as it shows a greater willingness by courts to recognize and give effect to foreign sovereign interests.

9.2.3 *Damages Claims: Discretionary Remedies for Defendants*

Finally, it should be noted that, even if the claimant can satisfy the rules of personal and subject matter jurisdiction of the forum discussed earlier, the defendant may have its own procedural remedies to thwart the claimant's recovery of damages. Most importantly, in common law countries, a defendant may seek a stay of local court proceedings on the ground that the local court is inappropriate to hear the matter. The precise formulation differs among countries, with English, Singapore, Hong Kong, and New Zealand law requiring the defendant to show that there is a more appropriate forum elsewhere for the case to be tried,[28] whereas in Australia the defendant must show that the local court is a "clearly inappropriate forum."[29]

In intellectual property cases, courts have generally taken the view that where a claimant has solely pleaded breach of a local right it is virtually impossible for the defendant to obtain a stay of court proceedings under either

[23] Jurisdiction of Courts (Foreign Land) Act 1989 (NSW).

[24] *Regie Nationale des Usines Renault SA v. Zhang* (2002) 210 *CLR* 491 at [76]; *Moti v. R* (2011) 245 *CLR* 456 at [49].

[25] Law Reform Committee of the Singapore Academy of Law, *Reform of the Choice of Law Rule Relating to Torts* (March 31, 2003), *available at* www.sal.org.sg/Lists/Law%20Reform%20Committee%20Reports/Attachments/16/reform_of_choice_of_law.pdf.

[26] *Id.* at [56]–[57], [111]. [27] *Id.* at [100].

[28] *See, e.g.*, in England, *Spiliada Maritime Corp v. Cansulex Ltd.* [1987] 1 AC 460; in Singapore, *JIO Minerals FZC v. Mineral Enterprises Ltd.* [2011] 1 *SLR* 391; and in New Zealand, *Club Mediterranée NZ v. Wendell* [1989] 1 *NZLR* 216.

[29] *Voth v. Manildra Flour Mills Pty. Ltd.* (1990) 171 *CLR* 538.

of the aforementioned tests. The reasoning is that the forum court is obviously better placed and equipped to adjudicate cases involving infringement of its own laws, when compared with a tribunal in a foreign country that must receive evidence of the foreign country's intellectual property law through the medium of expert witnesses. Such an approach not only puts the parties to greater expense but also carries a higher risk of inaccurate determinations as to the applicable law.[30]

Similarly, where an action is brought against a defendant resident in or carrying on business in the forum, even where both local and foreign infringements are pleaded, it would also be likely that a stay would be refused. The reasoning here is that a defendant residing and acting in its own jurisdiction – the forum – can hardly complain that it is an inappropriate place in which to be sued.

The operation of the doctrine of inappropriate forum in the context of a locally based defendant in which infringement of both local and foreign intellectual property rights is alleged can be seen in the recent English decision *Actavis Group HF v Eli Lilly*.[31] In *Actavis* the claimant sought declarations of noninfringement with respect to UK, French, German, Italian, and Spanish patents, all of which were derived from the same process and similar factual matrix. Eli had been validly served in England on the basis that it was carrying on business in the forum but argued nevertheless that England was an inappropriate forum to resolve the claims concerning the infringements of the foreign patents. The court rejected this argument, largely on the basis of the desirability of consolidation and avoiding fragmentation in cases involving multiterritorial infringements. England provided a single forum in which claims involving the five patents could be heard together, which would "reduce the likelihood of inconsistent decisions."[32] The strong links with the forum both in terms of the defendant's place of business and the fact that an infringement of a local intellectual property right had also been pleaded was enough to defeat the application to stay the claims for foreign infringement.[33]

Contrast these situations with the case of a claim being brought against a foreign-based defendant involving the infringement of *solely* foreign rights. Even if the hurdle of personal jurisdiction were overcome a court would be

30 *TS Production LLC v. Drew Pictures Pty. Ltd.* (2008) 172 *FCR* 473 at [21] (Finkelstein J) and at [44] Gordon J (with whom Stone J agreed); *Jedis Ltd. v. Vodafone New Zealand Ltd.* [2012] NZHC 2448 at [63]; *see also* Fawcett & Torremans, *supra* note 5, at 280, 287.

31 [2012] EWHC 3316.

32 *Id.* at [100].

33 *See also Lucasfilm Ltd. v. Ainsworth* [2008] EWHC 1878 (Ch) at [274] where a stay of English proceedings was refused in the case of a local defendant and alleged infringements of both local and foreign rights.

much more inclined to stay local proceedings in such a situation given the lack of connections to the forum and the greater expertise of a foreign court in applying its own law. Pertinently, in the *Jedis* case the New Zealand court noted that "different considerations may apply where [in an action for infringement of foreign rights] the defendant is outside the jurisdiction" as opposed to being "present or resident in the country where the claim was being heard."[34]

What the aforementioned principles on discretionary jurisdictional remedies show in relation to interoperability is that respect for a foreign sovereign's interests may also include deference to such country's courts in certain circumstances. Where a dispute solely involves intellectual property rights of that country and a defendant resident there, it would be an undue interference in the sovereignty of such a nation for the forum to retain jurisdiction.

9.2.4 *Damages Claims: Applicable Law*

Once the claimant has secured personal jurisdiction over the defendant with respect to its pleaded claims it must persuade the forum court to grant it relief under the law applicable to the action. In Commonwealth countries, such as Australia, England, and New Zealand, choice of law rules such as those that exist for torts and contracts do not apply in cases where infringements of statutory intellectual property rights are alleged. Consequently, claimants plead breaches of local laws only for local infringements (or foreign laws in the case of foreign infringements under the *Lucasfilm* principle), and the task for the court is to determine that there has been an infringement of the statute and that the infringement occurred in the country where the intellectual property right arose or was granted. The choice of law rule in such cases is the law of the country for which protection of the right is claimed (*lex loci protectionis*).[35] Such an approach applies in all cases in which a claimant seeks damages for infringement of a statutory right. So, for example, if a claimant sues for damages in Australia for infringement of an Australian copyright then Australian law will apply to all questions of liability and remedy.

The position is, however, less clear in the case of infringement of foreign statutory rights. If, for example, in England a claim for infringement of US

[34] *Jedis Ltd. v. Vodafone New Zealand Ltd* [2012] NZHC 2448 at [39]. In *Esquel Enterprises Ltd. v. Tal Apparel Ltd.* [2006] HKCFA 34 a stay was granted by a Hong Kong court of an action for infringement of a foreign patent, although both claimant and defendant had residential links with Hong Kong.

[35] *See, e.g.*, Commission Regulation 864/2007, on the Law Applicable to Non-Contractual Obligations (Rome II), art 8(1), 2007 O.J. (L 199) 40, 45.

copyright were pleaded, then US law would apply to the issue of liability as the law of the country of protection but on the issue of damages there appears to be a split in the common law world. In countries such as New Zealand and Canada a distinction is drawn between available heads of damages, which is a substantive matter, governed by the law applicable to liability, and the issue of quantification of damages, which is governed by the law of the forum as a procedural question.[36]

By contrast, in countries such as England, Australia, and most recently Singapore, the line is drawn differently between substantive and procedural matters on the matter of damages. According to the High Court of Australia in *John Pfeiffer Pty Ltd. v. Rogerson*,[37] all questions relating to the amount of damages are governed by the law of the cause of action. By contrast, matters regulating the mode or conduct of court proceedings are procedural and governed by forum law.[38] Similarly, art. 15(c) of the Rome II Regulation[39] provides that the applicable law of the noncontractual obligation shall "govern . . . the existence, nature and assessment of damage . . ." The effect of *John Pfeiffer* and the EU regulation is that both the questions of available heads of damages and assessment and quantification are resolved by the law applicable to the issue of liability. The Singapore Court of Appeal in *Goh Suan Hee v. Teo Cher Teck*,[40] while not finally deciding the issue,[41] expressed sympathy for the *Pfeiffer* view, saying that the traditional common law approach of treating quantification of damages as procedural was artificial and conducive to forum shopping.

The *Pfeiffer*/EU regulation approach has consequences for the conduct of litigation in those countries, as evidence must now be received from foreign law experts not only as to the substantive principles of intellectual property law but also regarding the quantum of damages a judge or jury would award in each case. Some commentators have suggested that such a process imposes an unreasonable forensic burden on courts and parties in terms of acquiring and analyzing expert evidence but those in favor of this approach argue that by seeking to replicate what the foreign court would do on the same facts this principle will help to prevent forum shopping.[42]

36 *Stewart v. Franmara Inc. (No. 2)* [2012] NZHC 1771; and *Somers v. Fournier* (2002) 60 OR (3d) 225.

37 (2000) 203 CLR 503 at [99].

38 *Id.*

39 For torts occurring before 11 January 2009 a position similar to that adopted in Canada and New Zealand applies: *see Harding v. Wealands* [2007] 2 AC 1.

40 [2010] 1 SLR 367 at [21].

41 *See The Reecon Wolf* [2012] 2 SLR 289 at [44].

42 *See generally*, Richard Garnett, Substance and Procedure in Private International Law 334–336 (2012).

The issue of the law applicable to the question of quantum of damages in the intellectual property context arose in the New Zealand decision *Stewart v. Franmara Inc (No. 2)*.[43] As noted previously, the court there accepted that it had the power to adjudicate a claim for infringement of a US patent. The claimant in that case also argued that US patent law allowed for an increase in damages where there had been willful behavior by the defendant and so any damages awarded by the New Zealand court should be doubled. The New Zealand court, however, found that that such provision in US law was a matter relating to a "measure or quantification of damages" and so was procedural and not applicable in the New Zealand proceedings. So, whereas a US court would have been able to award such increased damages had the matter been heard there, a New Zealand court could not do so. By contrast, an English, Australian, or Singaporean court would likely have applied the US provision as a substantive matter under their laws' narrower conception of procedure.

Where damages are sought for infringement of a nonstatutory intellectual property right, such as breach of confidence or passing off, the relevant choice of law rule will depend on the cause of action pleaded. Passing off is generally classified as a tort in common law systems and so the relevant choice of law rule for torts will be applied to determine recovery. In Australia this is the law of the place of the wrong, which in the context of passing off would be the law of the place where the goodwill of the claimant, misrepresentation by the defendant, and damage suffered by the claimant occurred.[44] In Singapore[45] and possibly New Zealand,[46] however, the "double actionability" rule applies, which provides that the law of the forum will apply where the wrong is "actionable" under both the law of the place of the wrong and the law of the forum, subject to an exception in favor of the law with the closest connection. In England, the law applicable to passing off is now determined by the Rome II Regulation. Article 6 of the Regulation identifies the law applicable to an action for "unfair competition" and provides that where an act of unfair competition affects exclusively the interests of a specific competitor then the rule in art. 4 applies, which is the law of the country where damage occurs.

43 [2012] NZHC 1771.

44 Fawcett & Torremans, *supra* note 5, at 870.

45 *EFT Holdings Inc v. Marinteknik Shipbuilders (S) Pte. Ltd.* [2014] 1 *SLR* 860.

46 The double actionability rule was endorsed by the High Court in *Baxter v. RMC Group plc* [2003] 1 *NZLR* 304, but in later cases it has been suggested that the law of the place of the wrong may apply as an alternative choice of law rule: *see Waterhouse v. Contractors Bonding Ltd.* [2012] NZHC 566 at [38].

In the case of breach of confidence, the claim may be classified as either contractual or equitable in nature depending on the facts. If characterized as contractual, then, under common law rules,[47] the law governing the contract will be applied, which will be the law chosen by the parties, and if no choice is made, the law with which the contract is most closely connected. If breach of confidence is regarded as an equitable right, then in Australia, New Zealand, and England the law of the forum would be applied, although in Singapore, owing to the influence of the work of the scholar Tiong Min Yeo,[48] the law of the closest analogous cause of action would most likely govern, which may be contractual or tortious, depending on the specific facts.

The complexity of the aforementioned rules on applicable law may pose a challenge to ASEAN courts and legislatures as they seek to develop a system of interoperability or coordination between their intellectual property laws. The trend, however, is clearly in favor of wider application of and greater deference to foreign law, which again is consistent with the idea of respect for other sovereigns.

9.3 INJUNCTIVE RELIEF

9.3.1 *Jurisdiction*

Another common remedy in infringement cases is an injunction to restrain the defendant from breaching the claimant's intellectual property right. Personal jurisdiction will again be established under common law principles where the defendant is resident, present for service, or carrying on business in the forum. Analogously, there have been a number of Australian cases in which local defendants have been the subject of injunction orders aimed at restraining the advertising of infringing material on foreign websites directed at Australian consumers.[49] If the defendant resides abroad then the claimant will have to satisfy the rules for service out of the jurisdiction, although in some common law jurisdictions there is an additional ground that the order is sought

[47] In England the matter is now governed by Commission Regulation 593/2008, on the Law Applicable to Contractual Obligations (Rome I), O.J. (L177) 6 which produces results broadly similar to that at common law.

[48] YEO TIONG MIN, CHOICE OF LAW FOR EQUITABLE DOCTRINES (2004).

[49] *ACCC v. Hughes* [2002] FCA 570; *ACCC v. Purple Harmony* [2001] FCA 1062; *see also Christian v. Société des Produits Nestlé SA (No 2)* [2015] FCAFC 153 at [47].

to restrain a wrong that has been committed or may be committed in the forum.[50]

A serious problem that is often encountered in the context of injunctions is that service of process outside the jurisdiction may be dismissed on the basis that any order subsequently made by the forum court could not be enforced and so would be futile. As will be discussed below at 9.6.2, it is still the case that in the majority of common law countries injunctive relief granted by foreign courts is not enforceable. The concern is that, unlike an award of damages, enforcement of an injunction may require judicial supervision and oversight that a court feels less willing and able to perform in the case of foreign orders. While service out will not automatically be refused in such cases, "the fact that an injunction granted . . . may prove difficult or even impossible to enforce . . . is a material consideration to be weighed against other circumstances relevant to the exercise of the court's discretion."[51] To strengthen a service out application in an injunction case, therefore, a claimant may seek to provide evidence (if it can be obtained) that the foreign court would enforce any injunctive relief awarded by the forum court.

Alternatively, the claimant may seek parallel or concurrent injunctive relief in multiple jurisdictions. In a recent case involving both Australia and Singapore, a software development manager employed by an Australian company (Bluescope) is alleged to have stolen trade secrets for use in her new role in Singapore. An injunction was granted by the Federal Court in Australia to restrain the former employee's use of the materials and now parallel injunctive relief has been sought in Singapore with the same objective. Parallel or concurrent injunction applications can be effective in a situation such as *Bluescope* where the local and foreign intellectual property rights are not territorially limited, such as in passing off and breach of confidence. Where, however, the claimant seeks an injunction to restrain infringement of a statutory intellectual property right such as a trademark or patent granted under the law of another country, such relief can be awarded only where the *Lucasfilm* principle is followed. In countries such as Australia and Singapore, which have not yet recognized such a power, the position is less clear, although equitable remedies such as injunctions have long been recognized as an exception to the *Moçambique* principle, which may provide another basis.[52] If a court in those countries were, however, to refuse to issue an injunction on justiciability grounds then

[50] *See, e.g.*, in the Australian state of New South Wales, Uniform Civil Procedure Rules 2005 Sch 6 (n).
[51] *Humane Society International Inc. v. Kyodo Senpaku Kaisha Ltd.* [2006] FCAFC 116 at [25].
[52] *Tritech Technology Pty. Ltd. v. Gordon* (2000) 48 IPR 52 at [28].

parallel and concurrent relief could be granted only if the claimant could show an infringement of local intellectual property rights in each jurisdiction in which an injunction was sought.

9.3.2 *Applicable Law*

The question of applicable law and injunctive relief has lately become more complex. First, it is universally accepted that in the case of interlocutory or interim injunction applications, the existence or availability of such relief is considered a procedural matter and governed by the law of the forum.[53] The reason for this conclusion is that interlocutory relief is part of the procedural machinery of a court and it would be practically inconvenient (if not impossible in some cases) if the court had to apply a remedy that did not exist within its own arsenal. The same analysis applies in the case of freezing or search orders.

Yet foreign law is not entirely irrelevant in interlocutory injunction cases. Where the injunction is sought to restrain infringement of a foreign tort, contract, or intellectual property right then the law applicable to the obligation will be applied to determine whether a breach has occurred, at least to the level of an arguable case. Once this requirement has been met, forum law is then applied to determine whether an interlocutory injunction should be granted on the facts, by reference to matters such as the balance of convenience.[54]

The position with respect to final injunctions, however, is less clear. Historically such relief has always been governed by forum law because of its origin in the medieval equitable jurisdiction based on conscience. Hence, even where foreign law governs the substantive cause of action, an injunction will be granted only if the conditions under forum law for its being ordered are satisfied.[55] Equally, an injunction will not be granted by the forum court even where it would have been issued under the law of the obligation.[56] More recent commentary has, however, cast doubt on this view,[57] arguing that equitable rights and remedies should no longer be automatically governed by forum law, but instead be subjected to the law of the nearest analogous cause of action. So, for example, in the case of an injunction sought to restrain an act of passing off or an infringement of a statutory intellectual property right, the

53 Garnett, *supra* note 42, at 299. 54 *Id.*
55 *Baschet v. London Illustrated Standard Co.* [1900] 1 Ch. 73.
56 *Warner Bros Pictures Inc. v. Nelson* [1937] 1 KB 209.
57 Yeo, *supra* note 48; and Adrian Briggs, *Conflict of Laws and Commercial Remedies*, in Andrew Burrows & Edwin Peel (eds.), Commercial Remedies: Current Issues and Problems 271 (2003).

law to be applied to determine whether the injunction should be granted on the facts should be the same law as would resolve the question of substantive liability. A similar position would therefore apply as in the case of damages under English, Australian, and Singaporean law.

The injunction is a common and important remedy in intellectual property cases but a traditional problem in cases involving foreign-based defendants has been enforcement. The needs of interoperability in the ASEAN region however, may be furthered by an increased use of parallel or concurrent relief as in the *Bluescope* case, and a greater willingness to apply foreign law in applications for injunctive relief.

9.4 DECLARATIONS AS TO VALIDITY OR EXISTENCE OF INTELLECTUAL PROPERTY RIGHTS

9.4.1 *Jurisdiction*

Occasionally the question of the *validity or subsistence* of a statutory intellectual property right will be raised, for example, where a claimant seeks a declaration that the defendant is not the owner of a copyright or that its patent was invalidly granted. Alternatively, the question of validity or subsistence may be raised by way of a declaration in a cross-claim in an action for infringement of an intellectual property right. An example of this situation is in a suit for breach of license where the licensor sues the licensee for breach and the licensee alleges in its cross-claim that the primary intellectual property right that is the subject of the license is invalid or does not exist. These situations may be distinguished from cases in which the issue of validity or existence arises "incidentally," such as in the context of a breach of license suit where the validity of the license is assumed for the purposes of the determination.

While the UK Supreme Court in the *Lucasfilm* case noted that there was a trend in favor of allowing suits to be brought for infringements of foreign intellectual property rights, where a party raises the issue of subsistence or validity, the position at common law is less clear. Under EU law, art. 24(4) of the Brussels I Regulation (recast) provides that where an issue of validity or registration of an intellectual property right that is granted by an EU member state such as a patent or trademark is raised, then the court of the state in which the right was granted will have exclusive jurisdiction over the question. The rationale for this view is that only the courts of the state in which the register is held have the power to make effective and enforceable orders in the case of invalidity being found. In the case of other intellectual property rights, however, such as copyright, which are not created by sovereign grant, EU law would appear to allow a claim challenging existence or ownership to be raised in a country other than where the right arose. In terms of the common law position, the Supreme Court in *Lucasfilm* suggested, *obiter*, that as regards registered rights, the same approach should be adopted as applies under EU law.[58] In relation to copyright, the court did not express a clear view, but noted pointedly that "the substantial dispute" in that case was about infringement rather than subsistence.[59]

In other common law countries, there seems to be a clear consensus that validity and existence questions concerning *all* foreign intellectual property rights are not justiciable. It will be recalled that in *Potter* the High Court of Australia's decision not to adjudicate a foreign patent infringement claim was at least partly motivated by the fact that the validity of the patent was put in issue. In two more recent Australian decisions, courts have suggested that claims for declarations as to ownership and existence of foreign copyright are not justiciable,[60] with Finkelstein J in *TS Production LLC v. Drew Pictures Pty. Ltd.*[61] noting that this was also the position under US law. Further in that case,[62] the fact that the Australian court could not determine the question of ownership of US copyright and a US court could not resolve the same issue concerning Australian copyright meant that a stay of Australian court proceedings on appropriate forum grounds had to be rejected. The majority's rejection of the application by the claimant for an antisuit injunction, restraining the defendant from pursuing its action in the United States, can logically be explained on the same basis. A proceeding in a court (whether local or foreign) can hardly be described as "vexatious and oppressive," "inappropriate," or "unconscionable" where that court was the only tribunal capable of giving the requested relief.[63]

In Singapore, the 2003 Academy of Law report into choice of law recommended adoption of the EU law approach, with claims for subsistence and ownership of foreign copyright being justiciable but not allegations questioning the validity or existence of registered rights.[64]

58 *Lucasfilm Ltd. v. Ainsworth* [2012] 1 AC 208 at [101], [106].

59 *Id.* at [103].

60 *Top Plus Pty. Ltd. v. K Square Pty. Ltd.* [2009] FMCA 900 at [40], [43]; and *TS Production LLC v. Drew Pictures Pty. Ltd.* (2008) 172 FCR 433 at [15], [19] (Finkelstein J).

61 *TS Production LLC v. Drew Pictures Pty. Ltd.* (2008) 172 *FCR* 433 at [18], citing *Vanity Fair Mills Inc. v. T Eaton Co. Ltd.* 234 F. 2d 633 at 647 (2d Cir. 1956).

62 *Id.*

63 Compare this analysis with *id.*, at [44] where the majority spoke simply of the "different rights in issue" in the US and Australian proceedings as being the principal basis for refusal of the order.

64 *See supra* note 25, at [111]

The different treatment of issues of validity and infringement of foreign intellectual property rights can, however, lead to problems of fragmentation of litigation. While it was argued in the preceding text that the goals of efficiency and consolidation of litigation are enhanced by allowing a claimant to bring all claims for multiterritorial infringements in a single proceeding, this objective cannot be achieved once validity or existence of a right is placed in contention and the court has no power to resolve the issue. Courts have traditionally had two options in this situation: they may either allow the infringement action to proceed and stay or ignore the defendant's cross-claim on validity or stay the entire action.

The advantage of the first approach is that the claimant retains the opportunity to have its rights vindicated by a court and denies the defendant the possibility of using a validity plea as a "Trojan horse" to undermine the claimant's action. The disadvantage of this approach, however, is that if proceedings for infringement go forward in the absence of consideration of the cross-claim, the defendant may still commence separate proceedings in the country where the right was granted seeking a declaration of invalidity. The existence of such multiple proceedings creates a real risk of inconsistent results: a court in country A finds an infringement of a patent granted by country B but country B's courts then hold the patent to be invalid. Such a situation obviously leaves the parties in a state of disarray as to their rights.

The English courts have responded to this dilemma in EU law cases by taking the pragmatic approach of staying any infringement proceedings where validity of a registered right in another EU country is raised as an issue on the basis that the English court no longer has any subject matter jurisdiction over the infringement claim.[65] Other EU courts, however, have not followed this approach and have allowed infringement actions to proceed notwithstanding that the issue of validity of a foreign registered right is raised but cannot be determined.[66]

The conflict has not been clearly resolved subsequent to the 2006 decision of the European Court of Justice (ECJ) in the *GAT* case.[67] In *GAT*, the ECJ held that where an issue as to the validity of a patent granted in another member state arose either in proceedings to invalidate the patent or as a defense to an infringement action, the court of the state in which the patent was registered has exclusive jurisdiction under art. 22(4) of the 2001 Brussels

65 *Coin Controls Ltd. v. Suzo International (UK) Ltd.* [1999] Ch. 33.

66 *See, e.g., Palamz v. Boston Scientific BV* [1998] FSR 199 at 21 (Hague DC 6th Sess. 1997).

67 Case C-4/03, *Gesellschaft fur Antriebstechnik mbH & Co KG* (GAT) *v. Lamellen und Kupplungsbau Beteiligungs KG* (LuK), 2006 E.C.R. I-6509; *see also* Case C-539/03, *Roche Nederland BV v. Primus*, 2006 E.C.R. I-6535.

I Regulation to determine the matter. While English courts have apparently interpreted this conclusion as an endorsement of the *Coin Controls* principle,[68] commentators have disagreed,[69] saying that the ECJ said nothing about the status of *infringement* proceedings in *GAT*. Instead, the effect of the decision is to require a court before which infringement proceedings are brought, in which the validity of a registered right is raised, to stay its proceedings to allow the court in the state of registration first to resolve the question of validity. After such determination has been made the infringement proceedings may resume in the first court – unless of course the right has been declared invalid. Such an approach is different from *Coin Controls* in that the court before which the infringement claim has been brought still retains jurisdiction over the matter. According to this view, the ECJ in the *GAT* case had authorized the splitting of proceedings between member state courts on the issues of infringement and validity.[70]

This excursus into EU law may seem slightly remote from the concerns of ASEAN countries. Yet, now that *Lucasfilm* and later cases have created the potential for courts to adjudicate infringements of foreign intellectual property rights, similar jurisdictional conflicts between courts in different countries over validity and infringement issues are likely to be inevitable and the EU experience may be instructive. Managing such jurisdictional conflicts would seem to be a key component of any scheme of interoperability or cooperation between regional nations.

9.4.2 *Applicable Law*

The applicable law rules in the case of declarations are similar to those governing injunctions. The issue was recently considered in the English decision *Actavis Group HF v. Eli Lilly*.[71] *Actavis* concerned claims for declarations of noninfringement of foreign patents and the court held that while foreign law

68 *See, e.g.*, *Knorr-Bremse Systems for Commercial Vehicles Ltd. v. Haldex Brake Products GmbH* [2008] EWHC 156 (Pat).

69 Fawcett & Torremans, *supra* note 5, at 371; and Adrian Briggs, *Jurisdiction over Defences and Connected Claims*, LMCLQ 447 (2006).

70 Note that in the later case of *Solvay SA v. Honeywell Fluorine Products Europe BV* (Case C-616/10, *Solvay SA v Honeywell Fluorine Products Europe BV*, 2012 E.C.R. I-445) the ECJ held that it would be permissible for a member state court to rule on the validity of a foreign patent as a preliminary question in a proceeding for interim relief and that such a ruling would not have *erga omnes* effect and require the cancellation of the patent by the office in the country of registration.

71 [2012] EWHC 3316 (Pat).

applied to determine whether the defendant's acts amounted to an infringement of each patent,[72] English law, as the law of the forum governed the question of whether the court had power to grant declaratory relief.[73]

9.5 CONTRACTUAL LICENSES

Much of what has been said above also applies to contractual licenses of intellectual property rights. In the license context, the claimant's remedies will normally be damages for breach of contract, specific performance to compel adherence to the license, or an injunction to restrain infringement. For the purposes of establishing personal jurisdiction, service out in contract cases is typically permissible where the contract is made or breached in the forum, governed by forum law, or involves a submission to the forum court's jurisdiction.

An issue that can arise in the context of international contracts (including licenses of intellectual property rights) is where the parties have included a jurisdiction or arbitration clause. Such clauses are often inserted in contracts to limit jurisdictional risk by stipulating in advance where, and before which tribunal, suits concerning the parties' rights and obligations under the license may be brought.

In the context of jurisdiction clauses, there is a well-accepted distinction between "exclusive" and "nonexclusive" jurisdiction clauses. Where a clause is a foreign exclusive jurisdiction clause, that is, where it identifies a forum in a foreign country for dispute resolution and precludes litigation elsewhere, then common law courts will normally stay local court proceedings in favor of trial proceeding in the foreign court unless the claimant can show exceptional reasons.[74] One such reason may be where the forum legislature requires the action to be brought in the forum courts by way of an overriding mandatory rule.[75] Such legislative rules are commonly enacted to protect persons with perceived lesser bargaining power, such as consumers and employees, but have less application in the intellectual property context.

There is an arguably even stronger legal regime for enforcement of arbitration agreements under the widely adopted New York Convention.[76] Where a party brings court proceedings in breach of an arbitration agreement, such proceedings will be stayed unless the agreement is found to be null and void, inoperative, or incapable of being performed.[77] An exception to arbitrability

[72] *Id.* at [31]. [73] *Id.* at [30]. [74] *The Eleftheria* [1970] P 94.

[75] *See*, in the Australian context, *Akai Pty. Ltd. v. People's Insurance Co. Ltd.* (1996) 188 CLR 418.

[76] United Nations Convention on the Recognition and Enforcement of Foreign Arbitral Awards, June 7, 1959, 330 UNTS 38.

[77] *Id.* art. II.

may, however, arise if the respondent seeks to challenge the validity of a registered right such as a patent. An arbitrator would have no power to determine this question, which could be resolved only by the courts in the state of registration, unless the parties otherwise agreed and the effect of any ruling on validity was only *inter partes* and not *erga omnes*.[78]

Courts' willingness to give effect to foreign jurisdiction and arbitration clauses in intellectual property licenses is also a key element in any system of interoperability between national legal orders, as it demonstrates confidence in the ability of the foreign tribunal to adjudicate the matter.

9.6 RECOGNITION AND ENFORCEMENT OF FOREIGN JUDGMENTS

A particular issue of importance to remedies in cross-border intellectual property cases is the recognition and enforcement of foreign judgments. The issue arises because often the defendant (particularly if served abroad) has no assets in the forum and the claimant must take any judgment award to a foreign country and execute against the property of the defendant there. In the case of foreign awards of damages Commonwealth countries (except for Canada) follow largely the same principles for recognition and enforcement based on 1933 UK legislation,[79] which purported to codify the common law.

In essence, for a foreign judgment to be recognized in a Commonwealth country (other than Canada) the defendant must have been either present for service in or have submitted to the jurisdiction of the foreign court. Submission in this context refers to active participation in the merits of the proceeding as opposed to simply appearing to contest the jurisdiction of the foreign court. Canadian courts and legislatures have taken an alternative approach: a foreign judgment may be enforced in the Canadian forum where the defendant had a "real and substantial connection" with the foreign jurisdiction.[80]

9.6.1 *Finality*

Furthermore, for a foreign judgment to be recognized, it must have been "final and conclusive." Finality in this context means that the judgment is not capable of being varied or amended by the court that pronounced it. The practical effect of this requirement is that judgments for interlocutory or injunctive

[78] *See Tomolugen Holdings Ltd. v. Silica Investors Ltd.* [2016] 1 SLR 373 at [96]–[98] (SGCA). I am grateful to Mark Lim, of the Intellectual Property Office of Singapore, for alerting me to this reference.

[79] Foreign Judgments (Reciprocal Enforcement) Act 1933 (Eng.).

[80] *Morguard Investments v. De Savoye* [1990] 3 SCR 1077 at 1107; Court Jurisdiction and Proceedings Transfer Act adopted in British Columbia, Saskatchewan and Nova Scotia.

relief are generally not enforceable across borders. Yet a line of authority has developed in common law countries whereby interim relief granted in other common law jurisdictions may be recognized by the granting of equivalent or parallel relief in the country of enforcement. So, for example, a freezing order was issued by an Australian court in support of similar relief granted by a Bahamas tribunal over the defendant's assets worldwide, including assets in Australia, to secure local assets in anticipation of a later application to enforce a Bahamas judgment debt in Australia.[81]

9.6.2 *Monetary Sum*

The other traditional common law requirement for recognition and enforcement of foreign judgments is that the judgment requires the defendants to pay a sum of money to the claimant, such as an award of damages. In situations where final nonmonetary relief such as injunctions, declarations, and orders for specific performance has been sought, this principle has historically been rigidly observed. In Canada, however, it has been recently suggested by the Supreme Court in *Pro Swing Inc v. Elta Golf Inc*[82] that the "fixed sum" rule is outdated in a time of increased technological change and modern communications and when national courts need to cooperate with one another in the resolution of transnational disputes. Consequently, in *Pro Swing* it was held that a foreign nonmonetary judgment may now be enforced in Canada where the foreign order (1) was clear and specific both as to its intended territorial scope and the obligations that it imposes on the defendant and (2) does not impose a burden on the Canadian justice system or the rights of third parties.[83]

The application of those principles to the facts of *Pro Swing* is useful to consider given that it was a cross-border intellectual property case. The claimant in *Pro Swing* was based in the United States and sued an Ontario-based defendant in a US court for trademark infringement arising from the defendant's alleged use of the claimant's mark on its website that was accessible to customers in the United States. The parties subsequently entered a settlement agreement that was endorsed by a consent decree of the US court. The decree restrained the defendant from marketing or selling golf clubs on its website that bore the claimant's trademark or a confusing similar variation of the mark. The claimant then brought a motion for contempt of court, alleging that the defendant was in violation of the consent decree, and the US court granted the further order. The claimant then sought enforcement of both the consent decree and

[81] *Davis v. Turning Properties Pty. Ltd.* (2005) 222 ALR 676.
[82] [2006] 2 SCR 612 (Can.). [83] *Id.* at [30].

the contempt order in Canada but a majority of the Supreme Court refused the application on the grounds that the orders were quasi-criminal in nature and the intended territorial scope of the injunctive relief was too uncertain. Specifically, there was no express provision in the settlement agreement that the restraint on the defendant was to operate worldwide and the court would not imply such a restriction, given that no "worldwide trademark protection" currently exists.

Despite a majority of the court in *Pro Swing* opting not to enforce the US injunction, the significance of this case is still great. For the first time a common law court has accepted that final injunctions, specific performance orders, and declarations in intellectual property cases may be recognized and enforced across borders. Courts in subsequent Canadian decisions have generally embraced the liberalization of *Pro Swing* and shown a willingness to enforce final nonmonetary relief. For example, in *United States of America v. Yemec*[84] the Ontario Court of Appeal enforced a permanent injunction issued by a US court. The injunction restrained a Canadian company from selling lottery tickets by telemarketing to US consumers allegedly in breach of the US Federal Trade Commission Act. The Canadian court found that the terms of the foreign injunction were clear and specific, in that "it would be obvious to the defendants what they cannot do in the US"[85] and that "a complete prohibition of telemarketing aimed at people in the United States is [not] unfair or unreasonable."[86] Injunctions to restrain breaches of consumer protection laws are analogous to orders prohibiting passing off or infringement of trademarks, and so this case has clear relevance to the cross-border intellectual property context.

Furthermore, a version of the *Pro Swing* principle has been adopted in the Australia–New Zealand Agreement on Trans-Tasman Court Proceedings and Regulatory Enforcement,[87] where final and conclusive nonmonetary judgments from each country may now be enforced in the other country's courts.[88] Principles of EU law have also long provided for recognition and enforcement of nonmonetary relief where it emanates from an EU or European Economic Area country.[89] It will be interesting to see if the foregoing developments lead

[84] (2010) 100 OR (3d) 321 (Can.); *see also Hartzog v. McGriskin* (2010) ONSC 5618 (Can.).
[85] *Id.* at [47]. [86] *Id.* at [48].
[87] Agreement between the Government of Australia and the Government of New Zealand on Trans-Tasman Court Proceedings and Regulatory Enforcement, [2013] ATS 32 (Austl.).
[88] *See* Trans-Tasman Proceedings Act 2010 (Cth) s 66 (Austl.).
[89] Commission Regulation 1215/2012, on Jurisdiction and the Recognition and Enforcement of Judgments in Civil and Commercial Matters (recast), art. 36(1), 2012 O.J. (L 351) 14.

to a more general trend in common law countries to recognize and enforce foreign final nonmonetary relief, which will be significant given the importance of such orders in intellectual property cases.

9.6.3 *Judgments Concerning Foreign Rights*

A difficult and largely unexplored topic in common law jurisdictions is the question of whether a court in country A is required to enforce a judgment of a court in country B, which, for example, has awarded damages for infringement of a patent registered in country A or C. If, after *Lucasfilm* and subsequent decisions, common law courts now have subject matter jurisdiction to adjudicate claims for infringements of foreign intellectual property rights, the issue of enforcing such judgments across borders is also likely to arise. There appears to be little direct authority on the question although both Australian legislation[90] and the editors of Dicey, Morris, and Collins on the Conflict of Laws[91] suggest that a judgment in which title or possession to "immovable property" in a foreign country was determined is not entitled to recognition and enforcement in the forum. Such a principle encapsulates the *Moçambique* rule discussed earlier but if the approach in *Lucasfilm* was adapted to the foreign judgment context, then presumably a foreign judgment for damages for infringement of a foreign intellectual property right would not fall within the scope of the prohibition. Arguably, to give full effect to the *Lucasfilm* principle, a corresponding change must be made at the stage of recognition and enforcement of foreign judgments.

In the case of claims for declarations as to invalidity and existence of foreign intellectual property rights, the problem of enforcement does not directly arise because no execution against property has to occur. A court, however, may be asked to "recognize" such a foreign judgment in the context of a plea of *res judicata* or *Anshun* estoppel. In such a circumstance the issue would arise: if, for example, an English court issued a declaration that no copyright subsisted under Singapore law with respect to a work as between parties A and B, then a Singapore court would have to determine whether it would recognize such a judgment in the context of proceedings in Singapore between A and B for infringement of the same copyright. Consistent with the analysis in *Dicey, Morris and Collins*, the Singapore court would not have to give effect to the English judgment as it concerned title to immovable property outside

[90] Foreign Judgments Act 1991 (Cth) § 7(3)(b) (Austl.). The position is similar as between Australia and New Zealand under the Trans-Tasman Proceedings Act 2010 (Cth) § 72(1) (Austl.).

[91] Dicey, Morris & Collins, The Conflict of Laws rule 47(2) (15th ed. 2012).

the country of origin but if a consensus were to develop among common law jurisdictions that subject matter jurisdiction exists with respect to claims concerning the existence of foreign copyrights, the position may change.

The recent draft Hague Convention on the Recognition and Enforcement of Foreign Judgments[92] may offer some scope for greater enforcement of judgments concerning foreign intellectual property rights. The draft text contains provisions allowing recognition where the foreign judgment concerns a question of infringement or validity of copyright under the law of the country of origin[93] or infringement of a registered right under such law.[94] Where the foreign judgment, however, rules on the validity of registered rights outside the country of origin it need not be recognized.[95] Yet, judgments for infringement or validity of copyright or infringement of registered rights outside the country of origin may still be recognized under the general grounds of recognition in art. 5(1)(a)–(e), including the situation where, for example, the defendant is a habitual resident of the country of origin.[96] The draft text also provides for recognition of final nonmonetary judgments,[97] a position consistent with the *Pro-Swing* case described earlier.

9.7 CONCLUSION

It is obvious that the topic of recognition and enforcement of foreign judgments is central to the theme of interoperability between legal orders. There can be no greater demonstration of a country's respect for another sovereign's legal system than a willingness to enforce its judgments and orders. The trend both in common law countries and international instruments is for increased recognition that hopefully will prove instructive to ASEAN countries as they devise new schemes of cooperation in the field of intellectual property rights.

92 The text of the draft Hague Convention on the Recognition and Enforcement of Foreign Judgments is *available at* https://assets.hcch.net/docs/42a96b27–11fa-49f9–8e48-a82245aff1a6.pdf.

93 *Id.* at art. 5(1)(l).

94 *Id.* at art. 5(1)(k).

95 *Id.* at art. 6(a).

96 *Id.* at art. 5(1)(a).

97 *Id.* at art. 3(1)(b).

PART III

INTELLECTUAL PROPERTY INTEROPERABILITY AT THE ADMINISTRATIVE/LEGISLATIVE LEVEL

The five chapters in this part examine the possibilities and impediments to agency cooperation. The chapters also foreshadow the comparative analysis in the later chapters. The first four chapters propose interoperability models in respect of copyright, geographical indications, trademark, and designs. The final chapter focuses on administrative issues.

First, in Chapter 10 Pisawat Sukonthapan advances a Thai perspective on the administration of the copyright system. Centering discussion on collective rights management, Professor Sukonthapan cautions that the diversity in collective management of musical works and performance rights across ASEAN member states is likely to pose impediments to the efficient management of these rights and have undesirable effects on local rights holders, as well as the overall development of a nation. She concludes that possible areas for enhancing the interoperability between and among the domestic copyright systems of ASEAN members include the ASEAN initiative of developing a copyright recordation system and an efficient copyright collective management system.

In Chapter 11, Lê Thi Thu Ha and Delphine Marie-Vivien offer an ASEAN perspective on geographical indications. Providing a comparative analysis of the domestic geographical indications laws of ASEAN countries, they explore possibilities for developing a more interoperable approach to geographical indication protections. Ha and Delphine conclude with suggestions on facilitating the registration and protection of geographical indications in the ASEAN region, including the development of online platforms.

Chapter 12 by Ignacio de Medrano Caballero addresses the challenges of connectivity and interoperability in the regional integration of the design and trademark systems. Examining the cooperation and collaboration between ASEAN and the European Union, particularly the ECAP program, the author underscores the importance of developing interoperable digital platforms. He concludes optimistically that the successful setting up of a regional Trademark Registration System will constitute a significant milestone toward achieving the ASEAN Economic Community.

In Chapter 13, Soh Kar Liang and Chew Phye Keat put forth a case for the practical application of the interoperability principle. Analyzing the strength and weaknesses of the international trademark registration system under the Madrid Protocol, Soh and Chew highlight important gaps in the ASEAN trademark filing landscape. Realizing that a middle ground solution is needed to fill this gap, they advance a proposal for developing a Pan-ASEAN trademark system.

This part concludes with a discussion in Chapter 14 by Jakkrit Kuanpoth on the challenges faced in the administration of the patent system in Thailand. Examining the difficulties faced by a developing country like Thailand in establishing an efficient patent system, the chapter notes that the lack of patent expertise in academic and educational institutions, as well as resource-scarcity of patent offices are major impediments to the interoperability agenda. Patent backlog and issues of patent quality have ensued as the patent offices in developing countries struggle to cope with the increasing volume of patent applications. The chapter makes an urgent call for technical assistance to develop the human resources, intellectual property infrastructure, and capacity building in developing countries.

10

Copyright Interoperability in ASEAN

Current and Future Issues

Pisawat Sukonthapan

10.1 INTRODUCTION

This chapter discusses current and future issues relating to the administration of copyright law within and between Association of Southeast Asian Nations (ASEAN) member states, with a particular focus on Thailand, this author's home country. Two decades ago, ASEAN member states signed the ASEAN Framework Agreement on Intellectual Property Cooperation[1] in Bangkok (1995 IP Framework Agreement) which covers inter alia cooperation in the fields of copyright and related rights.[2] Included among the cooperative activities under this 1995 IP Framework Agreement are those relating "to the implementation of the Trade-Related Aspects of Intellectual Property Rights (TRIPS) Agreement and other recognized international intellectual property conventions."[3]

Fifteen years later, the ASEAN Intellectual Property Rights Action Plan 2011–2015[4] noted that

> The ASEAN region is highly diverse and its transformation as a single bloc with a harmonized set of laws and procedures in IP has been a challenge. ASEAN continues to acknowledge the important role played by IP in social,

* The author acknowledges, with thanks, the kind assistance and suggestions given by Ms. Christina Asha Arnold, Mr. John Jacob Lucchi, and Ms. Srichan Chancheewa.

[1] *ASEAN Framework Agreement on Intellectual Property Cooperation* (December 15, 1995) [hereinafter 1995 IP Framework Agreement]. The text of the 1995 IP Framework Agreement is *available at* http://www.wipo.int/edocs/lexdocs/treaties/en/asean-ip/trt_asean_ip.pdf.

[2] Art. 3.1 of the 1995 IP Framework Agreement, *supra* note 1. Related rights are usually granted to performers, phonogram producers, and broadcasting organizations.

[3] Art. 3.3.b of the 1995 IP Framework Agreement, *supra* note 1.

[4] *ASEAN Intellectual Property Rights Action Plan 2011–2015* (July 31, 2011) [hereinafter 2011–2015 Action Plan], *available at* www.aseanip.org/Portals/0/PDF/ASEAN%20IPR%20Action%20Plan%202011–2015.pdf.

> technological, and economic progress. At the same time, recognizing that for ASEAN to fully utilize the benefits of IP as a tool that would help the region achieve economic integration by 2015, the [ASEAN Working Group on Intellectual Property Cooperation] has designed a unique way of contributing to this goal. Instead of trying to formulate a single set of laws and designing a harmonized regional system in IP, the AWGIPC has crafted its own means of integrating through a higher level of cooperation by undertaking programs and activities together, with [ASEAN member states] strengthening linkages with each other to improve their capacity, and participating in global IP structures, subject to the capacity and readiness of each ASEAN member state.[5]

In addition, ASEAN devised a "Work Plan" for copyright. It includes the following key aim:

> To make recommendations for legislative changes (where necessary) so as to facilitate access to and protection of copyright works; e.g., whether to incorporate provisions relating to parallel import and compulsory licensing for translation of work into national language. Other activities included ascertaining the difficulties faced by copyright owners, enforcement, and custom officers in copyright enforcement, examining the feasibility of establishing specialized IP courts and private criminal prosecutions. Other goals include creating a cross-border network of enforcement authorities to combat piracy and the establishment of collecting societies.[6]

We now have a draft of a new ASEAN Intellectual Property Rights Action Plan 2016–2025, which is discussed briefly at the end of this chapter.

In the author's view, the following key points can be distilled from initiatives within ASEAN in the copyright field:

- The varying levels of economic development among ASEAN member states are relevant to the ability of individual ASEAN members to comply with international standards in the copyright area.
- The lack of any plan to create a regional agreement to establish an ASEAN standard of copyright protection makes the need for individual ASEAN member states to comply with international standards more pressing. This will depend, however, on the readiness of the individual states, given their level of economic development.
- For ASEAN relations, important future issues include parallel importation; compulsory licensing for translations of work into national

[5] *Id.*, at clause 2.

[6] *See* Elizabeth Siew-Kuan Ng, *ASEAN IP Harmonization: Striking the Delicate Balance*, 25 Pace Int'l. L. Rev. 129, 145 (2013).

languages; the availability of private criminal prosecutions; the establishment and role of collecting societies; and the ASEAN Copyright Recordation/Notification Network.[7]

Taking these preliminary observations as a springboard, this chapter discusses the administration of copyright law in ASEAN, giving particular attention to Thailand. Section 10.2 discusses recent developments in the copyright law of Thailand. Section 10.3 turns to the important topic of collective rights management. And Section 10.4 briefly considers the ASEAN initiative to develop a copyright recordation system, in light of the new 2016–2025 Action Plan.

10.2 RECENT DEVELOPMENTS IN THE COPYRIGHT LAW OF THAILAND

The current copyright law of Thailand has been amended twice since its enactment in 1994.[8] Most recently, Thailand has adopted provisions that allow the reproduction or adaptation of copyright-protected works for visually-disabled people. These are permitted by the Marrakesh Treaty to Facilitate Access to Published Works for Persons Who Are Blind, Visually Impaired, or Otherwise Print Disabled.[9] Interestingly, these amendments were enacted without Thailand's accession to the Marrakesh Treaty, which has yet to occur. The amendment is, however, consistent with Initiative 7 of the ASEAN IPR Action Plan 2011–2015,[10] which anticipates "sharing on copyright exceptions and limitations for the visually impaired and persons with disabilities, including exploring best practices, and consultations with concerned interest groups in each [ASEAN member state] to discuss the necessity of implementing the initiative on a regional or on a per country basis." Initiative 7 also anticipates discussion and determination of an "ASEAN collective stand" on "copyright exceptions and limitations for the visually impaired and persons with disabilities." This example should illustrate the power of ASEAN initiatives in the copyright field. With the ASEAN Action Plan's encouragement, Thailand has begun to address the needs of visually impaired people without yet joining the Marrakesh Treaty itself.

In addition, Thailand has taken advantage of the flexibility in the TRIPS Agreement concerning parallel importation. The Copyright Act (No. 2)

7 *See* 2016–2025 Action Plan, Initiative 1 of Strategic Goal 1.

8 Copyright Act, B.E. 2537 (1994). The two amendments are Copyright Act (No. 2), B.E. 2558 (2015) and the Copyright Act (No. 3), B.E. 2558 (2015).

9 *Marrakesh Treaty to Facilitate Access to Published Works for Persons Who Are Blind, Visually Impaired or Otherwise Print Disabled*, June 27, 2013, 52 *I.L.M.* 1309 (2013), *available at* www.wipo.int/wipolex/en/treaties/text.jsp?file_id=301019.

10 *See* 2011–2015 IPR Action Plan, *supra* note 4.

introduces provisions on parallel importation (using international exhaustion of rights), as seen from section 32/1. This section stipulates that "[s]ale of an original or copy of a copyright work by a person legally acquiring ownership of the original or the copy of such copyright work shall not be deemed a copyright infringement."[11] This adoption is permitted by art. 6 of TRIPS, which states that "[f]or the purposes of dispute settlement under this Agreement, subject to the provisions of arts. 3 and 4 nothing in this Agreement shall be used to address the issue of the exhaustion of intellectual property rights."[12] The adoption of this provision should facilitate the free movement of goods into Thailand.

Thailand has also adopted provisions that reflect its intention to meet international standards, such as those contained in the World Intellectual Property Organization (WIPO) Internet Treaties, in the areas of the liability of internet service providers, rights management information, and technological measures.[13] The 1994 Copyright Act also lists sound recordings among works eligible for copyright protection,[14] and entitles phonogram producers to claim copyright fees for the uses of their sound recordings for communication to the public.

10.3 COLLECTIVE MANAGEMENT OF PERFORMING RIGHTS IN MUSICAL WORKS

Initiative 9 of the ASEAN IPR Action Plan 2011–2015 anticipated that collective management organizations (CMOs) – or collecting societies – would be formed in ASEAN member states by 2015.[15] This is an important initiative. CMOs may assist in achieving more streamlined access to and licensing of copyright-protected works, and with enhancing the opportunities for authors to secure an income from exploitation of the works both at home and abroad. Even so, the diversity in the collective management of musical works and performance rights across ASEAN member states is likely to continue to impose impediments to the efficient management of these copyrights. This has implications both for individual rights holders as well as having development

[11] The text of the Thai Copyright Act (No. 2) is *available at* http://web.krisdika.go.th/data/outsitedata/outsite21/file/COPYRIGHTACT_(NO.2),_B.E._2558_(2015).pdf.

[12] *Agreement on Trade Related Aspects of Intellectual Property Rights, April 15, 1994, Marrakesh Agreement Establishing the World Trade Organization*, Annex 1C, 33 *I.L.M.* 87–88 (1994) [hereinafter TRIPS], *available at* www.wto.org/english/tratop_e/trips_e/t_agm2_e.htm.

[13] *See* sects. 32/3, 53/1, 53/2, 53/4, 53/5, 70/1 of the Copyright Act, B.E. 2537, as amended by the Copyright Act (No. 2), B.E. 2558 (2015).

[14] Apparently, this followed the Copyright Act, B.E. 2521 (1978) that granted copyright protection to producers of phonograms/sound recordings.

[15] 2011–2015 Action Plan, *supra* note 4, at Initiative 9.

implications for ASEAN member states. If local rights holders cannot derive income from their works in other ASEAN member states – and, indeed, beyond ASEAN – then the potential for copyright income to contribute positively to individuals' economic welfare and member states' balance of payments will be impeded.

The copyright laws of a number of ASEAN member states now include provisions on collective rights management. For example, art. 56 of the Cambodian Copyright Act[16] provides that

> The author of work . . . can establish the collective management organization to protect and manage their economic rights.
>
> The establishment of collective management organization of author's right . . . must require the recognition of the Ministry of Culture and Fine Arts . . .

Section 8 of the Laos Law on Intellectual Property (as amended)[17] also covers collective management organizations. Article 114 (new), art. 115 (new), and art. 116 (new) stipulate that

> **Article 114 (new). Collective Management Organizations:** Collective management organizations are associations managing copyright . . . established on the basis of agreement among authors, copyrights owners . . . to operate in accordance with the law in order to protect copyrights . . .
>
> **Article 115 (new). Role of Associations Managing Copyright:** Associations managing copyright . . . shall perform the following roles:
>
> 1. To manage copyright . . . on behalf of authors, copyrights owners . . . ; to negotiate on licensing, the collection of remuneration on behalf of such persons, and to divide and distribute royalties, remuneration and other material benefits there from the allowance of exploiting the authorized rights;
> 2. To protect members' rights and legal benefits, including to represent the persons mentioned in item 1 above in legal proceedings, and to reconcile any dispute on their behalf.
>
> **Article 116 (new). Rights and Obligations of Associations Managing Copyright:** The associations managing copyright . . . shall have the rights and obligations as follows:
>
> 1. To establish encouraging creation activities and other social activities;
> 2. To cooperate with correlative national and international organizations on the protection of copyright . . . ;

16 *See* Law on Copyrights and Related Rights (2003), art. 56 (Cambodia).
17 Law No. 01/NA on Intellectual Property (2011), sect. 8 (Laos).

3. To make report on collective management to competent authorities;
4. Other rights and obligations according to the provisions of this Law.[18]

The concept of collective management of copyrights has also been introduced to Myanmar, as stipulated in Chapter XV of Myanmar's new draft copyright law.[19] The draft Chapter reads, in part, that "[t]he author and other owner of copyright: (a) may, apply to the Central Body together with the organizational set-up for granting permission to form a collective administration organization in categories of literary and artistic work."[20]

In Thailand, however, the legislative position is quite different. As of April 2016, the Thai government has not yet been able to pass special legislation to regulate or supervise collective management of copyrights and collective management organizations. Unfortunately, rights owners have not consolidated the management of copyrights in a way that would assist small businesses that are concerned with lowering transaction costs and dealing with multiplicity of copyright owners. The lack of specific legislation on collective management of rights does not prevent rights owners from forming collecting organizations/societies (generally, in the form of private companies established under the *Civil and Commercial Code*). As of September 2016, there were, at least, 31 CMOs in Thailand.[21] Among them is the Music Copyright (Thailand) Company Limited – MCT. Eight out of these 31 CMOs have fewer than 500 songs to offer – 380, 340, 281, 279, 260, 108, 76, and 33 songs.[22] Hoping to ensure fair and just prices, the Thai government has utilized the Act on Prices of Goods and Services, B.E. 2542 (1999)[23] by prescribing licensing of performing rights in songs[24] as a regulated service. For example, on January 27, 2014, the Central Commission on Prices of Goods and Services issued an Announcement on Submission of Rates of Royalties, Costs, Expenses, Rules, Procedures

[18] *Lao People's Democratic Republic – Law No. 01/NA of December 20, 2011, on Intellectual Property (as amended), available at* www.wipo.int/wipolex/en/text.jsp?file_id=310926.

[19] Myanmar's new draft copyright law has yet to be published as of December 9, 2016. A copy of the new draft copyright law is on file with the author.

[20] Section 63 of the draft Copyright Act (8th draft). This translation has been made available by Office of the Attorney General of the Union of Myanmar.

[21] *See* the list of CMOs on the Thai Department of Intellectual Property website, *available at* http://ipthailand.go.th/.

[22] For number of songs controlled by each of the CMOs, *see* the Thai Department of Intellectual Property, *Id.*

[23] An English translation of the 1999 Act on Prices of Goods and Services is *available at* www.asianlii.org/th/legis/consol_act/pogasa1992249/.

[24] The Announcement uses the term 'เพลง' (*pleng*) which should be broader that the term 'musical works'. *See* http://law.dit.go.th/Upload/Document/238fe81c-502a-44a4–9d5c-81b4013f5f32.pdf.

Nation	CISAC member's name	Status (as of January 2015): Associate = A; Provisional = P; Member = M	Repertoire: Music (MU)
Brunei Darussalam	BEAT	P	MU
Cambodia	-	-	-
Indonesia	PAPPRI	A	MU
	WAMI	P	MU
Lao PDR	-	-	-
Malaysia	MACP	M	MU
Myanmar*	-	-	-
Philippines, The	FILSCAP	M	MU
Singapore	COMPASS	M	MU
Thailand	MCT	M	MU
Viet Nam	VCPMC	M	MU

FIGURE 10.1 Members of CISAC: CMOs in ASEAN.

and Conditions Related to Licensing of Communicating Copyright Songs to the Public for Commercial Gain, B.E. 2557 (2014).[25] It will be interesting to see whether these steps improve the situation for Thai copyright owners and licensees.

We can get some sense of the true position on the collective management within ASEAN by considering the level of engagement with the International Confederation of Societies of Authors and Composers (CISAC), a leading, if not the leading, network of CMOs.[26] One of CISAC's key purposes is to "encourage the efficient collection and distribution of Royalties."[27] Through CISAC's international network of domestic CMOs, it is possible for collectively managed royalties to be collected abroad. As Figure 10.1 indicates, however, engagement with the CISAC system within ASEAN is incomplete.[28]

According to CISAC, affiliated CMOs do not exist in Laos or Cambodia. In Myanmar, there is an association called the "Myanmar Music Association (MMA),"[29] but it is not clear whether the MMA or other organizations (if any) represent owners of performing rights in musical works to collect royalty fees in return for the use of such rights; nonetheless the MMA does not appear to have joined CISAC.[30] It appears that MMA has not begun to function as a

[25] For the text of this Announcement, *see id.* For the form used, *see* Thailand Department of Internal Trade, Download Form, *available at* http://law.dit.go.th/.

[26] *See generally*, CISAC, *available at* www.cisac.org/.

[27] *See* cl. 5 of CISAC Statutes, June 6 2014, AG10–1275R6.

[28] For the list of CISAC members, *see* CISAC – Our Members, *available at* www.cisac.org/Our-Members.

[29] Limited information on the MMA may be obtained from its Facebook page, *available at* https://web.facebook.com/search/top/?q=myanmar%20music%20association).

[30] CISAC, *supra* note 28.

CMO to collect fees for the use of performing rights in musical works. This, combined with the lack of protections in Myanmar copyright law[31] for foreign-origin works, is likely to continue to make it difficult for Myanmar copyright owners or their organization(s) to conclude reciprocal representation contracts with CMOs abroad.

Within ASEAN some CMOs have sought to collect royalties by establishing bilateral agreements with CMOs in other member states. For example, the MCT of Thailand has concluded a reciprocal representation contract with the Composers and Authors Society of Singapore Ltd (COMPASS)[32] of Singapore. Another example is an agreement between MCT and the Music Authors' Copyright Protection (MACP)[33] of Malaysia. COMPASS has also concluded reciprocal contracts with CMOs in Malaysia (Music Authors' Copyright Protection – MACP), Indonesia (Karya Cipta Indonesia – KCI),[34] and the Philippines (Filipino Society of Composers, Authors and Publishers, Inc. – FILSCAP).[35] There is, however, no reciprocal contract between COMPASS and the Vietnam Center for Protection of Music Copyright (VCPMC).[36]

In sum, while the initiatives discussed in this section suggest that there is already some degree of cooperation in the management of performing rights within ASEAN, it is clear that CMOs is a context in which significant work is required to achieve "interoperability" in this key part of the popular entertainment market. Going forward, for ASEAN to realize the expectations in 2011–2015 ASEAN IPR Action Plan relating to collective management, it is hoped that member states will share information about policies and practices relating to the functioning of CMOs. In the author's view, this is particularly important for those ASEAN member states with CMOs that have workable and productive relationships with international CMO networks. This will be especially important for Cambodia, Laos, and Myanmar, and should help composers and authors to earn revenue from outside their countries. As an initial step, the governments of ASEAN member states should require CMOs managing performing rights in musical works to permit Cambodians, Laotians, and Myanmar nationals to join their networks.

31 Myanmar's Copyright Act of 1911 only provides protections for original literary, dramatic, and artistic works if they are either first published in Myanmar, or, if unpublished, are the work of a citizen or person otherwise inside of Myanmar at the time of creation. Copyrighted works from other nations are afforded no protection in Myanmar under this system. *See* Chapter II of the Copyright Act of 1911, *available at* www.wipo.int/wipolex/en/details.jsp?id=15713.

32 COMPASS, *List of Societies with Reciprocal Agreements with* COMPASS (November 15, 2016), *available at* www.compass.org.sg/cIndex244.aspx.

33 For information on MACP, *see* MACP – Affiliated Societies, *available at* www.macp.com.my/affiliated-societies.htm.

34 COMPASS, *supra* note 32. 35 *Id.* 36 *Id.*

10.4 COPYRIGHT NOTIFICATION AND RECORDATION

Included among the deliverables of the new 2016–2025 Action Plan is the plan to establish an ASEAN Copyright Notification/Recordation Network. The country champions are Thailand, Indonesia, and Administrator of ASEAN IP Portal (ASEC). This may prove to be a useful initiative. Although the Berne Convention precludes conditioning the subsistence and exercise of copyrights on compliance with formalities,[37] recordation can be a useful tool for those seeking to negotiate licenses for copyright-protected material. Consistent with Berne, recordation can never be a mandatory condition for exercising rights in copyright-protected works. However, if recordation enhances efficient marketing, it might be expected that copyright owners will be encouraged to use the system.

The Thai Department of Intellectual Property has established an office to receive information on works (including works of applied art) eligible for protection under the Thai Copyright Act of 1994 for the purpose of recordation. For this system to work, however, it will be crucial for the interface to include clear information as to how to use the system. For example, if this is truly to be an "interoperable" aspect of the ASEAN intellectual property system, consideration should be given to translating information about the system into English, which should then facilitate further translations into other languages used within ASEAN member states.

When the recordation system is fully operational, it should also include user-friendly information about the practical effect of recordation. It must be made very clear, for instance, that recording alone does not constitute the granting of copyright protection; nor does it provide reciprocal rights among other ASEAN member states. An ASEAN-wide recordation system may well prove to be a useful initiative, to the extent that it will assist with more efficient licensing of copyright-protected works. However, more work needs to be done to manage expectations as to the legal implications of copyright recordation.

10.5 CONCLUSION

From this brief survey, it is clear that there are many opportunities for further development of copyright law within ASEAN member states to enhance interoperability *between and among* the domestic copyright systems of ASEAN

[37] Art. 5 of the Berne Convention for the Protection of Literary and Artistic Works, September 9, 1896, S. Treaty Doc. No. 99–27 (1986) (as revised at Paris July 4, 1971 and amended September 28, 1979).

members. Because all ASEAN countries are members of TRIPS, there already exists a baseline of expectations. However, because of the different levels of development, with few exceptions, ASEAN member states have largely honored their TRIPS obligations in the field of copyright; some still hope to comply fully with TRIPS in the very near future.

Another context in which there will need to be better alignment is in the area of collective rights management. As discussed in the preceding text, the discrepancies in the substantive law as well as domestic practices are likely to continue to impede the efficient management of rights across borders. Similar issues might also arise in the context of copyright recordation. Although this initiative may enhance interoperability in the licensing of copyright-protected material, more work is required to ensure that the operational details of this proposal help fulfill its laudable expectations.

11

Notification and Registration System for Geographical Indications

Lê Thi Thu Hà and Delphine Marie-Vivien

11.1 INTRODUCTION

Shortly before the Trade-Related Aspects of Intellectual Property Rights (TRIPS) Agreement came into force, the importance of geographical indications was acknowledged in the Association of Southeast Asian Nations (ASEAN) context by their inclusion in the 1995 ASEAN Framework Agreement on Intellectual Property Cooperation. Even if many of the ASEAN countries had geographical indication protection prior to joining TRIPS (through unfair competition, consumer protection, food standards, or even appellation of origin), adhesion to the World Trade Organization (WTO) was for many ASEAN countries the occasion to adopt new legal protection schemes for geographical indications, following pressure from Old World countries in WTO's accession. As discussed in more detail in this chapter, ASEAN countries are also involved in numerous regional and bilateral free trade agreements (RTAs and FTAs), and have implemented a wide range of initiatives for the protection of geographical indications. ASEAN has thus become one of the most active areas for the protection of geographical indications in the world.

Geographical indications are defined in the TRIPS Agreement as "... indications which identify a good as originating in the territory of a Member, or a region or locality in that territory, where a given quality, reputation or other characteristic of the good is essentially attributable to its geographical origin."[1] This concept is a bridge between the earlier notions of Indication

* Research for this chapter was partly supported by the Swiss State Secretariat for Economic Affairs under the SECO/WTI Academic Cooperation Project, based at the World Trade Institute of the University of Bern, Switzerland.

[1] *See* Agreement on Trade-Related Aspects of Intellectual Property Rights, art. 22.1, April 15, 1994, Marrakesh Agreement Establishing the World Trade Organization, Annex 1C, 33 I.L.M. 87–88 (1994), *available at* www.wto.org/english/tratop_e/trips_e/t_agm0_e.htm [hereinafter TRIPS Agreement].

of Source and Appellation of Origin. This convergence of new concepts in the TRIPS Agreement cannot, however, stop the divergence between parties advocating stronger multilateral protection for geographical indications and parties favoring a less ambitious outcome, led respectively by the European Union (EU) and the United States.[2]

This chapter explores responses to these issues within ASEAN. It could be expected that creating a single market in ASEAN would similarly increase the availability of legal tools supporting that single market. In the field of intellectual property, such tools could include the harmonization of domestic legal frameworks and the facilitation of intellectual property protection within the ASEAN market itself, or through the creation of unique intellectual property rights that are valid and enforceable in all ASEAN countries.

This chapter provides an overview of these issues. Section 11.2 begins with a brief background to the protection for geographical indications in ASEAN countries and a comparative analysis of domestic laws in ASEAN countries. Section 11.3 describes possibilities for adopting a more interoperable approach to protection for geographical indications in ASEAN. Finally, Section 11.4 focuses on the possible ways to facilitate the registration and protection of geographical indications in the ASEAN region.

11.2 GEOGRAPHICAL INDICATIONS IN ASEAN: A NEW CONVERGENCE OR OLD DIVERGENCE?

Geographical indication protection has a long tradition in many of the ASEAN countries through unfair competition, consumer protection, food standards, or even appellations of origin. While the adhesion to WTO, and then to various RTAs and FTAs, was, for many ASEAN member states, the occasion to adopt new legal protection schemes, the convergence of new concepts in these legal frameworks has not stopped the divergence in geographical indication protection.

11.2.1 *ASEAN Integration of Geographical Indication Protection*

Among three main international treaties related to the protection of geographical indications before TRIPS,[3] ASEAN countries were members of only the

[2] Lê Thi Thu Hà, *The New Evolution of Protection of Geographical Indications*, 32(1) VNU J. Sci. Policy Manage. Stud. 68–78 (2016).

[3] The Paris Convention for the Protection of Industrial Property in 1883 [hereinafter the Paris Convention]; The Madrid Agreement for the Repression of False or Deceptive Indications of Source on Goods of 1891 [hereinafter the Madrid Agreement on Indications of Source] and

Paris Convention.[4] The restricted participation of ASEAN countries in these international treaties also meant that, prior to TRIPS, the integration of these nations with international systems for the protection of geographical indications was quite limited.

Once they became members of the WTO,[5] ASEAN countries undertook extensive reforms of their intellectual property laws. ASEAN countries are now reviewing their national legislation to go beyond TRIPS compliance. The World Intellectual Property Organization (WIPO) along with many international and regional organizations in which the EU plays a very active role are supporting these initiatives. As a result, seven out of ten ASEAN countries have *sui generis* regulated geographical indication protection. Among the remaining three countries (the Philippines, Brunei, and Myanmar) that protect geographical indications through certifications or collective trademarks under national trademark laws, the Philippines recently drafted Rules and Regulations on geographical indications (2014),[6] the draft Trademark Law of Myanmar[7] has been reviewed and approved in September 2014, and Brunei is planning to develop specific laws on geographical indications. Although less developed countries are given an extended transition period until July 2021 to protect intellectual property rights under the TRIPS Agreement, the establishment of legal frameworks to regulate geographical indications is already effective in Cambodia and Laos.

Besides changes in the substantive law relating to geographical indications, ASEAN countries have also been upgrading intellectual property offices to allow for geographical indication registration and the promotion of using geographical indications as tools for economic development. Nearly 200 products are currently being registered or are in the process of registration as geographical indications. Some countries allow and accept the registration and recognition for both national and foreign geographical indications (Thailand,[8]

The Lisbon Agreement for the Protection of Appellations of Origin and their International Registration [hereinafter the Lisbon Agreement].

4 All ASEAN countries are members of Paris Convention except Myanmar. The author considers the participation in Paris Convention of ASEAN members is due to the interest in other intellectual property subject matters such as trademark or patent, not geographical indication.

5 All ASEAN countries are now members of WTO since Laos's accession in February 2013.

6 The drafted proposed Rules and Regulations on geographical indications of the Philippines, *available at* www.ipophil.gov.ph/images/WhatsNew/Draft-Rules&Regulationsongeographicalindications.docx.

7 In this draft, Chapter 7 provides rules for geographical indications.

8 Eleven geographical indications protected in Thailand include Prosciutto di Parma Ham (Italy) Pisco Peru (Peru), Champagne (France), Brunello di Montalcino (Italy), Cognac (France), Scotch Whisky (UK), Napa Valley (USA), Tequila (Mexico), Barolo (Italy), and Barbaresco (Italy).

Vietnam,[9] Malaysia,[10] Cambodia, Laos, Myanmar, and Indonesia[11]). That said, although the number of foreign geographical indications registered in ASEAN is increasing, principally through trade relations with the EU, the protection of geographical indications originating from ASEAN countries in other, non-ASEAN countries is limited.[12]

Individual ASEAN member countries have been entangled in a network of RTAs/FTAs in the recent past.[13] Regarding the negotiations with the EU, the intellectual property rights template in most of these instruments reflects the EU's advocacy of a specialized system for the registration of geographical indications and of enhanced and extended protection for geographical indications.[14] These negotiations were launched in July 2007 with ASEAN as part of a possible move toward an EU-ASEAN FTA. However, these negotiations stalled. In December 2009, EU member states agreed that the Commission would pursue FTA negotiations in a bilateral format with ASEAN countries. Negotiations with Singapore and Malaysia were launched in 2010, with Vietnam in June 2012, with Thailand in March 2013, with the Philippines in December 2015, and with Indonesia in July 2016. Negotiations of an investment protection agreement are also underway with Myanmar. The European

9 Foreign geographical indications protected in Vietnam include Cognac (France), Pisco (Peru), Scotch Whisky (UK), and Isan Indigenous Silk Yarn (Thailand).

10 Foreign geographical indications protected in Malaysia include Cognac (France), Tequila (Mexico), Barolo (Italy), Prosciutto di Parma Ham (Italy), Pisco Peru (Peru), Champagne (France), and Scotch Whisky (UK).

11 Champagne is registered in Indonesia and Myanmar.

12 There are no official statistics defining the geographical indications originating from ASEAN in third-party countries. The author compiled and updated from different IP portals of ASEAN members and reports of regional geographical indications projects (ECAP/FAO/AFD).

- In Thailand, Khao Hom Mali Thung Kula Rong is registered in EU (2013), Isan Indigenous Silk Yarn is registered in Vietnam (2014), and three other applications of Kafae Doi Chaang (Coffee), Kafae Doi Tung (Coffee), and Khao Sungyod Muang Phattalung (Rice) are pending at the EU.
- Cambodia has only one geographical indications application Kampot Pepper pending at the EU.
- Vietnam also has one geographical indication Phu Quoc registered in EU but thirty-eight other Vietnamese geographical indications are protected in this market through the Vietnam-EU FTA-Buon Ma Thuot coffee and Moc Chau tea have been applied in Thailand.

13 Individual member countries of ASEAN are involved in a total of 156 FTAs in varying stages of development. The authors compiled the data from the ADB's statistics, *available at* https://aric.adb.org/fta-country.

14 Chuthaporn Ngokkuen & Ulrike Grote, *Challenges and Opportunities for Protecting Geographical Indications in Thailand*, 19(2) Asia-Pacific Dev. J. 93 (2012).

Commission finalized negotiations of an FTA with Singapore in October 2014 and with Vietnam in December 2015.[15] The two FTAs (EU–Singapore and EU–Vietnam) have some similarities, with the obligation to provide for a *sui generis* system comprising a register, an administrative process to evaluate the existence of a link with the origin, an objection procedure, legal means that permit the rectification and cancellation of entries on the domestic register, and the right of use of the geographical indication by any complying producer without further requirements.[16] Yet these principles of *sui generis* law are already implemented in most ASEAN countries, and thus these FTAs have had little impact on the homogenization of the legislation within ASEAN.

At a regional level, ASEAN has built an Intellectual Property Action Plan (2011–2015) identifying five strategic goals[17] that should contribute to the collective transformation of ASEAN into a competitive region for the use of intellectual property. ASEAN, as a bloc, is also entering into negotiations for additional RTAs and FTAs. Among six FTAs with Australia and New Zealand, China, the EU, India, Japan, and South Korea, currently, it is only the negotiations with the EU (having provisions concerning geographical indication protection) that are not progressing.

11.2.2 *The Framework for Geographical Indication Protection in ASEAN*

As with other intellectual property rights, there is no common legal framework for the protection of geographical indications at the regional level of ASEAN. As a result, the legal framework in each ASEAN country must be examined against the TRIPS Agreement. At this stage it is necessary to assess the differences between the domestic laws on three different points: definition and eligible indications; mean of protection; and scope of protection including the conflict between geographical indications and trademarks.

Definition and Eligible Indications

The definition of geographical indication in TRIPS has become the model for ASEAN countries[18]:

[15] *See* European Commission, *Association of South East Asian Nations (ASEAN)* (October 24, 2016), *available at* http://ec.europa.eu/trade/policy/countries-and-regions/regions/asean/.

[16] *See* European Commission, *Overview of FTA and Other Trade Negotiations* (October 2016), *available at* http://trade.ec.europa.eu/doclib/docs/2006/december/tradoc_118238.pdf.

[17] For the full text of the ASEAN IPR Action Plan 2011–2015, *see* ASEAN Secretariat, *ASEAN IPR Action Plan 2011–2015*, *available at* www.aseanip.org/Portals/0/PDF/ASEAN%20IPR%20Action%20Plan%202011–2015.pdf.

[18] *See* TRIPS Agreement, *supra* note 1, art 22.1.

> Geographical indications are . . . indications which identify a good as originating in the territory of a Member, or a region or locality in that territory, where a given quality, reputation or other characteristic of the good is essentially attributable to its geographical origin.

This definition differs from other concepts, such as Appellations of Origin[19] and Indications of Source.[20] The TRIPS definition is flexible enough to overcome the limitations set out by previous international conventions,[21] and has opened greater opportunities for the protection of geographical indications in the world.[22]

While appellations of origin are merely direct names indicating geographical places, geographical indications may be indirect names or indirect signs, such as images or symbols. In fact, the TRIPS Agreement has no requirement for geographical indications to be geographical *names*.[23] Chaiya salted eggs from Thailand would qualify, for example.[24] But a geographical name can of course also be the name of a geographical location, such as a territory, a city, a region (e.g., Nakonchaisri Pomelo of Thailand or Sarawak Pepper of Malaysia), the name of a mountain (e.g., Ngoc Linh ginseng of Vietnam), a valley, an island (e.g., Phu Quoc fish sauce of Vietnam) or any other place. Nor does the TRIPS agreement exclude iconic symbols or images[25] having a connection with certain locations, as the Eiffel Tower to designate French goods or the Petronas Twin Towers to designate goods from Malaysia (theoretical examples). In addition, the TRIPS definition excludes indications of source that do not specify any quality, reputation, or other characteristics of the product but instead signal only the geographical source of such products. This

[19] As defined in article 2 of the Lisbon Arrangement 1958, an "appellation of origin" is the "geographical name of a country, a region or a territory . . . used to indicate a product that originates from it and the quality and characteristics of which are exclusively or mainly due to the geographical environment, including the natural and human factors."

[20] The term "indication of source" is used in Paris Convention 1883 and Madrid Agreement 1891 but there is no definition in those two treaties. Article 1(1) of the Madrid Agreement contains language that clarifies what is meant by the term. The indication of source relates to the geographical origin of a product and not to another kind of origin, for example, an enterprise that manufactures the product. This definition does not imply any special quality or characteristics of the product on which an indication of source is used.

[21] Lê Thi Thu Hà, *Protection of Geographical Indications in the Context of Vietnam's International Economic Integration*, Information and Communication Publishing House (2011).

[22] Rangnekar Dwijen, The Socio-Economics of Geographical Indications: A Review of Empirical Evidence from Europe (UNCTAD/ICTSD Capacity Building Project on Intellectual Property Rights and Sustainable Development 2003).

[23] Bernard O'connor, The Law of Geographical Indications 52 (2004).

[24] Latha R. Nair & Rajendra Kumar, Geographical Indications: A Search for Identity 95 (2005).

[25] Bernard O'Connor, *supra* note 23, at 52.

requirement for the link between product quality and the geographical origin for geographical indications is weaker than the one required by appellations of origin.[26] Indications having one of the three above factors (such as only reputation) can be protected as a geographical indication.

Among the Philippines, Myanmar, and Brunei, only the Philippines law, while including geographical indications in the enumeration of recognized forms of intellectual property rights, does not give any definition of this subject.[27] The definition of geographical indication in Thailand,[28] Malaysia,[29] Singapore,[30] Cambodia,[31] Laos,[32] Indonesia, and Vietnam conforms to that of TRIPS, though there are some differences in the forms of expression used.

The definitions in Vietnamese law require the existence both of natural and human factors, either raw material must be sourced locally or the influence of the climate or natural elements must be demonstrated.[33] The definition of geographical indication in Indonesian law also specifies that geographical environmental factors, including both natural factors and human factors, can

26 See the Lisbon Agreement for the Protection of Appellations of Origin and their International Registration (1958).

27 Intellectual Property Code of the Philippines §4 (1997) "The term "intellectual property rights" consists of: a. Copyright and Related Rights; b. Trademarks and Service Marks; c. Geographic Indications; d. Industrial Designs; e. Patents; f. Layout-designs (Topographies) of Integrated Circuits; and g. Protection of Undisclosed Information."

28 The Geographical Indications Protection Act of Thailand, Chapter 1, §3: "Geographical Indication means name, symbol or any other thing which is used for calling or representing a geographical origin and can identify the goods originating from such geographical origin where the quality, reputation or other characteristic of the goods is attributable to the geographical origin."

29 The Geographical Indications Act 2000 of Malaysia, Chapter 1, §2: "geographical indication" means an indication which identifies any goods as originating in a country or territory, or a region or locality in that country or territory, where a given quality, reputation or other characteristic of the goods is essentially attributable to their geographical origin."

30 Geographical Indication Act 1998 of Singapore, Article 1: "geographical indication means any indication used in trade to identify goods as originating from a place, provided that (a) the place is a qualifying country or a region or locality in the qualifying country; and (b) a given quality, reputation or other characteristic of the goods is essentially attributable to that place."

31 The Law on Geographical Indications 2009 of Cambodia, Article 4: "Mark of Goods which include a Geographical Indication refers to a name, symbol or any other sign which is used for calling or representing a geographical origin and can identify the goods as originating in such geographical origin where the quality, reputation or other characteristic of the goods is essentially attributable to the geographical origin."

32 The Law on Intellectual Property 2011 of Laos, Article 4.22: "Geographical indication means a sign used to indicate a good as originating in the territory of a country or region or locality in that territory, where a given quality and reputation or other characteristic of the good is essentially attributable to its geographical origin."

33 The Law on Intellectual Property of Vietnam, Article 82.2 and Article 82.3.

be taken alone or in combination to justify the specific characteristics and quality of the goods bearing the geographical indication.[34] Because human factors can be considered alone, geographical indication can be protected for processed goods made out of nonlocal raw materials.

Under TRIPS, the concept of geographical indications is available for any kind of goods, including handicrafts. This is followed in all ASEAN countries,[35] with legislation in some countries including Thailand,[36] Malaysia,[37] and Singapore[38] expressly covering a wide range of natural, agricultural, handicraft, and industrial products. The newly drafted Rules and Regulations on Geographical Indications in the Philippines extends the protection of geographical indications to agricultural products, foodstuffs, any products of handicraft, or wines and spirits in the same way as Thailand, Malaysia, and Singapore do.[39] While the laws in Vietnam, Indonesia, Cambodia, and Laos are silent on this issue, these kinds of goods are, by default, protected as geographical indications in these countries. Examples of geographical indication for handicraft goods are conical hats from Hue (Vietnam), or Aranyik knives, Chantaburi sapphire, and Sukhotai gold (Thailand).

Thus, it is evident from these insights that the ten ASEAN countries have attempted to satisfy the definition of geographical indication stipulated in the TRIPS Agreement, but each has a different way of wording the requirements. There are different requirements regarding the requisite strength of the link with the origin, and different approaches to the necessity of human or natural factors.

HOMONYMS Homonymous geographical indications refer to geographical names that are spelled or pronounced alike but are located in different

34 The Law of The Republic of Indonesia 2007, Article 1.1: "A Geographical Indication shall mean a sign which indicates the place of origin of a good, which due to its geographical environment factors the nature, the people, or the combination thereof gives specific characteristics and quality on the goods produced therein."

35 Delphine Marie-Vivien, *The Protection of Geographical Indications for Handicrafts: How to Apply the Concepts of Natural and Human Factors to All Products*, 4(2) W.I.P.O.J. 191, 191–203 (2013).

36 The Geographical Indications Protection Act of Thailand, Chapter 1, §3: "goods" means articles which can be traded, exchanged or transferred, whether they are natural or are agricultural produce, including handicraft and industrial products.

37 The Geographical Indication Act 2000 of Malaysia, Chapter 1, §2: "goods" means any natural or agricultural product or any product of handicraft or industry.

38 The Geographical Indication Act 1999 of Singapore, Article 2: "goods" means any natural or agricultural product or any product of handicraft or industry.

39 The drafted Rules and Regulations on Geographical Indication 2014 of the Philippines, Article 1, Rules 2(b).

countries or different geographical regions within the same country. Almost all ASEAN countries' laws exclude homonymous indications from protection, while Indonesia and Vietnam are silent on this issue. Malaysia[40] and Singapore[41] expressly extend protection to homonymous indications of wines only. Thailand extends protection not only to wine but also to additional categories for which they offer protection similar to that for wines and spirit.[42] In Vietnam, there is no prohibition on registration of homonymous indications, and some homonymous indications could be protected after considering the practical conditions under which each indication could be differentiated or under the FTAs to which Vietnam is a signatory.[43] For ASEAN countries protecting geographical indication through the trademark system, however, it is assumed that homonymous indications could not be protected under this system even in relation to wines (as mandated by TRIPS).[44]

GENERIC NAMES The provision in art. 24.6 of TRIPS provides an exception to the obligation of protecting geographical indications for WTO members if that indication is "identical with the term customary in common language as the common name" for the goods or services in question in that member; that is, it has become the generic term for describing the goods or services in the local language. ASEAN countries all have this TRIPS provision, with the result that generic or customary geographical indications cannot be protected.[45]

40 The Geographical Indication Act 2000 of Malaysia, §7.1 "In the case of homonymous geographical indications for wines, protection shall be accorded to each indication."

41 The Geographical Indications Act 1999 of Singapore, §3.2(c) ". . . any use of a geographical indication, being a geographical indication which identifies a wine, in relation to a wine which did not originate from the placeindicated by the geographical indication."

42 The Geographical Indications Protection Act of Thailand, §29 "In case that the specific goods . . . have the same or homonymous geographical indication but different geographical origin, when registration of a geographical indication for those goods is effected, the use of geographical indication in this case shall be in accordance with the rules and procedures prescribed in Ministerial Regulations."

43 This is the case of homonym Pisco, which is granted protection as geographical indication for Peru in 2007, and is also recognized as protected geographical indication in the Vietnam-Chile FTA in 2014.

44 N.S. Gopalakrishnan, Prabha S. Nair, & Aravind K. Babu, Exploring the Relationship between Geographical Indications and Traditional Knowledge: An Analysis of the Legal Tools for the Protection of Geographical Indications in Asia (ICTSD Program on Intellectual Property Rights and Sustainable Development, International Centre for Trade and Sustainable Development 2007).

45 Thitapha Wattanapruttipaisan, *Trademark and Geographical Indications: Policy Issues and Options in Trade Negotiations and Implementation*, 26(1) Asian Dev. Rev. 166 (2009). *See also*, Chuthaporn Ngokkuen & Ulrike Grote, *supra* note 14, at 110, discussing Thai Jasmine rice.

The question of generic geographical indications is often addressed in FTAs.[46] Countries usually undertake to phase out the generic use of geographical indications as an important quid pro quo for advancing negotiations in other areas.[47] For example, the EU has made efforts to repatriate some forty-one names (with twenty-eight for wines and spirits), including champagne, which has been successfully protected in some ASEAN countries, including Thailand, Malaysia, Indonesia, Myanmar, and Vietnam.

Means of Protection: *Sui Generis* or Trademark System?

TRIPS does not dictate the legal means for geographical indication protection. Three approaches to this question can be identified. The EU, which has a long tradition of protecting geographical indications, has a *sui generis* system, that is, a register for geographical indications, an administrative substantive examination of the validity of the geographical indication (the existence of the link with the origin), an opposition procedure, and the right of use for all those who comply with the geographical indication specification. In addition, geographical indications are also protected under business law and unfair competition law.

As a result of their relationship with the EU, most ASEAN member states have followed the *sui generis* approach for geographical indications and a registration system. Only the Philippines, Myanmar, and Brunei provide for protection of geographical indications through their trademark systems. Yet they are all in the process of enacting *sui generis* regimes. Singapore affords protection through either specific geographical indication law or trademark law and passing off.[48]

Scope of Protection

The scope of protection under the TRIPS Agreement distinguishes between the minimum standard for geographical indications related to all products (art. 22.2), a higher level of protection for wines and spirits (art. 23.2), and an extra-additional protection only for wines (art. 23.1).[49] The additional protection for wines and spirits seems to be confined to these two categories only in

46 Evans G.E. & Michael Blakeney, *The Protection of Geographical Indications after Doha: Quo Vadis*? J. Int'l. Econ. Law (September 2006) 9 (3): 575–614.

47 *Id.*

48 The Law on Geographical Indications 1998 of Singapore, §12: "Nothing in this Act shall affect the rights of a person under the Trade Marks Act 1998 or the law relating to passing off."

49 TRIPS Agreement, *supra* note 1, art. 22.2, 23.2 and 23.1.

the laws of Vietnam,[50] Malaysia,[51] Singapore,[52] and Laos.[53] Thailand permits ministers to specify any goods as specific goods benefiting from additional protection by the issue of a Ministerial Regulation.[54] Indonesia and Cambodia grant additional protection to all kinds of goods. In some countries, the interpretations of these provisions are not yet clear because the law is only at an early stage of implementation and there has been no body of case law. Indeed the scope of protection of geographical indications in Vietnam seems to be above the standard protection under art. 22.2, with no need to prove the misleading of consumers to prohibit the use of the geographical indications. Moreover, with the negotiations on extending the additional protection to all products at the WTO,[55] the domestic legal framework might evolve to remove this divide.

In relation to trademarks, the TRIPS obligation on geographical indications is only to provide an effective means for the protection of geographical indications. Members have enough flexibility to design a system of protection in line with TRIPS, and this leads to a conflict of rights between geographical indications and trademark protections. The TRIPS Agreement provides a framework for the resolution of this conflict in art. 24.5. However, art. 24 can be

[50] The Vietnam Law on Intellectual Property 2009, art. 129.3.d prohibits "Using protected geographical indications of wines or spirits for wines or spirits not originating from geographical areas bearing such geographical indication, even where the true origin of goods is indicated or geographical indications are used in the form of translations or transcriptions, or accompanied by such words as 'category,' 'model,' 'type,' 'imitation' or the like."

[51] The Geographical Indication Act 2000 of Malaysia, §5.1.d prohibits "any use in the course of trade of a geographical indication identifying wines for wines not originating in the place indicated by the geographical indication in question or a geographical indication identifying spirits for spirits not originating in the place indicated by the geographical indication in question, even where the true origin of the wines or spirits is indicated or the geographical indication is used in translation or accompanied by expressions such as 'kind', 'type', 'style' or 'imitation.'

[52] The Geographical Indications Act 1999 of Singapore, §3.2.c & 3.2.d, prohibit "any use of a geographical indication, being a geographical indication which identifies a wine/spirit, in relation to a wine/spirit which did not originate from the place indicated by the geographical indication."

[53] The Law on Intellectual Property 2011 of Laos, art. 59.2, prohibits "a geographical indication . . . where related to wines or spirits, even in translation or accompanied by expressions such as 'kind', 'type', 'style', 'imitation' or the like."

[54] The Geographical Indications Protection Act of Thailand, §28 "Indication of the true geographical origin of the goods . . . shall include the use of the expressions 'kind', 'type', and 'style' including any similar expression or the like in conjunction with the geographical indication used with the goods."

[55] *See* General Council Trade Negotiations Committee, *Issues Related to the Extension of the Protection of Geographical Indications provided for in Article 23 of the TRIPS Agreement to Products other than Wines and Spirits*, WT/GC/W/546 and TN/C/W/25 (May 18, 2005), *available at* www.wto.org/english/tratop_e/trips_e/ta_docs_e/5_2_wtgcw546_e.pdf.

interpreted as an exception to both trademarks and geographical indications. This results in different interpretations in local jurisdictions according to their respective views on the matter.[56]

The ASEAN *sui generis* countries accept the coexistence of trademarks registered previously in good faith and geographical indications later registered. However, Thailand is unique, in that it supports the proposals submitted by the EU to the WTO,[57] while the Philippines has supported the approach of the United States.[58] In addition to these debates over how ASEAN countries should reform their domestic laws to better protect geographical indications, however, there is also a need for a greater emphasis on interoperability of geographical indications within ASEAN.

11.3 ESTABLISHING AN INTEROPERABLE SYSTEM FOR GEOGRAPHICAL INDICATIONS

Some countries have started to engage in a regional framework, building up an interoperable system to facilitate the protection of geographical indications among themselves. It is interesting to analyze these systems and see whether they can facilitate the protection of geographical indications in ASEAN countries. After outlining the wider international law context, this section discusses the EU and West African approaches to geographical indication protection. It then analyzes the possibilities for greater interoperability in the ASEAN context.

11.3.1 *International Notification and Registration Frameworks*

The TRIPS Agreement and the 2001 Doha Declaration offer a mandate for the establishment of a multilateral system of notification and registration of geographical indications for wines, later extended to spirits.[59] TRIPS does not, however, set out a timeframe for the completion of the negotiations and indicates that participation in the system may be voluntary. That approach has led to divergence between countries. Some countries are of the view that there is no agreement to negotiate other outstanding implementation

56 Lê Thi Thu Hà, *Conflit de protection de l'indication géographique et de la marque selon l'Accord ADPIC et le droit vietnamien*, EU ASEAN Partenariat, FEDUCI collection (2013).

57 Thailand is a signatory to EU's proposals submitted to WTO: JOB (02)/194; TN/C/W/14 and Add.1 and 2, and Corr.1; WT/GC/W/540/Rev.1 and Add.1 TN/C/W/21/Rev.1 and Add.1; JOB (05)/61 and Add.1–2; *see* WT/GC/W/546, TN/C/W/25, *supra* note 55.

58 The Philippines is a signatory to the proposals submitted to WTO by the United States, IP/C/W/386; IP/C/W/360, *see* WT/GC/W/546, TN/C/W/25, *supra* note 55.

59 This mandate is clearly given in art. 23.4 of the TRIPS Agreement and in para. 18 of the Doha Declaration.

issues.[60] Other countries take the position that there is a clear mandate to negotiate the issue.[61]

The United States has assumed the responsibility for supervising the minimum proposal known as the joint proposal (the name is based on the large number of countries that support it).[62] It is influenced by the trademark system, with the basic principle of creating a database of geographical indications from different countries. Participation is entirely voluntary, and the database will contain information on the name protected as a geographical indication, the concerned WTO member, the date on which the geographical indication was protected by the member, the expiration date, any agreement involved (if applicable),[63] and the identification of the area relevant to the geographical indication. These points appear to be the basic minimum of what defines a geographical indication.[64] Any objection is resolved at the national level because it is not considered necessary to establish a new procedure for resolving disputes internationally.[65] Members who choose to be part of the system must refer to the notified list of geographical indications "along with other sources of information."[66] The joint proposal is based on a tradition of protecting

60 *See* Communication from Argentina regarding paragraphs 18 and 12 of the Draft Ministerial Declaration, November 12, 2001, WT/MIN (01)/W/8, *available at* www/wto.org/.

61 *See* Communication from Bulgaria, Czech Republic, EU, Hungary, Liechtenstein, Kenya, Mauritius, Nigeria, Pakistan, The Slovak Republic, Slovenia, Sri Lanka, Switzerland, Thailand, and Turkey regarding paras. 18 and 12 of the Draft Ministerial Declaration, November 14, 2001, WT/MIN (01)/W/11, *available at* www.wto.org/.

62 The group of the proposed joint proposal has fluctuating contours and has increased significantly. Japan signed the first proposal submitted in 1999 (IP/C/W/133) with the United States and will be part of the seventeen signatories countries of the proposal of 2002 (IP/C/W/5, October 23, 2002): Argentina, Australia, Canada, Chile, Colombia, Costa Rica, El Salvador, Ecuador, the United States, Guatemala, Honduras, Japan, Namibia, New Zealand, the Philippines, the Dominican Republic, and China have not, but will sign the last proposal of 2005.

63 *See* Council for TRIPS, *Notification Possibilities Provided in Articles 1.3 and 3.1 of the TRIPS Agreement*, IP/C/W/5 (October 23, 2002), *available at* www.wto.org/english/tratop_e/trips_e/ipcw5_e.doc.

64 *See* Council for TRIPS, *Technical Cooperative Activities: Information from Other Intergovernmental Organizations*, IP/C/W/10 (August 7, 1995), *available at* https://docs.wto.org/dol2fe/Pages/FE_Search/FE_S_S006.aspx?Query=(%40Symbol%3d+ip%2fc%2fw%2f*+)+and+(+%40DocumentDate+%3e%3d+1995%2f01%2f01+00%3a00%3a00+)+and+(+%40DocumentDate+%3c%3d+1995%2f12%2f31+23%3a59%3a59+)&Language=ENGLISH&Context=FomerScriptedSearch&languageUIChanged=true#.

65 *See* Council for TRIPS, *Joint Proposal for a Multilateral System of Notification and Registration of a Geographical Indications for Wines and Spirits*, TN/IP/W/9 (April 13, 2004), *available at* https://docsonline.wto.org/dol2fe/Pages/SS/DirectDoc.aspx?filename=t%3A%2Ftn%2Fip%2Fw9.doc&.

66 *See* Council for TRIPS, *Proposal for a Multilateral System for Notification and Registration of Geographical Indications for Wines and Spirits based on Article 23.4 of the TRIPS Agreement*, IP/C/W/133 (March 11, 1999), *available at* https://docsonline.wto.org/dol2fe/Pages/SS/DirectDoc.aspx?filename=t%3A%2Fip%2Fc%2Fw133.doc&.

geographical indications through the trademark system and constructs a multilateral system that is least constraining. It requires a geographical indication applicant from the origin country to initiate all the procedures for protection of their geographical indication in every single country where protection is sought.

A more expansive concept of protection is set forth under the Lisbon Agreement, as well as the EU system.[67] The first EU (1998) proposal outlined a multilateral system that necessarily involved all WTO members, with all the existing geographical indications being already recognized and protected in their country of origin, along with applicable laws and proof of compliance according to the definition of the geographical indication.[68] This notification of a list was followed by a proposed notification of individual geographical indications that was similar to the joint proposal, but that also provided for the notification of available translations of the geographical indication. The EU proposal regarding an objection contrasts with the joint proposal, in that the differences and objections are resolved at an international level through direct negotiations between the concerned countries in terms of *absolute* grounds of refusal, known as reserves, with the *relative* grounds of refusal having been resolved at the national level. Possible reasons for absolute refusal include the noncompliance of the geographical indication with the definition in the TRIPS Agreement (art. 22.1), the question of homonyms (art. 22.4), and the generic nature of the geographical indication (art. 24.6). Relative grounds include the existence of prior rights (arts. 24.4 and 24.5). These cannot form the basis of a reservation at the international level by WTO members, but they can be invoked under domestic law.[69]

The system proposed by the EU implies a two-tier logic of examination. Acceptance of an application, after success at the first stage of the examination of absolute criteria at the international level, reduces further questions about the validity of the geographical indication (related to these criteria) in each country where protection is sought. These legal effects apply to all WTO members, regardless of whether they are a part of the system or not. However, the obligations of the participating members go beyond this: the registration of

67 Evans and Blakeney, *supra* note 46 at 607.

68 *See* Council for TRIPS, *Proposal for a Multilateral Register of Geographical Indications for Wines and Spirits Based on Article 23.4 of the TRIPS Agreement*, IP/C/W/107 (July 28, 1998), *available at* https://docsonline.wto.org/dol2fe/Pages/FormerScriptedSearch/directdoc.aspx?DDFDocuments/t/IP/C/W107.doc.

69 *See* Council for TRIPS, Geographical Indications, TN/IP/W/11 (June 14, 2005), *available at* https://docsonline.wto.org/dol2fe/Pages/SS/DirectDoc.aspx?filename=t%3A%2Ftn%2Fip%2Fw11.doc&.

a geographical indication on the multilateral register constitutes a rebuttable presumption of its eligibility for protection.

Hong Kong shares this concept of rebuttable presumption and has made a "middle" proposal.[70] This proposal is based on an entirely voluntary principle of participation, just as in the joint proposal. Any conflict between competing geographical indications is settled at the national level, in the same way as for joint proposals. Registration would provide *prima facie* evidence of ownership of the geographical indication, its conformity with the TRIPS Agreement, and the protection it enjoys in the country of origin.[71] The presumption does not apply to the recognition of geographical indications as a nongeneric name or to the issue of homonyms. All other grounds of validity of a geographical indication would be dealt with at the national level, leaving little scope to move to the international sphere. Since Doha, there has been absolute gridlock[72] on this issue, largely the result of the vastly divergent positions taken by the EU and United States. It means that under the TRIPS Agreement, there is no facilitation system for the protection of geographical indications at the international level that could help protection of geographical indications within ASEAN countries.

The Lisbon Agreement, as adopted in 1958 and revised in 1967, provides for a single international registration system for appellations of origin, administered by the International Bureau of the WIPO. The principle is that the appellation of origin of each of the signatory countries are automatically protected in all other signatory countries except in any country that has opposed it within one year from the receipt of the notification of registration.[73] As domestic legislation in many countries does not incorporate the concept of "appellations of origin" with parallel provisions, the Lisbon Agreement did not attract many members other than twenty-eight countries (and not even all EU countries). Indeed, the definition of appellation of origin sets higher criteria for recognition than those for geographical indication defined in TRIPS.[74]

[70] Stefania Fusco, *Geographical Indications: A Discussion on the TRIPs Regulation after the Ministerial Conference of Hong Kong*, 12 INTEL. PROP. L. REV. 197 (2008), *available at* http://scholarship.law.marquette.edu/iplr/vol12/iss2/1.

[71] *See* Council for TRIPS, *Multilateral System of Notification and Registration of Geographical Indications under Article 23.4 of the TRIPS Agreement*, TN/IP/W/8 (April 23, 2003), *available at* www.wto.org/english/tratop_e/trips_e/ta_docs_e/5_1_tnipw8_e.pdf.

[72] Malobika Banerji, *Geographical Indications: Which Way Should ASEAN Go?*, Boston College Intellectual Property & Technology Forum, *available at* http://bciptf.org/wp-content/uploads/2012/06/Geographical_Indications.pdf.

[73] *See* Lisbon Agreement, art 5.3.

[74] Art. 2.1(i) of Geneva Act defines "appellation of origin" as "any denomination protected in the Contracting Party of Origin consisting of or containing the name of a geographical area,

Taking the shortcomings of the Lisbon Agreement into consideration, the Geneva Act, as adopted in May 2015, expands the application of the system to geographical indications as defined in the TRIPS Agreement. It thus enlarges the system to include denomination of products having a weaker link with their geographical origin than those with appellations of origin. The definitions of geographical indication and appellation of origin include any words "consisting of or containing the name of geographical area, or another denomination known as referring to such area." The Lisbon system is characterized by the registration of names already protected at the national level through appellations of origin/geographical indications in an International Register, which automatically confers the high level of protection granted to geographical indication/appellation of origin by the Lisbon system in all countries party to the Agreement (except any contracting party that has refused the registration during the time limit provided by the Regulations).

Article 11 of the Geneva Act maintains the high level of protection in the initial Lisbon Agreement while providing more details about the scope of the protection. The Geneva Act prohibits any use of the geographical indication/appellation of origin with respect to goods of the same kind not originating in the geographical area of origin or not complying with any other applicable requirements for using the geographical indication/appellation of origin (such as specification), without having to prove any risk of the use being misleading. It also prohibits the use for dissimilar goods, if such use would indicate or suggest a connection between those goods or services and the beneficiaries of the geographical indication/appellation of origin, and would be likely to damage their interests, or because such use would be likely to impair or dilute in an unfair manner, or take unfair advantage of, the reputation the owner has in its geographical indication/appellation of origin. Any other practice liable to mislead consumers as to the true origin, provenance, or nature of the goods is also prohibited.

The Geneva Act also prohibits any imitation of the geographical indication/appellation of origin, even if the true origin of the goods is indicated, or if the geographical indication/appellation of origin is used in translated form or is accompanied by terms such as "style," "kind," "type," "make," "imitation," "method," "as produced in," "like," "similar," or the like. Where a later

or another denomination known as referring to such area, which serves to designate a good as originating in that geographical area, where the quality or characteristics of the good are due exclusively or essentially to the geographical environment, including natural and human factors, and which has given the good its reputation."

trademark is covered by the appellation of origin/geographical indication, a Contracting Party shall, ex officio if its legislation so permits or at the request of an interested party, refuse or invalidate the registration of that later trademark if use of the trademark would result in one of the situations covered by article 11.

An innovation from the initial Lisbon Agreement is that the application for international registration can be done by the Competent Authority of the Party or directly by the beneficiaries of the geographical indication/appellation of origin (i.e., the producers). This reflects the influence of TRIPS where the protection in a foreign jurisdiction can be applied by the users of the geographical indication themselves.

In conclusion, the Geneva Act of the Lisbon Agreement offers a very interesting tool to facilitate the protection of domestic geographical indications in countries that are members of the Union. As noted by Daniel Gervais, the system is very appealing, as it allows for objections against the registration for any reason.[75] Yet even if now it is easier for any country to become a member of the Lisbon System, it will take time before new countries join, and currently no ASEAN country (or ASEAN itself) is a member.

11.3.2 *Existing Regional Systems*

With very few countries being members of the Lisbon Union, some groups of countries have decided to set up regional systems for the protection of geographical indications. In particular, the EU has a fully integrated system, but also the West African countries have a system through the African Intellectual Property Organization (OAPI).

European Union

The EU aims to enhance the reputation of European wines and increase their market share both in the EU and worldwide. The first wine names were protected at EU level under legislation in the 1970s that required member states to identify and protect geographical indications and notify them to the European Commission, thereby protecting them in all member states.[76] After

[75] Daniel J. Gervais, *Traditional Knowledge: Are We Closer to the Answers? The Potential Role of Geographical Indications*, 15(2) ILSA J. Int'l. Comp. Law 551, 564 (2009).

[76] Frank Fay, *EU System for Geographical Indications for Agricultural Products and Foodstuffs*, WIPO/GEO/SOF/09/4 (June 11, 2009), *available at* www.wipo.int/edocs/mdocs/geoind/en/wipo_geo_sof_09/wipo_geo_sof_09_www_124276.pdf.

reform to the wine sector in 2008, an EU register for wine was established along similar lines as that for agricultural products and foodstuffs, and is currently in the process of being implemented. An additional list geographical indication has been established for aromatized wines, which is associated with the register for wine names. The first spirits were protected throughout the EU in 1989 legislation[77] by a list of names in an annex to the regulation, which serves as the register. Under Regulation 110/2008 on protection of geographical indications for spirits, there is no specific provision on application at the national level but only a registration procedure at the EU level. Wines are now protected through EU Regulation 1308/2013 following the same principle of a two-step registration procedure as for agricultural goods and foodstuffs.

For agricultural products and foodstuffs, an EU register was established in 1992. Once the geographical indication is registered at the EU level, the national transitional rights disappear. Indeed, no national rights shall coexist next to the EU Protected Designations of Origin (PDOs) and Protected Geographical Indications (PGIs). The EU system is mandatory for all members of the EU, with no possibility of a grant of only national PDOs or PGIs for the list of products annexed to the EU Regulation where the EU is competent. In the same light, only the EU is authorized to negotiate trade agreements on geographical indications and not the member states of the EU. Geographical indications are thus placed under the sovereignty of the EU and its member states.

West Africa

In Africa, among the twenty-three countries with *sui generis* geographical indication laws, seventeen[78] are members of the African Intellectual Property Organization (OAPI) and therefore have the same geographical indication law, namely the provisions of Annex VI to the Bangui Agreement.[79] It is, thus, the same unique legislation for intellectual property rights including geographical indication in the seventeen countries. All the member states of the OAPI are party to both the Paris Convention and the TRIPS Agreement. Burkina

77 Regulation (EEC) No 1576/89 of May 29, 1989 on Laying Down General Rules on the Definition, Description and Presentation of Spirit Drinks, 1989 O.J. (L 160).

78 Benin, Burkina Faso, Cameroon, the Central Africa, Chad, Congo Republic, the Democratic Republic of Congo, Côte d'Ivoire, Gabon, Guinea, Guinea Bissau, Equatorial Guinea, Mali, Mauritania, Niger, Senegal, and Togo are parties to the OAPI Agreement, which embodies the national laws of the member states of the African Intellectual Property Organization and, therefore, applies directly in each Member State.

79 African Intellectual Property Organization (OAPI), *Bangui Agreement* (amended on February 24, 1999), *available at* www.oapi.int/.

Faso, Congo, Gabon, and Togo are also Parties to the Lisbon Agreement. Under the Bangui Agreement,[80] any person wishing to register a geographical indication must file with the organization or the ministry responsible for industrial property. Once registered the geographical indication is then valid automatically in all members of the OAPI, becoming an independent legal title in each of the countries, governed according to the laws of that country.

11.3.3 *Challenges for ASEAN*

These two models of regional integration of geographical indication protection can contribute to the debate around the need for enhanced protections for geographical indication within ASEAN. Within ASEAN, government officials have become increasingly aware of the role of intellectual property rights in economic development. However, the same awareness of geographical indications has not yet reached out to producers, rural communities, businesses, and civil society.[81] Geographical indication protection itself builds up valuable reputations and goodwill for well-known local products.[82] Research on geographical indications protection has found several economic benefits including that it helps maintain the reputation of products and helps producers obtain premium prices.[83]

Owing to the general absence of collective organization for registered geographical indications, the lack of experience in the creation and management of such organizations (which is amplified by literacy and organizational weaknesses in rural areas as well as insufficient communication among producers, traders, and other actors), geographical indication protection is mainly a top-down approach, with authorities at local or national levels identifying and registering geographical indications. This top-down approach needs to be reconsidered, with the creation of producer/interprofessional organizations to guarantee the sustainability of geographical indication system development in ASEAN countries.

80 *Id.*

81 Food and Agriculture Organization of the United Nations [FAO], *FAO-AFD Project on the Promotion of Rural Development through Development of Geographical Indications at Regional Level in Asia*, GCP/RAS/281/FRA (August 1, 2013).

82 Sophie Reviron, *Geographical Indications: Creation and Distribution of Economic Value in Developing Countries*, Swiss National Center of Competence in Research (2009), *available at* http://phase1.nccr-trade.org/images/stories/publications/IP5/report_IP5_GI_Value_2009.pdf.

83 Carl Shapiro, *Premiums for High Quality Product as a Return to Reputation*, 98(4) Q. J. Econ. 659, 659–679 (1983).

Most geographical indications in ASEAN are linked to products related to agriculture, fisheries, crafts, and artisanal works, which are also some of the sectors that provide livelihoods to large sections of the poor. It is too early to examine the socioeconomic implications of geographical indication protection in ASEAN in detail, because almost all of the ASEAN countries are in the very first steps of building geographical indication protection systems. For Vietnam, except in the cases of Phu Quoc and Halong calamari (in which there has been an obvious change in the price of its products after the geographical indication registration), there seems to be no notable change in product pricing.[84] Thailand has emerged to be the most successful country at implementing geographical indication protections.[85] There has been a notable price change of products in Thailand after geographical indication registration,[86] and this allows other ASEAN countries to better understand the benefits provided by geographical indications for the unique and special products in those countries. Explicit economic gains are important, but the lack of use of geographical indications is a point of concern. ASEAN countries should consider this to be a development issue, recognizing that geographical indications are linked to the livelihoods of the people residing in the designated areas.

A key consideration for ASEAN countries in approaching geographical indications, as is the case with other forms of intellectual property rights, relates to the costs of setting up the institutional framework necessary for registering, administering, and enforcing geographical indications in the country. Considering their human, financial, and technical resource constraints, it is expected that in the short to medium term, the costs for establishing and running the system will be reasonable when considering the economic value that might attach to the use of said system. Technical and financial assistance may obviate some of these constraints in the short term.

There are also significant technical and capacity needs that have to be addressed at different levels of developing and using a geographical indication as well as when setting up a national protection system. During the past decade, intellectual property offices and geographical indication divisions in

84 Lê Hà, *supra* note 21.

85 Stephane Passerie, *FAO/AFD Project on the Promotion of Rural Development through Development of Geographical Indications at Regional Level in Asia*, Regional Workshop on "Making Geographical Indications Work for Rural Communities in Selected Asian Countries: Identify Products and Drafting of Disciplinary for Geographical Indication Registration," Cambodia (2014).

86 *Id.*, the price of Coffee Cherry Doi Chaang before/after registration is 4.50 baht/kg and 15 baht/kg, it continues increasing to 28–32 baht/kg. Price of pineapple Chiang Rai Phulae before/after registration is 8 baht/kg and 23 baht/kg (price at farm) and 35 baht/kg – 50 baht/kg (retail price), it reaches now 60 baht/kg.

Indonesia, Thailand, Vietnam, Laos, and Cambodia have gained expertise in identifying geographical indications and support the drafting of geographical indication applications following several cooperation and development projects.[87] As a result, they were able to accompany the registration of 200 national geographical indications. This is not yet the case for Brunei, and Myanmar, where a geographical indication division was either just created or needs to be created and where geographical indication officers are still being trained.

For most ASEAN countries, it is still a challenge to afford the costs of all these technical and capacity components. The increased efficiency of geographical indication administrations (both public and private) is a key means to support the sustainability of geographical indication systems, through improved protection, control, enforcement, commercialization, and valorization. It is therefore very important to favor nationally the creation of a cooperation mechanism between various agencies playing a role on national geographical indication development (such as intellectual property organizations, Departments of Agriculture, Fishery, and Tourism; export promotion; accreditation/control bodies; intellectual property enforcement authorities; consumer protection, etc.) through the support of national committees or working groups on geographical indications and memorandums of understanding. Cooperation between public and private entities (nongovernmental organizations, trade associations, etc.) involved in rural development and trade promotion also needs to be further developed.

11.3.4 *Harmonization of ASEAN Member States' National Legal Frameworks*

Improvements in intellectual property rights administration can be achieved by harmonizing national systems regionally and internationally. While TRIPS was the main model for implementing geographical indication laws in ASEAN countries (with some influences from bilateral cooperation and development projects with the EU, France, and Switzerland), another recent source of inspiration for domestic laws in ASEAN countries are the more than 156 RTAs/FTAs that reference geographical indications. RTAs/FTAs involving the EU typically have provisions concerning the establishment of registration and recognition of selected European geographical indications, while the

[87] Some examples for cooperation under ECAP Project, or under AFD or national programs such as National Program supporting Intellectual Asset Development in Vietnam (Program 68).

RTAs/FTAs that involve the US[88] focus on the use of trademark systems.[89] Participating in such agreements therefore not only means that countries are agreeing to amend their national intellectual property laws, but also means that they are likely to agree to standards that are far removed from their own economic and social needs.[90] While some of these FTAs might have some impacts on domestic legal frameworks, they are meant mainly to protect a list of geographical indications from signatory countries in other signatories' jurisdictions, thereby escaping from the long procedure of individually registering each geographical indication in the other signatories' jurisdictions.

The FTA between Vietnam and the EU includes a list of 169 EU geographical indications and 39 Vietnamese geographical indications.[91] The level of protection to be granted to these particular geographical indications is covered by the Agreement, with the same protection being accorded to Vietnam geographical indications and EU geographical indications. The extent of protection is higher than that provided in Vietnamese law, but lower than that provided in EU Regulations. There is a prohibition on the use of a geographical indication for goods not originating in the country, even where the true origin of the product is indicated or the geographical indication is used in translation or accompanied by expressions such as "kind," "type," "style," "imitation," or the like; and there is a prohibition on goods not produced according to the laws of the country of alleged origin using, in a way that misleadingly or unfairly indicates or suggests that the goods in question originate in a geographical area other than the true place of origin.

In the FTA between Vietnam and Singapore, the list of indications has to be validated, with the same scope of protection as that provided in the EU–Vietnam FTA. Taking only the particular geographical indications listed in the Agreement into consideration, it is difficult to conclude whether such provisions will influence the national legal framework and enable any harmonization of national legislation within ASEAN, and especially given that only two FTAs have been finalized. It can thus be concluded that ASEAN was

88 The US-Vietnam BTA were signed in 2001, the US–Singapore FTA implemented in 2007 and has been in force in January 2004. The US–Thailand FTA negotiations were launched in 2004 but suspended in 2006 following the dissolution of the Thai Parliament and the subsequent military-led coup.

89 Mohammed El-Said, *The Road from TRIPS-Minus, to TRIPS, to TRIPS-Plus: Implications of IPRs for the Arab World*, 8(1) J. WORLD INTELLECT. PROPERTY 53, 53–65 (2005).

90 Bryan Mercurio, *TRIPS-plus Provisions in FTAs: Recent Trends in Regional Trade Agreements and the WTO Legal System, in* LORAND BARTEL & FEDERIO ORTINO (eds.), REGIONAL TRADE AGREEMENTS AND THE WTO LEGAL SYSTEM 215–237 (2006).

91 The EU–Vietnam FTA, art. 6.

not a sufficiently solid partner for negotiations with the EU and that bilateral relations were easier to conclude, and this is partially explained by ASEAN not having the exclusive ability to negotiate FTAs in the name of its members (as opposed to the EU).

On the other hand, some countries are also negotiating with the United States, which focuses to a large extent on the elimination of domestic *sui generis* geographical indication protection systems and their replacement by trademark systems.[92] The "TRIPS-minus" geographical indication provisions can be found in US draft FTAs with Thailand[93] and Singapore.[94] However, the evolution of the geographical indication chapters in the FTAs with the United States has changed significantly over time. For example, while the fate of the recent Trans-Pacific Strategic Economic Partnership Agreement (TPP) remains uncertain, it is interesting to note that that agreement anticipates the transformation of geographical indication protection to an independent system.[95] The United States and the alliance adopted, for the first time, a full section for geographical indication recognition and protection.[96] If this approach takes hold, there may be less tension for ASEAN countries in geographical indication system implementation when negotiating with both the EU and the United States.

Many FTA/RTAs have been signed by members of ASEAN, but it is critical that none of the FTAs were directly negotiated by ASEAN but by individual member counties, which raises the issue of reinforcing ASEAN as a unique partner. At the international level (especially in the WTO forum), thanks to the power of numbers, ASEAN should have a significant impact on the direction of the multilateral trade agenda, whereas an individual member country could not have such an impact in the bilateral context.[97] ASEAN

92 Vivas-Eugui, D., & C. Spennemann, *The Treatment of Geographical Indications in Recent Regional and Bilateral Free Trade Agreements*, United Nations Conference on Trade and Development (UNCTAD)/International Centre for Trade and Sustainable Development (ICTSD) Project on Intellectual Property and Sustainable Development, Costa Rica (2006).

93 The Thailand–US FTA has launched negotiations since February 2006 and has not been concluded.

94 The Singapore–US FTA, *available at* https://ustr.gov/trade-agreements/free-trade-agreements/singapore-fta/final-text.

95 *See* Trans-Pacific Partnership Agreement, Article 18, *available at* https://ustr.gov/trade-agreements/free-trade-agreements/trans-pacific-partnership/tpp-full-text.

96 Lê Hà, *Conflict of Geographical Indications and Trademark: from TRIPS Agreement to EU-VN FTA: Challenges for Vietnam*, J. Laws, VNU (2016), online copy *available at* www.sblaw.vn/conflict-between-geographical-indication-and-trademark-protections-under-the-trips-agreement-and-vietnam-laws/.

97 Ross Buckley, Vai IO Lo, & Laurence Boulle (eds.), Challenges to Multilateral Trade: The Impact of Bilateral, Preferential and Regional Agreements (2008).

should thus stress its position to support the multilateral trade rules of the TRIPS Agreement under the auspices of WTO. It may be useful for countries to work closely with other "geographical indication alliances" in order to make the geographical indication issue more public. The target should be not only to improve information for consumers of ASEAN geographical indications (which may act ultimately as "ambassadors" of quality and know-how for all chain of production, and the region of origin, in the global market), but also to raise recognition from all parties about the importance of having domestic geographical indication better protected.

11.3.5 *Regional Geographical Indication Website and Mandatory Database*

Currently the visibility of geographical indication developments in ASEAN is relatively low. The absence of a common regional platform to mutualize specific information and developments related to geographical indication is a handicap to geographical indication visibility, exchange, and networking in the region. In that context, it is necessary to consider establishing a regional system for recognition of geographical indications through an online regional network.

Already, in ASEAN the common online geographical indications platform of the ASEAN member states aims to make the information of all registered geographical indications in the ASEAN region widely available and easily accessible to all interested stakeholders. ASEAN also now has a geographical indication database[98] developed by the Intellectual Property Offices of the ASEAN member states, with the support of the EU–ASEAN Project on the Protection of Intellectual Property Rights (ECAP, administered by the EU Intellectual Property Office). This website must be linked to the ASEAN portal and developed as a forum where all information and knowledge can circulate and where stakeholders can find information according to their interests. This will help achieve the following goals:

- To mutualize information on geographical indication national systems and develop a system dedicated to targeted audiences
- To promote geographical indications as a concept, the visibility of geographical indication products, and the practical benefits of geographical indications

[98] *See ASEAN GI Database*, ASEAN, *available at* www.asean-gidatabase.org/.

- To encourage information exchanges and discussion forums between geographical indication stakeholders (public–public, public–private, and private–private), business partners and other development partners.

ASEAN countries could through technical initiatives such as this strengthen their socioeconomic and cultural values and associated features such as the microenterprises they can spin off, and increase their attraction for tourism or investment. Further, there is a need to determine and codify the scientific attributes of these products on which legal verdicts can be based, instead of relying on subjective, connoisseur-determined statements on reputation, as is largely the case now. Such a register could be used to facilitate the protection of geographical indications within ASEAN, following one of the models proposed under the TRIPS negotiations, or (preferably) the model proposed by the Geneva Act of the Lisbon Agreement, which could be enforced with ASEAN to become a party to the Geneva Act.

11.4 CONCLUSION

Protection of geographical indications contributes to creating a bridge that marries the old and the new: the national imperative of creating awareness about traditional products and knowledge with the preparation to engage internationally with the trade of goods and ideas in the twenty-first century.

While it may be assumed that ASEAN countries can benefit from geographical indication protection, there is some evidence that geographical indication protection would generate significant challenges for ASEAN countries, such as the problems posed by a top-down approach to geographical indication protection, the costs of establishing and administering a geographical indication protection regime, the lack of harmonization between domestic legal frameworks, and the fact that there is no common regional Intellectual Property Office.

As this chapter has described, a variety of approaches to the protection of geographical indications exist at the international and regional levels. The two models of regional integration of geographical indication protection (EU and OAPI) can contribute to the debate of an enhanced protection for geographical indication within the ASEAN context.

12

Connectivity, Interoperability, and Regional Integration of the ASEAN Trademark and Design Systems

Ignacio de Medrano Caballero

12.1 INTRODUCTION

The significant efforts required to facilitate e-government connectivity and interoperability in trademarks and designs is one of the current challenges facing the Association of Southeast Nations (ASEAN) intellectual property offices. The challenges stem from language barriers, differences in institutional capacity, and different specifications of formats and varieties of categorizations within ASEAN countries.[1] There is therefore a pressing need for ASEAN intellectual property offices to exchange data in an interoperable manner in order to fulfill many of the key objectives set up in the ASEAN Intellectual Property Rights (IPR) Action Plan 2016–2025.

Organizational complexity, outdated and cumbersome procedures, and a lack of connectivity and cooperation between countries might also create electronic barriers that prevent citizens and businesses from using public services efficiently and that might impede the smooth functioning of a regionally integrated economic zone such as the ASEAN Economic Community (AEC). If these challenges are overcome, ASEAN member states will move closer to their goal of transforming ASEAN into an innovative and competitive region through the use of intellectual property, and ensuring that the region remains an active player in the international intellectual property community.

* The comments made in this chapter express the views of its author and do not necessarily represent the views of the EU Intellectual Property Office (EUIPO).

[1] On the interoperability of the European Trademarks and Designs Systems *see* Jane E. Fountain, *On the Effects of e-Government on Political Institutions*, *in* Daniel Lee Kleinman & Kelly Moore (eds.), Routledge Handbook of Science, Technology and Society 474, 462 (, 2014). *See also* Jane E. Fountain, Raquel Galindo-Dorado & Jeffrey Rothschild, *The Office for Harmonization in the Internal Market: Creating a 21st Century Public Agency*, 10(2) National Center for Digital Government Working Paper Series 38 (2010), *available at* http://scholarworks.umass.edu/ncdg/38.

Therefore connectivity and interoperability must be considered key driving factors for the achievement of the strategic goals in the intellectual property field included in the ASEAN Community Vision 2025.

12.2 INTEROPERABILITY OF THE ASEAN TRADEMARK AND INDUSTRIAL DESIGN SYSTEMS WITHIN THE ASEAN IPR ACTION PLAN 2011–2015

Within the five strategic goals laid out in the ASEAN IPR Action Plan 2011–2015, the first[2] and second[3] goals are the most relevant to improving the interoperability of ASEAN member states' trademark and registered design systems, as they aim at enhancing the capacity of the ASEAN intellectual property offices to enable them to deliver timely, quality, and accessible intellectual property services and develop regional infrastructures. The fifth[4] strategic goal also supports the improving of interoperability between ASEAN intellectual property offices by focusing on increasing cooperation between them and working toward convergence of practices.

Among the initiatives that have facilitated the interoperability and the regional integration of ASEAN trademark and industrial design systems are:

- The implementation of the "ASEAN Ethnic List of Goods and Services" to be used by ASEAN intellectual property offices to supplement the Nice Classification of goods and services. The original purpose of this list was to identify goods and services specific to ASEAN countries that could be submitted for inclusion in the Nice Classification. Under the IPR Action Plan 2011–2015, the objective of this list was modified. The ASEAN Ethnic List of Goods and Services was renamed as the ASEAN List of Goods (and Services), and is now part of a larger list known as ASEAN TMclass. The list was further developed from 2014 to 2016 by the ASEAN Task Force on Trademark Cooperation, which was established by the ASEAN Working Group on Intellectual Property Cooperation (AWGIPC) and

[2] A balanced intellectual property system that takes into account the varying levels of development of member states and differences in institutional capacity of national intellectual property offices to enable them to deliver timely, quality, and accessible intellectual property services to promote the region as being conducive to the needs of users and generators of intellectual property.

[3] Developed national or regional legal and policy infrastructures that address evolving demands of the intellectual property landscape and ASEAN member states participate in global intellectual property systems at the appropriate time.

[4] Intensified cooperation among ASEAN member states and increased level of collaboration among them to enhance human and institutional capacity of intellectual property offices in the region.

composed of senior officials from the trademark departments of ASEAN intellectual property offices.

- The ASEAN IP Portal,[5] which is a regional consolidated platform providing information about intellectual property for the entire ASEAN region and is one of the most important initiatives in this area. The ASEAN IP Portal was included in the third strategic goal and was launched in April 2013. It was first developed and managed by Thailand before being passed on to Singapore.[6] It provides information on ASEAN member states' intellectual property systems, comparative intellectual property–related data, and web links to ASEAN intellectual property offices. The ASEAN IP Portal includes an electronic application form for the ASEAN Patent Examination Co-operation (ASPEC) platform, for ASEAN TMview, and ASEAN Designview. In the future new features such as ASEAN TMclass might be introduced to enhance the portal.
- Another relatively new addition to the initiatives on regional interoperability is the development of a common filing form for trademarks, which is also part of the first strategic goal. This common filing form was originally part of the ASEAN IPR Action Plan 2004–2010, but was shelved before its completion. In 2014, it was brought back to the table in response to feedback from the private sector, which wanted filing of trademarks in the region to be simpler, and more harmonized between jurisdictions.
- Some initiatives with an international dimension are the commitment of the ASEAN member states to accede to two international agreements: the Protocol Relating to the Madrid Agreement Concerning the International Registration of Marks (Madrid Protocol),[7] and the Hague Agreement concerning the International Registration of Industrial Designs (Hague Agreement).[8] These two commitments resulted from the difficulties facing attempts to develop common regional trademark and design systems within ASEAN (pursuant to the first IPR Action Plan), and accession to international agreements was accepted by the ASEAN member states as a viable alternative to the development of a common regional system in the short term.

5 ASEAN, *ASEAN Intellectual Property Portal* (October 7, 2016), *available at* www.aseanip.org.

6 The hosting and management of the ASEAN Intellectual Property Portal followed the country acting as chair of the AWGIPC, however, the last chair (Brunei Darussalam) did not host the ASEAN Intellectual Property Portal, which has remained with the Intellectual Property Office of Singapore (IPOS).

7 On May 2017, Brunei Darussalam, Cambodia, Laos, Philippines, Singapore, and Vietnam are members of the Madrid Protocol.

8 On May 2017, Brunei Darussalam, Cambodia and Singapore are members of the Hague Agreement.

In 2014, the AWGIPC requested the World Intellectual Property Organization (WIPO) to assist in conducting an assessment study of the implementation of the action plan 2011–2015. This study was commissioned to identify the initiatives that would need to be carried over into the next action plan, those that would need to be refocused, and the key areas of intellectual property rights that would aid the regional economic integration of ASEAN. According to the assessment study done by two external consultants,[9] more than 80 percent of the 108 initiatives under the action plan 2011–2015 should have been completed by 2015.[10] This assessment study was also a preliminary step in the preparation for the next ASEAN IPR Action Plan 2016–2025, to ensure that the final design of this new plan was fully in line with the agenda of the AEC.

12.3 COOPERATION AND COLLABORATION IN TRADEMARKS AND DESIGNS BETWEEN ASEAN AND THE EUROPEAN UNION IN THE FRAMEWORK OF THE ASEAN INTELLECTUAL PROPERTY RIGHTS ACTION PLAN 2011–2015

The cooperation and collaboration within the context of the ASEAN IPR Action Plan 2011–2015 between the ASEAN member states and the European Union (EU) in trademark and design systems has been very fruitful. Intellectual property was included as one of the sectoral areas of cooperation between the EU and ASEAN in the Bandar Seri Begawan Plan of Action to Strengthen the ASEAN–EU Enhanced Partnership (2013–2017), and the EU agreed to continue providing technical assistance on intellectual property matters "as a means to contribute to enhancing the ASEAN intellectual property system."[11]

Since 2013, the intense and close cooperation between the EU and ASEAN[12] in the fields of trademarks and designs has been developed mainly under the

9 Ms. Liew Woon Yin, former Director General of the Singapore Intellectual Property Office (IPOS) and Mr. Mart Leesti, former commissioner of the Canadian Intellectual Property Office.

10 *See* Denis Croze, Director, WIPO Singapore Office (WSO), Presentation at the ASEAN Intellectual Property Association (ASEAN IPA) Conference in Kuala Lumpur (Malaysia): WIPO's Support of the ASEAN IP Ecosystem (March 5, 2016), *available at* www.aseanipa.org/attachments/article/653/02.%20Denis%20Croze-WIPO%20Support%20of%20ASEAN%20IP%20Ecosystem.pdf.

11 Point 2.2.5 of the Bandar Seri Begawan Plan of Action to Strengthen the ASEAN-EU Enhanced Partnership (2013–2017) agreed in 2012 at the 19th ASEAN-EU Ministerial Meeting, *available at* http://eeas.europa.eu/asean/docs/plan_of_action_en.pdf.

12 For previous examples of ASEAN cooperation with dialogue partners in the intellectual property field, *see* Elizabeth Siew-Kuan Ng, *ASEAN IP Harmonization: Striking the Delicate Balance*, 25 PACE INT'L L. REV. 129, 154 (2013).

ECAP III-Phase II program,[13] the EU–ASEAN intellectual property rights cooperation program implemented by the EU Intellectual Property Office (EUIPO).[14] The project was approved by the European Union and ASEAN in 2009 to support the objectives of the ASEAN Economic Community Blueprint.[15] The project is aimed at supporting the strategic goals identified in the ASEAN IPR Action Plan 2011–2015.[16] The cooperation program gained political support when the ASEAN economic ministers recognized the outcomes of the projects on trademarks and designs developed under the ASEAN IPR Action Plan 2011–2015 with the support of the ECAP III Phase II.[17]

ECAP III Phase II focuses on developing a common approach within the ASEAN region in the areas of trademarks, industrial designs, geographical indications, and intellectual property enforcement. The project consists of a series of coordinated activities at the regional level aimed at ASEAN as a whole, with a strong emphasis on regional cooperation, coordination, and harmonization among the ASEAN member states within the framework of the ASEAN Economic Community Blueprint.[18]

[13] The specific objective of ECAP III is to support ASEAN regional integration and further upgrade and harmonize the systems for IP creation, protection, administration, and enforcement in the ASEAN region. *See* ECAP III, *EU-ASEAN Project on the Protection of Intellectual Property Rights*, *available at* www.ecap-project.org/.

[14] Since March 24, 2016 the name of the Office for Harmonization in the Internal Market has been replaced by the European Union Intellectual Property Office by Commission Regulation (EU) 2015/2424, Amending Council Regulation (EC) No 207/2009 on the Community Trade Mark and Commission Regulation (EC) No 2868/95 Implementing Council Regulation (EC) No 40/94 on the Community Trade Mark, and Repealing Commission Regulation (EC) No 2869/95 on the Fees Payable to the Office for Harmonization in the Internal Market (Trade Marks and Designs) (Text with EEA relevance), 2015 O.J. (L 341) 21.

[15] *See* Dr Surin Pitsuwan, Secretary-General, A *Welcome Address at the ECAP III-Phase I 1st Steering Committee* (July 14, 2010), *available at* http://asean.org/?static_post=welcome-address-by-he-s-pushpanathan-deputy-secretary-general-of-asean-for-asean-economic-community-at-the-1st-steering-committee-meeting-of-the-asean-project-on-the-protection-of-intellectual-propert.

[16] The renewed collaboration was started in 2013 with the EUIPO as the new implementing agency.

[17] The ASEAN Economic Ministers, at their 47th Meeting held on August 22, 2015 in Kuala Lumpur, Malaysia, recognized with satisfaction the work done by the ASEAN member states in the field of IP, such as the adoption of Common Guidelines on Substantive Examination; the finalization of the ASEAN List of Goods and Services; and the launch of on-line search tools, namely, ASEAN TMview, ASEAN TMclass, and ASEAN Designview, *available at* www.asean.org/storage/2015/12/JMS-AEM-47-Final-22–08–2015_3.pdf.

[18] At the Second ASEAN-EUIPO Heads of IP Offices Meeting held in Alicante, Spain, on October 2, 2015 a joint summary of the meeting was adopted, acknowledging the importance of trademarks, industrial designs in the economies of the ASEAN region and the European Union and the essential role of these intellectual property rights in ensuring that ASEAN and European businesses continue to flourish. The intention to continue to strengthen their joint efforts

Finally, the EU under ECAP III Phase II has provided technical assistance for ASEAN member states to prepare for their accession to the Madrid Protocol and the Hague Agreement. The project provided for on-the-job training on the Madrid Protocol procedures for trademark officials of interested ASEAN intellectual property offices, IT support, training courses focused on providing improved knowledge of the Madrid Protocol system, and awareness sessions focused on sharing knowledge on the use of the Madrid system to help the business community obtain protection in export markets. Several training and awareness raising sessions on the Madrid Protocol and the Hague Agreement were organized in coordination with other dialogue partners of the AWGIPC, in particular within the frameworks of the ASEAN Australian New Zealand Free Trade Area (AANZFTA) programs for Madrid and WIPO.

12.4 INITIATIVES FOR THE CONVERGENCE OF EXAMINATION PRACTICES OF ASEAN TRADEMARKS AND DESIGNS

The ASEAN Common Guidelines for the Substantive Examination of Trademarks, adopted by the AWGIPC (Common TM Guidelines) on December 2014 and the ASEAN Common Guidelines on the Substantive Examination and Registration of Industrial Designs (Common ID Guidelines) exemplify interoperability efforts to arrive at a higher level of convergence of administrative practices among ASEAN intellectual property offices.

12.4.1 *The ASEAN Common Guidelines on the Substantive Examination of Trademarks*

The first strategic goal of the ASEAN Intellectual Property Rights Action Plan 2011–2015 states that "a balanced IP system that takes into account the varying levels of development of member states and differences in institutional capacity of national IP Offices to enable them to deliver timely, quality, and accessible IP services to promote the region as being conducive to the needs

towards improving the protection of intellectual property, specifically trademarks, designs and geographical indications, including IT tools and databases, and developing innovative mechanisms directed at creating more appropriate conditions for the protection and use of those rights to support balanced and highly effective intellectual property systems for the economic development of the ASEAN region and for the benefit of stakeholders in general, and the business community, was also reaffirmed. *See* ECAP III, *Second ASEAN-OHIM Heads of IP Offices – Joint Summary of the Meeting* (October 2, 2015), *available at* http://ecap-project .org/activities/second-asean-ohim-heads-ip-offices-joint-summary-meeting.

of users and generators of IP." One of the initiatives to fulfill this goal[19] was to develop a manual of substantive examination to be used by ASEAN trademark examiners, the Common TM Guidelines. The guidelines were drafted taking into account the laws, regulations, and available jurisprudence of the ASEAN countries that are relevant to the examination of trademark applications.

In 2014, in order to enhance the quality, consistency, and transparency of the work undertaken by ASEAN intellectual property offices, the Common TM Guidelines were drawn up by a group of senior trademark experts from the Offices. The Guidelines were created and implemented in several phases:

- First, a project consultant undertook missions to all the ASEAN intellectual property offices (May–June 2014) and had consultations with the competent authorities in each of the Offices regarding the desired content of the guidelines.
- Second, a regional meeting of the ASEAN trademark experts on substantive examination was organized in Bangkok in July 2014 to allow them to work on the elaboration of the guidelines. The group, consisting of senior trademark experts from all the ASEAN intellectual property offices, agreed on a draft text and provided examples and suggestions to supplement and further elaborate specific parts of the draft text. The inputs were used as basis for a revised version of the draft guidelines, which was completed in September 2014.
- Third, the revised version of the guidelines was circulated to all the ASEAN intellectual property offices in October 2014. Each Office had the opportunity to provide further inputs during that month. The final draft of the guidelines was then submitted to the ASEAN intellectual property offices in November 2014 for consideration by the Task Force on Trademark Cooperation,[20] which endorsed the draft guidelines at its meeting in Makati City in November 2014. After this endorsement, the guidelines were finally approved and adopted by the AWGIPC in December 2014.
- The guidelines were elaborated in English. Translation of the Common TM Guidelines has been already completed to Bahasa Indonesian and Thai. Translation works into national official languages of other interested ASEAN intellectual property offices (Khmer, Laos, and Vietnamese) is currently ongoing.

[19] Initiative 1.2 led by Cambodia and Philippines, ASEAN, *ASEAN Intellectual Property Rights Action Plan 2011–2015* (July 31, 2011).

[20] Constituted under the AWGIPC.

- In 2014,[21] 2015,[22] and 2016[23] regional workshops addressing officials from all the ASEAN intellectual property offices were organized with the support of ECAP III to train them in the implementation of common criteria embodied in the Common TM Guidelines.
- Finally, the AWGIPC agreed on November 2016 to make the Common TM Guidelines publicly available.

The Common TM Guidelines are not binding on the participating offices and do not purport to reflect the current practice in all those offices. While much of the matter covered in the national laws and practice of the ASEAN countries is consistent in substance with the Guidelines, some divergence may remain with respect to certain specific points. The Guidelines are a useful tool for ASEAN intellectual property offices to use in achieving a higher level of consistency in the decisions of their trademark examiners and help to reduce the average turnaround time for the registration of trademarks, with consequential benefits for the business community. They might also serve as a valuable training material for new or junior examiners.

Further development and use of these Common TM Guidelines is expected to stimulate gradual convergence of the standards and criteria for the examination of trademarks in the ASEAN countries. The Guidelines are meant to be a dynamic reference document for both trademark examiners and applicants, as the document reflects the evolving practices applied by the ASEAN intellectual property offices.

12.4.2 *ASEAN Common Guidelines on the Substantive Examination of Industrial Designs*

The development of the ASEAN Common Industrial Designs (ID) Guidelines is one of the deliverables included in the initiative 2 of the new ASEAN Intellectual Property Rights Action Plan 2016–2025[24] but its drafting already started under the previous Action Plan 2010–2015:

- The first ASEAN Industrial Design Consultation Meeting was held in June 2015,[25] with senior design experts from the ASEAN intellectual property offices discussing a first draft text of the ASEAN Common ID Guidelines. The design experts provided inputs and examples during the

[21] Kuala Lumpur (Malaysia) from November 24 to 27.
[22] Luang Prabang (Laos P.D.R.) June 23 to 25.
[23] Nay Pyi Taw (Myanmar) from February 24 to 26 and Jakarta (Indonesia) from August 22 to 24.
[24] *Id.* at deliverable 2.5 lead by Philippines and Viet Nam.
[25] Langkawi (Malaysia) from June 2 to 5, 2015.

meeting, which were used to supplement and further elaborate specific parts of the text on the basis of which a revised version of the draft guidelines was completed in September 2015.

- The revised version of the guidelines was circulated to all ASEAN IP Offices in October 2015 to give the opportunity to the design experts to provide further input.
- The final draft of the guidelines was then submitted to the ASEAN IP Offices in November 2015 for consideration by the design experts, who endorsed the common guidelines in December 2015.
- In 2016[26] two regional workshops from the ASEAN intellectual property offices was organized to train senior design examiners on the implementation of the draft common guidelines on substantive design examination.
- The ASEAN Common ID Guidelines have been endorsed and adopted by the AWGIPC in 2017.

The creation of the Common ID Guidelines was aimed at enhancing the quality, consistency, and transparency of the work undertaken by ASEAN intellectual property offices. It is also a practical tool for the training of design examiners and a useful reference document for professional advisors. Like its trademarks counterpart, the draft ASEAN Common ID Guidelines took into account the laws, regulations, and available jurisprudence of ASEAN countries relevant to the examination and registration of industrial design applications. The internal guidelines and manuals used by some of the ASEAN intellectual property offices to examine design applications were also considered, as well as international standards and best practices.[27]

The implementation of the Common ID Guidelines in the ASEAN countries is a challenge at present by the fact that there are some major differences between the systems for the examination and registration of industrial designs in the region. Some of those differences are anchored in national laws and will require legislative action to be changed. However, greater convergence can be achieved at the level of administrative standards and internal directives to achieve consistency in the practices of those national offices in the context of the registration and maintenance of ID rights.

The Common ID Guidelines are intended to supplement the national internal guidelines and manuals, and to support a convergence of the design examination standards and criteria applied by member states' designs offices.

[26] Bali (Indonesia) from January 24 to 26, 2016 and Ha Noi (Vietnam) September 7 and 8, 2016.

[27] In particular, the European Community Guidelines for Examination in the EUIPO on Registered Community Designs – Examination of Applications for Registered Community Designs 2015, and Examination of Design Invalidity Applications 2015.

They are not legally binding on the participating offices and do not purport to reflect all the current practices in all those offices. While much of the matter covered in the national laws and practice of the ASEAN countries is consistent in substance with these common guidelines, some divergence may remain with respect to certain specific points. Further development and use of these Guidelines is expected to stimulate gradual convergence of the standards and criteria for the examination and registration of industrial designs in the ASEAN countries.

12.5 INITIATIVES FACILITATING THE CONNECTIVITY AND INTEROPERABILITY OF THE ASEAN TRADEMARK AND DESIGN SYSTEMS

ASEAN TMview, ASEAN Designview, and ASEAN TMclass are online tools developed by the ASEAN intellectual property offices with the support of ECAP III, and are good examples of e-government initiatives of interoperability among the ASEAN intellectual property offices.

12.5.1 *ASEAN TMview*

ASEAN TMview is the common online trademark information platform of the ASEAN member states. It aims to make ASEAN trademark data widely available and easily accessible to all interested stakeholders. ASEAN TMview offers free of charge online access to information on more than 3.5 million[28] trademark registrations and applications in the nine participating ASEAN countries. The platform fulfils multiple roles for users, and provides a means to deepen harmonization between ASEAN intellectual property offices by sharing resources and information. ASEAN TMview focuses on developing and supporting a "common trade mark search engine tool": an online consultation tool to allow users to search for trademarks in the registers of each of the nine ASEAN intellectual property offices.[29] One goal of this tool is to facilitate users to conduct easy searches before filing a trademark application to determine if the proposed trademark is in conflict with any current applications or registered marks in any of the ASEAN intellectual property offices.

At the ASEAN Trademark, Information Technology, and Industrial Design Consultation Meeting in May 2016, it was agreed that the Intellectual Property Office of the Philippines (IPOPHL) will be responsible on behalf of all the

[28] 3,539,692 trademarks as at December 23, 2016.

[29] Myanmar will be integrated in the tool once the trade mark law is approved and they have developed their national trade marks database.

ASEAN intellectual property offices for the management of ASEAN TMview itself. The other ASEAN intellectual property offices will be responsible for regular data transference to ASEAN TMview as well as the quality of the data on their databases accessible through TMview.

12.5.2 *ASEAN Database of Classified Goods and Services for the Registration of Trademarks (ASEAN TMclass)*

ASEAN TMclass provides a way to identify acceptance by ASEAN intellectual property offices of the terms to be included in a trademark application. This centralized resource provides users with access to the classified goods and services offered by all ASEAN offices and to find equivalent terms in the different ASEAN languages and varying expressions for goods and services in the classification database. ASEAN TMclass gives access to more than 13,800 standard terms and enables users to search for and verify the correct classification of those terms for goods or services in accordance with the criteria established by the International Classification (the Nice Agreement). They can also verify whether a particular term is accepted by any of the participating Offices and get translations of those terms into the available working language of these Offices.

The use of ASEAN TMclass helps ensure the correct classification of goods and services, thus improving the quality of applications filed with ASEAN intellectual property offices and thereby reducing the examination time needed for trademark applications. The content of the ASEAN TMclass database was agreed by the TM Task Force on Trademark Cooperation and now includes, in addition to the latest version of the Nice Alphabetical List, the ASEAN List of Goods and the Common EU–Madrid List.[30] The terms are translated into the national languages of interested ASEAN countries and uploaded in the ASEAN TMclass database as soon as they are accepted and validated by the Offices.

ASEAN TMclass has now been integrated in the online filing systems and internal electronic administration systems of some ASEAN intellectual property offices, thereby increasing the quality of applications filed and reducing the time taken to examine applications.[31] At the ASEAN Consultation Meeting it was agreed that the Malaysian Intellectual Property Office will take on the

30 This list consists of terms that are in common between the EU Harmonized Database and the Madrid Goods and Services.

31 On April 25, 2016, the Intellectual Property Office of the Philippines (IPOPHL) launched its new electronic filing system for trademark applications developed in collaboration with ECAP III Project, known as the IPOPHL eTMFile and linked to ASEAN TMclass. In the future,

responsibility for the management and maintenance of the ASEAN TMclass tool and database.[32]

12.5.3 *ASEAN Designview*

ASEAN Designview is the common online industrial design information platform of the ASEAN member states aimed at making ASEAN industrial designs data widely available and easily accessible. It offers free of charge online access to 160,000[33] registered industrial design registrations and applications in the nine participating ASEAN countries.

At the ASEAN Trademark, Information Technology, and Industrial Design Consultation Meeting in May 2016, it was agreed that the Intellectual Property Office of the Philippines (IPOPHL) will be responsible for the management and maintenance of ASEAN Designview.

12.6 THE EVOLUTION TO A MORE COMPETITIVE ASEAN IN THE FIELD OF INTELLECTUAL PROPERTY UNDER THE KUALA LUMPUR DECLARATION ON ASEAN 2025 AND THE ASEAN ECONOMIC COMMUNITY BLUEPRINT 2025

The Kuala Lumpur Declaration "ASEAN 2025: Forging Ahead Together" and the ASEAN Economic Community Blueprint 2025 were adopted by the ASEAN Heads of Government on the November 22, 2015.[34] The inclusion of intellectual property rights in these documents highlights the political importance given by the ASEAN leaders to, cooperation, interoperability, and connectivity and in the field of intellectual property rights.

First, to achieve an AEC by 2025, the ASEAN Community Vision 2025 emphasizes the need for ASEAN to become "highly integrated and cohesive;

other ASEAN intellectual property offices might integrate ASEAN TMclass within their trade mark administration systems and electronic filings.

[32] 6th Trademarks, 4th Information Technology and 2nd Industrial Designs Consultation Meeting held in Kuala Lumpur, Malaysia (May 17–19, 2016). The final details about the handover of the tool were discussed and agreed during the 7th Trademarks and 5th Information Technology Consultation Meeting held in Siem Reap, Cambodia (October 24–26, 2016).

[33] 159,848 ID on December 23, 2016 from the nine participating ASEAN countries. The data from Myanmar will be made available once their national database of designs has been established.

[34] ASEAN Secretariat, *ASEAN 2025: Forging Ahead Together* (November 30, 2015), *available at* www.asean.org/storage/2015/12/ASEAN-2025-Forging-Ahead-Together-final.pdf.

competitive, innovative and dynamic; with enhanced connectivity and sectoral cooperation."[35] Therefore, connectivity is one of the central, unifying, and crosscutting projects of the AEC.[36] The core aims were already set out in the 2010 Master Plan on ASEAN Connectivity, with the overall objective to bring businesses, people, and institutions closer together by eliminating barriers. The Master Plan underlined that, while hard infrastructure is important, an enabling regulatory framework and a shared identity also play crucial roles in connecting ASEAN countries with each other and with the rest of the world. Since connectivity is included among the factors of the ASEAN Community Vision 2025 and it is linked to sectoral cooperation, it must also be considered a driving factor for the strategic goals in the intellectual property field.

Second, the ASEAN Economic Community Blueprint 2025 includes specific references to intellectual property. It states:

> Intellectual Property (IP) has an important role in contributing to the achievement of national and regional socio-economic development goals. Protecting intellectual property rights (IPR) is critical for ASEAN member states to move higher up in the technology ladder, in encouraging transfer of technology, and in stimulating innovation and creativity. The approach in the next 10 years will be based on the need to support the economic development in the region through effective use of IP and creativity. National IP regimes should achieve full technical and procedural convergence, and IP Offices have adopted modern business models and practices that enable provision of efficient and effective "world class" services to clients at the national and regional levels. The future landscape will be more competitive and productive, as IP is one of the contributory factors towards enhancing the volume and value of exports, flows of domestic and foreign direct investment and improved global competitiveness rankings.[37]

In this context, one of the most important means of achieving full technical and procedural convergence among ASEAN intellectual property systems is to enhance connectivity and interoperability among ASEAN intellectual property offices in cooperation with dialogue partners and other public and private stakeholders.

[35] Points 9 and 10.3 of the ASEAN Community Vision 2025, *available at* www.asean.org/storage/images/2015/November/aec-page/ASEAN-Community-Vision-2025.pdf.

[36] High Representative of the Union for Foreign Affairs and Security Policy, *Joint Communication to the European Parliament and the Council – The EU and ASEAN: A Partnership with a Strategic Purpose* (Brussels, May 18, 2015), at Point 2, JOIN (2015) 22, *available at* http://eur-lex.europa.eu/legal-content/EN/TXT/PDF/?uri=JOIN:2015:22:FIN&from=EN.

[37] Point 30 of the ASEAN Economic Community Blueprint 2025, *supra* note 34, at 72.

Third, the ASEAN Economic Community Blueprint 2025 includes the following strategic measures on intellectual property,[38] which are relevant to increasing the connectivity and the interoperability of ASEAN trademark and industrial design systems:

- Strengthen IP offices and build IP infrastructure, in order to ensure the development of a more robust ASEAN IP system.[39]
- Develop regional IP platforms and infrastructure.[40]
- Expand the ASEAN IP Ecosystem.[41]

Therefore the vision and objectives for 2025 make specific reference to the development of regional intellectual property platforms and infrastructure to facilitate the interoperability of member states' trademark and designs systems. The new regional strategy for the period from 2016 to 2025 has been developed within the framework of this vision and by building on the successes and learning points of the previous ASEAN Intellectual Property Rights Action Plan 2011–2015.

12.7 CONNECTIVITY AND INTEROPERABILITY OF THE TRADEMARK AND DESIGNS SYSTEMS UNDER THE ASEAN INTELLECTUAL PROPERTY RIGHTS ACTION PLAN 2016–2025

The AWGIPC adopted in 2016 an ASEAN Intellectual Property Rights Action Plan 2016–2025[42] to develop the broad visions in the AEC Blueprint 2025 into specific initiatives for the ASEAN member states to implement. Among the four strategic goals of the Plan, it is important to highlight the first one, which states that "a more robust ASEAN IP System is developed by strengthening IP

[38] Point 31 of the ASEAN Economic Community Blueprint 2025, *supra* note 34, at 74.

[39] Specific measures referred to are: (a) Improve IP services, particularly in the areas of patents, trademarks and industrial designs; (b) Expand work-sharing activities among ASEAN member states to reduce the workload of IP Offices and duplication of activities. *Id.* at 72.

[40] Specific measures referred to to are: (a) to improve service delivery of ASEAN member states through connected online services, including patent, trademark and design search systems, and online filing systems; (b) to improve and centralize the management of the ASEAN IP Portal by ensuring that IP information, including statistical data, is accurate and regularly updated (e.g. number of filings, registrations, grants, pendency periods); and (c) to adopt information technology (IT) modernization so as to improve quality of services, including the development of an automated translation system for sharing of patent information, and regional patent and trademark databases. *Id.* at 73.

[41] *E.g.*, by enhancing engagement with private sector, intellectual property associations, and other stakeholders within the region and external parties. *Id.*

[42] *See ASEAN Intellectual Property Rights Action Plan 2016–2025* published in English and Thai by the Thai Department of Intellectual Property, September 2016.

Offices and building IP Infrastructures in the region." The second provides for "regional IP platforms and infrastructures are developed to contribute to enhancing the AEC." These two goals are particularly relevant for the regional integration and interoperability of the ASEAN Trademark and Design Systems.[43]

The four strategic goals are further elaborated in nineteen key initiatives.[44] Not all of the key initiatives appear to be equally relevant for all ASEAN member states since some countries may not have national priorities that align with the regional priorities as set out in these initiatives. Uptake of the initiatives by member states may therefore be reduced. In this respect a particularly difficult challenge to successful promotion of the initiatives is the different levels of development of the ASEAN member states. The initiatives are sufficiently flexible to accommodate these concerns, however, and the challenge will eventually become less critical over the course of time as member states continue to converge in their practices and their systems to interoperate and evolve as a region.

12.7.1 *Initiatives under the First Strategic Goal Related to the Interoperability of the ASEAN Trademark and Design Systems*

Under the first strategic goal, there are several key initiatives to improve the connectivity and interoperability of ASEAN trademark and designs systems:

- First, the action plan aims to improve patent, trademark, and industrial design services.[45] For this purpose the action plan mandates an analysis of the intellectual property systems of each member state to identify issues that may impact on the delivery of intellectual property services such as backlogs of applications, so that appropriate measures may be taken to improve the delivery of those services. The plan also emphasizes

[43] The third strategic goal being "an expanded and inclusive ASEAN IP Ecosystem is developed" and the fourth "regional mechanisms to promote asset creation and commercialization, particularly geographical indications and traditional knowledge are enhanced."

[44] *See* presentations at the ASEAN Intellectual Property Association (ASEAN IPA) Conference in Kuala Lumpur (Malaysia): Abdul Aziz Ismail, Deputy Director General (Industrial Property), MyIPO, Presentation at the Annual Meeting and Conference of the ASEAN IPA: *AWGIPC to Share the Strategic IPR Action Plan 2016–2025 – Where Do We Go from Here?* (March 5, 2016), *available at* www.aseanipa.org/attachments/article/653/01.%20AWGIPC-ASEAN%20IP%20Plan.pdf and Denis Croze, Director, WIPO Singapore Office (WSO), Presentation at the Annual Meeting and Conference of the ASEAN IPA: *WIPO's Support of the ASEAN IP Ecosystem* (March 5, 2016), *available at* www.aseanipa.org/attachments/article/653/02.%20Denis%20Croze-WIPO%20Support%20of%20ASEAN%20IP%20Ecosystem.pdf.

[45] Initiative 1 of the ASEAN Intellectual Property Rights Action Plan 2016–2025 [hereinafter 2016–2025 Action Plan].

the need to expand and update regional intellectual property databases, namely ASEAN TMview and ASEAN Designview (discussed earlier).

- Second, a plan to improve the timeliness and quality of intellectual property services[46] is expected to be put in place. A noteworthy initiative focuses on updating industrial design manuals and identifying similarities and differences in practices among member states[47]. The development of the ASEAN Common ID Guidelines[48] as well as regularly updating, as may be necessary, the Common TM Guidelines[49] (discussed earlier).
- Third, to explore the feasibility of harmonizing formality requirements for trademarks and industrial designs across the region,[50] the Action Plan suggests a feasibility study be undertaken to ascertain the plausibility of harmonizing formality requirements in these areas, and that member states consider implementing the results of that study.

12.7.2 *Possible Initiatives under the Second Strategic Goal Related to the Interoperability of ASEAN Trademark and Design Systems*

Under this second strategic goal, several initiatives are worth mentioning:

- First, there is an initiative to improve service delivery through connected online services, including trademark and industrial design search systems, and online filing systems.[51] Two possible projects under this initiative are the implementation of online filing for trademarks and industrial design applications and a possible feasibility study looking at standardizing trademark registration requirements within ASEAN.
- Second, there is an initiative emphasizing the need for member states to adopt modern information technologies to improve the quality of their services, including the development of an automated translation system, electronic correspondence and dossier systems for trademarks, and online filing and updating the regional industrial design and trademark databases.[52] One of the deliverables focuses on ensuring that information held by ASEAN intellectual property offices relating to trademarks and industrial designs is easily accessible to the public and relevant stakeholders.
- Third, there is an initiative to improve and centralize the management of the ASEAN IP Portal by ensuring that intellectual property information

[46] *Id.* at Initiative 2. [47] *Id.* at deliverables 2.1 and 2.3 led both by Philippines.
[48] *Id.* at deliverable 2.5 led by Philippines and Viet Nam.
[49] *Id.* at deliverable 2.6 led by Philippines.
[50] *Id.* at Initiative 4. [51] *Id.* at Initiative 9. [52] *Id.* at Initiative 10.

(including statistical data) is accurate and regularly updated.[53] This continues the development of the ASEAN IP Portal as the most important common platform for facilitating the interoperability of intellectual property systems in ASEAN.

12.8 REGIONAL INTEGRATION OF THE ASEAN TRADEMARK AND DESIGN SYSTEMS

The ambitious goal[54] of setting up a regional trademark system in ASEAN was first suggested in 1995 the ASEAN Framework Agreement. Article 1.5 states that

> Member states shall explore the possibility of setting up of an ASEAN trademark system, an ASEAN Trademark Office, if feasible, to promote the region-wide protection of trademark bearing in mind developments on regional and international protection of trademarks.

Subsequently in 1998, the Ha Noi Plan of Action included similarly ambitious objectives on intellectual property cooperation, including[55]

- Establishing an ASEAN Regional Fund for Trademark and Patent by the year 2000.
- Establishing a regional trademark and patent registration system or establishing a regional trademark or patent office (on a voluntary basis).

The later ASEAN Intellectual Property Rights Action Plan 2004–2010 included a goal of developing an ASEAN trademark system to function as a framework for simplification, harmonization, registration, and protection of relevant intellectual property rights. The activities to be accomplished were less ambitious than previous plans, noting the need for "the consideration of the suitability of a regional trademark system as compared to membership in international system."

Owing to the divergence between the intellectual property systems in the region and varying levels of development between member states, these ambitious aspirations were not fulfilled, however. Under the ASEAN Intellectual Property Rights Action Plan 2011–2015, the commitments of member states were deliberately lowered from the aspirations of previous plans, as part of

[53] *Id.* at Initiative 11.
[54] *See* Elizabeth Siew-Kuan Ng, *supra* note 12, at 138.
[55] Art. 2.7 B and D of the Hanoi Plan of Action adopted by ASEAN at the Sixth Summit in Hanoi in December 1998.

more deliberate efforts to lay the groundwork for the future development of a more harmonized intellectual property system in ASEAN.

The ASEAN Intellectual Property Rights Action Plan 2016–2025 anticipates the possibility of some harmonization of trademark formality requirements with ASEAN by suggesting a feasibility study be carried out to that effect.[56] Even more important, the new Action Plan also foresees to conduct a feasibility study for an ASEAN TM Registration System.[57]

Some authors have suggested that there is too much difference between the trademark systems of individual ASEAN member states for such a system to be workable, and that time must be taken to let some nations' systems develop further.[58] Other authors consider the actual creation of a single system too ambitious given the current degree of integration and harmonization of ASEAN trademark systems.[59]

It seems to be even more difficult to establish a regional system for industrial designs, considering the different types of substantive examination procedures existing in the ASEAN region. The ASEAN Intellectual Property Rights Action Plan 2004–2010 included as a target developing an ASEAN Design System to act as a framework for simplification, harmonization, registration, and protection of relevant intellectual property rights. The activities to be accomplished were described as follows: "If decision made to proceed by regional route, various studies to be carried on harmonization areas and proposals, preparations of framework agreements and regulations relating to the ASEAN Designs System." This ambitious target was dropped in the subsequent Action Plan 2011–2015. The current Action Plan 2016–2025 does not anticipate a feasibility study of an ASEAN regional design system.

Even if there are obvious institutional, operational, and political difficulties facing the creation of an ASEAN IP Office to administer an ASEAN TM Registration System, the feasibility study foreseen at the ASEAN Intellectual Property Rights Action Plan 2016–2025 can provide sufficient elements that advocate for the creation of such a regional system. Two issues to be developed within the feasibility study in the framework of the institutional setup of an ASEAN IP Office might be first, the self-funded nature of the Office with the fees collected from the users of the system and second, the coexistence of national trademark systems with the regional system. In this context the EU

[56] *Id.* at Initiative 4.1 led by Philippines. [57] *Id.* at Initiative 9.2 led by Philippines.

[58] *See, e.g.*, Siraprapha Rungpry & Oliver Knox, The ASEAN Economic Community: Good News for Trademark Owners? 36 WORLD TRADEMARK REV. 55 (2012).

[59] *See, e.g.*, Edy Santoso & Martin Roestamy, *ASEAN's Lack of Integration in Trademark Registration Related to ASEAN Economic Community (AEC) by 2015*; 18 J. LAW POLICY AND GLOBALIZAT. 15 (2013).

trademark[60] and design[61] systems administered by a self-funded EU agency as it is the EUIPO (and that coexist with the European national trademark and designs systems) might be seen as an inspirational example among others for a future ASEAN IP Office in charge of administering ASEAN regional trademark and designs systems.

12.9 CONCLUSION

In a global economy, users expect that systems to protect their trademarks and designs are different at territorial levels, but that those systems offer the same standards of service. Therefore, coexistence of varying procedures must be complemented by connectivity and interoperability among systems. The connection and interoperability between the different ASEAN intellectual property offices has been considered the way to facilitate access to information on existing trademark and design rights protected in the ASEAN member states. In this context, collaborative activities and exchanges are necessary for building greater coherence and interoperability throughout ASEAN intellectual property systems.

Efforts on interoperability and e-government mean interoperable platforms now have the potential to unleash unprecedented speed, efficiency, and quality in the delivery of public services. ASEAN intellectual property offices have already started the development of common platforms under the ASEAN Intellectual Property Rights Action Plan 2011–2015, and these developments will continue under the Action Plan 2016–2025.

Furthermore, ASEAN intellectual property offices are currently reducing administrative burdens and costs, introducing digital services and improving business processes. There is a very interesting possibility that the ASEAN IP Offices will become, under the ASEAN IPR Action Plan 2016–2025, what Professor Jane E. Fountain defined as "digitally mediated institutions," that is, "political institutions that use a portfolio of digital information, systems and tools internally and across boundaries"[62] or "government organizations

[60] Established by Council Regulation (EC) 207/2009 of February 26, 2009 on the Community Trade Mark, 2009 O.J. (L 78) as amended by Regulation (EU) 2015/2424 of December 16, 2015.

[61] Established by Council Regulation (EC) 6/2002 of December 12, 2001 on Community Designs, 2001 O.J. (L 3) as amended by Council Regulation 1891/2006 of December 18, 2006.

[62] Jane E. Fountain, *Bringing Institutions Back In to Strategic Management: The Politics of Digitally Mediated Institutional Change* 4 (National Center for Digital Government, University of Massachusetts Amherst, Working Paper No. 43, 2011), *available at* http://scholarworks.umass.edu/cgi/viewcontent.cgi?article=1039&context=ncdg.

characterized by a high degree of digital infrastructure and widespread use of digital applications and tools."[63]

This approach to regional integration within ASEAN is more realistic than previous approaches. After ambitious goals to set up regional trademark and design systems the ASEAN IPR Action Plans 2011–2015 and 2016–2025 contain more specific and balanced objectives that take into account the different levels of development of the ASEAN member states. Paraphrasing the Schuman Declaration of May 9, 1950,[64] the ASEAN trademark and design systems will not be made all at once, or according to a single plan. They will be built through concrete achievements which first create de facto solidarity.

The different initiatives taken by the ASEAN member states to align their trademark and design examination practices, and the projects to develop the connectivity and interoperability of the ASEAN trademark and design systems are tangible and concrete achievements. These initiatives and projects enable a higher degree of convergence between national trademark and designs systems, and will facilitate the creation in the future of regional ASEAN trademark and design systems. In this context, the feasibility study for the creation of an ASEAN TM Registration System foreseen at the ASEAN Intellectual Property Rights Action Plan 2016–2025 might provide sufficient elements that advocate for the setup of such a regional TM Registration System that will, in turn, constitute a significant milestone in the achievement of the AEC. The further member states progress along this path in the intellectual property sector, the more effective and harmonized the AEC will become.

63 Jane E. Fountain, *On the Effects of e-Government on Political Institutions, supra* note 1, at 462.

64 The Schuman Declaration of May 9, 1950 is believed to be the founding text of European integration. It was delivered by Robert Schuman, the French Foreign Minister and inspired by Jean Monnet. *See* Robert Schuman, Foreign Minister, France, *Declaration at the Salon de l'Horloge at the Quai d'Orsay in Paris: Declaration of 9 May* (May 9, 1950), *available at* www.robert-schuman.eu/en/declaration-of-9-may-1950.

13

Proposal for a PAN-ASEAN Trademark Registration

A Case for the Practical Application of the Interoperability Principle

Soh Kar Liang and Chew Phye Keat

13.1 INTRODUCTION

This chapter seeks to put in concrete terms a proposal that clearly embraces the Interoperability Principle elsewhere explained and championed in this book, taking into account the journey of Association of Southeast Asian Nations (ASEAN) in seeking stronger intellectual property cooperation among ASEAN member states via the ASEAN Working Group on Intellectual Property Cooperation (AWGIPC).[1] The ASEAN Intellectual Property Association (ASEAN IPA)[2] has been a close companion of the AWGIPC on that journey and feels that this proposal can contribute substantially to bring IP cooperation in ASEAN to the next level.

13.2 THE BEATEN PATH OF HARMONIZATION

The ASEAN Framework Agreement on Intellectual Property Cooperation in 1995 (Framework Agreement) held great promise for increased cooperation with an avowed goal of harmonization of the intellectual property laws and systems within the ASEAN member states with the intention of even considering the possibility of an ASEAN patent and trademark system with an

[1] The AWGIPC is a working group of senior officers of the respective intellectual property offices of the ASEAN member states created pursuant to the ASEAN Framework Agreement dated December 15, 1995 on Intellectual Property Cooperation.

[2] The ASEAN Intellectual Property Association was established in conjunction with the government sector AWGIPC under the ASEAN Framework Agreement on Intellectual Property Cooperation to promote private sector cooperation in intellectual property. It was granted official NGO status by the ASEAN Secretariat in 1998.

accompanying ASEAN Patent and Trademark Office.[3] All this was deemed necessary as ASEAN moved steadily into deeper and deeper economic integration.

The path to harmonization beaten by the AWGIPC (which incidentally was created by the Framework Agreement) went through many phases commencing with the Hanoi Action Plan (1999–2004) and moving on to the ASEAN IPR Action Plan 2004–2010 and followed by the ASEAN IPR Action Plan 2011–2015. At the time of writing, a more ambitious and longer duration ASEAN IPR Action Plan 2016–2025 has been launched (in conjunction with the announcement of the ASEAN Economic Community at the end of 2015) and is currently in various stages of concretization with respect to its strategic goals and specific initiatives.

What became apparent in the journey toward ASEAN intellectual property harmonization that intended to accompany ASEAN economic integration was that harmonization was harder than it looked on paper, with serious challenges arising from the different legal systems, different intellectual property capabilities, and different levels of intellectual property awareness and cultural sensitivities that made up the potpourri of the ASEAN community (more elaborately discussed elsewhere in this book). At times harmonization seemed a lost cause but there was nevertheless always a strong resolve to further strengthen intellectual property cooperation especially in terms of facilitating the filing and registration of intellectual property rights across the ASEAN member states through a common filing system.

13.3 THE SEARCH FOR A COMMON PLATFORM

Arising from this state of affairs there was a convergence of (1) the need for finding the path back to harmonization with (2) the push for ASEAN member states to accede to the various international intellectual property treaties and agreements. Some of these treaties and agreements were on substantive matters such as the World Trade Organization–sponsored Agreement on Trade-Related Aspects of Intellectual Property Rights (TRIPS) and the Berne Convention. But others were actually designed to facilitate centralized filings by way of establishing common platforms. A country acceding to such treaty was obliged to adapt its own rules and system to become consistent with that of the common platform. The Patent Cooperation Treaty (PCT) became the

[3] ASEAN, *ASEAN Framework Agreement on Intellectual Property Cooperation*, art. 1.4 & 1.5 (December 15, 1995), *available at* http://asean.org/?static_post=asean-framework-agreement-on-intellectual-property-cooperation-bangkok-thailand-15-december-1995.

first of such treaties to be accepted by the AWGIPC and thence to be acceded by the ASEAN member states. An ASEAN national could by using the PCT secure a patent application in another ASEAN member state (or any other PCT country for that matter) through the initial filing process offered by the PCT. Technically, this process in a narrow sense achieved harmonization within ASEAN albeit as part of a global harmonization framework for patent filing.

Then came the Madrid System[4] for trademarks (which was mandated in the 2010–2015 Action Plan) further discussed in the text that follows. Brunei, Cambodia, Laos, Singapore, Philippines, and Vietnam have already acceded to the Madrid System and the other ASEAN member states are pending accession to the same (which is also further discussed later). For completeness, it must be mentioned that the 2016–2025 Action Plan envisages a similar destination for industrial designs via the Hague Agreement for Industrial Designs. For the purposes of this chapter it is submitted that the Madrid System provides a springboard from which a trademark system designed for intra-ASEAN trademark filings could play a role to demonstrate ASEAN intellectual property interoperability.

13.4 ENTER THE MADRID SYSTEM

The Madrid System offers an international trademark application system that allows a national of any of its contracting parties to submit a single trademark application to secure trademark protection in other contracting parties. To achieve this, the Madrid System imposes minimum standards on contracting parties in relation to many aspects of a trademark application, including trademark representation, classification of goods and services, and examination turnaround time.

An international application is typically submitted to the applicant's own national trademark office as a receiving office that ensures initial administrative compliance before relaying the application to the international bureau of the World Intellectual Property Organization (WIPO) to process. Once WIPO clears the formality requirements of the application, the trademark is formally entered on an international register and the application forwarded to each contracting state designated on the application form for local examination. Since an international application has the effect of a national application in

[4] Protocol Relating to the Madrid Agreement Concerning the International Registration of Marks, June 27, 1989, S. Treaty Doc. No. 106–41, *available at* www.wipo.int/wipolex/en/wipo_treaties/text.jsp?file_id=283484 [hereinafter Madrid System].

each contracting state, a side effect of the Madrid System is that the applicant need not appoint a trademark agent in each contracting state (and incur the corresponding costs) for the purpose of submitting the international application. Only when a contracting state issues a refusal does the need to engage a trademark agent in that contracting state arise. If a contracting state fails to issue a refusal within a prescribed period or if it issues a refusal that is subsequently withdrawn, that contracting state is required to grant local trademark protection to the international registration.

Despite the potential convenience and cost benefits of the Madrid System, it has certain limitations that applicants must contend with. In particular, it is not possible to include the contracting state of the applicant in the international application. Instead, an international application must be based on an earlier application in the contracting state of the applicant. Should this basic/home application, or its resulting registration, become withdrawn, lapsed, renounced, finally rejected, revoked, canceled, or invalidated within five years of the international registration, the protection granted in a contracting state may no longer be invoked.[5] Mechanisms exist to mitigate this risk of "central attack" to some extent.[6] However, it presents a valid concern to applicants and owners of international registrations under the Madrid System and the preceding Madrid Agreement.

Further, although the cost of trademark agents in the designated contracting state of an international application under the Madrid System may potentially be avoided, it does not necessarily translate to an apples-to-apples cost comparison with individual national applications. The official fees charged against each designated contracting state in an international application are not the same as those charged against direct national applications with contracting parties.

Official fees charged by a trademark office are in the local currency of that trademark office. Fees under the Madrid System on the other hand are fixed in Swiss francs and do not vary actively with fluctuations in exchange rates. It may be noted from Figure 13.1 that national official fees and designation fees for the same country may be distinctly different.

In addition, unlike national applications, international applications under the Madrid System also incur extra fees charged by the receiving office and WIPO. The basic fee charged by WIPO is fixed but the fee charged by a national trademark office as receiving office varies. As illustrated in Figure 13.2, the initial overheads incurred by an international application even before taking into account designation fees could amount to hundreds

[5] *Id.* art. 6(3). [6] *See, e.g., id.* art. 9*quinquies*.

Countries	National	Madrid Protocol designation	Difference	% Difference
Philippines	PHP3,760 (≈ USD75)	CHF95 (≈ PHP4,690)	↑ PHP930 (≈ USD19)	↑ 24.7%
Singapore	SGD341 (≈ USD240)	CHF272 (≈ SGD384)	↑ SGD43 (≈ USD30)	↑ 12.6%
Vietnam	VND840,000 (≈ USD37)	CHF101 (≈ VND2,262,836)	↑ VND1,422,836 (≈ USD63)	↑ 169%

FIGURE 13.1 Official fee comparison between national trademark application in 1 class and the designation fee of an international application in 1 class for the Philippines, Singapore, and Vietnam. Exchange rates obtained from xe.com on November 22, 2016.

Countries	Receiving office	Basic fee (CHF653)	Initial overheads
Philippines	PHP2,182	≈ PHP32,223	≈ PHP34,405 (≈ USD691)
Singapore	SGD250	≈ SGD921	≈ SGD1,171 (≈ USD823)
Vietnam	VND1,500,000	≈ VND14,605,182	≈ VND16,105,182 (≈ USD710)

FIGURE 13.2 Official fee overheads of an international application filed through the trademark offices of the Philippines, Singapore, and Vietnam as receiving office. Exchange rates obtained from xe.com on November 22, 2016.

of US dollars. A prospective applicant for trademark registration will have to weigh the aforementioned pros and cons, including the issue of costs, before an appropriate decision may be made about filing an international application.

It should also be highlighted that the Madrid System currently has 98 contracting parties covering 114 countries.[7] Membership is growing steadily.

7 The Madrid System refers to the Madrid Agreement which entered into force in 1892 and the newer Madrid Protocol which entered into force in 1995. Together, the contracting parties to the Madrid Agreement and the Madrid Protocol constitute the Madrid Union.

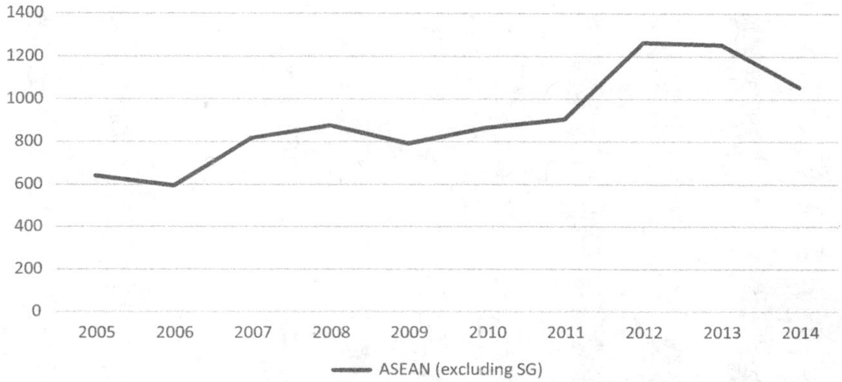

FIGURE 13.3 Trademark applications filed in Singapore by ASEAN nationals (except Singapore nationals) including national applications and Madrid System designations from 2005 to 2014. Data are derived from IPOS statistics at www.ipos.gov.sg/AboutIP/IPResources/Statistics.aspx (last accessed on November 22, 2016).

Even if all the ASEAN member states were to become contracting parties of the Madrid System, ASEAN will in all foreseeable likelihood represent fewer than 10 percent of the members and votes of the governing assembly over the Madrid System.[8] In the event that ASEAN desires to respond to trademark challenges that are specific or unique to ASEAN member states, the Madrid System may not be a suitable avenue to do so swiftly and effectively.

13.5 THE UNBRIDGED GAP

Figure 13.3 shows that trademark applications into Singapore by ASEAN nationals have seen an increase in momentum since 2005. The number of applications in 2013 is almost double that of 2005. It is expected that corresponding statistics in the other ASEAN member states will exhibit a similar upward trend reflective of the growth of intra-ASEAN trade and investment, and the emergence of an intra-ASEAN intellectual property ecosystem. Businesses within ASEAN are starting to realize the importance of trademark protection, not just within national boundaries but also in the larger ASEAN hinterland. There is a growing need to protect the trademarks of ASEAN businesses within ASEAN.

[8] *See* Madrid System, *supra* note 4, art. 10, regarding the responsibilities and proceedings of the governing assembly.

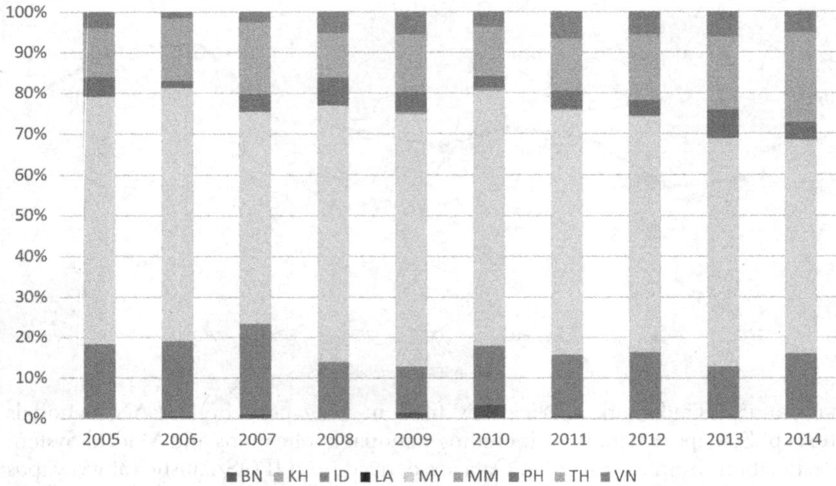

FIGURE 13.4 Distribution by national origin of trademark applications filed in Singapore by ASEAN nationals (except Singapore nationals) including national applications and Madrid System designations from 2005 to 2014. Data are derived from IPOS statistics at www.ipos.gov.sg/AboutIP/IPResources/Statistics.aspx (last accessed on November 22, 2016).

Interestingly, Figure 13.4 shows that there has been little change in the distribution of national origin of the ASEAN applicants of trademark applications filed in Singapore during the same period. In other words, the percentage of Singapore applications originating from each of its ASEAN neighbors has remained relatively stable despite the growing number of applications. Even though Vietnam and the Philippines respectively joined the Madrid System in 2006 and 2014, their piece of the pie of trademark applications into Singapore has not noticeably increased. This suggests that ASEAN nationals are filing trademark applications in Singapore (and in all likelihood the other ASEAN member states) regardless of the availability of international applications under the Madrid System.

It is submitted that most ASEAN nationals are small and medium-sized enterprises with resources that limit their interests primarily to the local or regional ASEAN markets. Their primary trademark interests are correspondingly also focused within ASEAN. If an ASEAN national finds the common platform of an international application under the Madrid System unsuitable for supporting its trademark interests, its only recourse is to undertake the filing of national applications. A middle ground solution does not presently exist and it appears a gap has to be filled.

13.6 THE PAN-ASEAN SYSTEM

As can been seen from the discussion in Section 13.3, the quest for a common platform to support the protection of trademarks within ASEAN is leading all its member states down the path toward the Madrid System. Although designed with an objective of harmonization, the Madrid System was not crafted with the special needs of ASEAN member states foremost in mind. Sections 13.4 and 13.5 explored the limitations faced by the Madrid System in meeting the need of ASEAN nationals to protect their trademarks within ASEAN.

ASEAN IPA took upon itself an exploratory quest for a common platform that could better meet the needs of ASEAN nationals in seeking trademark protection within ASEAN. This chapter proposes the establishment of a Pan-ASEAN trademark administrative system as an outcome of that quest, which it is felt fits nicely into the framework of interoperability.

There is of course nothing preventing ASEAN from adopting more than one common platform. The Madrid System potentially provides an effective common platform for non-ASEAN nationals to seek trademark protection within each ASEAN member state, and should serve ASEAN nationals well to correspondingly extend their trademark protection beyond ASEAN shores. However, to protect an ASEAN national's trademarks within ASEAN, the Pan-ASEAN system potentially offers a preferable tailored solution.

13.6.1 *What It Can Offer*

In a nutshell, the proposed Pan-ASEAN system is a common platform for ASEAN nationals to apply for registration of their trademarks across multiple ASEAN member states incorporating at least the following key features:

- Single Application: A one-stop interface for preparing and submitting an application to secure trademark registration in multiple ASEAN member states (a Pan-ASEAN Application).
- Applicant and State of Origin: The applicant of a Pan-ASEAN Application must be a national of an ASEAN member state (that ASEAN member state will hereafter be referred to as the "State of Origin"). If manually submitted over-the-counter, the application should be submitted to the trademark office of the State of Origin (Origin TMO).
- Representation: The representation requirements should be the same as those of a local application at the Origin TMO. If an applicant may submit a local application without engaging a representative, he should also be able to do so for a Pan-ASEAN Application before the Origin TMO. If an

applicant is represented, such representative must be qualified to practice before the Origin TMO.

- Application Form: The application form for a Pan-ASEAN Application should
  - Designated States: Enable an applicant to designate the ASEAN member state for which trademark registration is sought (Designated States). There should not be a minimum number of Designated States designated in an application. There should also not be a requirement that any particular Designated State(s) should be designated.
  - Standard Goods and Services: Provide a standard list of goods and services acceptable to all Designated States for selection by the applicant.
  - Formal Requirements: Collect all necessary data to meet the formal requirements of a local application in the Designated States. No additional data requirements should be imposed by any Designated State.
- Priority Claim: A priority claim in the Pan-ASEAN Application shall be treated as a priority claim in each Designated State in accordance with Article 4 of the Paris Convention for the Protection of Industrial Property. As with the Madrid System, formalities prescribed in Section D of that Article should not be mandated (e.g., provision of a certified priority document).[9]
- Application Date: The application date accorded to the Pan-ASEAN Application is treated as the application date in each Designated State.
- Distribution: The Origin TMO confirms the Pan-ASEAN Application and its application details before it is distributed for local processing by each Designated State.
- Local Processing: Each Designated State undertakes the further processing of the Pan-ASEAN Application as if it were a direct local application in that Designated State. The first communication from the trademark office of that Designated State (e.g., provisional refusal) shall be issued directly to the applicant (or representative, as the case may be). Further communication shall be subject to all local address for service and representation requirements of that Designated State.
- Registration: Each Designated State is responsible for issuing its own registration certificate in relation to a Pan-ASEAN Application as if it were a direct local application.
- Renewals and Recordals: The Pan-ASEAN system is not intended to cater to such administrative processes. The applicant of a Pan-ASEAN

[9] *Id.* art. 4(2).

Application or the owner of a local registration arising from a Pan-ASEAN Application is required to deal with the relevant Designated State as appropriate in the same manner as if the trademark application had been filed directly in that Designated State.

- Oppositions and Other Contentious Proceedings: The Pan-ASEAN system is not intended to cater to these proceedings. These should be initiated and managed with the relevant Designated State as appropriate.
- Subsequent Applications: Subsequent applications for the same mark may be filed as fresh Pan-ASEAN Applications and processed accordingly. Unlike the Madrid System, it is not necessary for the concept of a subsequent designation application to exist in the Pan-ASEAN system because the Pan-ASEAN system does not support a register and grant of registration is completely a national process under the purview of each Designated State.[10]
- Madrid System Benchmark: A Designated State should also be a contracting party of the Madrid System to demonstrate that it has met the benchmarks set by the Madrid System and will be required to uphold these benchmarks in relation to a Pan-ASEAN Application. No Designated State shall impose local requirements on a Pan-ASEAN Application that it does not similarly impose on a Madrid System application.

As can be seen from the preceding outline, the Pan-ASEAN system streamlines the administration of trademark application across the ASEAN member states in a way highly suitable for implementation by employing modern computerization technologies. It does not envisage a separate regional trademark register and does not seek to create trademark rights that overlap with that granted by local trademark systems. The proposed streamlining provides good opportunities for economy of scale, pooling of resources, and harmonization of administrative processes. This will foreseeably promote a trend of convergence and interoperation of systems and practices, not only among trademark administrations in ASEAN, but also among its users.

A direct trademark application process presents three stages from filing the application to processing the application to issuance of registration. An international application under the Madrid System introduces additional steps to a direct application. In place of filing a local application, there are three

10 Under the Madrid System, grant of protection to a mark is a two-stage process. First, Article 3 provides for immediate international registration as soon as goods and services are properly indicated. Second, Article 4 provides for grant of protection in each designated contracting state (if no refusal is notified, or if refusal is properly notified but subsequently withdrawn) as if registration was granted to a national application.

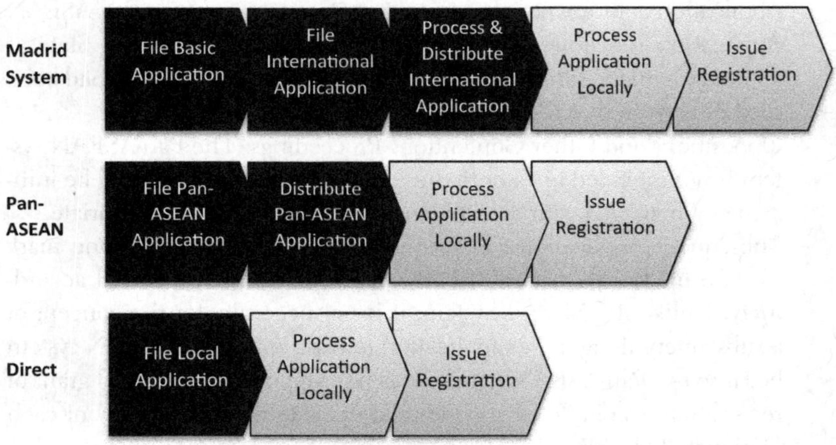

FIGURE 13.5 Schematic outline of trademark application process under the Madrid System, Pan-ASEAN and a typical direct application in an ASEAN nation.

stages of filing a basic/home application, filing an international application, and processing and distribution of the international application. A Pan-ASEAN process also replaces the initial filing step of a direct application with the filing of the Pan-ASEAN application but is administratively simpler than an international application under the Madrid System. A schematic outline of the three processes is illustrated in Figure 13.5.

13.6.2 *Is ASEAN Ready?*

Some may ask whether ASEAN is ready to consider, implement, and benefit from a Pan-ASEAN trademark system. A concept paper was presented to the ASEAN Working Group on Intellectual Property Cooperation (AWGPIC) as far back as 1998 supporting the institution of an administrative trademark system for ASEAN as a precursor to an ambitious ASEAN Trademark akin to a European Trademark.[11] Unfortunately, the idea was ahead of its time and did not take flight. Various reasons were postulated, ranging from opposition by local trademark practitioners afraid for their livelihood, lack of urgency,

[11] The concept paper was incorporated into the Hanoi Plan of Action which was endorsed by the heads of all ASEAN member states at the 6th ASEAN Summit. It was declared at that Summit that ASEAN will implement a regional trademark filing system by 2000.

lack of political will to discharge the efforts of associated regulatory changes, to distractions by other economic problems.[12]

Regardless of which reason played a more significant part at that time, the global environment, regional developments, and overall intellectual property sophistication of the ASEAN member states and their nationals have come a long way since 1998. It is submitted that conditions are vastly different now and ASEAN is more ready than ever because

- ASEAN has the motivation to do so;
- ASEAN has a model to serve as a springboard; and
- ASEAN has the momentum to carry it through.

Motivation

The need for ASEAN to pay attention to intra-ASEAN businesses is well supported by recent data.[13] Since 2007, there has been a steady growth in net inflow of foreign direct investment into ASEAN. By 2015, intra-ASEAN investment had reached 22 billion USD, making it the largest source of foreign direct investment inflow into ASEAN. The next highest sources were EU-28 at 20 billion USD and Japan at 17.6 billion USD.[14] The total inflow for 2015 was about 121 billion USD.[15] Contrasted with 2007, the intra-ASEAN investment inflow was only about 8 billion USD over almost 80 billion USD in total inflow.[16] In absolute terms, intra-ASEAN investment inflow has almost tripled from 2007 to 2015, while in percentage terms, it has almost doubled from about 10 percent to 18 percent. It is not surprising that intra-ASEAN trademark applications may be on the rise.[17]

ASEAN recognizes the important role that intellectual property plays in ASEAN's national and regional socioeconomic development goals.[18] Its emphasis on serving intra-ASEAN, as opposed to extra-ASEAN, businesses is evident in the ASEAN Economic Community Blueprint. The Blueprint exhorts all ASEAN national intellectual property offices to achieve full technical and procedural convergence to enable efficient and effective world class

12 Weerawait Weerworawit, *The Harmonisation of Intellectual Property Rights in ASEAN*, *in* C. Antons, M. Blakeney & C. Heath (eds.), Intellectual Property Harmonisation within ASEAN and APEC 215 (2004).

13 ASEAN Secretariat, *ASEAN Economic Community Chartbook 2016*, *available at* http://asean.org/storage/2012/05/13Content-AEC-Chartbook-2016.pdf.

14 *Id.* at 44. 15 *Id.* at 43, 44. 16 *Id.*

17 *See id.* at 44 and experience of Singapore in Figure 13.3.

18 ASEAN Secretariat, *ASEAN Economic Community (AEC) Blueprint 2025*, *available at* www.asean.org/storage/images/2015/November/aec-page/AEC-Blueprint-2025-FINAL.pdf.

services to clients *at national and regional levels*.[19] It identifies several strategic measures to strengthen intellectual property offices and build intellectual property infrastructure to ensure the development of a more robust system, which include[20]

- Improving intellectual property services in the area of trademarks, among other things;
- Expanding work-sharing activities among ASEAN member states to reduce workload and duplication of activities; and
- Promoting improvement of timeliness and output quality of intellectual property services.

Several other strategic measures with a view to developing regional intellectual property platforms and infrastructure were also identified. These include[21]

- Developing new networks of integrated intellectual property services for the region
- Improving service delivery of ASEAN member states through connected online services for searching and filing
- Improving and centralizing the management of the ASEAN IP Portal
- Adopting information technology modernization to improve service quality, including development of regional trademark databases

The implementation of the proposed Pan-ASEAN trademark system is not only consistent with all these objectives and strategic measures, but is in all likelihood also resonant with and complementary to their effect and efficacy.[22]

Model

At least as early as 2004, perhaps owing to the lack of progress in the implementation of a regional ASEAN Trademark system, ASEAN member states started diverting their attention to joining the Madrid System as an alternative.[23] Singapore was the first of the ASEAN member state to join in 2000. Vietnam, Philippines, Cambodia, and Laos followed in 2006, 2014, 2015, and 2016 respectively. Brunei is the latest to join and officially became a contracting state of the Madrid System on January 6, 2017. Indonesia, Malaysia, and Thailand are working toward accession in the near future. Only Myanmar, which has yet to implement a national trademark registration system, is expected to lag behind the rest.

[19] *Id.* at para 30. [20] *Id.* at para 31.i. [21] *Id.* at para 31.ii. [22] *See id.* at 2.

[23] ASEAN Secretariat, *ASEAN Intellectual Property Rights Action Plan 2004–2010*, *available at* http://asean.org/?static_post=asean-intellectual-property-right-action-plan-2004–2010.

The Madrid System provides a common platform for securing trademark rights in its contracting parties designated in a single international application. Nationals of all ASEAN member states are required to submit a common form to apply for an international application. The application form is submitted to the applicant's national trademark office as receiving office. National trademark offices of all ASEAN member states are required to comply with certain common standards. For example, an application may be refused only on grounds applicable under the Paris Convention, grounds of refusal must be stated,[24] and notification of refusal must be given within a time limit prescribed under the Madrid System.[25] National workflows associated with processing of an application (whether as receiving office or designated contracting state) and databases must be customized to interoperate with that of the World Intellectual Property Organization's international trademark workflow and database.

It is immediately apparent that the Madrid System platform shares certain conceptual similarities with the Pan-ASEAN system platform, in particular, the provision of a common platform for securing trademark rights in multiple designated jurisdictions using a common form. The Madrid System imposes minimum standards and best practices (e.g., refusal turnaround, workflow engineering, and interoperation between a receiving office and designated contracting parties) which the Pan-ASEAN system will similarly be pegged to and benchmarked against.

ASEAN member states that have joined the Madrid System would have met or even surpassed its minimum standards and best practices. Naturally, systems, processes, know-how, and experience in achieving the interoperation of the Pan-ASEAN system would have been substantially established as well. The journey toward a Pan-ASEAN system is already almost complete before it even begins. Sixty percent of ASEAN member states are already part of the Madrid System. With 90 percent accession clearly visible over the horizon, implementation of a Pan-ASEAN system is a very low hanging fruit of ASEAN intellectual property interoperation indeed.

Momentum

It is without a doubt that embarking on the Madrid System as a common goal of the ASEAN member states has translated to a significant alignment of capability and readiness for the Pan-ASEAN system. Any livelihood concerns of local trademark practitioners that could encourage opposition to the Pan-ASEAN system has become water under the bridge by virtue of the inevitable institution of the Madrid System throughout all the ASEAN member states.

[24] Madrid System, *supra* note 4, art. 5(1). [25] *Id.* art. 5(2).

Any absence of political will to roll up the sleeves of regulatory change has been put to rest by the active legislative reform in recent years throughout the ASEAN member states.

As a result of legislative progress in each ASEAN member state arising from the Madrid System, ASEAN has demonstrated that it is now ready for harmonization of trademark processes, systems, and standards of one-stop multijurisdictional common trademark platforms. The momentum of progress is now presenting ASEAN with an easily grasped opportunity to possess a regional trademark filing system in the Pan-ASEAN system.

The way forward for ASEAN is one of increasing cooperation among ASEAN member states. The AWGIPC has been actively providing government sector leadership in intellectual property matters in collaboration with private sector agencies such as the ASEAN IPA for the last twenty years. The collaborative efforts of the ASEAN member states represented in the AWGIPC has led to sophisticated online tools in the form of ASEAN TMview[26] and ASEAN TMclass[27] that are beneficial to the trademark community in ASEAN. The Pan-ASEAN system offers ASEAN a chance to scale up to the next level of intellectual property maturity.

13.6.3 *The "Best of Everything"*

The proposed Pan-ASEAN system complements the Madrid System in ASEAN by incorporating its positive elements in a parallel system for ASEAN nationals to apply for trademark registration within ASEAN. Unlike the Madrid System, it does not require a basic/home application and does not implement a register. As such, not only is it less administratively complex, but it also avoids the concerns of central attack endemic to the Madrid System. The Pan-ASEAN system could potentially be a "best of everything" approach to implementing a regional system for ASEAN.

Administering the System

It is proposed that the administration of the Pan-ASEAN system should be managed substantially by an online system. The key features of the online system may be considered in relation to each of the four stages of a Pan-ASEAN application identified in Figure 13.5.

26 *See* ASEAN Intellectual Property Portal, *ASEAN TMview*, *available at* www.aseanip.org/Services/ASEAN-TMview.

27 *See* ASEAN Intellectual Property Portal, *ASEAN TMclass*, *available at* www.asean-tmclass.org/ec2/.

- File Pan-ASEAN application. The online system should permit applicants to securely complete and submit the application form via common Internet browsers. Details and payment may be automatically validated and processed by the system in the usual manner of modern e-commerce/e-filing platforms.
- Distribute Pan-ASEAN application. Once application and payment details are confirmed, the system should automatically distribute the application to each of the Designated States via an agreed data interchange format (e.g., XML). Distribution of the payment collected by the State of Origin should also be apportioned and remitted to each Designated State according to an agreed scheme.
- Process application locally. The local system of each Designated State may be configured to automatically translate the agreed data interchange format to its local format (whether in electronic or physical form) as necessary. The issuance of a first communication from the trademark office of a Designated State to the applicant (or representative, as the case may be) may be effected by uploading it onto the online system, which should automatically relay the communication. Once the applicant receives the communication and complies with local address/agent requirements, further correspondence with that trademark office may occur in the usual manner of a national application without intermediation of the online system.
- Issue registration. The issuance of registration should follow the usual process of a national application without intermediation of the online system.

Location

When the idea of an ASEAN trademark system was first proposed two decades ago,[28] a difficult issue to address was where the seat of administrative governance of that system should be located.[29] It was a quagmire of social, economic, and political concerns that was ultimately never resolved. Viewed through the lens of modern technology and developments in the internet space, it is questionable whether a physical "seat of power" is even required anymore. The present age of ubiquitous cloud-based computing, server virtualization, and computerized workflow management has significantly reduced the need for

[28] *See* Madrid System, *supra* note 4.

[29] Christoph Antons, *Harmonization and Selective Adaptations as Intellectual Property Policies in Asia, in* C. Antons, M. Blakeney & C. Heath (eds.), Intellectual Property Harmonisation within ASEAN and APEC 119 (2004).

business and activities to be tied to the physical realm. In many instances, the resources required to operate a robust online system have become geographically agnostic. It is submitted that the same may now be said about the need for a specialized physical governmental office to exist in order to implement, operate, and administer the Pan-ASEAN system.

Governance

Although a physical Pan-ASEAN trademark office is not required, responsibility over the governance and supporting administrative functions of the Pan-ASEAN system will still have to be discharged. The ASEAN secretariat is responsible for providing greater efficiency in the coordination of ASEAN organs and of implementing ASEAN projects and activities.[30] The Pan-ASEAN system would appear to be within its purview. One of the main offices below the ASEAN Secretariat is the ASEAN Economic Community Department, which is tasked with collectively transforming the ASEAN region into a knowledge- and innovation-driven regional economy. The Pan-ASEAN system appears well aligned with such a goal.

In addition, the AWGIPC comprises representatives from the intellectual property offices of all the ASEAN member states. The AWGIPC has been working on developing the intellectual property ecosystem in the ASEAN region for the last two decades. It has tremendous experience to provide leadership in the governance and management of the Pan-ASEAN system. With the revitalization of goals set in the ASEAN Economic Community Blueprint 2025, the AWGIPC is well placed to direct and oversee the implementation and management of the Pan-ASEAN system.

Fee Model

The Pan-ASEAN system will require financing at three key levels:

- Governance. Based on the above, it is foreseeable that much of the cost associated with managing and providing leadership to the administration of the Pan-ASEAN system is unlikely to be significant and can be largely assumed by the ASEAN Secretariat and the AWGIPC.
- Operating systems. A budget will have to be set aside to design, develop, and maintain the online system required to operate the Pan-ASEAN system. The capacity for undertaking such a project has reached a far more mature state than twenty years ago, and the associated cost and effort are likely to be well within manageable means. Many of the ASEAN

[30] ASEAN, *About ASEAN Secretariat, available at* http://asean.org/asean/asean-secretariat/.

member states have been delivering online e-filing services to their own nationals for some years and will be able to contribute their experience to the collaborative effort.

- Administrative operations. The actual tasks of operating the Pan-ASEAN system will largely be executed by intellectual property offices of ASEAN member states acting in the capacity of receiving office. Although there are administrative tasks associated with the handling of applications distributed to a Designated State, these are likely to be readily weaved into the routine workflow of the relevant intellectual property office receiving applications directly, through the Madrid System or through the Pan-ASEAN system.

In view of the foregoing, the official fees relating to a Pan-ASEAN system may be rationalized according to the following proposed structure:

- Receiving Office handling fee. Each ASEAN member state may impose a flat handling fee in its local currency on an application, just like the corresponding receiving office handling fee under the Madrid System.[31] The handling fee should be independent of the number of classes or number of items in the specification. The handling fee may differ among the ASEAN member states to account for different local overhead costs with the intention of cost recovery rather than profit generation.
- Designation fee. Each Designated State selected in an application should attract a designation fee in the same manner that an application under the Madrid System would attract designation fees (though not in the elaborate manner of individual,[32] supplementary,[33] and complementary[34] fees). It is proposed that the designation fee for each Designated State should be identical to the official fee which that Designated State may charge for a corresponding national application. A simple designation fee pegged to the national official fee is a much simpler structure than the Madrid System's complex of individual, supplementary, and complementary fees. It also helps to promote the Pan-ASEAN system as a cost-effective mechanism for ASEAN nationals to extend trademark protection within ASEAN.

The system should also reference an exchange rate table that is updated periodically for converting the official fees of all Designated States to the local currency of the Receiving Office at the time payment is collected from the

[31] Madrid System, *supra* note 4, art. 8(1). [32] *Id.* art. 8(7)(a).
[33] *Id.* art. 8(2)(ii), art. 8(7)(a)(i). [34] *Id.* art. 8(2)(iii), art. 8(7)(a)(ii).

Fees	International Application	Pan-ASEAN Application	Direct Application
Receiving Office Handling Fee	Yes	Yes	No
Basic Fee	Yes	No	No
Filing/Designation Fee	Yes	Yes	Yes
Second Part/Registration Fee	Maybe	No	Maybe

FIGURE 13.6 Fee structure comparison under the Madrid System, Pan-ASEAN and a typical direct application in an ASEAN nation.

applicant. The same mechanism may be employed when designation fees are remitted by the Receiving Office to the relevant Designated States.

It is proposed that the Pan-ASEAN system does not accommodate the option for Designated States to adopt a two-part designation fee structure.[35] This ensures that there is full transparency of costs upfront, standardizes practices across Designated States, as well as helps to simplify national processing of a Pan-ASEAN application by avoiding an additional fee collection step. It is noted that even though the Madrid System allows a two-part individual fee structure, only two of its current ninety-eight contracting parties have opted for it. Many contracting parties that collect official fees for filing and registration of a national application separately have opted to consolidate both sets of official fees upfront on filing under the Madrid System. For example, both Philippines and Vietnam collect official fees for filing and registration of a national application separately, but have opted to impose a single individual designation fee under the Madrid System.

Unlike the Madrid System, no basic fee payable to a central administration body is proposed for the Pan-ASEAN system. This is because the Pan-ASEAN system does not have a register and is not designed to require a physical central administration body.

An overview of the fee models of a Madrid System international application, Pan-ASEAN Application and a typical national application are presented in Figure 13.6.

The proposed fee model of the Pan-ASEAN system is intended to offer simplicity, certainty, and affordability to ASEAN nationals in its use.

35 Under Rule 34(3)(a) of the Common Regulations applicable to Madrid System applications, a contracting party may split the individual fee into two parts, the first part payable at the time of filing the international application and the second part to be paid later. Only two contracting parties, Cuba and Japan, have implemented a two-part individual fee.

13.7 CONCLUSION

ASEAN's journey toward harmonization of its intellectual property laws has evolved into a search for common platforms. In the trademark realm, the Madrid System has arisen as the gold standard for ASEAN member states to aspire to. Although it is an effective common platform for large companies with global interests to harness, ASEAN businesses that are predominantly small and medium-sized enterprises with more regionally anchored interests will benefit more from a Pan-ASEAN trademark application system. It was proposed in this chapter that such a system is feasible, resonates with the objectives of the ASEAN Economic Blueprint 2025 and complements the wider Madrid System which all ASEAN member states have determined to join as contracting parties.

The Pan-ASEAN trademark application system targets ASEAN nationals as beneficiaries rather than non-ASEAN nationals. It borrows from the model of the Madrid System with critical systemic and procedural customizations such as doing away with a basic/home application and decentralized management. A fee model that supports the financing needs of governance, operating systems, and administrative operation, but yet offers simplicity, certainty, and affordability to ASEAN nationals was also proposed. The Pan-ASEAN trademark application system, if accepted by the ASEAN member states, will be an important milestone in the search for common platforms. It is submitted that the extensive efforts to accommodate the Madrid System have already paved the way and stacked the crates for ASEAN. Having come this far in the journey to intellectual property integration as part of the economic integration of ASEAN, this Pan-ASEAN trademark application system demonstrating the viability of ASEAN intellectual property interoperability would appear to be a natural step to take in the name of ASEAN solidarity.

14

Challenges for Protection and Administration of Intellectual Property

Thailand's Perspective

Jakkrit Kuanpoth

14.1 INTRODUCTION

The move toward increased integration of Association of Southeast Asian Nations (ASEAN) intellectual property systems may usher in significant changes to intellectual property laws and administration within individual ASEAN nations. Both regional and domestic intellectual property administration are engaged by an interoperability agenda, including the idea of intellectual property interoperability within ASEAN. Even without top-down harmonization, interoperability is premised on a greater degree of cooperation. To that end, initiatives such as the ASEAN Working Group on Intellectual Property Cooperation aim to increase efficiency in intellectual property administration and reduce costs in implementing intellectual property laws.[1]

Even so, intellectual property rights are still issued or granted by competent national authorities, and national courts will still have jurisdiction to determine infringement and validity of intellectual property rights. Accordingly, while regional (and international) developments will continue to exert a significant influence on the substance of intellectual property laws within ASEAN nations, key issues relating to domestic implementation will remain. In this brief chapter, I focus on the administration of patents in Thailand. Like many developing nations, Thailand faces acute difficulties in the area of patent examination, most of which arise from the resources that are available

[1] The ASEAN Working Group on Intellectual Property Cooperation was formed in 1996 and its work is currently based on the ASEAN Intellectual Property Rights Action Plan 2011–2015. The ASEAN Intellectual Property Rights Action Plan 2016–2025 is currently in the works. The goal of the ASEAN Working Group is to transform ASEAN into an innovative and competitive region through the use of intellectual property for their nationals and ensuring that the region remains an active player in the international intellectual property community. *See* ASEAN Intellectual Property Portal, *About AWGIPC, available at* www.aseanip.org/About-Us/About-AWGIPC.

to support the patent system. The discussion that follows highlights some of the difficulties arising from different levels of development and capacity in the intellectual property space.

14.2 PATENT ADMINISTRATION

The Department of Intellectual Property (DIP), established within the Ministry of Commerce in May 1992, is in charge of the implementation of intellectual property laws in Thailand with the exception of the Plant Variety Protection Act B.E. 2642 (1999) (which is administered by the Ministry of Agriculture). The DIP's duties and responsibilities are registering patents, trademarks and the licensing of intellectual property rights; developing systems, patterns, and means to protect intellectual property; promoting effective use of intellectual property and technology information for the purposes of education, research, and development; commercialization; and studying, analyzing, and recommending policies on intellectual property to the Thai government.[2]

To establish an effective patent system is challenging for developing countries such as Thailand, as they typically lack sufficient intellectual property expertise in their national academic or educational institutions. The lack of expertise in this field at such a level means a country will not have adequate well-trained professionals with technical competence for the substantive examination of patent applications. In addition, in the Thailand context, these problems are exacerbated because the DIP is generally underfunded and the maximum salary for its staff is not high. This means that it can be very difficult for Thailand's resource-scarce patent office to recruit, prepare, and maintain a group of competent patent examiners. While an efficient patent office generally requires at least 200 examiners to guarantee proper examination in all technical fields,[3] there are currently 42 patent examiners at the Thai Patent Office. Although the number of patent examiners employed by the DIP Patent Office has increased in recent years, from 24 in 2001 to 42 in 2010, the number is still too small to guarantee the quality and efficiency of patent examination. The situation is even worse considering the fact that only 17 out of the total 42 examiners are involved in the examination of patent applications for inventions in the fields of chemistry, biotechnology, pharmaceuticals, and engineering.

[2] *See Thai Department of Intellectual Property, Annual Report 2015, available at* www.ipthailand.go.th/images/AR_DIP_2015_Final.pdf.

[3] R.M. Sherwood, V. Scartezini & D. Siemsen, *Promotion of Inventiveness in Developing Countries through a More Advanced Patent Administration*, 39(4) IDEA J. LAW TECHNOL. 473, 480 (1990).

The rest are involved in examining applications for designs and petty patents.[4] These problems have become more acute, as examiners are called on to assess increasingly complex inventions. In Thailand, for example, 11.9 percent of the patent examiners currently employed by the DIP have a bachelor's degree in science, and the remainder hold a master's degree. The majority have little experience in patent examination. Of the total, 35.7 percent have between ten and fifteen years' experience, and the rest have work experience of less than ten years.[5]

It can be difficult to hire patent examiners quickly from the labor market. Partly, this is because a specialized profession of patent attorneys does not exist in Thailand. Relatedly, the law is silent about what type of qualifications a patent representative has to possess. As a result, attorneys at law are the only ones qualified to represent clients in the prosecution of patent applications. Such attorneys are generally law graduates and most of them do not have a technical degree, especially because there is no graduate school for the professional training of patent attorneys. The importance of essential details of the patented invention is crucial, but without technically skilled representatives applications will not contain sufficient details about the invention. And the inadequate and incomplete disclosure in patent applications makes it impossible for the public to utilize the patented information efficiently.[6]

Patent examiners at the DIP are hired at the government pay scale, which is uncompetitive with nongovernmental jobs. For example, the starting salary of a DIP's patent examiner is THB 12,000 (approximately 300 USD) per month, while an examiner with five to ten years' experience receives the maximum salary of THB 50,000 (approximately 1,666 USD) per month.[7] The DIP enjoys less flexibility than its counterparts in some other ASEAN countries such as Singapore and Malaysia, where the patent offices are now autonomous entities.[8] The DIP is still regarded as a source of income for the Thai government, and most of its income generated from application and maintenance fees must be remitted to the Revenue Department. This means it is unable to use the surplus income for providing pay incentives to well-performing examiners.[9] Because of its limitations, the Thai Patent Office has struggled to recruit competent examiners, and as a result it is unable to deal with dramatic increases in the number of applications.

4 Kenan Institute, Comparative Assessment of Patent and Trademark Offices in South-east Asia 116 (2011).

5 *Id.* at 14.

6 *Id.* at 121, *see also* Frederick M. Abbott, Carlos M. Correa & Peter Drahos (eds.), Emerging Markets and the World Patent Order 319 (2013).

7 *Id.* at 117.

8 *Id.* at 67, 102, 114.

9 *Id.* at 125–126.

Like many patent offices, the DIP is facing a dramatic increase in the number of applications.[10] This, combined with the personnel issues just described makes it difficult to offer technical examinations in all fields, particularly in new areas of technology such as biotechnology and pharmaceuticals. The problem of patent backlog for developing countries like Thailand has become even more acute owing to the weak institutional capacity in patent administration. The DIP has struggled to cope with the increasing volume of patent applications. From 2005 to 2009, the DIP received approximately 10,000 patent applications each year.[11] The majority of the applications were design patent applications. Only about 15 percent were applications for a patent on the invention.

The period of patent granting in Thailand is, on average, from three to five years, which can be much longer for patent applications in complex fields. It is estimated that the period taken to obtain a patent for invention in areas of physics and biotechnology generally takes five to nine years owing to the lack of examiners in those fields of technology.[12] The number of applications per examiner has also been growing in recent years. In 2009, each examiner was expected to process an average of 254 applications per year at an approximate rate of an application for every working day.[13]

Thailand has attempted to increase its patent quality and to reduce the administrative burden on the Patent Office by seeking international collaboration. The DIP has outsourced search and examination of patents to foreign patent offices. Examples of collaboration include outsourcing to the Intellectual Property Office of Singapore,[14] the Australian Patent Office,[15] and a pilot patent prosecution highway program with the Japan Patentice.[16] While the outsourcing option provides a relatively low-cost and high-quality examination, it has created a language problem as the patent law of Thailand requires all applications to be drafted in Thai. In practice, the DIP, owing to limited

[10] London Economics, Economic Study on Patent Backlogs and a System of Mutual Recognition (Report Submitted to the UK Intellectual Property Office) vii, 1 (2010), *available at* www.gov.uk/government/uploads/system/uploads/attachment_data/file/328678/p-backlog-report.pdf.

[11] Kenan Institute, *supra* note 4, at 118. [12] *Id.* at 121. [13] *Id.*

[14] Intellectual Property Office of Singapore, *Singapore and Thailand Collaborate to Serve Innovators in Patent Protection* (October 27, 2015), *available at* www.ipos.gov.sg/MediaEvents/Readnews/tabid/873/articleid/325/category/Press%20Releases/parentId/80/year/2015/Default.aspx.

[15] *See* Peter Drahos, The Global Governance of Knowledge: Patent Offices and Their Clients 41–42 (2010).

[16] Japanese Ministry of Economy, Trade and Industry *JPO Strengthens Cooperative Relationship with the Department of Intellectual Property, Ministry of Commerce in Thailand* (December 25, 2015), *available at* www.meti.go.jp/english/press/2015/1225_04.html.

resources and facilities, gives greater weight to the patent grants for the same invention in other countries. Because of this practice, a claimed invention that has been granted a patent by a foreign patent office, particularly in developed countries that are considered more capable of thoroughly examining applications, is almost guaranteed a patent right in Thailand.

In theory, patent databases and patent documentation provide a wealth of information for local scientists. In reality, the patent specifications provided by the applicant are generally a translation of the patent application filed in a foreign country by the same applicant. The DIP's patent examiners have faced difficulties dealing with the large number of translated documents. A number of patent applications filed in Thailand are technically incomplete and poorly translated, which makes it difficult for the examiners to read and understand the technical descriptions of the applications. Poorly translated applications may also lead to errors in the determination of the patent examiner and may result in an invalid patent being granted.

14.3 CONCLUSION

ASEAN member countries can be characterized by striking asymmetries in intellectual property policies and different levels of legal, social, and economic environments and administrative capacity. Thailand still struggles to improve its capabilities for implementing intellectual property laws. As long as a middle-income ASEAN country such as Thailand is unable to develop an efficient intellectual property system, there can be no doubt that the less-developed ASEAN members will find it more difficult to operate intellectual property regimes efficiently and at lower cost. While programs initiated by ASEAN such as ASPEC and the IP Portal[17] should help to address the major problem of disparate capacities among member countries' intellectual property offices, the ASEAN nations still require support for human resources development, capacity building, and policy and institutional improvements.

Most ASEAN members have urgent needs in technical assistance for the development of their human resources and intellectual property infrastructure. Technical assistance is also required to help develop the intellectual property regimes and policies in ASEAN nations. Technical collaboration should be

[17] For more information on ASPEC and the ASEAN IP Portal, *see* Elizabeth Siew-Kuan Ng, *Intellectual Property Interoperability in ASEAN and Beyond: An Integration Model, in* ELIZABETH SIEW-KUAN NG & GRAEME AUSTIN (eds.), INTERNATIONAL INTELLECTUAL PROPERTY AND THE ASEAN WAY: PATHWAYS TO INTEROPERABILITY, Chapter 1.

available to help set up national intellectual property strategies, which identify the country's strengths and weaknesses affecting their capacity for regime development. Remedies should be found for weak areas and areas of strength should be further enhanced with a view to attaining a successful and efficient intellectual property system. Developing ASEAN countries also require technical collaboration and capacity building for curricula development in national educational institutions and universities, and similar collaboration in the preparation of capacity-building programs for the judiciary and legislative authorities. This will allow all of them to keep abreast of worldwide developments in the field and sustain further development and growth in their intellectual property systems.

PART IV

BEYOND INTEROPERABILITY

The three chapters in this part explore different kinds of interoperability models. First, in Chapter 15 Annette Kur examines the administration of trademark law within the European Union context. In Chapter 16, Reto Hilty and Roberto Romandini share lessons learned from the European experience on developing a common patent system. In Chapter 17, Pablo Wegbrait and Carlos Garaventa examine the experience of Latin America in attempting to achieve greater interoperability between different jurisdictions in the region.

It is readily apparent that the interoperability models discussed here are quite different. The European Union has achieved the very kind of harmonization and economic integration that is no longer on the table in the ASEAN context. As Professor Kur discusses, however, even with complete integration of trademark law at the EU level, there may still be differences in how the (harmonized) law is applied in practice at the domestic level. The EU trademark system is also characterized by a parallelism, with the Community Trademark and the harmonized national laws working in tandem. Within the EU trademarks context, there are still important points of detail to work through. Even so, with the European Union, the trademark system reflects a commitment to convergence. A similar viewpoint was expressed by Reto Hilty and Roberto Romandini in the European patent law context. Whilst highlighting the achievements of the European Union in creating a unitary patent system and a unified jurisdiction – a process that has taken nearly fifty years – they nonetheless emphasize that the European model is not to be blindly followed. Instead, it should be a reference for learning and for evaluating what may be transplanted from Europe and what may not.

A very different picture emerges in Latin America. Within the broader Latin American context, there does exist one example of an integrated system: the Comunidad Andina de Nacione (Andean Community of Nations – CAN).

The Andean community has, however, lost a number of key members, and, as a result, the scope of its influence is diminishing. An alternative vehicle for integration, has been the Mercado Común del Sur (MERCOSUR). However, as Wegbrait and Garaventa describe, very little has been achieved in the intellectual property context under the aegis of MERCOSUR.

The analysis of the Latin American situation presented by Wegbrait and Garaventa draws attention to a key dynamic in the interoperability context: politics. The EU project emerged from a mutual desire to ameliorate the excesses of nationalism that led to the atrocities of World War II. While BREXIT and the rise of nationalist political parties within Europe have tested these commitments, the institutional structures remain firmly in place. In Latin America, however, the path toward integration was significantly impeded by the rise of a politics informed by a deep suspicion of the claimed benefits of the kind of economic consensus that has driven the dynamics of globalization, and the progress toward an ever more integrated European Union. Wegbrait and Garaventa's chapter provides a useful reminder that for intellectual property interoperability, like other forms of economic integration, politics can be another key force at play.

15

The EUIPO Convergence Program

A Model for ASEAN?

Annette Kur

15.1 INTRODUCTION

Since the 1990s trademark law in the EU member states is largely harmonized. The provisions governing signs eligible for protection, protection requirements, scope, and limitations of protection have been aligned both horizontally between the member states and also vis-à-vis the overarching trademark system applying on the EU level. The legal instruments employed to achieve those goals were the Trademark Directive (TMD), first enacted in 1989, and now recast as directive (EU) 2015/2436, and the Community Trademark Regulation (now: EU Trademark Regulation, EUTMR) of 1994, amended by Regulation (EU) 2015/2424, with the codified text entering into force on October 1, 2017 as Regulation (EU) 2017/1001. The recent reforms further enhance the overall level of alignment. In addition to new substantive issues such as transfer of marks, harmonization has been extended to procedural issues, such as application formalities and procedures for opposition and cancellation.[1]

However, even near-complete harmonization (or even unification) of the legal rules governing trademark law in the EU and its member states does not guarantee that those rules are applied consistently in practice. Indeed, practitioners often complain about the discrepancies experienced when filing applications or enforcing trademark rights in different member states and/or under the EUTMR. To improve the situation, the so-called convergence

[1] Somewhat less prominent, but equally successful has been the development in the field of industrial designs. The two-tiered structure of regulation is the same as in trademark law, i.e., national laws are harmonized on the basis of the Design Directive (Directive 98/71/EC of the European Parliament and of the Council of October 13, 1998 on the Legal Protection of Designs, 1998 O.J. (L 289) 28), and the Community Design Regulation (CDR) of 2002 (Council Regulation (EC) No. 06/2002 on Community Designs, 2002 O.J. (L 3) 1) has created a system of uniform protection applying directly on the EU level. As a novel feature, the CDR also embraces an Unregistered Community Design right (UCD).

program has been launched by the EU Intellectual Property Office (EUIPO) under its old name OHIM. While it is tailor-made to the relevant structures and issues under EU law, the question shall be posed as to whether the basic concept on which the convergence program relies might possibly also serve as a model in other regions such as Association of Southeast Asian Nations (ASEAN), where substantive harmonization beyond the international minimum is not on the agenda.

15.2 THE CONVERGENCE PROGRAM IN THE EU CONTEXT

15.2.1 *Legal and Administrative Framework*

As noted in the introduction, European trademark legislation pertains to two different levels. On the national level, member states are obliged to align the provisions of national laws with the mandatory rules enshrined in the TMD. Additionally, the EUTMR provides an autonomous system pertaining to the EU level. In the core aspects of substantive contents – and, after the legal reforms, also in most procedural aspects – the trademark systems on the national and the EU level run exactly parallel, with only a few exceptions that are pointed out in the text that follows.

Administration of the respective systems lies with the competent authorities and courts. In the case of the national systems, these are the national (or, in case of the Benelux States, regional) offices in charge of administering registration of industrial property rights (trademarks as well as designs and, as a rule, patents). The decisions of those offices are subject to judicial supervision under the pertinent national rules. Furthermore, in case of infringements, injunctions and remedies can be claimed in the national courts.

In case of the EUTM system, administration was consigned to a special agency created for the purpose under the Office for Harmonisation in the Internal Market (OHIM). Apart from its activities related to trademarks the Office also administers the registration of Community Designs on the basis of the Community Design Regulation (CDR) of 2002; it is the seat of the European Observatory on Infringements of Intellectual Property Rights (Observatory), and hosts the registry of orphan works in Europe. With the activities spanning so many different fields – and with more tasks waiting in the pipeline – the name of the Office was changed in the 2015 trademark law reform to EU Intellectual Property Office (EUIPO). EUIPO decisions are subject to judicial review by the General Court and, on points of law, by the Court of Justice (CJEU). In case of infringement of EUTMs, the competent courts are those designated by each member state as "Community Trademark Court(s)" within the respective territory.

15.2.2 *The Need to Promote Convergence*

In the first version enacted in 1989, the TMD was expressly confined to approximation of national laws in matters that "most directly affect the functioning of the internal market."[2] This left a certain margin for national systems to deviate from each other and from the system established on the Community level. For instance, it was (and still is) left to the member states whether they protect trademarks through use in addition to the (mandatory) route of acquiring protection through registration. Furthermore, apart from a single provision regarding licenses, the property aspects of national marks were not regulated; third, a number of provisions in the TMD were of an optional nature only, such as the obstacle for protection resulting from filing of applications in bad faith, or extended protection granted to national marks having a reputation. Lastly, and quite important in practice, procedural rules were practically entirely exempted from harmonization.[3]

While the restriction of harmonization to issues of relevance to the functioning of the internal market was a deliberate decision by the legislature that could be addressed only by further legislative measures such as the 2015 TMD recast, it was noted with some discontent among users of the European trademark system that even where the substantive provisions were exactly the same, their application tended to diverge in practice. To some extent this was due to the fact that the wording of the provisions was not unambiguous, so that clarity had to be sought through the instrument of reference of pertinent questions to the CJEU. Indeed, the number of such references in the years following the operationalization of the EU trademark system was remarkably high, with a peak of rather fundamental issues being decided around the end of first decade of this century.

However, even where the objectives and wording of provisions were clear enough – or where judgments by the CJEU had been given – it turned out

2 Directive 89/104/EEC of the Council of 21 December 1988 to Approximate the Laws of the Member States Relating to Trade Marks, 1989 O.J. (L 40) 1, Recital No. 3 of the preamble.

3 By contrast with the absence of explicit or mandatory rules in the TMD on the aspects just mentioned, the CTMR did provide a full-fledged protection regime including licences, transfer, and other property-rights aspects as well as rules of procedure. However, a gap was left in the otherwise unitary system insofar as the CTMR – just as the EUTMR – do not provide their own catalogue of sanctions, with the exception of injunctive relief. Where damages or corrective measures are claimed, national law applies instead.

that harmonized practice was by no means guaranteed. This became most visible when trademark applications were accepted in one or several national systems, but were rejected in others, or when marks registered nationally were rejected by OHIM. It is true that such differences can be the "natural" result of the fact that while marks can be descriptive or nondistinctive for linguistic reasons in certain parts of the EU, they appear as mere phantasy words, and are therefore registrable, in other parts where the respective language is not known or understood. Also, one must consider that decisions are made by humans, not by automats, and that each one involves a certain amount of subjective appraisal which, in particular in close cases, will inevitably provoke different opinions, even among persons serving in one and the same tribunal or authority.

Although certainly correct as such, those arguments were not fully capable to dissipate the uneasiness building around the experience of divergent office practice. First, language differences can hardly explain discrepancies between decisions taken by national offices on the one hand and OHIM (now: the EUIPO) on the other: as the latter must take all official EU languages into account, different outcomes can only result from different interpretations of the same rules. The same applies if the distinctive character of nonverbal marks, such as product shapes, colors per se, surface decoration or graphical symbols, is assessed differently in different national systems or on the EU level. Second, regarding the "human factor," it is true that a certain margin of divergences will inevitably arise whenever decisions involve subjective assessments; however, this becomes a structural problem where individual tendencies appear to solidify into a kind of consolidated office practice that diverges from the respective tendencies developed and observed by others.

Vexing as the issue may be, there is little that can be done in the strict terms of enforcing black letter law. The national systems, represented by the national offices, and the EUTM system represented by OHIM/the EUIPO coexist on the same systemic level; that is, there is no hierarchical order with the EU system taking the lead. Thus, decisions taken by the national authorities are amenable only to national judicial control; they are not subject to scrutiny and eventual correction by EU institutions. It is true that in case of doubts about the correct interpretation of EU law national courts *can*, and if no further appeal is possible, they *must* refer the question to the CJEU; however, that does not detract from the liberty of national decision-making bodies to reach their own conclusions in concrete cases. Thus, it has been held in numerous judgments both by national courts and by the General Court and the CJEU that decisions taken by OHIM (now: the EUIPO) do not prejudice those of national authorities and vice versa; they are only of informational value.[4]

This was the situation that motivated OHIM to address the issue of diverging practices and how they can be avoided in the framework of liaison meetings with representatives from the national offices. As the talks proved useful, they were institutionalized from 2011 under the name of "convergence program." In the course of the 2015 law reform the efforts to promote convergence were even expressly anchored in Article 152 EUTMR. The convergence program has thus gained the status of a firmly established feature of the European trademark (and design) system.

15.2.3 *Aims and Issues*

The Program

Promoting convergence was expressly mentioned as a policy goal in the 2011–2015 Strategic Plan launched by OHIM. It was conceived as a roadmap "to foster the progressive achievement of a European interoperable and collaborative network of trade mark and design offices."[5] The plans involved regular exchange of information and discussion on potentially problematic issues as well as the establishment of digital infrastructure enabling access to common information platforms and interactive communication tools. As the main benefits to be gained for users, the following points are highlighted[6]:

- Clarity and transparency: shared communication initiatives to keep stakeholders informed of advancements in a timely manner, with unified information.
- Quality and usability: effective and efficient access to protection offered by registration systems both at the national and EU levels.
- Legal certainty: increased legal certainty due to greater consistency in decisions made at the national and EU levels.
- Time and cost savings: potential reductions in application processing times and cost savings for both intellectual property offices and applicants.

4 *See, e.g.*, Case C-238/06, *Develey Holding v. OHIM*, 2007 E.C.R. I-09375, 65–68.

5 *OHIM Strategic Plan 2011–2015*, at 64, *available at* https://euipo.europa.eu/tunnel-web/secure/webdav/guest/document_library/contentPdfs/about_ohim/strategic_plan/strategic_plan_en.pdf.

6 *Id.* at 41. *See also* European Trade Mark and Design Network, *Converging Practices*, *available at* www.tmdn.org/network/converging-practices.

In regards to establishing a common infrastructure for digital communication and exchange of information, means were provided under the 2011–2015 Strategic Plan by the so-called Cooperation Funds. Regarding convergence in its core meaning, that is, alignment of national practices, the Convergence Program has become a regular item on the agenda on the periodic liaison meetings held at the EUIPO with representatives of the national offices and selected user associations. To further the discussions and provide a solid background in national practices, working groups are established to investigate specific issues that are identified as critical under convergence aspects. Based on the preparatory work done in the groups, workshops are then held to discuss and consider the issues with the aim to arrive at a set of recommendations for common practices. The national offices remain free to adopt the recommendations, eventually reflecting them in their own internal guidelines; however, they are also free to maintain their previous practices or even abstain from the discussions altogether.

Until now, the following topics were identified as relevant under the convergence program:

- CP1. Harmonization of trade mark classification practice of goods and services
- CP2. Convergence of class headings
- CP3. Absolute grounds for refusal for figurative trademarks with purely descriptive words or expressions
- CP4. Scope of protection of trademarks exclusively in black, white, and/or shades of gray
- CP5. Relative grounds – Likelihood of confusion (impact of nondistinctive/weak components)
- CP6. Convergence on graphic representations of designs
- CP7. Harmonization of product indications

Another regular item on the convergence program agenda concerns the monitoring of the implementation and continuation of the common practices established.

Institutionalization in the 2015 Law Reform

As indicated earlier, the Convergence Program was considered important enough to be firmly anchored in the EUTMR in the course of the 2015 law reform. Pursuant to Article 152(1) EUTMR, the EUIPO "and the central industrial property offices of the Member States . . . shall cooperate with each other to promote convergence of practices and tools in the field of trademarks and designs." Those efforts shall in particular cover administration and promotion of the unitary trademark and design systems, convergence of practices and tools in the fields of trademarks and designs, support of the tasks assigned to the EUIPO in regards to orphan works and the Observatory, and the exchange of technical expertise and assistance in all the areas covered. Specific projects to be pursued in that framework are defined by the management board on proposal of the executive director (formerly: president) of the EUIPO. The national offices have the right to opt out, restrict, or temporarily suspend their participation in the projects thus defined, by filing a written statement explaining the reason for their reservation. Once they have committed to participate, they must contribute effectively to the common goal. As an incentive, up to 15 percent of the yearly revenue of the EUIPO can be given in financial support to the participating offices, in the form of grants or in-kind contributions. Finally, Article 152(6) highlights the importance of concerted activities in the fight against counterfeiting. Thus, cooperation shall extend to awareness-raising including education and training activities as well as implementation of established standards and practices.

Specific Issues

Of the fields of activities where convergence has led to tangible results, two shall be presented here in some more detail. The first concerns classification: as every practitioner knows, this is of huge practical importance for the smooth handling of applications, in particular where more than one jurisdiction is covered. Internationally a common tool is provided for the purpose in the form of the Nice Classification Agreement. However, owing to constant economic developments the taxonomy established by the Nice Agreement may become incomplete or flawed and must be monitored and, where necessary, revised and complemented to remain operable; furthermore, language must be checked time and again to ensure that the meaning of terms is exactly the same in all languages used in offices participating in a common system. In addition, a particular problem arose in the EU when the OHIM announced, by communication of its previous president, that use of class headings from the Nice Agreement in trademark applications filed at OHIM would be interpreted as claiming protection for all goods and services listed in the respective Nice classes, irrespective of whether, under a "natural" understanding of the class heading, one would actually expect certain goods or services to be covered. That practice was criticized in some member states as resulting in blurred and unnecessarily broad protection. In the guise of an actual trademark conflict, the issue was finally referred to the CJEU. The Court shared the criticism and ordered that while use of class headings cannot be prohibited in principle, it must be ensured that it is clear and precise enough to indicate with sufficient certainty the exact subject matter covered ("means what it says").[7]

The CJEU decision in that case – the wording and repercussions of which are now reflected in Article 33 EUTMR – as well as divergences observed in the classification practice of national offices independently from the subject of class headings form the backdrop for the first two items in the convergence program. Pursuant to the EUIPO's own communications in this matter, the harmonization of trademark classification practice in particular can serve as "a great example of the synergy between the Cooperation Fund and the Convergence Programme." Thus, inter alia a common database of almost 65,000 acceptable terms that are implemented and maintained currently by 26 offices including the EUIPO has been established. For the purposes of that database, a taxonomy was created to structure goods and services hierarchically by means of smaller groups within each NICE goods and service class, so as to better reflect the market reality. Furthermore, a common list of acceptable and nonacceptable general indications of the Nice Class Headings was published, and the reasons indicated, in a common communication.

The second issue to be presented here concerns the legal effects of marks registered in black and white, or in shades of gray. Compared to classification, it is more confined in its dimensions; nevertheless, it has also led to quite controversial debates. The question is whether, if a figurative sign is registered without any particular color being indicated in the application, and/or the representation of the sign is only in black and white or shades of gray, this has the effect that protection of the sign extends to reproduction of the figurative element in any color, or whether it is restricted to the black and white/shades of gray configuration shown in the documents filed. The issue is of relevance inter alia because pursuant to European trademark law likelihood of confusion does not have to be established in case of "double identity," that is, when the conflicting signs as well as goods and services to which they pertain are identical. Thus, for example, identity of signs – and thereby one crucial element of "double identity" – can be asserted only between a figurative sign filed in black and white and an identical configuration filed (or used) in, for example, bright red if black and white registrations were assumed to cover all colors, as was indeed the traditional attitude prevailing in many EU member states

[7] Case C-307/10, *Chartered Institute of Patent Attorneys v. Registrar of Trade Marks*, 2012 E.C.R. 361.

as well as, originally, at OHIM.[8] However, following the discussions in the convergence workshop, OHIM's practice as well as that in a number of EU member states was changed; according to the current guidelines, colors must be expressly claimed for a figurative sign.[9]

At least initially, the result of the convergence efforts on this point was received quite critically among practitioners as well as in certain member states, some of which even chose not to participate at all in the pertinent discussions. The argument of critics is that registration in black and white is meant to cover the configuration as such, independent of particular colors, just as registration of word marks covers the word as such, irrespective of the font or style in which it is written. While that is a tenable argument, it is not necessarily convincing: different from word marks, figurative marks are essentially visual, and for the visual impression, color is an element of crucial importance that arguably should not be ignored when identity of signs is assessed. Thus, good arguments can be found for one and the other side; there is no clear way of telling right from wrong in this regard. Under the aspect of convergence, the only important thing in such cases is to agree on a common solution, even if that means abandoning one's previous practices. And, after all, the difference this makes in actual conflicts is not so grave: Even if a particular configuration registered in black and white is reproduced in a different color and thus does not count as identical, the degree of similarity vis-à-vis the protected sign

8 *See, e.g.*, Ladas & Perry, *European Union – New Practice on Black and White and Color Trade Marks* (July 16, 2014), *available at* http://ladas.com/education-center/european-union-new-practice-black-white-colour-trade-marks/ where it is reported that: "The European Trade Mark and Design Network has published a new common practice communication which took effect in all participating EU countries and OHIM on various dates with the last on July 16, 2014. Sweden, Denmark and Norway have opted out of the Common Practice because of legal constraints and Italy, France and Finland did not participate. The Common Practice aims to harmonise the practice between the different approaches of national offices in the EU regarding the scope of protection given to trade marks registered in black and white or greyscale. The new practice applies retrospectively to pending applications and proceedings. The former practice at OHIM and in many national offices was that if a mark was registered in black and white, the registration also protected colour variations of the mark."

9 *See Guidelines for Examination of European Union Trade Marks* (EUIPO), Part C Section 2 Chapter 4, para 2.4, *available at* https://euipo.europa.eu/ohimportal/en/trade-mark-guidelines. Without referring to the EUIPO Guidelines or the Convergence Program, the German Federal Supreme Court in a 2015 decision (Bundesgerichtshof [BGH] [Federal Court of Justice] March 12, 2015, Case No. I ZR 153/14 (*translated in* 47 International Review of Intellectual Property and Competition (IIC) 114 (2016)) held that the reproduction of the BMW sign in the exact colors used by BMW on its cars was not identical, but only similar to the registered sign, which had been filed in black and white.

and thus the likelihood of confusion caused are typically very high, so that infringement results in any case.

15.2.4 *From "Convergence Program" to the "Trade Marks and Designs Network"*

Boosted by the Convergence Program and fueled by means of the Cooperation Funds, the plans to establish powerful communication tools and enhanced digital infrastructure, the "European Trade Marks and Design Network (ETMDN)" has been established to carry the EUIPO's Strategic Plans further into the 2020s. According to the website established for promoting the activities of the network, the ETMDN is "the hub that connects National and Regional Intellectual Property Offices, User Associations and other IP Organisations, which work together to achieve a true trade mark and design system in Europe. This means that common practices, services, and tools are focused on the needs of IP professionals and rights holders." In essence, what this means is that the work commenced under the Convergence Program is continued and deepened with the goal of weaving an ever more close-knit mesh of common guidelines and working routines so that users, in the end, will hardly experience any differences in the handling and assessment of matters, irrespective of whether protection is claimed in any member state or on the EU level.

15.3 THE ASEAN CONTEXT

15.3.1 *Overview*

Before embarking on the question of whether and to what extent the EU experience with regard to convergence could be of any interest in the ASEAN context, the differences between the two supranational systems must be highlighted. Contrary to the EU and its predecessors (EEC; EC), ASEAN was not conceived with a view to establishing a common market. The foremost reason for its establishment was to ensure independence and mutual respect of its members, so as to leave to each one the space and freedom to concentrate on nation building, thereby enhancing the economic and political welfare in all of them. The cooperation initiatives launched in the framework therefore concerned primarily culture, education, and environmental concerns. However, trade and development, including economic integration, have also become an issue over time, and as a key factor of economic development and growth, intellectual property found its place on the agenda.

However, unlike in Europe, substantive harmonization of intellectual property laws is not of immediate interest. One reason is that the ASEAN countries are very diverse with regard to their economic strength and state of development. The group comprises developing countries with a very low GDP per person, threshold countries on diverse stages of development, and highly developed countries such as Singapore. Moreover, independence and sovereignty of political decisions constitute core elements of the particular "ASEAN Way" of supranational cooperation. From that perspective, supporting each other's use of existing flexibilities presents a more adequate approach than imposing centrally developed solutions that may be ill fitting to a country's particular socioeconomic situation.

On the other hand, even with a somewhat reserved attitude toward substantive harmonization within ASEAN, the European experiences with the Convergence Program are not completely irrelevant or unusable. First, despite the lack of regional harmonization, a basic stock of common rules has been established through the Agreement on Trade-Related Aspects of Intellectual Property Rights (TRIPS) and other instruments of international law. Second, even where laws differ in a number of details, mutual information and consultation among authorities in geographically adjacent countries makes sense, where the problems faced in certain areas are essentially the same, and where finding an appropriate solution requires taking a conceptual approach anchored in the general tenets of intellectual property (or, in the cases considered here, of trademark) law rather than emphasizing national policy prerogatives, or taking account of cultural or linguistic particularities.

In the following an attempt is made to identify, before the background of international trademark protection minima, certain areas where cooperation similar to the European convergence activities could prove useful, with the accent lying on mutual information and assistance rather than on pursuit of harmonization goals.

15.3.2 *International Minima*

Overview

Contrary to the Paris Convention, which confined international protection standards to constellations of particular relevance for cross-border trade, TRIPS reached behind borders by imposing a fairly high level of common substantive provisions. Thus, whereas the Paris Convention left it to the member states to define the notion of signs eligible for protection, Article 15 of TRIPS stipulates that, with the exception of signs that are not perceptible visually, all forms of signs must be registrable that are capable of distinguishing goods or services as to their commercial origin. Furthermore, regarding scope, protection must be granted at least against likelihood of confusion which, in case of double identity, must be presumed; furthermore, if a mark is well known, protection must extend to use for dissimilar products, if a mental link is established thereby to the proprietor of the mark that is detrimental to his interests. Other common rules concern the admissibility of limitations of the right conferred, in particular regarding use for descriptive purposes, the duration of protection, the use requirement, and transfer and licensing. Of particular interest in recent discussions is also the prohibition in Article 20 of TRIPS to "unreasonably" encumber use of marks.

Apart from that, some key rules anchored in the Paris Convention are of continuous interest, such as protection under Article 6bis for unregistered well-known marks vis-à-vis goods for identical or similar goods or services; Article 6ter about protection of state flags, symbols, and hallmarks; or Article $6^{septies}$ concerning unauthorized registration of marks by an agent or representative.

Furthermore, in addition to establishing the parameters of substantive law, international law also provides some important procedural instruments: the Madrid system (consisting of Agreement and Protocol) facilitates acquisition of trademark rights abroad through a process of international registration handled through the World Intellectual Property Organization (WIPO). As indicated earlier, for administrative purposes trademark registries often rely on the classification scheme set forth in the Nice Classification Agreement as its basis. Finally, of more recent date, the Trademark Law Treaty (TLT) and the Treaty of Singapore (STLT) seek to streamline and disencumber the registration of trademarks abroad.

Membership of ASEAN Countries

All ASEAN member states by now have adhered to the World Trade Organization (WTO) Agreement, including TRIPS. With the exception of Myanmar, all ASEAN members are also bound to the latest (1967) version of the Paris Convention by direct accession; for Myanmar, the obligation to comply with Article 1 to 12 and 19 of the 1967 text of the Paris Convention results from Article 2(1) TRIPS. While that results in complete conformity insofar as substantive obligations under international law are concerned, the picture is more fragmented with regard to international registration and procedural rules.[10] Only

[10] This is different in the three regional (economic) powers China, Japan, and Republic of Korea that are sometimes addressed, together with the ASEAN states, as "ASEAN plus three": All three states have adhered to the Madrid Protocol and the Nice Agreement. Japan and the

five of the ten ASEAN states (Cambodia, Laos, the Philippines, Singapore, and Vietnam) are members of the Madrid Protocol. The Nice Classification Agreement has been ratified by only two member states (Malaysia and Singapore). However, this does not mean that the structure and basic contents of the international classification scheme are not also used by the registries of other states as well, independent of formal membership. Finally, the TLT and STLT were ratified by only one ASEAN member state each (Indonesia and Singapore respectively). The picture could change, however, as the "endeavor to adhere" to the TLT or STLT increasingly figures as an element included in bilateral or regional trade agreements.

15.3.3 *A Way Forward: Some Suggestions*

In accordance with the philosophy reflected in the ASEAN Way, convergence efforts are of interest in the ASEAN context not as a tool for perfecting harmonization, but rather as a vehicle promoting discourse, mutual information, and, where feasible, paving the way to pragmatic solutions facilitating acquisition and enforcement of rights abroad and thus encouraging cross-border trade and investments while preserving member states' cultural, political, and economic autonomy. As a first step toward that goal, an investigation must be conducted regarding the current commonalities and divergences between national trademark laws and procedures, flagging out areas where common interests exist in resolving parallel issues accruing under the respective laws. Without being able to predict the outcome of such investigations, the following issues could be of relevance:

- With regards to substantive law, information could be exchanged concerning the conditions of "unconventional" marks, in particular three-dimensional shapes and colors per se. It is submitted that both types of signs – in contrast with nonvisible signs such as sounds or smells, which can be exempted from protection for good – must be eligible for registration, capable as they are in principle of distinguishing goods or services of one entrepreneur from those of another. However, the application of concrete protection requirements – that is, whether a shape or a color per se is sufficiently distinctive to be registered – is notoriously difficult to handle. Especially where offices lack specific experience with such signs, mutual

Republic of Korea have also adhered to the TLT and the STLT, while China has signed, but not ratified, both treaties.

information and exchange of experience might prove useful. Another "classical" topic for communication and debates could be the conditions for protection of unregistered well-known marks, and how their status is verified in practice. Further potential issues under substantive law concern the conditions for registration of geographical names or the names of persons (living or deceased), the question of how the registration of foreign descriptive or generic terms should be handled (with the possible establishment of an information platform to verify the meaning of foreign terms), or how to apply article 6ter Paris Convention (exclusion of flags, state symbols, or hallmarks; eventually leading to the establishment of a reference database containing terms or signs that, because of their political, cultural, or religious meaning should preferably not be registered in other ASEAN countries).

- With regard to procedural issues, the fact that most ASEAN countries have not adhered to the Nice Agreement leaves ample room – and arguably presents a solid case – for developing a common structure and taxonomy of terms to be used by the national registries. While it makes sense to basically anchor that structure in the overall scheme provided by the Nice Agreement, the details could be worked out on a mutual basis, with the correctness of language being checked on a regular basis, and with specific account being taken of the markets and consumption patterns in the ASEAN region. Furthermore, even absent widespread membership in the TLT or STLT, the use of formalities could be discussed, and common practices could be developed regarding filing requirements, renewals, changes in ownership or address and so forth, as well as reinstitution in case of delay.

After the relevant issues – not necessarily those listed in the foregoing – have been identified, a working agenda needs to be drafted and regular meetings must be scheduled that, based on detailed documentation and explanation of national practices, undertake to elaborate general concepts or guidelines serving as roadmaps toward more transparent and, where feasible and desirable, more homogeneous practices. While such roadmaps cannot possibly be binding in any manner, national offices should be encouraged to take them into account for their decisions and working routines.

Furthermore, while national offices remain independent, in the longer run cooperation could lead to the establishment of common digital platforms facilitating centralized management of trademark applications and registrations extending over several ASEAN states. Without creating a hierarchical order, such platforms could provide a central, multilanguage entrance point to the different systems for (prospective) trademark proprietors, and it could at the same time serve as a communication hub for the participating offices, similar, though not identical, to the ETMDN presented earlier.

15.4 CONCLUSION

For all its diversities the ASEAN region presents a fascinating picture of a world region in motion. In the best of scenarios that motion would lead to growing prosperity and enhanced public welfare in all countries alike. While intellectual property is but one factor among many others influencing the direction and speed of future developments, providing stable and adequately balanced conditions for acquisition and use of such rights within individual countries as well as in a group of countries linked by their regional vicinity as well as by a set of common core interests is of no small importance as a step toward the common goal. In that context, the experience gained through cooperation among EU member states on the sublegislative level, under the caption of "Convergence Program" could provide food for thought and an incentive to set up a concrete, realistic working program in the context of ASEAN.

16

Developing a Common Patent System

*Lessons to Be Learned from the European Experience**

Reto Hilty and Roberto Romandini

16.1 INTRODUCTION

The relationship between the European Union (EU) and the Association of Southeast Asian Nations (ASEAN) cannot be that of pioneer and follower. Too different are the nature, structure, and functions of the two entities, too distant and remote the cultural and political contexts in which they operate. However, the two organizations[1] do have some common purposes, such as maintaining peace and promoting integration among the respective member states, in particular by building a common market.[2] In achieving that they also face similar hurdles, such as different levels of development and different legal traditions, languages, and backgrounds among the countries involved.

Therefore, the ASEAN states, when considering whether and how to build a common patent system, can indeed look to the European experience, but *cum grano salis*. The European experience is not a model to be followed blindly,

* For an extended version of this chapter *see* Reto Hilty & Roberto Romandini, *Developing a Common Patent System – Lessons to Be Learnt from the European Experience, available at* https://www.ssrn.com/link/Max-Planck-Innovation-RES.html.

[1] Both ASEAN and the EU are international organizations established by intergovernmental agreements. However, the EU presents some specific features that ASEAN lacks, such as including supranational organizations with the ability to create norms that apply directly to individuals, a judicial system, a parliament, and an executive organ with enforcement powers. On the legal status of ASEAN from an international law point of view, *see* Simon Chesterman, *Does ASEAN Exist? The Association of Southeast Asian Nations as an International Legal Person*, 12 SING. YEAR BOOK INT'L. L. 199 (2008).

[2] *See* Association of Southeast Asian Nations (ASEAN), Charter of the Association of Southeast Asian Nations, art. 1.5, November 20, 2007 (entered into force December 15, 2008). According to the ASEAN Charter, one of the purposes of ASEAN is to create "a single market and production base which is stable, prosperous, highly competitive, and economically integrated, with effective facilitation for trade and investment." There must also be a "free flow of goods, services and investment, as well as facilitated movement of business, persons, professionals, talents and labour; and freer flow of capital." *See id.*

but rather a reference for learning what has been done in similar situations in order to evaluate what may be transplanted from Europe to Southeast Asia and what may not.[3] To that end, it will also be useful not only to know the current structure of the European patent system, but also to consider the alternatives discussed in the past century and the reasons why some solutions were adopted and others rejected.

The timing for such analysis seems appropriate. The European integration process is going through a profound crisis. In the field of patent law, however, the EU is about to complete the process of integrating national systems initiated some fifty years ago. The entry into force of the Agreement on a Unified Patent Court (UPCA),[4] expected for 2018,[5] and the subsequent applicability of EU Regulations 1257/2012[6] and 1260/2012,[7] will introduce a unitary patent system and a unified jurisdiction in parts of the EU[8] – a goal that has been pursued since 1949.[9] However, owing to the political compromises accepted by the EU institutions, this fundamental reform has not, according to some observers,[10]

3 *See also* for a similar cautious approach to adopting the EU model of regional competition law to the ASEAN Framework: Josef Drexl, *The Transplantability of the EU's Competition Law Framework into the ASEAN Region* 10–13, 23–25 (Max Planck Institute for Innovation & Competition Research Paper No. 16–11, 2016), *available at* https://ssrn.com/abstract=2841161.

4 Agreement on a Unified Patent Court, June 20, 2013, 2013 O.J. (C 175) 1 [hereinafter UPCA].

5 The entry into force of the system requires that thirteen Contracting Member States, including the United Kingdom, France, and Germany, ratify the agreement. The United Kingdom has confirmed its intention to ratify the UPCA despite the planned Brexit, at a meeting of the EU Competitiveness Council of November 28, 2016: *see* Ben Martin, *UK to Ratify EU Patent System Despite Brexit*, THE TELEGRAPH (November 28, 2016), *available at* www.telegraph.co.uk/business/2016/11/28/uk-ratify-eu-patent-system-despite-brexit/. On the possible effect of Brexit on the UPCA, *see* Richard Gordon & Tom Pascoe, *Opinion re the Effect of 'Brexit' on the Unitary Patent Regulation and the Unified Patent Court Agreement*, EIP (September 12, 2016), *available at* www.eip.com/assets/downloads/gordon-and-pascoe-advice-upca-34448129-1-.pdf.

6 *See* Regulation (EU) 1257/2012 of the European Parliament and of the Council of December 17, 2012, Implementing Enhanced Cooperation in the Area of the Creation of Unitary Patent Protection, 2012 O.J. (L 361) 1.

7 *See* Regulation (EU) 1260/2012 of the Council of December 17, 2012, Implementing Enhanced Cooperation in the Area of the Creation of Unitary Patent Protection with Regard to the Applicable Translation Arrangements, 2012 O.J. (L 361) 89.

8 More precisely, the Patent Package will be applied only in those countries that will have ratified the UPCA; *see* Regulation (EU) 1257/2012, *supra* note 6, at art. 18(2). Spain has not signed the UPCA and does not take part in the enhanced cooperation.

9 *See* Parliamentary Assembly of the Council of Europe, Committee on Economic Affairs and Development, *Creation of a European Patents Office*, Doc. 75 (September 6, 1949), *available at* www.assembly.coe.int/nw/xml/XRef/Xref-DocDetails-EN.asp?FileID=34&Lang=EN; Aurora Plomer, *A Unitary Patent for a (Dis)United Europe: The Long Shadow of History*, 46(5) INT'L. REV. INTELL. PROP. & COMPT. L. 508, 511–512 (2015).

10 *See, e.g.*, Jochen Pagenberg, *Die EU-Patentrechtsreform – zurück auf Los?*, 6 GRUR 582 (2012); Ingve Björn Stjerna, *Die Beratungen zum "Einheitspatent" und der zugehörigen Gerichtsbarkeit – Auf dem Weg ins Desaster*, MITTEILUNGEN DER DEUTSCHEN PATENTANWÄLTE 54

occurred in a completely satisfactory way. Further, several legal uncertainties still surround the unified jurisdiction.

16.2 REASONS FOR CREATING A COMMON PATENT SYSTEM

Before addressing how to create a patent system common to different sovereign states, it may be worth exploring the reasons for doing so. There are two sets of motives why a group of countries may consider sharing activities in the administration of their patent systems, or even pooling together the power to grant and protect patent rights. The first set can be labeled "economy of scale" or "efficiency" driven motives.[11] In particular, the aims are to reduce the costs for the states of administering a national patent system, and for the applicant of getting protection through national patent applications; to mitigate the backlogs of pending applications and the delays arising from multiple filings; to prevent a duplication of work throughout the various patent offices; to compensate for the potential lack of expertise of national offices (or to reduce the costs associated with an attempt to mitigate such lack of expertise); and to compensate for the lack of expertise of national courts in judging validity and infringement matters, as well as to reduce costs for enforcing patents or removing them in the territories concerned. Countries of every size can take advantage of economies of scale. It is clear, however, that those with a small or mid-sized market would benefit significantly from cooperation.[12]

A second set of reasons for sharing patent administration duties are by contrast specific to countries willing to establish a common market.[13] The

(2012); Luigi Mansani, *Riflessioni di Giuristi Europei sul Brevetto Unitario*, CONTRATTO E IMPRESA EUROPA 510, 514 (2012); Vincenzo di Cataldo, *Competition (or Confusion?) of Models and Coexistence of Rules from Different Sources in the European Patent with Unitary Effect: Is There a Reasonable Alternative?* 4 QUEEN MARY J. INTELL. PROP. 195 (2014); Hanns Ullrich, *Select from within the System: The European Patent with Unitary Effect* (Max Planck Institute for Intellectual Property & Competition Law Research Paper No. 12–11, 2012).

11 *See* Hon. Bruce A. Lehman, Chairman, International Intellectual Property Institute (IIPI), Presentation on behalf of the Singapore Intellectual Property Office: *Addressing the Crises of the Global Patent System* (October 3, 2004), *available at* http://iipi.org/wp-content/uploads/2010/07/Singapore1005.pdf; Brice C. Lynch, *International Patent Harmonization: Creating a Binding Prior Art Search within the Patent Cooperation Treaty*, 44 GEO. WASH. INT'L L. REV. 403, 415 (2012); ALEXANDER STACK, INTERNATIONAL PATENT LAW: COOPERATION, HARMONIZATION AND AN INSTITUTIONAL ANALYSIS OF WIPO AND THE WTO 47–48 (2013).

12 In view of the increase in worldwide patent applications it is not surprising, however, that forms of cooperation are conducted also by countries with large patent offices and national markets, as the Trilateral Cooperation between UPTO, EPO and JPO shows; *see* Dongwook Chun, *Patent Law Harmonization in the Age of Globalization: The Necessity and Strategy for a Pragmatic Outcome*, 93 J. PAT. & TRADEMARK OFF. SOC'Y. 127, 151–152 (2011).

13 *See* on integration-driven harmonization: STACK, *supra* note 11, at 58 (with reference to cases of unilateral harmonization, but his analysis applies also to cases of multilateral harmonization).

motivating factor in this case is to avoid a division of the common market into distinct geographical areas: those in which patent protection exists, and those in which such protections do not exist at all. Such a division can result from a variety of factors.

First, differences in national laws can mean that a specific subject matter is eligible for protection in one country and not eligible in another. Second, even if the laws of the states concerned are the same, the patent applicant could refrain from investing money in multiple filings for economic reasons. He could, for instance, decide to pursue protection only in the jurisdiction(s) in which he has more interest. Third, even if the laws are identical and the applicant decides to file the application in all countries that are part of the common market, a different application of the rules by the examiners could result in the patent being granted in one country, but rejected in another. Additionally, the patent could be issued in all of the countries, but with a different claim wording. Fourth, even if the patent has been granted with identical claims in all countries, a fragmentation of the protection can arise in the case of litigation when the national courts issue conflicting decisions on the same patent. Some courts may uphold the patent; others might declare it invalid in full or in part; and still others may find the patent to be valid and infringed, infringed but not valid, or valid but not infringed.[14] Because of all of these factors, a specific economic activity can, in some parts of the common market, be reserved for the patentee. In other territories, it could be patent-free from the outset or could become such, if the patent has been found invalid or not infringed.[15]

Such a division of the common market between patent-protected and patent-free areas would in turn lead to two further consequences.[16] On the one hand, competitors of the patentee could market the products or offer the process claimed by the patent in the territory where no patent protection exists, but not in the parts of the common market where a patent is in force. On the other hand, the patentee could market the products in the territory where the patent is in force, but could find it inconvenient to do so in the territory where protection does not exist. Indeed, to be competitive in the patent-free markets, the patentee should likely offer a lower price than the one offered in the territory where patent protection exists. However, such price reduction in the patent-free markets would then expose the patentee or his licensee to the

[14] *See also* Joseph Straus, *The Present State of the Patent System in the European Union as Compared with the Situation in the United States of America and Japan*, EUR 17014 EN, 5–6 (1997).

[15] *Id.*

[16] *See* the considerations of the patent proprietor in Case C-44/98, *BASF AG v. Präsident des Deutschen Patentamts*, 1999 E.C.R. I-06269, Reason No. 13.

risk of parallel imports in the territories where the patent is in force.[17] Indeed, the Court of Justice of the European Union (CJEU) has correctly considered the regional exhaustion of intellectual property rights[18] a necessary feature of a common or single market. If a rights holder could invoke national intellectual property rights to prevent the import of products marketed with his consent from another participating country into the single market, the patentee "would be able to partition off national markets and thereby restrict trade between the Member States."[19] While such a power is not necessary according to the CJEU to enjoy "the substance of the exclusive right"[20] deriving from the parallel patents, it would clash with the fundamental principles of EU law, such as the free movement of goods and services.

Likewise, the risk of parallel imports could jeopardize the opportunity for the patentee to obtain – in the countries where the patentee can rely on patent protection – a higher price than would be possible in a regime of full competition. This would undermine the (possible) incentive function of the patent system. This risk, in turn, could become a reason for the patentee to limit his marketing activities to the part of the common market where his patents are enforceable. Such an effect on the marketing activities of the rights holder would counteract the integration goal of EU law. It could even reduce the availability of the products concerned in the patent-free markets.

If the political aim of a group of states is to create a single market and prevent obstacles from arising in the efficient flow of patented goods without weakening the alleged incentive function of patent protection, then a common patent system and a regime of regional exhaustion are two complementary tools in achieving such a result.

16.3 HOW TO CREATE A COMMON PATENT SYSTEM FOR DIVERSE STATES: MODELS EXPLORED AND SOLUTIONS ADOPTED IN EUROPE (1949–2012)

Having considered the reasons why a common patent system may be opportune, let us now turn to the ways of creating it. From a purely theoretical

[17] Straus, *supra* note 14, at 6–7.

[18] On the concept of exhaustion, *see* Christopher Heath, *Exhaustion and Patent Rights, in* Patent Law in Global Perspective 419, 421 (Ruth L. Okediji et al., eds., 2014).

[19] *See* Case 15/74, *Centrafarm v. Sterling Drug Inc*, 1974 E.C.R. 1147, Reason No. 12.

[20] *See* Case 238/87, *Volvo AB v. Erik Veng (U.K.) Ltd.* 1988 E.C.R. 6211, [1989] 4 C.M.L.R. 122.

perspective, the measures taken into consideration in Europe after World War II may be described as follows[21]:

- The harmonization of domestic rules
- The mutual recognition of national patents
- The establishment of a regional patent office
- The creation of a unified patent system

Each of these approaches may include several variants. For the sake of simplicity, we will mention only those that have been discussed in Europe.

16.3.1 *Harmonization*

By the term *harmonization*, we mean measures that obligate lawmakers to enact domestic provisions that are consistent with a harmonizing model, without creating a new title of protection alongside or instead of national patents. Conversely, the term "unification" refers to a source of law that either replaces domestic provisions with uniform rules directly applicable to a title or protection already provided for under national law, or creates and regulates, *ex novo*, a title of protection not provided for under national law. Such uniform rules must then be applied either by national offices or regional organizations, or both, to the new title of protection.

Harmonization of the national rules represents a less ambitious step toward a common patent system. Indeed there can be varying degrees of harmonization.[22] But, regardless of the breadth and scope involved, a common element to the various harmonizing acts that distinguishes them from unification is that the objects of harmonization – the national laws – remain independent of each other.[23] The same holds true for the rights and obligations created under the national laws.

[21] On the different methodologies for harmonizing national law or creating regional intellectual property systems *see* Christopher Heath, *Methods of Industrial Property Harmonisation – The Example of Europe*, *in* INTELLECTUAL PROPERTY HARMONIZATION WITHIN ASEAN AND APEC 39, 44 (Christopher Antons et al., eds., 2004); Patrick Smith, *Harmonisation, Regional Collaboration and Small Patent Offices*, *in* INTELLECTUAL PROPERTY HARMONIZATION WITHIN ASEAN AND APEC, *id.*, at 227, 229.

[22] For example, one harmonizing act could limit itself to simply defining principles. In this case, the national lawmakers would have the discretion to flesh out these guidelines with concrete, specific rules. On the other hand, the harmonizing act can also dictate an exhaustive and self-sufficient regulation that the various lawmakers must implement under their national laws, without room for variation.

[23] *See* on the concept of harmonization Martin Boodman, *The Myth of Harmonization of Law*, 39 AM. J. COMP. LAW 699 (1991); with reference to the European experience, Eva J. Lohse, *The Meaning of Harmonisation in the Context of European Union Law: A Process in Need*

Harmonization of patent law in the aforementioned manner occurred relatively early in Europe. In 1963, several years before the European Patent Convention (EPC) was signed,[24] the member states of the European Council agreed upon the Convention on the Unification of Certain Points of Substantive Law on Patents for Invention of 27 November 1963[25] (Strasbourg Patent Convention, SPC). The SPC did not create a regional patent office or a regional patent. Rather, it aligned some substantive aspects of the Contracting States' domestic laws governing national patents. The SPC was ratified only by eight European states, and it has now been almost forgotten by courts and practitioners.[26] Seldom indeed do handbooks refer to its provisions. Even more rarely do the national courts' judgments mention it.[27] Nevertheless, its doctrinal and practical meaning could hardly be overestimated. There are several reasons for this.

First, the SPC exhaustively regulated the patent-eligible subject matter, (optional) exceptions to patentability, the mandatory requirements for protection (novelty, inventive step, and industrial applicability), and the scope of protection conferred by the patent. In this respect, it was more comprehensive than the Agreement on Trade-Related Aspects of Intellectual Property Rights (TRIPS),[28] which leaves room and discretion for the Members to define the requirements for inventive step, novelty, and industrial applicability. In addition, TRIPS does not even mention the issue of the scope of protection. As far as exceptions to patentability are concerned, it just adopts the wording of the SPC with some slight changes.[29]

Second, the SPC triggered an effective harmonization of the national laws of all EU Members, not only of the signatories. Indeed, the EPC follows

of Definition, *in* THEORY AND PRACTICE OF HARMONISATION, 282 (Mads Andenas & Camilla Baasch Andersen, eds., 2012).

24 Convention on the Grant of European Patents (European Patent Convention), October 5, 1973, 1065 U.N.T.S. 255, 13 I.L.M. 268 [hereinafter EPC].

25 European Treaty Series No. 47.

26 But *see* in this regard the excellent contribution of Christopher Wadlow, *Strasbourg, the Forgotten Patent Convention, and the Origins of the European Patents Jurisdiction*, 2 INT'L. REV. INTELL. PROP. & COMPET. L. 123 (2010).

27 References to the SPC are more often in the case law of the EPO, although the latter is not bound by the treaty. Since the provisions on patentability of the EPC are derived from the SPC, such references are done mostly in the context of historical interpretation. *See*, for instance, with reference to art. 53(b) EPC and art. 2(b) SPC, Case G 1/98, *In re Transgenic plant/NOVARTIS II* (December 20, 1999), Reasons for the decision VII, No. 5.

28 Agreement on Trade-Related Aspects of Intellectual Property Rights, April 15, 1994, 1869 U.N.T.S. 299 [hereinafter TRIPS Agreement].

29 *See* art. 27(2) and art. 27(3) TRIPS Agreement, and art. 2 SPC. The exclusion for medical methods under art. 27(3) TRIPS is not provided for by SPC, but it was influenced by EPC, *supra* note 24, at art. 52(4) EPC 1973, *see* now art. 53(c) EPC 2000.

the provisions of the SPC. The former did not create any obligation for the Contracting States to harmonize the rules governing national patents in accordance with the rules governing European patent applications. Its purpose was unification according to the abovementioned definition – that is, creating an office with the authority to grant European patents and receive European patent applications, as well as adopting uniform rules thereon. Despite that, all Contracting States voluntarily aligned their domestic acts regulating national patents to the substantive provisions of the EPC. In this way, they also gave effect to the SPC.

Third, also because of the EPC, the SPC exercised influence over several regional agreements as well as many Asian and South American laws.[30] Accordingly, the requirements for protection and the exceptions to patentability as defined by the EPC and the SPC found their way *de facto* in almost all primary jurisdictions, with the significant exception of the United States.

There were still some aspects of substantive law – such as the rights conferred by the patent and the limitations to them – that were not addressed either by the SPC or by the EPC. However, the harmonization of these aspects was obtained spontaneously through another convention, the Community Patent Convention of 1975 (CPC).[31] This convention was not directly binding for national patents and never entered into force. Like the EPC, it did not have the purpose of approximating national law. Instead, it strived to create a uniform set of rules applicable to the Community patent.[32] Nevertheless, the Contracting States took its provisions as a normative model to regulate – with respect to national patents – the right to prohibit direct or indirect infringement, as well as other aspects not included in the SPC and the EPC. As was the case with the SPC, the influence of the CPC went well beyond European borders. Several countries adopted provisions with identical wording for defining the rights conferred by the patent and their limitations. And so did the TRIPS Agreement, as far as the rights conferred by the patent with respect to direct infringement are concerned.[33]

As a result of this unique situation, the law governing national patents was virtually identical in all EU member states from 1979 onwards, with a few

[30] *See* for references in Hilty & Romandini, *Developing a Common Patent System – Lessons to be Learnt from the European Experience*, at 10, *available at* www.ssrn.com/link/Max-Planck-Innovation-RES.html.

[31] Convention for the European Patent for the Common Market of December 15, 1975, 1976 O.J. (L 17) 1 (EC) [hereinafter CPC].

[32] *See id.*, at art. 1(2).

[33] *See* TRIPS Agreement, *supra* note 28, at art. 28.

anecdotal exceptions. This "cold harmonization"[34] was reached through traditional intergovernmental agreements instead of legislative acts of the EU. This had significant practical implications for the application of the harmonized domestic norms. Since the EU was neither a party to the SPC nor of the EPC, the CJEU had no authority to interpret the provisions of either one. Consequently, the CJEU has never ruled on matters of novelty, inventive step, or industrial applicability.

In a harmonization approach, the patent rights remain national. They are granted by national authorities, limited to national borders, and litigated before national courts. Harmonization affects only the wording of the domestic provisions applicable to the national patents. This wording must be consistent with the harmonizing act.

If one considers the two primary motivating factors for developing a common patent system, which are laid out in the previous section, a mere harmonization cannot satisfy any of the economy- or efficiency-driven motivations because it does not tackle the problem of insufficient expertise of the national offices; it does not eliminate the necessity of multiple filings; it does not reduce the costs, either for the applicants or for the states; and it does not reduce the duplication of work or backlogs in the national offices. Nevertheless, one might at least presume that harmonization could prevent a division of the common market. Harmonization could ensure that equal conditions for obtaining and defending patents apply in all national markets covered by the harmonized rules. Consequently, an applicant would first be able to get a patent for the same subject matter and then enforce it against a specific product or service offered by a competitor, with the same outcome in all the countries participating in the common market. Identical rules should also produce identical outcomes in the granting procedure and the litigation proceedings, thereby preventing fragmentation.

However, as shown by the experience with the national law of the EU members or even the direct application of the uniform law of the EPC through national courts, these expectations are not justified. For a number of reasons, the mere harmonization of domestic rules cannot prevent a division of the common market in areas where patent protection exists and areas where patent protection is absent. First, harmonization of national rules does not eliminate the need for multiple filings. Therefore, an applicant could decide

34 "Cold" because it was not imposed by binding rules, since neither the EPC nor the CPC obligated the signatories to amend the law governing national patents. *See* Kurt Haertel, *The Harmonizing Effect of European Patent Law on National Patent Laws*, 14 Int'l. Rev. Intell. Prop. & Compet. L. 719 (1983); Stefan Luginbuehl, European Patent Law: Towards a Uniform Interpretation 8 (2011).

to apply for a patent only in some countries in order to, for example, reduce the costs, or for lack of economic interest. Second, identical wording does not necessarily ensure that the application of the rules to the same set of facts will produce the same decision in different jurisdictions. This is at least true in European patent law, where the rules governing three fundamental issues require a value judgment (*Werturteil*) from the decision maker. We are referring to the following questions: whether the invention is obvious; whether the description of the patent is sufficient to allow the person skilled in the art to practice the invention without undue inventive efforts; and whether a product or a process that does not reproduce literally the asserted patent claim may, nevertheless, still infringe the patent under the doctrine of equivalence. These value judgments do not imply a discretionary power of the courts or the Patent Office. Nor do they mean that for the aforementioned questions two opposite answers are equally right and possible. Such value judgments do, however, leave room for different evaluations between instances of the same jurisdiction as well as instances of different jurisdictions.

This holds true even if the various national courts or instances interpret the relevant provisions in the same way and apply them with the same methodology, such as the substantive provisions for assessing validity of the patent. Indeed, the national courts, when applying arts. 52–57 and 123 EPC, tend to follow the settled case law of the Boards of Appeal of the European Patent Office (EPO). As a principle of interpretation, uniform conventional law has to be applied autonomously and uniformly in the territories covered by the treaty.[35] There is a legal duty on national courts to take into account foreign interpretations and practice concerning the uniform provisions,[36] including the practice and the decisions of the EPO. This is also appropriate on a

[35] *See* LUGINBUEHL, *supra* note 34, at 4; Kurt Haertel & Dieter Stauder, *Zur Auslegung von internationalem Einheitsrecht*, 2 GRUR INT. 85 (1982). Karl Bruchhausen, *Interpretation and Application of European Patent law and Harmonized National Patent Law*, 14 INT'L. REV. INTELL. PROP. & COMPET. L 732 (1983). *See also* UN Convention on Contracts for the International Sale of Goods (CISG), art. 7, April 11, 1980, 1489 U.N.T.S. 3, *available at* www.uncitral.org/pdf/english/texts/sales/cisg/V1056997-CISG-e-book.pdf.

[36] *See* Case G 0005/83, *Second Medical Indication/EISAI* (December 5, 1984), O.J. 1985, 64 (observing that "the establishment of harmonized patent legislation in the Contracting States must necessarily be accompanied by harmonized interpretation. For this reason, it is incumbent upon the European Patent Office, and particularly its Boards of Appeal, to take into consideration the decisions and expressions of opinion of courts and industrial property offices in the Contracting States"). *See also German Federal Supreme Court (Bundesgerichtshof)*, INT'L. REV. INTELL. PROP. & COMPET. L. 396 (1987), "Rabies Virus" 12.02.1987, Case No. X ZB 4/86 (stating that "since the harmonization of national and European provisions of substantive patent law should serve the creation of largely identical patent law, care must also be taken that the interpretation in the national and international area be as uniform as possible").

practical level, since it would be contradictory to grant a patent (by the EPO) according to a specific standard and evaluate its validity (by the national courts) according to a diverging standard based on domestic tradition. Indeed, EPO organs and national courts have to apply the same substantive provisions in granting, opposition, and revocation procedures.[37]

Nevertheless, uniform interpretation cannot ensure uniform application of rules with an evaluative language in a concrete case. A trivial example can clarify this apparently paradoxical statement. If one considers again the requirements for an inventive step, the national practices in continental Europe are uniform. In assessing whether a claim is inventive or not, national judges usually resort to the "problem-solution approach" developed by the EPO.[38] As a consequence, continental courts consider an invention obvious within the meaning of art. 56 EPC only when the person skilled in the art could have found a suggestion, a prompt, or a motivation in the prior art for modifying the closest prior art as proposed by the patent in suit. Despite this methodological and interpretative consistency, conflicting decisions within and among different jurisdictions are possible. The explanation for this is in the very structure of the norm defining the requirement for inventive step. The concept of obviousness implies a margin of appreciation that no methodology or protocol can definitively eliminate, however consistently it is applied.

For all of these reasons, harmonization is not sufficient to prevent market fragmentation. It can, however, pave the way for the adoption of more effective solutions, such as mutual recognition models.[39]

16.3.2 *Mutual Recognition of Patents Granted by National Authorities*

A stronger measure toward the creation of a common patent system is to agree on a system of mutual recognition.[40] Under this approach an applicant needs to file an application in only one country to get protection in all the remaining members of the agreement. There are two primary ways to achieve this. The first method is to provide that national patents granted by one state should be automatically recognized by the other states, with the patents being granted according to the national law of the authority chosen by the applicant. However, the grant generates titles of protection that have effect in the territory

37 *See* EPC, *supra* note 24, at arts. 100, 138.

38 *See* references to the case law in Hilty & Romandini, *supra* note 30, at 13.

39 Harmonization is also useful, even if not necessary, for other forms of cooperation, such as sharing search and examination results; *see* Chun, *supra* note 12, at 148–156.

40 *See* Chun, *supra* note 12, at 163; on mutual recognition in general, *see also* Heath, *Methods of Industrial Property Harmonisation*, *supra* note 21, at 44–45.

of each member state participating in the system of mutual recognition. The grant may generate a bundle of national rights subject to the national law of each member state or a unitary right. The Convention of Friendship and Good Neighborhood between Italy and San Marino[41] is an example of the former option, the treaty between the Swiss Confederation and the Principality of Liechtenstein on patent protection[42] an example of the latter.

The second way of implementing a system of mutual recognition is to provide that any national patent office grant, in addition to a national patent, a regional patent. Such a regional patent will be valid in all states of the agreement. This grant will occur on the basis not of national law, but of common rules laid down in an agreement among the participating countries. The latter solution was proposed and analyzed within the first official European Council efforts to create a common European patent system. It was also discussed as an alternative to the creation of a regional patent office. The proposal was made by Eduard Reimer,[43] lawyer, law professor, and first president of the German patent office, and permits two variants: the regional patent may consist of a bundle of territorially limited rights, or a unitary right. In other words, it is possible to create a unitary right without having a regional patent office, just as it is possible to establish a regional patent office without having a unitary patent. The two solutions may coexist, but the latter does not require the former, and vice versa.

A system of mutual recognition of the national patents has clear advantages. It does not require the creation of a new organization. The system would make use of existing authorities. It eliminates the problem of multiple filings for the states concerned and prevents a duplication of work across different patent offices. It reduces the costs for the applicant seeking protection in the common market. At the same time the measure has some shortcomings. It does not avoid the problem of insufficient expertise in the national patent offices that perform the substantive examination. It is likely to create patents with the same territorial scope, legal term, and content, but of different value and quality depending on which national patent office grants the rights. It could

[41] *See Convenzione di amicizia e buon vicinato tra l'Italia e San Marino*, art. 43, March 31, 1939, WIPO, *available at* www.wipo.int/wipolex/en/other_treaties/details.jsp?treaty_id=836.

[42] Treaty between the Swiss Confederation and the Principality of Liechtenstein on Patent Protection (Patent Treaty), December 22, 1978, 1980 O.J. EPO, 407.

[43] A modified version of the first Proposal Reimer of 1953 "Plan Reimer No. 1" is published in EDUARD REIMER, EUROPÄISIERUNG DES PATENTRECHTS 259–277 (1955). According to art. III § 8 of the Proposal only patent offices that performed a substantive examination of the patent applications should have been allowed to grant European patents. *See also* Wadlow, *Strasbourg*, *supra* note 26, at 131–133.

encourage forum shopping by applicants, triggering a "race to the bottom" among national authorities to become the most patent-friendly agency, and increase the number of monopoly rights of dubious validity.

Against this background, it is not surprising that such a solution was met with significant resistance within the Expert Group that was entrusted with the preparation of the Draft of a Convention on European Patent Law,[44] and that it was eventually rejected. This attitude has not changed since then. In a survey conducted as recently as 2006 by the European Commission among European stakeholders, the proposal to create a system of mutual recognition was almost unanimously opposed because, among other reasons, "individual National Patent Offices" were "seen to apply diverging rules and standards resulting in patents having very unequal value."[45]

16.3.3 *Creation of a Regional Patent Office*

The creation of a regional office is a move toward a common patent system stronger than the mutual recognition model. It is a more useful means of realizing economies of scale in granting patent protection in a specific region.[46] However, it does not necessarily imply stronger integration. Indeed, by establishing a common organization physically located in the same place and with multinational staff, the participating member states are able to ensure a uniform procedure and examination for the entire region; recruit staff who, with their skills and technical backgrounds, can provide a better examination in all technical fields; and reduce duplication of work, multiple filings, and costs for the participating member states (and applicants).

But from the viewpoint of integration, the mere creation of a regional patent does not prevent a division of the common market in patent-free and patent-protected territories. It does not even make it less likely. Instead, further measures should be implemented, including

- The abolition of national patents
- The creation of a unified jurisdiction and the establishment of a supranational title of protection, so that only one institution can decide on infringement or validity with respect to the same infringing act

44 *See* Wadlow, *Strasbourg, supra* note 26, at 129.

45 European Commission, *Consultation on Future Patent Policy in Europe – Preliminary Findings: Issues for Debate*, at 15 (July 12, 2006), *available at* http://ec.europa.eu/internal_market/indprop/docs/patent/hearing/preliminary_findings_en.pdf.

46 *See* Smith, *supra* note 21, at 233; Christian H. Nguyen, *A Unitary ASEAN Patent Law in the Aftermath of TRIPS*, Pacif. Rim Law and Policy J., 8 (March 1999), at 468.

- The reduction of the formalities necessary for maintaining protection after the grant of the regional patent in all national states

Although the creation of a regional office does not imply the creation of a unitary common market for inventions and patent rights, it has some clear advantages. The normative model is compatible with various degrees of discretion of the member states in pursuing their own innovation policy. The treaty establishing the patent office could indeed regulate the regionally issued patent in the post-grant phase before the member states. But it does not need to do so. It is equally possible to leave the states completely free to define which rights and scope of protection the patent granted by the regional office should confer with effect on their territory, or what defense or revocation grounds a defendant can invoke in proceedings before their national courts.

The creation of a regional patent office does not require harmonization of national law. It does not even postulate the introduction of uniform rules for the post-grant existence of the regional patents. The latter can increase the efficiency of the system and the value of the patent. Nevertheless, it is not a requirement for the operation of the office. The European experience is consistent with these assumptions.

The European Patent Office and the European Patent

Europe could agree relatively easily on the creation of a regional patent office, at least if one considers the opposition to the project for a unified system in the last sixty years. In 1973, thirteen European states agreed on the European Patent Convention. The treaty was open to all European countries, not only members of the European Union. Until now 38 states have signed and ratified the Agreement.[47]

The Convention established the European Patent Office (EPO) and created an autonomous system of procedural and substantive provisions for granting patents with effect in the Contracting States. The procedure provides for an examination of the invention described and claimed in the European patent application. In each European patent application the applicant may designate the countries for which protection is sought.[48] The patent application has to be filed in one of the official languages of the EPO, namely, English, French, or German.[49] The choice of the language of the application also defines – with some questionable exceptions – the language of the proceedings before the EPO.[50]

47 An updated list of Contracting States is *available at* www.epo.org/law-practice/legal-texts/html/guidelines/e/foreword_6.htm.
48 EPC, *supra* note 24, at art. 79. 49 *Id.* at arts. 14(1), 14(2).

The examination is carried out by the European Patent Office, an international body with staff recruited among the citizens of the Contracting States and with headquarters in Munich. The examination also includes the requirements for protection[51] and the exceptions to patentability[52] as defined by the EPC. After examination of the patent application, the EPO can decide either to reject the patent application or to grant the European patent.

The European patent has in all designated states the effect of a national patent.[53] After its grant, the patent is subject to the jurisdiction of the national courts. This does not imply, however, that the European patent consists of a "bundle of national patents," as is sometimes observed in the literature. This definition was adopted by Kurt Haertel, one of the fathers of the Convention, but it referred to the first preliminary draft for a convention establishing a European System for the Grant of Patents of 1969.[54] According to this Draft, after grant, the European patent would have been fully subject to the law governing national patents in each Contracting State,[55] so that a distinction between titles of protection granted by the European or the national office was indeed irrelevant. This original draft was intended to interfere as little as possible with the discretion of the Contracting States to set their own standard of protection. Therefore, it avoided enacting uniform substantive provisions applicable to European patents after their grant.

However, such a minimalist approach was rejected in favor of the so-called "maximal solution." This maximal solution is reflected in art. 2(2) of the EPC, according to which the European patent is subject to the rules governing national patents unless otherwise provided in the Convention.[56] The Convention, however, applies to the most important aspects of the patent. Indeed, the EPC regulates exhaustively the scope of protection conferred by the title.[57] It dictates the term of the patent and the criteria for computing such term.[58]

50 *Id.* at art. 14(3). 51 *Id.* at arts. 54–57 (novelty, inventive step, and industrial applicability).

52 *Id.* at art. 53. 53 *Id.* at art. 2(2).

54 Convention Establishing a European System for the Grant of Patents, 1 IIC 80 (1970).

55 *See* art. 2(2) of *id.*, according to which "subject to the provisions of this Convention the European patent shall, in each of the Contracting States for which it is granted, have the effect of and be subject to the same conditions as a national patent granted by that State. This shall apply in particular to the term of the patent, the grounds of revocation and the exercise of the rights attached to the patent." *See* on this first preliminary Draft Kurt Haertel, *The Draft Conventions for a European System for the Grant of Patents and for the European Patent for the Common Market*, 1 INT'L. REV. INTELL. PROP. COMPET. L. 289 (1970); Romuald Singer, *The European Patent Enters a New Phase*, 1 INT'L. REV. IND. PROP. COPYR. L. 19 (1970).

56 *See* LUGINBUEHL, *supra* note 34, at 2, 4.

57 EPC, *supra* note 24, at art. 69. *See also* Protocol on the Interpretation of art. 69 EPC of 5 October 1973 as revised by the Act revising the EPC of 29 November 2000.

58 EPC, *supra* note 24, at art. 63.

Further, it defines the effect of process claims with respect to products directly obtained by the claimed process.[59] It also determines the binding version of the patent in national proceedings.[60] The treaty regulates exhaustively the revocation grounds, and allows national judges to revoke the patent only on the basis of the same uniform provisions applied by the examiner in granting it.[61] The EPC also provides for some procedural rights that the patent proprietor may exercise in national revocations proceedings, such as the right to limit the patent.[62] Therefore, the European patent is a bundle of rights only in the meaning that the EPC does not mandate a unitary effect and does not provide a unified jurisdiction, but leaves it to the Contracting States to establish them.[63] However, after grant the European patent is more than a simple national patent and maintains its European character and normative autonomy.[64]

The EPC and the Integration of National Markets

Since the start of its activity in 1978, the EPO has attracted a significant amount of filings by multinational applicants. The establishment of a regional patent office in Europe, in this specific respect, may be considered a success. Further, the EPO has not only ensured a uniform practice in granting patents, but it has also developed a significant body of case law, to which the national courts have resorted to solve similar legal issues that arise in domestic proceedings. The jurisprudence of the EPO has contributed to a greater uniformity in Europe. Nevertheless, if one analyzes the EPC it becomes clear that the purpose of the agreement was not to favor market integration, but only to simplify the procedure for the applicant and reduce duplication of work among the EPC Contracting States, without significantly interfering with the states' sovereignty.[65]

Three features of the treaty support this conclusion. First, in order to obtain protection, the patentee is required to file a translation into the official language of the Contracting State that has exercised the option provided for

59 *Id.* at art. 64. 60 *Id.* at art. 53.

61 *Id.* at art. 138 referring to arts. 52–57, art. 123, and art. 60. 62 *Id.* at art. 138(3).

63 *See* art. 149a and art. 142 EPC.

64 This has practical implications. For instance, by implementing Directive 98/44/EC of the European Parliament and of the Council of July 6, 1998 on the Legal Protection of Biotechnological Inventions, 1998 O.J. (L 213) 13, some EU members – such as Italy, France, or Germany – adopted some limitations to patent-eligibility that the Directive 98/44/EC itself does not expressly provide for. Such provisions are relevant only for national patents. They may not apply to European patents without violating art. 138 of the EPC.

65 *See* Johannes Bob van Benthem, *The European Patent System and European Integration*, 24(4) INT'L. REV. INTELL. PROP.& COMPET. L. 435, 436 (1993).

under art. 65 of the EPC (the so-called translation requirement). According to this provision, the member states have the authority, but not the obligation, to require such a translation. All the EPC Contracting States made use of this option when implementing the treaty in 1978. Only thirty-two years later, with the London Agreement,[66] were applicants able to obtain partial relief.[67] Second, the EPC follows a principle of coexistence. The European patent has not replaced national rights, and the EPO has not replaced national offices. The applicant remains free to file a national application or a European application, or both. It might even be possible, if allowed under national law, for the same invention to be protected by a European and a national patent for the same territory.[68] Third, as already mentioned, after grant the EPC leaves the title of protection to the jurisdictional competence of the national courts, which decide on validity and infringement issues with effect in their territory.

Against this background, despite the filing of a European application, a division of the common market remains possible. It might follow (1) from the decision of the applicant to designate only some of the Contracting States; or (2) from conflicting decisions of the national courts with respect to the patents litigated.

Such a result was not a foregone conclusion of the negotiation over a regional patent system. The first drafts of a convention on European patent law discussed within the EEC provided for a unified jurisdiction and a unitary right, and not only for a regional patent office and common grant procedure.[69] But this ambitious plan was abandoned because of several political difficulties, and the approach eventually taken by the EU states was to conclude two different treaties.[70]

A first agreement was only to create a regional office and provide a common procedure for the grant of patents.[71] This treaty would have constituted a special agreement under the meaning of art. 19 of the Paris Convention, and would have been open to participation by both EU and non-EU members.

66 *See* Agreement dated October 17, 2000 on the Application of art. 65 of the Convention on the Grant of European Patents, 2001 O.J. EPO 549.

67 Still, nineteen EPC members did not join that Agreement, including states with significant markets such as Spain, Italy, and Poland.

68 *See* EPC, *supra* note 24, at art. 139(3) EPC.

69 *See Avant-projet de convention relatif à un droit européen des brevets élaboré par le groupe de travail "brevets,"* European Commission Working Paper (1962), *available at* http://aei.pitt.edu/14064/. *See* on the draft, Franz Froschmaier, *Some Aspects of the Draft Convention Relating to a European Patent Law*, 12 Int. & Comp. L. Q. 886, 887–888 (1963).

70 *See* Thomas R. Nicolai, *The European Patent Convention: A Theoretical and Practical Look at International Legislation*, 5 Int'l. L. 135, 140 (1971).

71 *See* van Benthem, *supra* note 65, at 436.

A second agreement would have provided for a unified jurisdiction over the patents granted on the basis of the first agreement, thus conferring a unitary effect on them and uniform rules for their enforcement.

The first agreement became the EPC, and the second agreement the Community Patent Convention (CPC).[72] But whereas the EPC was adopted because of the will of the Contracting States and the pressure of the industry, the CPC was not. Only now, after fifty years and several proposals, were the EU states able to agree on a common unified jurisdiction. The relevant question in this regard is why the European industry was so keen on obtaining a regional patent office, while at the same time it failed to push for a unified jurisdiction.

The reasons are various and complex. We discuss only one of them. In all probability, a company does not need to get a patent in all EU countries to get protection in the common market or to enforce the patent in all countries to stop an EU-wide infringement. Instead, it seems reasonable to assume that it can be sufficient to get the patent in a few countries – Germany, France, the United Kingdom, and Italy – and enforce it just in one – Germany or France. This assumption is supported by statistical data,[73] and seems plausible both from the economic and the legal points of view.

From an economic perspective, it can be inconvenient for pan-European infringers, even if the injunction is limited to a specific country, to create two different lines of products – one in which the patent exists, and the other where it does not. Indeed, if they lose a significant market, they may need to try to invent around the patent or attempt to obtain a license. This is at least true for industries in which the economies of scale are significant.[74]

72 *See* CPC, *supra* note 31.

73 From the available data on patent validation and litigation in Europe we may infer three conclusions. First, the validation rate of European patents is greater than 50 percent only in three countries (Germany, the United Kingdom, and France). In the remaining EPC states – with the possible exception of Italy – the rate is less than 40 percent; *see* Harhoff, D., K. Hoisl, B. Reichl, and B. van Pottelsberghe de la Potterie, *Patent Validation at the Country Level – The Role of Fees and Translation Costs*, Res. Policy 38, 1423–1437 (2009). Second, patent litigation is concentrated in very few countries. Germany has the highest number of cases; France follows at a great distance. Third, parallel litigation (same patents, same embodiment, and same parties) seems to be rare in Europe. For instance, only 2 percent of the patents litigated in Germany end up being enforced or challenged in other European countries; *see* K. Cremers, M. Ernicke, F. Gaessler, et al., *Patent Litigation in Europe*, Eur. J. Law Econ. 1 (2016). As a consequence, even if in all the mentioned parallel proceedings a German and a foreign court would render conflicting judgments, the share of cases decided differently at least by two courts of two different member states would still be very limited.

74 *See* Confederation of the Finnish Industries, *Report on the Reform of the European Patent System: On the Impact of the Unitary Patent and the Unified Patent Court (UPC) on Finnish Companies*, at 77 (April 2014), *available at* http://ek.fi/wp-content/uploads/Finnish-Report-on-UPC1.pdf.

From a legal perspective, even where such a strategy of product differentiation as a reaction to an injunction in Germany or France might be economically convenient, it would be very risky. Indeed, if a patent has been found to be literally[75] infringed and valid in Germany, similar outcomes are to be expected in France, the Netherlands, the United Kingdom, or Italy. This is due to the fact that national courts apply the same provisions and follow very similar interpretations. Therefore, the national courts are hesitant to ignore a precedent concerning the same patent and the same set of facts from another jurisdiction.[76] It seems reasonable to assume that for a plaintiff or a defendant in Europe to win in Germany might, in most cases, create a good basis for a community-wide settlement.

If this assumption is correct, then one could conclude that the protection afforded in Europe under the current system is not significantly lower than the protection afforded in the United States, China, or other unified jurisdictions. This raises the question of why and for what purpose a fully unified patent system may still be needed in Europe and elsewhere.

16.3.4 *Creation of a Fully Unified Patent System*

There are three possible reasons why a group of states may opt for a fully unified patent system. The first and likely most important reason is to integrate their national markets. Such a step is appropriate if the states participating in a common or single market are willing to integrate themselves at a higher level. Indeed, no federation has maintained state patents after a unitary market was finally established.[77] The second motivation is strictly interrelated with the former, and it involves the pursuit of a common patent and innovation policy.

The third reason for introducing a unitary patent system is to increase the efficiency of enforcement, revocation, and administration of patent rights and the quality of the related court judgments. In an ideal environment, a unified patent system makes it possible for the rights holder to block infringement and for the alleged infringer to remove the exclusivity right with only one action in the whole market. It should also make it possible for even smaller countries to benefit from specialized bodies that issue judgments and deal with patent

75 The situation is more complex in the case of an alleged equivalent infringement. National practices have a different methodology, since the EPO does not deal with the matter and does not offer a case law to be followed.

76 *See* GRUR, *Response to the European Commission Questionnaire on Future Patent Policy* (March 14, 2006), at 10; *see also* Hilty & Romandini, *supra* note 30, at 22 with further references.

77 *See* for the evolution in the United States with respect to state patents: Pasquale J. Federico, *State Patents*, 13 J. PAT. & TRADEMARK OFF. SOC'Y. 166 (1931).

matters. Specialized judges are indeed only a small resource in the field of patents, even in the most developed countries.

The reasons for adopting a unified patent system also anticipate the perceived shortcomings of such a measure.[78] First, if the states involved present significant differences in their development and industrial structures, then they could also have diverging needs and views regarding the optimal level of protection. However, as adopting a common currency requires a group of states to give up the option of pursuing an autonomous monetary policy, the adoption of a fully unified patent system requires that the states give up the option of pursuing an autonomous patent policy.

Indeed, on the one hand, it would be impossible for the states concerned to unilaterally impose their own standards of patent protection within the community of states. Such standards would be the result of intergovernmental negotiations, rather than an internal democratic process. On the other hand, it would hardly be meaningful to maintain a national patent system under a domestic law that diverges from the unified patent system in the standards of patentability, in the scope of protection, or in the rights conferred. Such a national system would attract users only if it offered a level of protection at least equivalent to that of the unified system. If the protection were weaker, then the applicant could easily circumvent the limitations provided by domestic law for domestic patents by obtaining a supranational unitary patent and enforcing it before the unified jurisdiction. Diverging, competition-friendly solutions in national law would attain only a symbolic political meaning. Furthermore, they could have a discriminatory effect on applicants who cannot afford to take the route of the unitary supranational patent. The only meaningful divergences would be those directed to the grant of some substantive or procedural advantages to the applicants for national patents. Consequently, any flexibility with regard to an independent national policy would be strongly reduced.

Second, even if all the participating states presented a similar degree of development, similar needs, and similar attitude toward the optimal asset – so that they could agree on a level of protection which matched the national references of all participants – the unification of the patent system would imply a loss. Indeed, the effects surrounding the patent system are unclear. Therefore, the *perceived* optimal level of protection is not necessarily the *real* optimal level of protection for a specific territory or industry.[79] To ascertain

[78] *See* in general on benefits and costs of law unification in the specific field of patents Stack, *supra* note 11, at 35–38; John F. Duffy, *Harmony and Diversity in Global Patent Law*, 17 Berkeley Tech. L.J. 685, 685, 703–709.

[79] *See* Stack, *supra* note 11, at 35–38 and 158–159.

that would require experimentation in the lawmaking and case law of several member states. Such an option is excluded under a unified patent system in the participating countries. Even if the lawmaker could theoretically design the content of the national rights *ad libitum*, domestic players would remain exposed to the unified system. This eliminates any basis for meaningful domestic experimentation.

These two criticisms are well described in the literature. Of course, they have a strong logical impact. The European experience could show that the two mentioned shortcomings can be attenuated in the implementation of a unified system, and that they are likely overestimated in the view of diachronic and synchronic normative experiences.

But before we proceed further with these hypotheses, we ought to clarify the concept of a unified patent system and the possible variants of the model and finally give some information about the final design upon which the European states could agree.

The Concept of a Unified Patent System

By a unified patent system we mean a body of law that governs for a group of countries the grant, enforcement, and revocation of patents having a unitary effect throughout their territories. Unitary effect means that the patent covers the territories of the states in question as a single entity without borders of protection.[80] In that territorial entity the patent provides uniform exclusivity rights.

The unitary character of the patent has two consequences. On the one hand, the patent may be transferred, revoked, or allowed to lapse only for the whole territory of the states concerned. On the other hand, by considering whether the patent is infringed or not, the acts performed by the same entity in the regional territory may be aggregated, as this is possible regarding a national patent with respect to the acts performed in the national territory in which the national patent has effect.[81] The injunction may be requested and granted for the whole territory covered by the unitary right. The damage claim may include losses incurred in the whole region, so far as a causal link with the contested acts exists.

A corollary of a unified system is that one patent application is sufficient to obtain a patent with effect in the whole territory. One action is sufficient

80 *See* Roberto Romandini & Alexander Klicznik, *The Territoriality Principle and Transnational Use of Patented Inventions – The Wider Reach of a Unitary Patent and the Role of the CJEU*, 5 Int'l. Rev. Intell. Prop. & Compet. L. 524, 530–537 (2013).

81 *Id.*

to revoke or enforce the patent with effect in all the participating states. An administrative and jurisdictional structure that allows such a unified grant, enforcement, or revocation of the patent is the necessary premise and implication of a unitary right.

The Possible Subvariants of a Unified Patent System

Within the very broad definition of unified patent system provided in the previous subsection, various differentiations are possible.[82]

As for the nature of the organs of the unified jurisdictions one could distinguish between several different systems. One approach exclusively relies on national bodies for granting the unitary patents and deciding on their validity and infringement. Another relies exclusively on supranational bodies to grant the unitary patents and to decide on questions of validity and infringement on an ad hoc basis. Yet another approach entrusts some administrative or jurisdictional functions to national authorities, and delegates other administrative or jurisdictional functions to regional supranational institutions again on an ad hoc basis.

In the European experience, a unitary intellectual property system relying exclusively on national authorities was never considered. Even under the prudent proposal of *Reimer*, the national patent offices would have granted the (regional) patent, whereas a supranational body – a court defined significantly as "European Court of Justice" – would have decided on their revocation or infringement.[83] The European experience does, however, provide several examples belonging to the other two submodels indicated earlier.

The Proposal for a Community Patent Regulation[84] (CPR) designed a system in which two supranational bodies – the European Patent Office[85] and the Community Intellectual Property Court[86] – decide on the granting,[87] revocation, and infringement[88] of unitary patents. This model left no room for the

[82] *See* the analysis by Christopher Wadlow, *An Historical Perspective II: The Unified Patent Court*, *in* THE UNITARY EU PATENT SYSTEM 33, 38–41 (Justine Pila & Christopher Wadlow, eds., 2015).

[83] *See* REIMER, *supra* note 43, at 92, 270 and 274 (art. 3 § 20 and §§ 26–31 of the "Plan Reimer no. 1"). According to the Reimer Proposal, it would have been possible to start infringements actions also before the national courts, but the latter would not have power to revoke formally the patent with *erga omnes* effects.

[84] *See* European Commission, Proposal for a Council Regulation on the Community Patent of August 1, 2000, COM/2000/412 final, O.J. (2000) C 337 at 278 [hereinafter CPR].

[85] *See id.* at art. 1.

[86] The Community Intellectual Property Court should have been established by way of an amendment to the EC treaty and it would have been an integral part of the European Union jurisdictional system.

[87] *See* CPR, *supra* note 84, at art. 1.

[88] *See id.* at art. 30(1) and art. 30(3).

national courts and authorities, as far as validity and enforcement of the patent were concerned.

The European Union Trade Mark Regulation[89] (EUTMR), by contrast, provides an example of a combined system. A regional authority grants the right[90] and is competent for its revocation.[91] National courts – performing the function of EU Trade Mark Courts[92] – are competent for infringement actions[93] and counterclaims for invalidity.[94] Further examples of this combined system can be found in the Community Plant Variety Regulation[95] and the Community Design Regulation.[96]

There are similarly different ways of centralizing the institutions involved in the unitary patent process.[97] One way is to utilize a fully centralized system, in which only one administrative body and one judicial body decide over grant, validity, and enforcement. Another way is to fully decentralize, and have several bodies in each participating country be able to grant the right or decide on its validity and infringement. Or an intermediate model could be used, combining different degrees of centralization or decentralization of the administrative and jurisdictional functions.

A centralized model has the advantage that, by excluding decentralized organs – such as the national courts – from the operation of the system, it can ensure uniform specialization in the jurisdiction and higher consistency in the case law. However, it implies a greater political, legislative, and financial burden for the establishment of the centralized jurisdiction and administration. Indeed such a system requires first the adoption of a fully self-sufficient procedural regulation, and the establishment of the centralized bodies. Second, it presents the problem of how to finance the court and/or the office. Third, it reduces the epistemic community of specialists dealing with the intellectual property rights concerned. Fourth, since the centralized bodies will be established in one or a few locations, the system can lead to a concentration of expertise and specialist work in the countries hosting

89 Council Regulation 207/2009 on the Community Trade Mark, 2009 O.J. (L 78) 1 (EC), amended by the Regulation (EU) 2015/2424 of the European Parliament and of the Council of December 16, 2015 [hereinafter EUTMR]. The codified version of EUTMR will enter into force on October 1, 2017, see Council Regulation No. 2017/1001 of June 14, 2017 on the European Union trade mark 2017 O.J. (L 154), 1 (EU).

90 *See id.* at art. 2 establishing an Office for Harmonization in the Internal Market (now: European Union Intellectual Property Office).

91 *Id.* at art. 56. 92 *Id.* at art. 95. 93 *Id.* at art. 96(a). 94 *Id.* at art. 96(d).

95 *See* Council Regulation No 2100/94 of 27 July 1994 on Community Plant Variety Rights, 1994 O.J. (L 227) 1, 1–30 (EC).

96 *See* Council Regulation No 6/2002 of December 12, 2001 on Community Designs, 2001 O.J. (L 3) 1, 1–24 (EC).

97 Wadlow, *Historical Perspective, supra* note 82, at 38.

them.[98] Professionals and specialists located in countries not hosting the centralized bodies might suffer competitive disadvantages. Lastly, centralization sacrifices local accessibility to justice to the goal of full uniformity in adjudication.

Various models can also be applied to the separation or consolidation of jurisdictional functions. Indeed one could distinguish among three different systems. One could be based on a principle of strict separation, where one body decides on validity and another body decides on infringement without the latter being allowed to question the reach of the claim with prior-art-based arguments. In this model, not only is a counterclaim for revocation of the patent inadmissible, but also the invalidity defense is excluded and the prior art defense strongly limited. A second model uses a combined system, where the same judge may hear validity and infringement, and finally a third model utilizes a system based on a principle of moderate separation, where one body decides on validity and another body decides on infringement, but the latter – although not able to admit and decide over a counterclaim for revocation – can consider prior art or invalidity defenses.

A principle of rigid separation is nowadays still followed only by the Community Plant Variety Regulation.[99] Also at the national level, the principle of rigid separation is the exception. In Europe, only Germany adopts it. Systems that were following the German model in Europe or Asia have in the meantime mitigated it, either by case law or by legislative action, and have allowed either the invalidity or the prior art defense in infringement proceedings. Reasons for this development are likely the perceived imbalances of a principle of strict separation and the increase of global filings. Indeed a strict separation of invalidity and infringement issues provides the rights holder with key advantages in the enforcement of the patent. As long as the majority of the right holders are domestic companies, a lawmaker could have an interest in providing them with such advantages. However, even in the most developed World Trade Organization member states the patents owned by foreigners outnumber the patents owned by residents. As a consequence, the pressure for granting procedural advantages to rights owners is clearly weakening.[100]

98 *See* with respect to the possible establishment of an ASEAN Office: Imke Pente, *Lipstick, Innovation, and Preferences – A Developmental-Intergovernmental Approach to Economic Policy Transfer from the EU to ASEAN*, 134 *et seq* (2014) (PhD dissertation, Freie Universität Berlin).

99 *See* Council Regulation 2100/94 on Community Plant Variety Rights, arts. 105 and 20, 1994 O.J. (L 227) 1 [hereinafter CPVR].

100 This may explain why the principle of separation is in decline, at least as practiced in Germany, where it is still confronted with doubts and reservations coming not only from academia, but also among practitioners and counsels. *See* Katrin Cremers et al., *Invalid but Infringed? An Analysis of Germany's Bifurcated Patent Litigation System* (Max Planck Institute

Finally, with respect to the relationship with the national patent system, the regional lawmaker could again either allow both coexistence and double protection, or allow coexistence but prohibit double protection, or simply exclude both. The last solution would be the most consistent with the purpose of creating a single market. But, not surprisingly, it has never been implemented in Europe for any of the unitary intellectual property rights. Reasons for the resilience of the national rights are manifold and cannot be addressed here.[101] The European experience at any rate shows that, even in a regime of coexistence, some caution can prevent possible strategic use of the multilayered system of protection. For instance, the Community Plant Variety Regulation has allowed coexistence, but has prohibited double protection.[102] The Community Trade Mark Regulation has allowed both coexistence and simultaneous protection, but has prevented double litigation.[103] Surprisingly, despite the proclaimed goal of simplifying the defense against ungrounded claims for companies active in Europe, the European lawmaker has not addressed this issue when designing the unified patent system.

The European Unified Patent System: Main Features and Open Issues

The Unitary Patent Package includes three legal instruments: Council Regulation (EU) No 1257/2012 on unitary patent protection (Unitary Patent Regulation, UPR)[104]; Council Regulation (EU) No 1260/2012 of December 17 2012, implementing enhanced cooperation in the area of the creation of unitary patent protection with regard to the applicable translation arrangements; and the Unified Patent Court Agreement (UPCA).

The UPR and Regulation No 1260/2012 aim to create unitary patent protection and discipline the applicable translation regime. They are an integral part of the Union Legal Order. The CJEU will have jurisdiction to give preliminary rulings on their interpretation.

The UPCA has the purpose of creating a unified jurisdiction by establishing a Unified Patent Court (UPC). The EU is not a party to the treaty, and the latter is not part of the Union Legal Order. Preliminary references to the CJEU with respect to the application of the UPCA will, nevertheless, still be

for Innovation & Competition Research Paper No. 14–14, 2014), *available at* http://ssrn.com/abstract=2504507.

101 *See* on the issue Hugh Laddie, *National I.P. Rights: A Moribund Anachronism in a Federal Europe?*, 23(9) Eur. Intell. Prop. Rev. 402 (2001).

102 *See* CPVR, *supra* note 99, at art. 92.

103 More precisely, it has prohibited two civil actions from being brought against the same party on the basis of identical community and national trademarks with respect to identical or similar products. *See* EUTMR, *supra* note 89, at art. 109.

104 *See* Regulation (EU) 1257/2012, *supra* note 6, at 1.

possible.[105] This will be the case when the UPCA implements provisions of the Union Legal Order or when the operation of the UPCA provisions can interfere with principles of union law or fundamental EU rights.

The unitary patent is not a new title of protection that applicants may request by filing a patent application. The unitary patent is instead a classic European patent issued by the EPO. Until the patent is granted, nothing will change for applicants or third parties. The only innovation that the UPR implies for the EPC system is that it grants the owner of a European patent the right to request, within a deadline of one month after publication of the decision to issue the European patent, a unitary effect in the states taking part in the enhanced cooperation.[106] European patents for which such a request was filed and that benefit from such effect pursuant to the Regulation can be called Unitary Patents.

The UPC, however, is a completely new institution under international law. It includes a Court of First Instance, a Court of Appeal, and a Registry.[107] The Court of First Instance shall comprise a central division headquartered in Paris,[108] with sections in London and Munich,[109] as well as local and regional divisions in the Contracting States. The Court of Appeal will be based in Luxembourg and will consist of a single division.

Within the territory of the Contracting States the UPC will have exclusive jurisdiction over all infringement and revocation actions concerning European patents with or without unitary effect. Local (or regional) divisions will have jurisdiction over actions for actual or threatened infringement of European patents,[110] as well as counterclaims for the revocation of the asserted European patents.[111] The central division will have exclusive authority over actions for declaration of non-infringement,[112] actions for revocation of the patent[113] and, in some limited cases, also over actions for infringement of the patents brought against a defendant domiciled outside the territory of the Contracting States.[114] The Court of Appeal will have jurisdiction over appeals against decisions or orders issued by the Court of First Instance.[115]

If one considers the possible variants available for the unified jurisdiction as discussed in the previous sections, one cannot blame the European lawmaker

[105] *See* UPCA, *supra* note 4, at arts. 20 and 21.

[106] *See* Regulation (EU) 1257/2012, *supra* note 6, at art. 9(1)(g); Decision of the Select Committee of the Administrative Council of December 15, 2015 adopting the rules relating to Unitary Patent Protection (SC/D 1/15), Rule 6(1), 2016 O. J. EPO (A 39).

[107] *See* UPCA, *supra* note 4, art. 6(1). [108] *Id.* at art. 7 (2).

[109] *See id.* at art. 7 (2). [110] *Id.* at art. 33(1)(a). [111] *See id.* at art. 33(3).

[112] *See id.* at art. 33(4). [113] *See id.* [114] *See id.* at art. 33(1)(b). [115] *See id.* at art. 73.

for not experimenting with incremental variations of old projects for a Community Patent. Admittedly, most of these incremental modifications follow the more recent Draft for a European Patent Litigation Agreement (EPLA).[116] However, other innovations are the result of more recent negotiations. In any case, the Unitary Patent Package seems to have looked more for intermediate solutions between opposite models than for more radical functional choices, such as those adopted under the CPC or the CPR.

The European patent system can indeed be considered a centralized, but geographically distributed one. Each Contracting State can host a local division if it wishes to do so.[117] But such local divisions are part of a single Court,[118] the UPC, which will apply the same rules of procedure in each division.[119]

The European patent system has a supranational character, since its two main bodies – the EPO and the UPC – are international authorities created by international treaties. At the same time, it maintains internally some national elements. Indeed, the UPCA provides for a predominantly national composition of the local divisions. These will consist of two judges from the country hosting the division and one foreign judge conversant in the language of the local division.[120] This predominantly national composition of the panels of the local divisions should allow the latter to hear infringement actions in the language of the country hosting them.[121] Further, the UPCA provides for transitional rules, according to which national courts will still have jurisdiction over classic European patents for several years.

Lastly, the system can be considered a consolidated one, but with the option of a discretionary separation. Indeed, counterclaims for revocation before the seized local division are admissible.[122] Local divisions can decide on both validity and infringement. However, they can also decide to refer the counterclaim for revocation to the central division.[123] In the latter case, the local division has the option to stay the proceeding or to proceed further with the infringement claim.

One optimistic view might be to consider the system a successful example of how to join the advantages of centralization and consolidation by utilizing *ad hoc* supranational bodies that can hear both validity and infringement cases,

[116] Wadlow, *supra* note 82, at 33, 38 and 43. *See also* EPO Working Party on Litigation, *Draft Agreement on the Establishment of a European Patent Litigation System* (February 16, 2004), *available at* http://documents.epo.org/projects/babylon/eponet.nsf/0/B3884BE403F0CD8FC125723D004ADD0A/$File/agreement_draft_en.pdf.

[117] *See* UPCA, *supra* note 4, at art. 7(3).

[118] *See id.* at arts. 6(1), 7(1).

[119] *See id.* at art. 41.

[120] *See id.* at art. 8(3).

[121] *See id.* at art. 49(1).

[122] *See id.* at art. 33(3).

[123] *See id.* at art. 33(3)(b).

with the benefits of jurisdictional decentralization by creating local divisions and admitting an optional bifurcation. Pessimists might fear, however, that the system as designed will have the disadvantages of the opposing models that it attempts to combine. Indeed, if the local divisions develop a national approach for specific procedural or substantive issues, this could jeopardize the uniformity of the procedure and the equal treatment of all defendants (who cannot choose the venue).[124] If the local divisions generously interpret the rules of competence based on the *locus delicti* or concerning multiple defendants, they could extend the room for the plaintiffs to choose their favourite venue. Such a development would jeopardize the function of the local divisions to ensure a reasonable proximity of the Court of First Instance to the parties and the relevant facts of the case. Or rather, the principle of proximity would benefit only the patentee, since the UPCA has excluded the option for competitors to bring actions for non-infringement before the local divisions.[125] Therefore, whether or not these rules will provide for uniform treatment of parties, as well as reducing room for competition among local divisions in attracting plaintiffs with patent-friendly practices, will depend largely on their interpretation. In this regard, the UPCA has taken some precautions against a re-nationalization of the procedure. The Court of Appeal can intervene relatively early in order to prevent diverging practices. Indeed, it is entitled to grant leave to appeal not only against final judgments, but also against all the procedural orders adopted by the Court of First Instance.[126]

There are several aspects of the new system that have been viewed as problematic.[127] As it will stretch the limits and purpose of this chapter to address this criticism in detail, we simply mention some of these criticisms. First, neither the Regulation nor the UPCA have regulated the relationship between national and unitary patent protection. It is therefore consistent with EU and international law to allow the same invention to be made the subject of both a European patent with unitary effect and a national patent. It is equally possible to allow the same party to enforce both patents against the same competitor, the European Patent with unitary effect before the UPC, and the national patents before the national courts. This outcome is problematic. The purpose of the UPCA is to improve not only the enforcement of patents, but

[124] *See* Marco Ricolfi, *La 'biforcazione' tra azioni di validità ed azioni di contraffazione: Ragioni teoriche e problemi applicativi*, 22 Il diritto industriale 10 (2014).

[125] *See* UPCA, *supra* note 4, at art. 33(4). But if an infringement action is pending before the local division, the action for declaration of non-infringement can be brought only before the same local division. *Ibid.*

[126] *See id.* at art. 73(2)(b)(ii).

[127] *See* literature quoted in note 10.

also the defense against unfounded claims and invalid patents.[128] However, national lawmakers have the option to mitigate the problems that may arise from the absence of a European regulation on this issue. Indeed, the Contracting States could prohibit a double protection – for instance, by adopting a rule corresponding to art. 92 of the Community Plant Variety Regulation – or they could reduce the room for a doubling of litigation – for instance by adopting in the national law a rule corresponding to art. 109 of EUTMR, as proposed in Germany.[129] Both approaches would be UPCA and EPC consistent.

Second, one of the purposes of the agreement is to avoid distortion of competition. The language regime adopted is inconsistent with this objective. The trilingual system implies advantages for some companies and disadvantages for others. Under the UPCA and the EPC, for example, a German or French company may file an application in French or German, and can defend it in French or German before the central division of the UPC and before the EPO. Before the EPO, this company is exposed to opposition not filed in German. But in most of the cases such oppositions are filed in English, which is the language of technology and business and provides no advantage to the opponent. The same company, by contrast, can file its opposition in French and in German against Italian, Spanish, or Polish competitors that file a European patent application before the EPO, even if the latter chooses English as the language of the proceeding. These Italian, Polish, or Spanish companies will bear the costs related to the translation of the arguments and materials submitted by the opponent, even if the opposition is completely ungrounded. In addition, they will need a representative able, at least, to understand German (or French) in order to defend them effectively.

An English-only solution would have made the whole system fairer and more reasonable. It also would have likely allowed a different and simpler regulation with respect to translation arrangements.[130] Of course, it would have required an amendment of the EPC. The reduction of costs and the gain in efficiency would have been worth the reform.[131]

[128] *See* Preamble of the UPCA, *supra* note 4 ("wishing to improve the enforcement of patents and the defence against unfounded claims and patents which should be revoked").

[129] *See* Roberto Romandini, Reto Hilty & Matthias Lamping, *Stellungnahme zum Referentenentwurf eines Gesetzes zur Anpassung patentrechtlicher Vorschriften auf Grund der europäischen Patentreform*, 6 GRUR INT. 554, 554–555 (2016).

[130] The transitional provisions of Regulation No 1260/2012, *supra* note 7, in the transitional period will indeed not reduce the cost for translations with respect to European patents requested and granted for all EU states.

[131] Some minor adjustments are possible without amending the EPC. So for instance, it is still possible to amend Rule 1 of the Implementing Regulations to the EPC and provide that if the patentee has chosen English as the language of the proceeding, then the opposition must

Third, the system seems to provide some incentive for the Court to develop a plaintiff-friendly practice.[132] Local divisions with at least fifty patent cases per calendar year will have two legally qualified judges, both of whom "are nationals of the Contracting Member State hosting the local division concerned."[133] Divisions with fewer than fifty cases will sit in a composition where only one of the judges is a national of the state concerned, and the other two members of the panel are allocated from the pool of judges pursuant to art. 18 of the UPCA. This means that the judges of the local division will be reallocated to the central division if the local division does not have sufficient work. Further, the court is designed as a self-financing institution. Such self-financing will depend largely on the court fees paid by the plaintiffs. As a consequence, the court will rely on handling as many cases as possible to finance itself.[134]

Fourth, the UPR does not include any provisions related to the rights conferred by the patent and the scope of protection. In these two aspects, it refers to national provisions that apply to European patents with unitary effect. Since the national law includes the UPCA and the latter refers to the EPC, art. 5 of the Regulation refers indirectly to arts. 25–30 of the UPCA as far as the rights conferred by the patent are concerned, and to art. 69 of the EPC with regard to the scope of protection. Article 69 EPC adopts an exhaustive and self-sufficient approach to the scope of protection. The UPCA, by contrast, contains some lacunae in the law of infringement and its remedies. This is true for joint, accessory, and intermediary liability, the nature of the damage claim resulting from them, the causal link between damage and contested acts, the statute of limitations and estoppel, and prior user rights. It is also true for the compulsory licenses regime. The Contracting States remain fully free to define the scope and reasons for compulsory licensing.[135] Of course, the uniform law provided by the UPCA is far more detailed than the ones contained in the Community Trade Mark Regulation or in the Community Design Regulation, both of which include even broader references to national law. But

also be filed in English. By contrast, if the language of the proceeding is German or French, it should still be possible for third parties to file an opposition in English.

132 *See* Hilty et al., *Comments on the Preliminary Set of Provisions for the Rules of Procedure of the Unified Patent Court*, at 2 (Max Planck Institute for Intellectual Property & Competition Law Research Paper No. 13–16, 2013), *available at* https://ssrn.com/abstract=2337467.

133 UPCA, *supra* note 4, at art. 8(3).

134 Hilty et al., *supra* note 132, at 2.

135 *See* Regulation (EU) 1257/2012, *supra* note 6, at Recital 10; *see also* Clement Salung Petersen et al., *The Unified Patent Court (UPC), Compulsory Licensing and Competition Law*, NORDISKT IMMATERIEELT RÄTTSKYDD 324 (2014), *available at* https://ssrn.com/abstract=2489006.

while the latter relies on national courts for its operation, the UPCA relies on the UPC, which is an international court.

Lastly, the European unified patent system lacks a single final court that can answer legal questions with a general binding ruling.[136] The interpretation of the EPC, for instance, will be in the hands of three organs: the Enlarged Board of Appeal of the EPO, the Court of Appeal of the UPC and, to a lesser degree, the European Court of Justice, as far as the EPC rules that implement Union Law are concerned. No provision of the UPCA or of the EPC clarifies the relevance for the EPO of the judgments of the Court of Appeal. Symmetrically, no provision of the UPCA clarifies the relevance for the UPC of the opinions of the EPO Enlarged Board of Appeal.[137]

As far as the CJEU rulings are concerned, the UPCA ensures that they are binding for the UPC under the same conditions and with the same effects as they bind national judges.[138] The EPC, by contrast, does not contain a similar provision. Nor does it formulate a general dynamic referral to Union law as the UPCA does. As a result, the organs of the EPO cannot refer preliminary questions to CJEU and do not consider themselves formally bound by CJEU rulings.[139]

The lack of a court with mandatory authority over interpretation of the EPC for all instances of the system should not be deemed a significant flaw. A similar gap exists under the current national enforcement regime. Despite that, national courts and EPO organs have developed an interpretative practice with respect to the EPC, which is in most cases consistent. The national

[136] *See* for an in-depth analysis Federica Baldan & Esther van Zimmeren, *The Future of the Unified Patent Court in Safeguarding Coherence in the European Patent System*, 52 CML Rev. 1529 (2015).

[137] But even the local and central divisions of the UPC seem to be formally free to depart from interpretations of the EPC adopted by the Court of Appeal. Pursuant to art. 75 of the UPCA and Rule 243 of the UPC Rules of Procedure (October 19 2015) (RoP), if the Court of Appeal decides to refer back a case to the Court of first instance, then the latter shall be bound by the referring decision of the Court of Appeal and by its *ratio decidendi*. The concept of *ratio decidendi* is not defined by the RoP, but it shall include indeed also the specific statutory interpretation that leads the Court of Appeal to reach a specific conclusion on the case. *Ex contrario* one could argue that such a binding effect does not exist, when the Court of First Instance is faced with a similar legal issue, but not in the same case referred back by the Court of Appeal. In the EPC system, by contrast, the Board of Appeals cannot deviate from an interpretation of the EPC contained in a previous opinion of the Enlarged Board of Appeal. If the Board of Appeals intends to do so, then it is obliged to refer again the legal question to the Enlarged Board of Appeals; *see* Rules of Procedure of the Boards of Appeal, art. 21, 2016 O.J. EPO 378.

[138] *See* UPCA, *supra* note 4, at art. 21.

[139] Case G 0002/06 (Use of Embryos/WARF) (November 25, 2008), 2009 O.J. EPO, 306, Reason no. 4; *see also* T 2221/10 (Culturing Stem Cells/TECHNION) (February 4, 2014), Reasons no. 37–39, *available at* www.epo.org/law-practice/case-law-appeals/recent/t102221eu1.html.

courts follow the settled case law of the Board of Appeals of the EPO. Equally spontaneously the Boards of Appeals of the EPO have followed the case law of the CJEU by interpreting the provisions of the EPC implementing the Directive on the legal protection of biotechnological inventions.[140]

The lack of a final court with authoritative jurisdiction over all the interpretative issues concerning the EPC could even turn out to have some positive effects. It could create some room for judicial dialogue and experimentation.[141] Further, it will incentivize the UPC and EPO organs to carefully craft their legal opinions. The latter will be followed only when they are persuasive and not because they are binding.

16.4 EU VERSUS ASEAN

In this last section we intend to briefly mention some possible common features and diverging elements between the current situation facing ASEAN and the situation in Europe in 1973, when the EU States agreed upon the EPC. Further, we will briefly address the issue of whether or not the different integration models discussed in Europe can accommodate these differences. Of course, instead of providing answers, the next sections only propose a few suggestions.

16.4.1 *Europe and ASEAN: Common Elements and Differences in the Field of Patents*

At first sight, the EU system can provide a normative model for ASEAN, since, like Europe, ASEAN includes common-law and civil-law countries, has many different languages among its member states and intends to build a single market with a free flow of goods and services. At the same time, the situation of the ASEAN states in the field of patents presents some differences compared to that of European countries at the time the latter established their regional patent office.[142]

First, when the European countries decided to create a regional patent office, the majority of the national patent applications by their national patent

[140] *See* T 2221/10, *id.*; Stefan Luginbuehl, *An Institutional Perspective I: The role of the EPO in the Unitary (EU) Patent System, in* THE UNITARY EU PATENT SYSTEM 55 (Justine Pila & Christopher Wadlow, eds., 2015) at 54–55.

[141] *See* discussion on judicial percolation and the role of the Federal Circuit in US by Craig Allen Nard & John F. Duffy, *Rethinking Patent Law's Uniformity Principle,* 101 NW. U. L. REV. 1619, 1646–1650.

[142] *See also* in depth, the analysis by Pente, *supra* note 98, at 138–147.

offices originated from applicants located in Europe. So if we consider the statistics concerning filings in the patent offices of Germany, the United Kingdom, France, and Austria, in each of them more than 60 percent of the patent applications were from European applicants.[143] For this reason the regional patent office would have served mostly the European industry. This assumption was confirmed by the filing data of the EPO. If we consider the first three years of activity of the EPO, more than 60 percent of the patent applications originated from applicants domiciled in an EPC country.[144] Even in 2015, the applications from EPC countries were still 47 percent of the total number of applications filed that year.[145]

By contrast, in the case of the ASEAN states, the mutual filings between them are limited. In each patent office the overwhelming majority of the applications are filed by applicants located in a non-ASEAN country.[146] Against this background, one may conclude that the establishment of a regional Patent Office in the ASEAN states would serve and benefit mostly foreign applicants. Since the number of mutual filings is low, it would also not significantly reduce transaction costs for ASEAN companies.

Second, the level of income and the industrial development of the EPC countries that were also members of the EEC at that time (1973) were relatively similar.[147] The same holds true for the rules governing the economy and the market. The situation is here again quite different in ASEAN countries.[148] Some states, such as Singapore, have some of the most developed economies in the world. Other members, such as Vietnam and Thailand, are still developing. These differences make it likely for the countries to have diverging options and priorities in policy issues.[149]

143 *See* for statistical data Hilty & Romandini, *supra* note 30, at 37–38.

144 In 1978, 2,421 out of 3,599 applications to the EPC came from EPC Contracting States (67.15%), *see* 1979 O.J. EPO 215; in 1979, 7,352 out of 11,020 applications (66.72%), *see* 1980 O.J. EPO 258; in 1980, 11,347 out of 17,505 applications (64.82%), *see* 1981 O.J. EPO, 279.

145 EPO, Annual Report 2015 – European Patent Applications, *available at* http://documents.epo.org/projects/babylon/eponet.nsf/0/4C30F69F33211B6EC1257F6A0049308F/$File/european_patent_applications_en.pdf.

146 *See* for statistical data and sources Hilty & Romandini, *supra* note 30, at 38.

147 *Id.*

148 Michael Plummer, *The ASEAN Economic Community and the European Experience* (ADB Working Paper Series on Regional Economic Integration No. 1, Asian Development Bank, July 2006), *available at* www.adb.org/sites/default/files/.../wp01-plummer.pdf.

149 *See* on the socioeconomic differences in the ASEAN Region as obstacles for the creation of a regional patent institution ASEAN Working Group on Intellectual Property Cooperation (AWGIPC), ASEAN *Intellectual Property Rights Action Plan 2011–2015*, at 2 (July 31, 2011), *available at* www.aseanip.org/Portals/0/PDF/ASEAN%20IPR%20Action%20Plan%202011–2015.pdf.; Pente, *supra* note 98, at 138–142.

Third, when the EU countries started negotiating the SPC and the EPC they were completely free to decide which requirements and which exceptions to patentability should apply. The same holds true for the other aspects of the substantive patent law. The situation of the ASEAN states is different. On the one hand, TRIPS defines a framework common to all ASEAN members, which could facilitate cooperation. On the other hand, a body of patent provisions has been included in some FTA agreements, which could be an obstacle to integration. These FTA agreements bind only some of the ASEAN members,[150] and their intellectual property provisions may complicate the negotiation for a regional patent agreement.[151]

Finally, when the EU members decided to establish the EPO, a positive attitude toward patents was prevailing in Europe. At least most of the literature was convinced that a common patent system would benefit the development of the European industry. Today the situation is markedly different. The pendulum has swung in favor of a more critical stance toward the patent system. This cultural change can trigger political resistance against harmonization in this field.

All this makes it unlikely that in the short term the ASEAN states will agree to create a unified patent system, where granting and enforcement would be subject to uniform rules under the operation of a single office and single court. Nevertheless, such differences could and should not prevent an intermediate step toward this goal.

16.4.2 *Building a Common Patent System and Diverging National Preferences*

The ASEAN states had already considered the possibility of creating a regional patent office in 1995.[152] In the 2000s this option lost political support; instead of creating a supranational office, the states eventually preferred to agree on ASPEC,[153] a milder form of regional cooperation, and to support accession to

150 *See* Trans Pacific Partnership Agreement (TPP), concluded on October 4, 2015 and signed so far only by four ASEAN members (Singapore, Vietnam, Malaysia, and Brunei Darussalam).

151 *See*, for instance, art. 13.11(2) of the Malaysia/Australia Free Trade Agreement (MAFTA), concluded on March 22, 2012 (mandating a twelve-month grace period for any disclosure made by the inventor); *see also* art. 18.37 TPP (obliging the members to provide protection for "use inventions" through a "use" or "method of" claim).

152 *See* Nguyen, *supra* note 46, at 466–469.

153 The ASEAN Patent Search and Examination Cooperation (ASPEC) provides for a sharing of search and examination results between the patent offices of nine participating states. The procedure requires a request by the applicant in the office of the participating ASEAN state where a patent application is first filed. However, the decision whether or not to grant a patent

the Patent Cooperation Treaty (PCT). The main reason suggested in the literature for this change was sovereignty concerns. In view of the socioeconomic disparities the ASEAN States were not ready to accept unification of domestic patent laws and to reduce the role of the national patent agencies.[154] Despite this development, it is the opinion of the authors that the establishment of a regional patent office is still a viable option for ASEAN. This evaluation may sound optimistic, but it is based on three considerations.

First, the establishment of a regional patent office does not require a full harmonization of patent law. More precisely, it does not require that the members of the regional organization give up the option to provide for specific exceptions to patentability based on policy or moral reasons, or the power to define the substance of the rights and their limitations. What a regional office needs for its meaningful operation is that the three positive requirements for protection – novelty, inventive step, and industrial applicability – be uniform for all designated countries. By contrast, exceptions to patentability provided under national law can still be maintained and applied to the national designation of the regional application or to the national fraction of the regional patent. Such exceptions can be considered in the granting procedure by requiring a different set of claims according to the designated countries. Alternatively or in addition, they can be taken into account in the revocation procedures by providing the courts of the designated member states with the power to apply exclusions from protection to the national fraction of the regional patent granted. The European experience offers examples for both solutions.[155]

Second, the differences among the patent laws of the ASEAN states are already marginal nowadays, as far as the positive requirements for patent eligibility are concerned. The main differences among their laws concern the grace period, which is longer in some countries[156] and shorter in

remains in the hands of the respective national patent offices. *See* Elizabeth Siew-Kuan Ng, *ASEAN IP Harmonization: Striking the Delicate Balance*, 25 Pace Int'l. L. Rev. 149–150 (2013).

154 *See* Pente, *supra* note 98, 134–137; Siew-Kuan Ng, *supra* note 153, at 158.

155 On the one hand, art. 167 of the EPC 1973 allowed the Contracting States to prohibit product protection for chemical compounds for a transitional period of ten years; in this case the EPO could have granted in derogation to art. 118 of the EPC a European patent with a different set of claims with respect to the countries that made use of this option. On the other hand, the first drafts of the EPC provided for the power of the Contracting States to declare void European patents on the basis of national law. *See supra* Section 16.3.3.

156 *See* for instance § 14(3) of the Patents Act 1983 (Act No. A291 of 1983) (My.), providing for a twelve-month grace period including any disclosure that "was by reason or in consequence of acts committed by the applicant" or "was by reason or in consequence of any abuse of the rights of the applicant."

others,[157] and the claims to new uses of a known substance, that are admitted in some jurisdictions and prohibited in others.[158] The required harmonization to overcome these divergences would not necessitate radical changes to the patent systems of the ASEAN states.

Third, it is true that the establishment of a regional patent office would imply some limitations to the sovereignty of the members. But one must not compare such limitations with an ideal world where each country has the resources and the expertise necessary to develop its own standard of patentability and to conduct an efficient examination of the applications filed with the national office. In the current situation, many national offices are not able to examine in a reasonable time the patent applications filed. Significant backlogs affect the majority of national patent offices, mainly because of a lack of resources and skilled staff. As a result many offices, and among them also some of the ASEAN States, contemplate *de facto* or *de jure* simplified granting procedures, where the national office takes into account the examination conducted by other authorities, such as the EPO, the USPTO, or the JPO.[159] Although statistics are not available, it is likely that the foreign grant in most of the cases influences significantly the decision of the examiner whether or not to grant the patent. The same may hold true for the PCT examination report issued by a foreign International Searching Authority. Therefore, if the creation of a regional patent office would limit the sovereignty *within* the members of the regional organization, it would reinforce it against the influence that *de facto* foreign practices exercise on the respective national patent offices. It would also create the necessary technical infrastructure to allow the member states to develop jointly an independent patent examination practice and standard of patentability, as the EPO has done in Europe for the past fifty years.[160]

Of course, such a regional patent office would likely increase (for most of the ASEAN states) the number of foreign-owned patent rights. A regional patent office would likely attract more customers than the PCT or the ASPEC currently do. This would also mean an increase in the legal hurdles for domestic manufacturers. But whether this is a positive or negative development depends

[157] *See* Law on Intellectual Property of Socialist Republic of Vietnam, supplemented and amended under Resolution No. 51/2001/QH10 of December 25, 2001 (Vn.), providing for a six-month grace period including only scientific presentation of the inventor beyond the case of abusive disclosures through third parties. *See* for further references Hilty & Romandini, *supra* note 30, at 41–42.

[158] *Id.* [159] For instance, *see* Patent Act 1983, *supra* note 156, at § 29A(2).

[160] *See also* the analysis (expressing however some reservations from the point of view of developing countries against the establishment of regional patent offices in favor of other networking models) Drahos, The Global Governance of Knowledge – Patent Offices and their Clients, 324–332 (2010).

on the general opinion on the effects of the patent system in a specific national market. One might consider a significant increase in foreign filings as positive. It creates opportunities for knowledge transfer and foreign investment. Others might see it as a source of concern. At least in the middle phase a weak patent protection can be seen as a comparative advantage for domestic manufacturers. However, international law leaves sufficient flexibilities[161] for lawmakers to limit in the post-grant phase the effects of the regional patents in order to accommodate specific national policies. A regional patent agreement does not need to constrain such flexibilities. The use of the latter by the national states would neither disturb the operation of a regional office, nor diminish the advantages of its creation.

161 *See* Max Planck Institute for Innovation & Competition, *Declaration on Patent Protection – Regulatory Sovereignty under TRIPS*, 45 Int'l. Rev. Intell. Prop. & Compet. L. 679 (2014) (with commentary by Lamping).

17

Integration in Intellectual Property in Latin America

Carlos Adrián Garaventa and Pablo Wegbrait

17.1 INTRODUCTION

This chapter discusses the principal harmonization attempts in intellectual property law and policy that have occurred within Latin America. These developments need to be considered in the wider context of economic integration in the region. Analyzing Latin American integration is a complicated task: throughout history there have been various (continuing) attempts to accomplish Latin American or, at least, South American, integration. The most important achievements resulted from a factor external to the continent's will or, rather, an international factor: globalization was the great driving force for Latin American governments (especially South American governments) to come together in pursuit of a more efficient global strategy. In turn, the growth of world markets and of free trade, combined with the technological revolution that had already started, led to the question of how intellectual property rights should be uniformly protected around the world.

As this chapter discusses, relatively little progress has been made in Latin America toward integration of domestic intellectual property systems. The most promising vehicle for achieving legal integration in the region, the Comunidad Andina de Naciones (Andean Community of Nations – CAN), offers the strongest mechanisms for achieving legal integration in the intellectual property context, but it has been losing members to the Mercado Común del Sur (MERCOSUR). MERCOSUR's two intellectual property protocols have not, however, come into force. Another key factor in this region is the broader political context, including an emerging resistance to the kinds of economic commitments that led to developments such as the Agreement on Trade-Related Aspects of Intellectual Property Rights (TRIPS). As we discuss in the text that follows, broader political issues have imposed significant impediments to further progress toward economic integration more broadly, as well as in the specific field of intellectual property.

17.2 DEVELOPMENTS IN LATIN AMERICAN INTEGRATION

In the 1990s, the Latin American integration model drew from the largely successful European integration experience.[1] International trade was the principal catalyst, with individual nations focusing on opening up markets, tariff reductions, liberalization of imports, and growth through increase in exports.[2] However, principally as a result of the significant social and economic differences between both continents, South American integration was, in its details, devised differently from the European model,[3] and has not been especially successful. At the structural level, a key development has been the departure of key member states from the CAN. Chile withdrew in 1976.[4] In 2006, Venezuela left to join the MERCOSUR,[5] and Bolivia later followed suit (even though its acceptance process to the MERCOSUR has not yet concluded) while Colombia and Peru are participating in the Pacific Alliance.[6] Thus, the growth of the MERCOSUR and the Pacific Alliance occurred as the CAN began to disintegrate. While MERCOSUR's membership has grown, it lacks the important characteristics of the CAN (direct integration and supremacy of laws) that are characteristic of the EU model. Finally, 2010 marked the creation of the Community of Latin American and Caribbean States (CELAC), which replaced the former Group of Rio. This had both positive and negative implications; on the positive side, it implied replacing what was until then just an international forum for a new integration process with the goal of establishing a confederation of Latin American states; however, Venezuela's protagonism in the process meant the paralyzation of commercial negotiations with North American countries (especially the United States). These complexities, and

[1] Fermi Landi & Fabio Alberto, La Integración Social Sudamericana vs. La Integración Económica Europea 16 (2012).

[2] Julián Kan, Del Comercialismo a la Repolitización del Vínculo Regional. Gobiernos, Sindicatos y Corporaciones Empresarias en el Rediseño de la Integración Latinoamericana 2 (2014).

[3] Landi & Alberto, *supra* note 1, at 27.

[4] Alberto J. Cerda Silva, *Copyright Convergence in the Andean Community of Nations*, 20 Tex. Intell. Prop. L.J. 429, 430 (2012).

[5] Gian Luca Gardini, *MERCOSUR: What You See Is Not (Always) What You Get*, 17(5) Eur. L.J. 683, 683 (2011).

[6] Gordon Platt, *Pacific Alliance: Another Brick in the Supertrade Block*, 27 Glob. Finance 10 (2013).

shifting alliances in the South American context, have made it impossible to achieve economic integration of the kind seen in the European Union.

We have also seen important shifts in regional politics, and in the appetite for economic integration. In the early years of the millennium, Latin American governments supported a policy change that rejected many of the policy commitments of the Washington Consensus. Most immediately, this change in direction contributed to the failure of the Cancun's Doha Round in 2003. An important symbol of that policy change was the Buenos Aires Consensus, a political declaration signed by the Presidents of Argentina (Néstor Kirchner) and Brazil (Luiz Inácio Lula da Silva).[7] This document advanced a set of positions shared by Brazil and Argentina on the ability of each nation to develop autonomous economic policies and a more equitable distribution of wealth. As such, the Buenos Aires Consensus reflected an emerging resistance in Latin America to the 1990s policies associated with globalization, and a determination of individual nations to exert greater control over flows of capital in the region.[8] These developments continued in the following years. For example, during the 2005 IV Americas Summit in Mar del Plata a group of South American Presidents (headed by Argentina, Brazil, and Venezuela) raised strong opposition to the Free Trade Area of the Americas (FTAA), signaling a definitive rejection of that proposal.[9]

17.3 INDUSTRIAL PROPERTY WITHIN THE CAN: AN INTEGRATION PROCESS IN THE PROCESS OF DISINTEGRATION

These developments are significant when it is recognized that the CAN is the only supranational space in Latin America to achieve a sufficiently high degree of integration of community law.[10] Andean community law is characterized by the principles of automatic or direct incorporation, direct effect, applicability by national courts, and supremacy.[11] Two of these, direct incorporation and supremacy, shed important light on why the more ambitious attempts at harmonization within Latin America through MERCOSUR have failed.

7 Gary Prevost, *Contesting Free Trade: The Development of the Anti-FTAA Movement in the Streets and Corridors of State Power*, 21(3–4) J. Dev. Soc. 369, 370 (2005).

8 *Id.*

9 *Id.* at 385–386; and Marcel Nelson, A History of the FTAA: From Hegemony to Fragmentation in the Americas 111 (2015).

10 Ricardo Schembri Carrasquilla & Cayetano Núñez, *La Comunidad Andina de Naciones (CAN)*, 16 J. Law UNED 563, 669 (2015).

11 Calogero Pizzolo, Derecho e Integración Regional 143 (2010).

"Direct" incorporation (also known as "automatic" or "immediate" application) consists of the requirement of domestic ratification of community law. In other words, community law enters into force simply by having been adopted by the competent body and by having been published by the supranational body. Based on this characteristic, scholars speak about a monist system of community law.[12] "Supremacy" is fundamentally important to achieving legal harmonization within an integration process. Because regional integration is an association of states with different legal systems, the only way to have all members abide by the same rules is to create a common legal system that ranks higher than the members' domestic legal systems.

The Court of Justice of the Cartagena Agreement (the predecessor of the CAN's Court of Justice) developed these principles for the first time in a 1988 case, which, incidentally, concerned trademark law. The Court held that

> . . . trademark regulation . . . corresponds to the category of resolutions that have been identified as self-executing whose main feature is that they are directly applicable and in an identical manner in all Member States. . . . Therefore, [it] prevails in principle over any national regulation, prior or subsequent thereto, as far as it is compatible with domestic law. A different interpretation would make it impossible to attain the goal of integration processes, which is to accomplish a harmonized system for all community members.[13]

The CAN not only has developed an advanced community law system, but it has also regulated industrial and intellectual property in detail. Decision 351 dated December 17, 1993 (D351) legislates on intellectual property rights and Decision 486 dated December 1, 2000 (D486) deals with industrial property rights. Section 4 of Decision 351 sets forth that "The protection granted by this Decision shall accrue to all literary, artistic and scientific works that may be reproduced or disclosed by any known or future media . . . " This is extended to software in section 23, the protection of which may not be less than life of authors plus fifty years after their death (section 18). Decision 351 also contemplates moral and economic rights (sections 11 and 13), as well as their exceptions (sections 21 and 22) and it even establishes the guidelines to be followed by collective management organizations (Chapter XI). Finally, it regulates the activity of public offices specialized in the registration of works and, apart from making clear that it is not mandatory, it establishes that registration shall be merely declaratory and shall not itself confer rights (sections 52 and

[12] Leandro E. Ferreyra, *Aspectos constitucionales y culturales del Derecho Comunitario*, LECCIONES Y ENSAYOS. NÚM. 87 239 (2009).
[13] Court of Justice of the Cartagena Agreement: Process 2-IP-88 (May 25, 1988).

53). Decision 486 regulates rights concerning patents, trademarks, industrial models, and designs, as well as all aspects concerning unfair competition in industrial property rights. The Decision does not, however, establish anything novel with respect to the TRIPS Agreement. In fact, Decision 486 brings the Andean law in line with TRIPS.

While the CAN boasts a complete regional system in industrial and intellectual property, this integration process is undergoing an accelerated *disintegration* process, owing to the departure from CAN of a number of key states. As discussed in the next section, attempts at intellectual property integration within the MERCOSUR context have largely failed.

17.4 LEGAL HARMONIZATION IN THE MERCOSUR: TWO MORE TREATIES THAT ITS MEMBERS DECIDED NOT TO JOIN

MERCOSUR is the most advanced vehicle for economic integration within the Latin American context.[14] Its importance lies in two factors: first, it connects the most important South American economies; second, it is the economic regional block with the highest growth expectations in the region (measured by the countries that want to become its members).[15] The MERCOSUR was established in 1991 pursuant to the Asunción Treaty and it ultimately became a subject of international law in 1994 with the adoption of the Ouro Preto Protocol. Its original members were Argentina, Brazil, Paraguay, and Uruguay; Venezuela joined in 2012. It is currently expected that members will vote for Bolivia's admission, which would deprive the CAN of another of its members.

Two industrial property protocols were adopted by the MERCOSUR, one concerning trademarks,[16] the other industrial models and designs.[17] Because, however, the MERCOSUR does not apply the principles of Community Law (unlike the CAN), these protocols require unanimous ratification of each member state for their entry into force. To date, neither of these two industrial property protocols has been ratified, suggesting that industrial property harmonization has ceased to be a priority for the member states. Even so it is useful to provide a brief outline of what these two protocols set out to achieve.

14 Because there are other larger regional blocks such as, for example, the *Unión de Naciones Sudamericanas* (UNASUR), which are political, rather than economic, integration processes.

15 Even though, since its recent creation, the Pacific Alliance competes in equal terms with the MERCOSUR because it is the most sought-after integration process.

16 Protocolo Sobre armonización de normas sobre propiedad intelectual en el MERCOSUR, en materia de marcas, indicaciones de procedencia y denominaciones de origen.

17 Protocolo de armonización de normas en materia de diseños industriales.

The Protocol for the Harmonization of Intellectual Property Norms within the MERCOSUR concerning Trademarks, Designations and Appellations of Origin (Trademark Protocol) does not purport to achieve total harmonization at the legislative level in the area. It seeks only to establish minimum protection standards for those matters that may have the greatest degree of influence in the integration process.[18] Section 5 of the Trademark Protocol defines a mark as "any sign capable of distinguishing goods and services in commerce." This language largely resembles the definition of "trademark" under Argentine law; but it then drifts away from the provisions of Argentine law and, following Brazilian legislation, requires a trademark to be "visually perceptible" (section 5.2 of the Trademark Protocol). Section 6.1 of the Trademark Protocol establishes a type of mark not contemplated under Argentine law,[19] but which is recognized in other MERCOSUR members, the "3D mark," which provides trademark protection for product packaging. Taken together, these provisions imply scent and motion marks were meant to be excluded.

The Trademark Protocol also sets forth the principle of attribution for ownership of trademark rights, that is to say, trademark rights exist only through registration. However, section 8 sets forth an exception, establishing that

> The first trademark applicant shall have better rights to the mark, except if such right is claimed by a third party who has used the mark publicly, peacefully and in good faith, in any State Party, during at least six months, as long as it applies for the mark at the time of filing the claim.

As far as the applicant is concerned, the Trademark Protocol is more lenient than other domestic legislation. For example, under Brazilian law, an application for a mark may be filed only if it is directly related to the applicant's business or industry. However, the Trademark Protocol establishes that applicants shall be required only to have a "legitimate interest" (section 7). Section 9 establishes grounds for refusing trademark registration, but does not distinguish between absolute and relative grounds.[20] Section 10 provides that trademarks shall be valid for ten years and may be renewed indefinitely for subsequent equal periods, which was already included in all legislation of the member countries.

[18] Elis Salis, *El protocolo de marcas del Mercosur y el sistema de marcas argentino*, Tem. Der. Indust. Compet. Núm. 3 215 (1999).

[19] However, section 1 of the Argentine Trademark Act allows registration of any sign with "distinctive capacity," which means that types of trademarks not specifically contemplated in the law may still be registered, as long as they may be considered "distinctive."

[20] Within the MERCOSUR region, Uruguay is the only country to make that distinction.

Section 11 of the Protocol appears to introduce a dilution standard, by including "risk of association" in the grounds available for establishing trademark confusion. On its face, this allows trademark owners to oppose any trademark that may jeopardize them in any manner as a result of a dilution of the trademark's distinctive character. Another interesting provision is contemplated in section 13, referred to as exhaustion of rights, which is of great importance if we take into consideration that the MERCOSUR's main goal is the stimulation of international trade. However, the Trademark Protocol does not indicate whether it adopts national, regional, or international exhaustion.

Section 14 of the Protocol concerns the invalidation of trademarks granted in violation of sections 8 and 9, which may be declared at the administrative level, unlike Argentine and Paraguayan laws, which set forth that invalidation may be declared only by a judge. Moreover, it establishes that "any interested party" may file for invalidation. But invalidation may be declared not only at the administrative level: cancellation is also administrative when the trademark owner has not used it in any of the MERCOSUR member countries within the five-year period preceding cancellation. It should also be noted that the Protocol allows for partial cancellation of a trademark registration, when it is not used to identify some of the goods or services it covers, adopting a system similar to the one applied in the European Union (section 15).

Section 19 of the Protocol also includes grounds for the protection of designations and appellations of origin.[21] The Protocol defines designations of origin to mean the "geographic name of a country, city, region or place of its territory, known as an extraction, production or manufacture center of a certain product or rendering of a certain service." An appellation of origin "shall be the geographic name of a country, city, region or place of its territory, which identifies goods or services whose qualities or characteristics result exclusively or essentially from the geographic medium, including natural and human factors." In turn, section 20 sets forth that designations and appellations of origin may not be registered as trademarks.[22] This also provides another cause for invalidation, in addition to those enumerated in section 14.

[21] By including designations of origin, the Protocol seems to have adopted the lightest form of protection for geographical names, if we consider that the strictest form are appellations of origin, which require for the product's reputation to result exclusively or essentially from the geographic *medium*. Geographical indications require that the product's reputation result from the geographic *origin*. However, designations of origin are less strict because they require only that the geographic name be known as the relevant geographic center. In other words, it appears that the Protocol establishes broad protection for geographical names.

[22] Without prejudice to this provision, MERCOSUR countries would likely not bar trademark registration of designations or appellations of origin when the applicant is the association or entity of producers from the region where the designation or appellation of origin was created.

Like the Trademarks Protocol, the Harmonization Protocol on Industrial Designs has not come into force. Section 5 of the Design Protocol provides that "Industrial designs shall be protected as long as they are original creations consisting of a plastic form or destined to provide a special appearance to an industrial product conferring ornamental character thereto." An interesting aspect of this definition is that it includes not only industrial designs, but also models, because it protects "original creations consisting of a plastic form or destined to provide a special appearance to an industrial product." In this regard, scholars consider that a "plastic form" is a three-dimensional creation,[23] which means that the definition of section 5 covers industrial designs.

When we analyze the exclusions in section 9 of the Protocol, however, especially the one in section 9.2, another element should be added to the definition: industrial designs and models are prototypes that may be manufactured in a series. Two other elements of this definition deserve a more detailed explanation. The first of these is "original creations"; in this regard, section 8.1 of the Design Protocol establishes that they must "differ significantly from known industrial designs." We may conclude that the foregoing means that the industrial design (and the model) must be novel, which is confirmed when we read sections 8.1.1 and 8.1.2. The second element refers to the "ornamental character" that the design (or model) must confer to the product; this relates to section 9.1, which excludes protection for designs that contribute only a functional or technical improvement to the product, that is, the novel contribution must be exclusively related to an aesthetic aspect. Argentine case law (whose legislation also demands for designs to have an ornamental character) has established that "not only objects that are ornamental strictly speaking, but which also constitute an aspect or form incorporated to the product in a manner to make it more appealing and to impact the sense of sight and, consequently, attract consumers"[24] should be protected as designs. The protocol requires industrial designs and models to be novel and have industrial applicability (section 8). Moreover, they must not be essentially determined by technical or functional considerations; they must not be purely artistic or not serve for the manufacturing of a product; and they must not be offensive to public policy or morals (section 9).

Section 11 of the Design Protocol determines the rights of owners of a design in the following terms: "preventing third parties, without their consent, to manufacture, sell or import articles bearing or incorporating a design which is a

[23] José Manuel Otero Lastres, El Modelo Industrial 98 (1977).

[24] Federal Appellate Court for Civil and Commercial Matters, Division III, *Pasolde Ltd. v. Fadete S.A.* (August 20, 1982).

copy, or fundamentally a copy, of the protected design, when those acts are carried out for commercial purposes." The foregoing means that the exclusive rights do not cover third party acts carried out in the private sphere and without a commercial purpose, as well as experimenting, teaching and research activities (section 12 of the Design Protocol). In addition, section 14 establishes that the protection term shall be ten years, with the option to renew for one additional five-year period. Section 6 provides that "the protection granted to industrial designs does not affect the protection that the design might deserve pursuant to other intellectual property protection regimes." For example, nothing would prevent the owner of an industrial model that functions as product packaging to also apply for protection of a 3D trademark pursuant to section 6.1 of the Trademark Protocol.

The Design Protocol further regulates exhaustion of the right; however, like the Trademark Protocol, it does not specify the type of exhaustion that it adopts: national, regional, or international (section 13). Finally, like the Trademark Protocol, section 17 of the Design Protocol establishes that invalidation of the industrial design (or model) may be requested at the administrative level; but it also establishes that there is no statute of limitations to file for invalidation in two situations: "a) when the design was obtained in bad faith; and b) when the substantive requirements for protection have not been met" (section 17.1). The Design Protocol is as broad as the Trademark Protocol and it enables "any interested person" to file for invalidation (section 3.1).

17.5 MORE EMPTY PROMISES: THE CELAC AND A NEW APPROACH TO INDUSTRIAL PROPERTY IN THE REGION

The CELAC is an intergovernmental integration process created in February 2010, even though its origins go back further in time. In fact, the CELAC's predecessor was the so-called Rio Group, which put together Latin American states interested in bolstering commercial integration. However, after the Rio Group carried out the XXI Latin American and Caribbean 2010 Unity Summit, it was dissolved into the CELAC. This new intergovernmental initiative stems from an integration model completely different from that used by its predecessor and had very different objectives, such as strengthening the sovereign powers of Latin American states or promoting development in the region, without neglecting social issues.

An important development of the CELAC occurred in 2015, shortly after Ecuador took over the pro tempore presidency. During the III Meeting of Ministers and Higher Officials in Science, Technology and Innovation of the CELAC, held in September of that year, it was made known that the priority of Ecuador's administration would be to "encourage a process towards the definition of common regional policies in areas concerning science, technology and research, within an approach of regional sovereignty."[25]

One of the aspects that Ecuador intends to tackle in order to achieve this goal is harmonization of industrial property policies in the region. Therefore, the ministers of the CELAC have been entrusted with developing a new legal framework in line with the goals of the regional block; the ministers consider that this initiative differs from the TRIPS Agreement, which they consider reinforces technological dependence.[26]

While this is very recent, we may foresee what could happen within the CELAC if we analyze the changes that Ecuador implemented in its domestic legislation. While Ecuador has recognized industrial property rights for many years, it was only in 1998 that the national administration began to take the matter seriously, with the creation of the National Ecuadorian Institute of Intellectual Property (Instituto Ecuatoriano de la Propiedad Intelectual – IEPI).[27] Ecuador responded to the traditional approach in the matter that TRIPS had followed. However, once Rafael Correa took office, a series of legislative amendments were introduced. One of the first amendments was section 387, which sets forth that one of the responsibilities of the state shall be "To promote the generation and production of knowledge, to foster scientific and technological research, and to upgrade ancestral wisdom to thus contribute to the achievement of the good way of living (sumak kawsay)."[28]

An important achievement of President Correa's administration was to create an exception to copyright to freely transform any literary work to any system allowing access to those works for the visually impaired. Together with Uruguay and Brazil, Ecuador took this initiative to the World Intellectual Property Organization (WIPO), and it became one of the catalysts for the Marrakech Treaty to Facilitate Access to Published Works by Visually Impaired Persons and Persons with Print Disabilities,[29] adopted in 2013.

This significant achievement led the Ecuadorian government to pursue its reform efforts of intellectual property legislation more vigorously. That is how, as of 2013, the government began to draft a bill for an Organic Code of Social Economics of Knowledge, Creativity and Innovation (known also as

[25] Sally Burch, *Soberanía Cognitiva y Tecnológica, e Integración*, AM. LAT. MOV. NÚM. 507 1 (2015).

[26] *Id.* at 2–3.

[27] CÉSAR ECHEZURÍA, PROPIEDAD INTELECTUAL 148 (2014).

[28] The concept of *Sumak kawsay* comes from Latin American indigenous peoples and refers to the balance between human beings with their community and nature, which enables the achievement of a better standard of living.

[29] ECHEZURÍA, *supra* note 27, at 156–157.

"Código Ingenios"). As of 2014, and more actively during 2015, the government published official versions of the Code. In October 2016, the Ecuadorian congress approved the Code, which includes rules for knowledge sharing, incentives for innovation, provisions for fostering Ecuadorian patents and the use of free software among the population. The Code also refers to biopiracy and the protection of traditional knowledge.[30]

17.6 THE PROSUR: AN ALTERNATIVE TO REGIONAL INTEGRATION?

The Sistema de Cooperación sobre Aspectos de Información Operacional y de Propiedad Industrial (PROSUR – System of Cooperation on Aspects of Operational Information and Industrial Property) constitutes an alternative integration mechanism, different from the attempts made (and promised to be made) in the different supranational Latin American integration processes. The members of the PROSUR are Argentina, Brazil, Chile, Colombia, Ecuador, Paraguay, Peru, Surinam, and Uruguay, and it is financially supported by the Inter-American Development Bank. It is worth noting that the PROSUR is not an industrial property integration process, but an intergovernmental group comprising the highest authorities of the public offices involved in the matter.

Even though the negotiations for the PROSUR's establishment began in 2010, it was finally incorporated in 2012 with the execution of the Memorandum of Understanding among the member states in the Santiago de Chile round. The Memorandum sets the following goals:

> 1. Data Exchange among the different Parties and operational cooperation on proceedings, with the aim of creating a common platform which unifies and simplifies access to information and industrial property registries; 2. Cooperation in the use of information technologies for the comprehensive resolution of common problems, avoiding the multiplication of efforts and achieving more efficient and sustainable solutions in the region; 3. Exchange of information about new developments in the industrial property protection system in the respective countries; 4. Exchange of experiences and technical and/or scientific knowledge, about the role of the Parties and governmental entities which promote and implement policies for the development of competitiveness, entrepreneurship and innovation; 5. Exchange of experiences, knowledge and abilities in the general administration of the Parties, including human resources, training and quality control; 6. Exchange of experiences and knowledge about the supply of technical information to the user and

[30] *See* www.snna.gob.ec/dw-pages/Descargas/CODIGO_INGENIOS.pdf

the industrial, business, scientific and university communities, for the scientific and economic development of the parties; 7. Exchange of experiences and experts involved in educational industrial property projects reinforcing academic practice in the countries.

As may be seen, legal harmonization is not within the PROSUR's goals; rather, it purports to generate an exchange mechanism among the different industrial property offices. However, in accordance with section 4 of the Memorandum, nothing prevents the PROSUR, if it is a successful initiative, from entering into new agreements with broader scope including — among other aspects — the promotion of legal harmonization. However, considering that in all these years the PROSUR could barely achieve the establishment of its internal structure, it will likely be necessary to wait years to see any results.

17.7 CONCLUSION

Latin American integration processes have always sought to resemble the European experience as much as possible; however, the governments of the region have not learnt the lesson that Jean Monnet's neo-functionalism taught: little steps. Unlike the paused and strategic integration process carried out in the European Communities, Latin America always proposes grand objectives that are never accomplished or integration treaties are signed, which nobody will enforce. Even when things are done correctly – as is the case with the CAN – the process can disintegrate simply because of disagreement between different leaders.

In our view, the integration process in the continent and all intellectual property harmonization proposals are frail. The CAN's disintegration, the lack of political will within the MERCOSUR and the CELAC's empty promises makes us deposit our hopes in PROSUR, which, considering past experiences, could also end in failure.

PART V

SPECIAL SECTION: ASEAN INTELLECTUAL PROPERTY MATRIX

The intellectual property matrix in this part is prepared by the members of the ASEAN Intellectual Property Association and summarizes the intellectual property laws and frameworks in the ten ASEAN member states. It is divided into six sections. The first section sets out the general information pertaining to the role of the courts including an outline of the appellate process for intellectual property civil disputes, as well as the basis of the legal systems (i.e., civil or common law system) in the various ASEAN countries. It also indicates whether specialist intellectual property courts and alternative dispute resolution processes are available in each of the member states. The section concludes with information on ASEAN countries' membership in international intellectual property treaties, such as the Berne Convention, Budapest Treaty, Hague Agreement, Madrid Protocol, Marrakesh Treaty, Paris Convention, Patent Cooperation Treaty, Singapore Treaty on the Law of Trademarks, TRIPS Agreement, UPOV, WIPO Copyright Treaty, WIPO Performance and Phonogram Treaty, as well as, regional cooperative agreements.

The second section focuses on trademark law. Specifying whether nontraditional trademarks, such as color, sound, smell and so forth are registrable in the ASEAN countries – it also highlights whether trademarks are examined on absolute or relative grounds. The availability of protection for unregistered well-known marks, common law tort of passing-off, duration of trademark protection, groundless threats of infringement action, as well as remedies and enforcement are also outlined.

The third section centers on patent law. Displaying the approaches of the ASEAN member states in respect of the search and examination process, it includes information on opposition proceedings and the availability of post-grant amendments. The overlap between patent and competition law in respect of "tie-in" and "tie-up" clauses are also highlighted. Data on translation requirements, availability of compulsory licenses, civil and criminal enforcement are also captured in the matrix. The section concludes with information on the availability of utility models.

Design law is set forth in the next section. Presenting details on the search and examination procedures, opposition proceedings and whether registration is mandatory to obtain design protection, it also sums up whether protection is available for graphic user interfaces, partial designs, and unregistered design rights. Summarizing the availability of civil and criminal enforcement actions including border enforcement measures, it concludes with the overlap between design and copyright law.

The next two sections deal with copyright law and other related rights, such as trade secrets, privacy, and personal data protection. The copyright section captures information on subject-matter of copyright protection, duration of protection for copyrighted works, as well as works in electronic form. The availability of safe harbor protection for internet service providers, notice takedown, technological protection measures, and copyright management information protection are also discussed. The section concludes with enforcement of copyright including the availability of groundless threats of infringement actions.

18

ASEAN Intellectual Property Matrix

ASEAN Intellectual Property Association

SECTION 1 – GENERAL

General	Brunei Darussalam	Cambodia	Indonesia	Laos	Malaysia	Myanmar	Philippines	Singapore	Thailand	Vietnam
Basis of legal system Civ: Civil law Com: Common law	Com	Civ	Civ	Civ	Com	Com	Civ	Com	Civ	Civ
Outline of appellate process for IP civil disputes CA: Court of Appeal CoC: Commercial Court CFI: Court of First Instance FC: Federal Court HC: High Court MC: Municipal Court PC: Provincial Court RC: Regional Trial Court SC: Supreme Court SuC: Superior Court TC: Township Court	HC →CA	MC / PC →CA →SC	CoC →SC	PC →CA →SC	HC →CA →FC	TC →DC →HC →SC	RC →CA →SC	HC →CA	CFI →SC	DC →PC →SuC
Availability of specialist IP courts	×	×	×	×	✓	×	✓	×	✓	×
Availability of ADR options at IP office, court, IP tribunal proceedings	✓	✓	✓	✓	✓	×	✓	✓	✓	×
Availability of IP statutes										
• Trademarks	✓	✓	✓	✓	✓	×	✓	✓	✓	✓
• Patents	✓	✓	✓	✓	✓	×	✓	✓	✓	✓
• Copyright	✓	✓	✓	✓	✓	✓	✓	✓	✓	✓
• Designs	✓	✓	✓	✓	✓	×	✓	✓	✓	✓
International IP treaty memberships										
• Berne Convention	✓	×	✓	✓	✓	×	✓	✓	✓	✓
• Budapest Treaty	✓	×	×	×	×	×	✓	✓	×	×
• Hague Agreement	✓	×	×	×	×	×	×	✓	×	×
• Madrid Protocol	×	✓	×	✓	×	×	✓	✓	✓	✓

FIGURE 18.1 ASEAN intellectual property matrix: Section 1 – General.

	Brunei Darussalam	Cambodia	Indonesia	Laos	Malaysia	Myanmar	Philippines	Singapore	Thailand	Vietnam
General										
• Marrakesh Treaty	×	×	×	×	×	×	×	✓	×	×
• Paris Convention	✓	✓	✓	✓	✓	×	✓	✓	✓	✓
• Patent Cooperation Treaty	✓	×	✓	✓	✓	×	✓	✓	✓	✓
• Singapore Treaty on the Law of Trademarks	×	×	×	×	×	×	×	✓	×	×
• TRIPS Agreement	✓	✓	✓	✓	✓	✓	✓	✓	✓	✓
• UPOV	×	×	×	×	×	×	×	✓	×	✓
• WIPO Copyright Treaty	×	×	×	×	✓	×	✓	✓	×	×
• WIPO Performances and Phonograms Treaty	×	×	✓	×	✓	×	✓	✓	×	×
Regional IP cooperative agreements										
• ASEAN Patent Examination Cooperation (ASPEC)	✓	✓	✓	✓	✓	×	✓	✓	✓	✓
• Trans-Pacific Partnership Agreement (TPP)	✓	×	×	×	✓	×	×	✓	×	✓

FIGURE 18.1 (*cont.*)

SECTION 2 – TRADEMARK

	Brunei Darussalam	Cambodia	Indonesia	Laos	Malaysia	Myanmar	Philippines	Singapore	Thailand	Vietnam
Trademark										
Registered professionals who may practice before Trademark Office										
• Lawyer	✓	×	×	✓	×	✓	✓	✓	✓	×
• Trademark agent	NA	✓	NA	NA	✓	NA	NA	NA	NA	NA
• IP agent	NA	NA	✓	✓	NA	NA	NA	NA	NA	✓
Existence of Trademark Register	✓	×	✓	✓	✓	×[1]	✓	✓	✓	✓
Registrable non-traditional trademarks										
• Colour	✓	×	✓	✓	×	NA	✓	✓	✓	×
• 3D/shape	✓	✓	×	✓	×	NA	✓	✓	✓	✓
• Sound	×	×	×	×	×	NA	×	✓	✓	×
• Smell	×	×	×	×	×	NA	×	×	×	×
Examination on absolute grounds	✓	✓	✓	✓	✓	NA	×	✓	✓	✓
Examination on relative grounds	✓	✓	✓	✓	✓	NA	✓	✓	✓	✓
Opposition before/after registration	Before	After	Before	After	Before	NA	Before	Before	Before	Before
Declaration of use/non-use required to maintain registration	×	✓	✓	×	×	NA	✓	×	×	×
Is registration mandatory for protection	×	✓	✓	✓	×	NA	✓	×	✓	×
Availability of protection for unregistered well-known marks	✓	✓	✓	✓	✓	✓	✓	✓	✓	✓

[1] only declarations

FIGURE 18.2 ASEAN intellectual property matrix: Section 2 – Trademark.

	Brunei Darussalam	Cambodia	Indonesia	Laos	Malaysia	Myanmar	Philippines	Singapore	Thailand	Vietnam
Trademark										
Availability of protection for unregistered marks (eg, passing off/unfair competition)	✓	✓	×	✓	✓	✓	✓	✓	✓	✓
Term of protection (years)	10	10	10	10	10	NA	20	10	10	10
Enforcement										
• Availability of border enforcement measures	✓	✓	✓	✓	✓	✓	✓	✓	✓	✓
• Availability of trade description action	✓	✓	×	×	✓	✓	✓	✓	✓	✓
• Availability of criminal action	✓	✓	✓	✓	✓	✓	✓	✓	✓	✓
• Availability of provisional relief (interim/interlocutory injunctions or equivalent)	✓	✓	✓	✓	✓	✓	✓	✓	✓	✓
• Availability of civil search orders (at common law, the Anton Piller procedure)	✓	✓	✓	✓	✓	✓	✓	✓	✓	✓
• Risk of groundless threat action	✓	✓	×	✓	✓	×	✓	✓	✓	✓

FIGURE 18.2 (*cont.*)

SECTION 3 – PATENT

	Brunei Darussalam	Cambodia	Indonesia	Laos	Malaysia	Myanmar	Philippines	Singapore	Thailand	Vietnam
Patent										
Registered professionals who may practice before Patent Office										
• Lawyer	✓	✓	×	✓	×	NA	✓	✓	✓	×
• Patent agent	NA	NA	NA	NA	✓	NA	✓	✓	✓	NA
• IP agent	NA	NA	✓	✓	NA	NA	NA	NA	NA	✓
Existence of Patent Register	✓	✓	✓	✓	✓	×[1]	✓	✓	✓	✓
Absolute novelty required	✓	✓	✓	✓	✓	NA	✓	✓	✓	✓
General unconditional grace period available for prior disclosure	×	✓	×	×	×	NA	✓	×	×	×
Are there non-patentable subject matter	✓	✓	✓	✓	✓	NA	×	✓	✓	✓
Substantive search & examination required	✓	✓	✓	✓	✓	NA	✓	✓	✓	✓
Substantive search & examination satisfied by foreign substantive search & examination result	✓	✓	✓	✓	✓	NA	✓	✓	×	✓
Opposition before/after registration	NA	Any time	Before	Before	NA	NA	Before	After	Before	Before
Availability of post-grant amendments	✓	×	✓	×	✓	NA	✓	✓	×	✓
Maximum term of protection (years from filing date)	20	20	20	20	20	NA	20	20	20	20
Availability of patent term extension	✓	×	×	×	×	NA	✓	✓	×	×

[1] only declarations

FIGURE 18.3 ASEAN intellectual property matrix: Section 3 – Patent.

	Brunei Darussalam	Cambodia	Indonesia	Laos	Malaysia	Myanmar	Philippines	Singapore	Thailand	Vietnam
Patent										
Is registration mandatory for protection	✓	✓	✓	✓	✓	NA	✓	✓	✓	✓
Are pre-grant annuity payments required	×	✓	✓	✓	×	NA	×	×	×	×
Requirement for English specification to be translated into local language	×	✓	✓	✓	×	NA	×	×	✓	✓
"Tie-in" and "Tie-up" clauses are dealt with under patents or competition law CL: competition law	NA	NA	NA	NA	NA	NA	NA	CL	NA	NA
Mandatory local first filing required	✓	×	✓	×	✓	NA	✓	✓	×	✓
Availability of compulsory licences										
• Third party	✓	✓	✓	✓	✓	×	✓	✓	✓	✓
• Government	✓	✓	✓	✓	✓	×	✓	✓	✓	✓
Enforcement										
• Availability of border enforcement measures	×	✓	×	✓	×	×	✓	×	×	✓
• Availability of criminal action	✓	✓	✓	✓	×	×	✓	×	✓	×
• Availability of provisional relief (interim/interlocutory injunctions or equivalent)	✓	✓	✓	✓	✓	✓	✓	✓	✓	✓
• Availability of civil search orders (at common law, the Anton Piller procedure)	✓	✓	✓	✓	✓	✓	✓	✓	✓	✓

	Brunei Darussalam	Cambodia	Indonesia	Laos	Malaysia	Myanmar	Philippines	Singapore	Thailand	Vietnam
Patent										
• Risk of groundless threat action	✓	✓	×	✓	✓	×	×	✓	✓	✓
• Availability of utility model registration	×	✓	✓	✓	✓	×	✓	×	✓	✓

FIGURE 18.3 (*cont.*)

SECTION 4 – DESIGN

Design	Brunei Darussalam	Cambodia	Indonesia	Laos	Malaysia	Myanmar	Philippines	Singapore	Thailand	Vietnam
Registered professionals who may practice before Design Office										
• Lawyer	✓	✓	✗	✓	✗	NA	✓	✓	✓	✗
• Design agent	NA	NA	NA	NA	✓	NA	NA	NA	✓	NA
• IP agent	NA	NA	✓	✓	NA	NA	NA	NA	NA	✓
Existence of Design Register	✓	✓	✓	✓	✓	✗[1]	✓	✓	✓	✓
Absolute novelty required	✓	✓	✓	✓	✓	NA	✓	✓	✓	✓
General unconditional grace period available for prior disclosure	✗	✓	✗	✗	✗	NA	✓	✗	✗	✗
Are there non-registrable designs?	✓	✓	✓	✓	✓	NA	✓	✓	✓	✗
Substantive search & examination required	✗	✓	✓	✓	✗	NA	✓	✗	✓	✓
Opposition before/after registration	Before	Any time	Before	After	Before	NA	Before	NA	Before	Before
Maximum term of protection (years from filing date)	15	5	10	15	25	NA	15	15	10	15
Is registration mandatory for protection	✓	✓	✓	✓	✓	NA	✓	✓	✓	✓
Availability of protection for graphical user interfaces	✗	✓	✓	NA	✓	NA	✓	✓	✓	✗
Availability of protection for partial designs	✗	✓	✓	NA	✓	NA	✓	✓	✗	✗
Availability of protection for unregistered designs	✗	✗	✗	✗	✗	NA	✗	✗	✗	✗

[1] only declarations

Design	Brunei Darussalam	Cambodia	Indonesia	Laos	Malaysia	Myanmar	Philippines	Singapore	Thailand	Vietnam
Enforcement										
• Availability of border enforcement measures	✗	✓	✗	✓	✗	✗	✓	✓	✗	✓
• Availability of criminal action	✓	✓	✓	✓	✗	✗	✓	✗	✓	✗
• Availability of provisional relief (interim/interlocutory injunctions or equivalent)	✓	✓	✓	✓	✓	✓	✓	✓	✓	✓
• Availability of civil search orders (at common law, the Anton Piller procedure)	✓	✓	✗	✓	✓	✓	✓	✓	✓	✓
• Risk of groundless threat action	✓	✓	✗	✓	✓	✗	✗	✓	✓	✓
Can design protection and copyright protection coexist in relation to a design	✓	✓	✗	✓	✗	✓	✓	✗	✓	✓

FIGURE 18.4 ASEAN intellectual property matrix: Section 4 – Design.

SECTION 5 – COPYRIGHT

Copyright	Brunei Darussalam	Cambodia	Indonesia	Laos	Malaysia	Myanmar	Philippines	Singapore	Thailand	Vietnam
Registered professional who may practice as agents										
• Lawyer	NA	✓	×	NA	✓	✓	✓	NA	✓	✓
• Copyright agent	NA	NA	NA	NA	✓	NA	NA	NA	NA	NA
• IP agent	NA	NA	✓	NA	NA	NA	NA	NA	NA	✓
Subject matter protected by copyright										
• Literary works	✓	✓	✓	✓	✓	✓	✓	✓	✓	✓
• Artistic works	✓	✓	✓	✓	✓	✓	✓	✓	✓	✓
• Dramatic works	✓	✓	✓	✓	✓	✓	✓	✓	✓	✓
• Musical Works	✓	✓	✓	✓	✓	✓	✓	✓	✓	✓
• Others	✓	✓	✓	✓	✓	✓	✓	✓	✓	✓
Existence of copyright register	×	✓	✓	✓	✓	✓	✓	×	✓	✓
Is registration mandatory for protection	×	×	×	×	×	×	×	×	×	×
Maximum term of protection for literary, artistic, musical and dramatic works (years from death of author)	50	50	75	50	50	50	50	70	50	50 (75 for dramatic works)
Availability of safe harbour protection for ISPs	×	✓	×	×	✓	✓	×	✓	✓	✓
Availability of take down notices against ISPs	×	✓	×	×	×	✓	×	✓	×	✓
Availability of TPM (Technology Prevention Measures) protection	✓	✓	×	✓	✓	✓	×	✓	✓	✓

Copyright	Brunei Darussalam	Cambodia	Indonesia	Laos	Malaysia	Myanmar	Philippines	Singapore	Thailand	Vietnam
Availability of CMI (Copyright Management Information) protection	✓	✓	×	✓	×	✓	×	✓	✓	✓
Existence of licensing agent register	×	×	×	×	✓	✓	✓	×	×	×
Availability of moral rights	✓	✓	✓	✓	✓	✓	✓	✓	✓	✓
Availability of performers' protection	✓	✓	✓	✓	✓	✓	✓	✓	✓	✓
Enforcement										
• Availability of border enforcement measures	✓	✓	✓	✓	✓	×	✓	✓	✓	✓
• Availability of criminal action	✓	✓	✓	✓	✓	✓	✓	✓	✓	✓
• Availability of provisional relief (interim/interlocutory injunctions or equivalent)	✓	✓	✓	✓	✓	✓	✓	✓	✓	✓
• Availability of civil search orders (at common law, the Anton Piller procedure)	✓	✓	✓	✓	✓	✓	✓	✓	✓	✓
• Risk of groundless threat action	×	✓	×	✓	✓	×	×	✓	✓	✓
• Infringer's knowledge affects damages claimable	✓	×	✓	✓	✓	✓	✓	✓	✓	×

FIGURE 18.5 ASEAN intellectual property matrix: Section 5 – Copyright.

SECTION 6 – OTHERS

	Brunei Darussalam	Cambodia	Indonesia	Laos	Malaysia	Myanmar	Philippines	Singapore	Thailand	Vietnam
Other related rights										
Availability of trade secrets/confidential information protection	✓	✓	✓	✓	✓	✖	✓	✓	✓	✓
Availability of right of privacy protection	✓	✓	✖	✖	✓	✖	✓	✖	✖	✓
Availability of personal data protection	✓	✓	✖	✖	✓	✓	✓	✓	✖	✓

FIGURE 18.6 ASEAN intellectual property matrix: Section 6 – Other related rights.

This work is the joint effort of various contributors from the ASEAN Intellectual Property Association:

Coordinator/editor: Soh Kar Liang (Ella Cheong LLC, Singapore)

Design/format: Jo-Ann See (Amica Law LLC, Singapore), Lee Ai Ming (Dentons Rodyk & Davidson LLP, Singapore), Murgiana Haq (hslegal LLP, Singapore), Soh Kar Liang (Ella Cheong LLC, Singapore), Tan Kee Leng (KL Tan & Associates, Singapore)

Contributors: Aisha Alkaff (Ahmad Isa & Partners, Brunei), Khiew Mealy (Sok Siphana & Associates, Cambodia), Dwi Anita Daruherdani (Daruherdani & Partners, Indonesia), Caroline Francis (Ram Rais & Partners, Malaysia), Khine Khine U (Khine Khine U Law Firm, Myanmar), Moe Mynn Thu (Rouse & Co, Myanmar), Thein Aung (Myanmar Trademark & Patent Law Firm, Myanmar), Rico V Domingo (Law Firm of RV Domingo & Associates, Philippines), John Paul Gaba (Angara Abello Concepcion Regala & Cruz Law Offices, Philippines), Jo-Ann See (Amica Law LLC, Singapore), Darani Vachanavuttivong (Tilleke & Gibbins International Ltd, Thailand), Wiramrudee Mokkhavesa (Tilleke & Gibbins International Ltd, Thailand), Pham Nghiem Xuan Bac (Vision & Associates, Vietnam).

Index